The UNIVERSITY CHALLENGE

Quiz Book

The

UNIVERSITY
CHALLENGE

Quiz Book

*Over 3,500 challenging questions
from Britain's most difficult quiz*

Compiled by
Steve Tribe

10

Published in 2010 by BBC Books, an imprint of Ebury Publishing.
A Random House Group Company.

Questions and answers © ITV Studios Ltd 2010
Editorial arrangement and contribution © Woodlands Books Ltd 2010

University Challenge is an ITV Studios Production for BBC Two.
Produced in association with The College Bowl Company © ITV Studios Ltd 2010

Licensed to BBC Books by ITV Studios Global Entertainment Ltd

The Random House Group Limited Reg. No. 954009

Addresses for companies within the Random House Group can be found at
www.randomhouse.co.uk

A CIP catalogue record for this book is available from the British Library.

ISBN 978 1 84607 856 9

The Random House Group Limited supports the Forest Stewardship Council® (FSC®), the leading
international forest certification organisation. All our titles that are printed on Greenpeace approved
FSC® certified paper carry the FSC® logo. Our paper procurement policy can be found at
www.randomhouse.co.uk/environment

Commissioning editor: Albert DePetrillo
In-house editor: Joe Cottington
Project editor: Steve Tribe
Production: Phil Spencer

Printed and bound in the UK by CPI Group (UK) Ltd, Croydon, CR0 4YY

To buy books by your favourite authors and register for offers, visit www.rbooks.co.uk

Contents

Preface
and
Acknowledgements

Welcome to your opportunity to test your knowledge against the best and worst that British television's most fiendish quiz show has to offer, and see just how well you'd really do if you were up against the frighteningly knowledgeable hopes-for-the-future fielded by our universities over the last five decades.

You may be playing as part of a team or in a tournament, in which case: enjoy the contest, and good luck reaching the final (but maybe get rid of that plastic monkey-faced mascot). Or you might be dipping in and out, on your own or with your family, and beginning to boggle at the sheer breadth of learning and general knowledge and the wider cultural and political awareness required of each winning team. Just relish the sheer fun of having your brilliance confirmed (and the gaps in your knowledge painfully revealed). And, one day soon, you'll read some ill-informed newspaper space-filler about universities 'dumbing down', and exams being easier, and kids these days not knowing half the things Everybody Knew back in Some Golden Age... Take a look at this book then, or watch an edition on BBC Two, and remember: you can't trust *anything* you read in the press...

This book is a testament to the astounding dedication, erudition and resourcefulness of the programme's long-serving question-setters: Christine Ansell, Stephen Battersby, Tom Benson, Olav Bjortomt,

Neville Cohen and Janet Barker, Janet Crompton, Matthew Dolan, Saira Dunnakey, Phil Jones, Sara Low, Chris Miller, Charles Oakley, Elissa Phipps, Sean Prendiville, Stan Shaw, Beth Vokurka, and John Willcox. Their hard work – fact-checking, double-checking, cross-checking, and verifying – is contained in these pages.

I'm grateful to Peter Gwyn and all at ITV Studios for letting me scavenge through their vast database of questions and answers, transcripts and statistics. And to Jeremy Paxman, erudite quizmaster, for allowing me to quote so many of those little moments that enliven the show each week.

Thanks also to Albert DePetrillo, Joe Cottington, Nick Payne, Ed Griffiths, Kevin Morgan, James Goss and Antoinette Burchill.

Steve Tribe
August 2010

Round One

'Two teams have the
opportunity over the next half-hour
to reassure taxpayers everywhere
that money on higher education
isn't being wasted, and whichever
of them does so more convincingly
wins a place in the second round.'

THE RULES

The match begins with a starter question, worth 10 points, which must be answered on the buzzer and without conferring.

The first team correctly to answer a starter question then gets three connected bonus questions, worth 5 points each. The team may confer before the team captain gives their answer.

If a contestant interrupts a starter question with an incorrect answer, his or her team suffers a 5-point penalty, and the opposing team is given the whole question.

In the event of a tie, the match is decided by a single starter, with the winning team being the first to answer a starter correctly. Should either team incorrectly interrupt a tie-break starter, they incur a 5-point penalty, which automatically loses them the match.

Match One

1. Your starter for 10:
Trebbia, Trasimene and Cannae are among the military victories of which commander of antiquity? Born in 247 BC, his name means 'the grace of the god Baal'.

> **Three bonus questions on poetry:**
> In each case, identify the eighteenth- or early nineteenth-century poet who wrote the following lines:
> (a) 'To see a world in a grain of sand, / And a heaven in a wild flower, / Hold infinity in the palm of your hand, / And eternity in an hour...'
> (b) '... I fear thy skinny hand! / And thou art long, and lank, and brown, / As is the ribb'd sea-sand.'
> (c) 'Nothing beside remains: round the decay / Of that colossal wreck, boundless and bare, / The lone and level sands stretch far away.'

2. Your starter for 10:
Born in Fife in 1954, which novelist uses his middle initial 'M' to distinguish his science-fiction writing from his mainstream novels?

> **Three bonus questions on jewellery in Shakespeare:**
> (a) In which play by Shakespeare is a bracelet stolen from the King of Britain's daughter Imogen while she sleeps, in an attempt to ruin her reputation?
> (b) The stolen bracelet was a love token from Imogen's

husband Posthumus, who received what item of jewellery from her, before they bade each other farewell with vows of fidelity?

(c) What archaic name for a red gemstone, now more commonly used for a boil or abscess, appears in both *Cymbeline* and *Antony and Cleopatra* in references to the decoration of the chariot of Phoebus, the sun god?

3. Your starter for 10:
Named after an ancient Indo-European people, which historic region of south-eastern Europe is bounded by the Black Sea, the Aegean Sea and the Balkan mountains, and includes parts of Bulgaria and Greece and the whole of the European part of Turkey?

Three bonus questions on arrows:
(a) The story of a fellowship of outlaws during the Wars of the Roses, *The Black Arrow* is an 1888 work by which novelist?

(b) In the *Aeneid*, who fires the poisoned arrow from the walls of Troy which, guided by Apollo, fatally wounds Achilles in the heel?

(c) *Time's Arrow*, in which a German doctor during the Holocaust experiences time in reverse, is a Booker-shortlisted work by which author?

4. Your starter for 10:
Appearing along with figures from her entourage and the painter himself, the Infanta Margarita is the central figure in which 1656 group portrait by Diego Velazquez? Its original title was *The Family of Philip IV*.

Three bonus questions on symbiosis:
(a) The symbiotic association of *rhizobium* bacteria with the roots of legumes is the basis of which process, essential to agriculture?

(b) What name is given to a mutualistic association of a fungus with the roots of a higher plant, such as that formed by a truffle and a host tree?

(c) The type of symbiosis in which one organism shares the home or nest of another with no ill-effects to the host is known by what specific name?

5. Your starter for 10:
Designed by Sir Nigel Gresley, which Class A3 Pacific steam locomotive bore the British Railways number 60103 after 1948 and the London and Northeastern region number 4472 prior to 1948?

Three bonus questions on post-Soviet states:
In each case, name the country in which the following 'revolutions' took place:

(a) Carrying long-stemmed roses as a sign of peace, Mikhail Saakashvili and his supporters entered the parliament building and demanded the resignation of President Eduard Shevardnadze in the Rose Revolution of 2003.

(b) Which country saw the Orange Revolution of 2004, in which protesters successfully challenged a presidential run-off election that had given victory to the pro-Russian Prime Minister, Viktor Yanukovych?

(c) Which country saw the Tulip Revolution of 2005, after which President Askar Akayev fled by helicopter to neighbouring Kazakhstan?

6. Your starter for 10:
Used since the fourteenth century to mean the purchase of the liberty of a slave, what word is now more commonly understood to mean deliverance from sin and its consequences by the atonement of Jesus?

Three bonus questions on plants and their properties:

(a) Its name derived from a Tongan word meaning 'bitter', what non-alcoholic but intoxicating drink is made from the pepper plant *piper methysticum*, native to Polynesia?

(b) What name is given to the evergreen shrub *catha edulis* of Arabia and Africa, whose leaves are used as a narcotic when chewed or made into a drink?

(c) Which nut is commonly chewed in much of West Africa and is the source of the name of a carbonated soft drink?

7. Your starter for 10:

A senator for 47 years, Edward Kennedy, who died in 2009, lost his only attempt to secure the Democratic presidential nomination against which opponent, who was also the incumbent president?

Three bonus questions on US politicians:

(a) To what political office was Dean Rusk appointed in 1961, as a result of which he played a leading role in the Cuban Missile Crisis the following year?

(b) Which Secretary of State resigned from Jimmy Carter's administration in 1980 over the failed attempt to rescue US hostages in Tehran?

(c) Who was appointed Secretary of State under Richard Nixon in 1973, holding the post concurrently with that of National Security Advisor?

8. Your starter for 10:

Which Greek historian's work is the source of the lines paraphrased in an inscription on the main post office building in New York city: 'Neither snow nor rain nor gloom of night shall stay these couriers from the swift completion of their appointed rounds'?

Three bonus questions on a polysyllabic term:

(a) Futures, options and warrants are examples of which type of financial instrument or arrangement, whose value stems from and is dependent upon the value of an underlying variable asset, such as a commodity, currency, or security?

(b) What is the derivative of the function cos2(x) + sin2(x)?

(c) In mechanics, what name is given to the derivative with respect to time of an object's velocity?

9. **Your starter for 10:**
    What name is commonly given to those parasitic flatworms of the class *digenea* that live, as adults, in the liver and other organs of various hosts, including sheep and humans?

    Three bonus questions on social networking websites:

    (a) In 2005, Rupert Murdoch's News Corporation bought which website? It allows users to share their musical tastes and had become associated with the discovery of new musical talent.

    (b) In August 2009, MySpace gained control of the social music discovery technology used on rival sites such as Facebook by acquiring which Seattle-based music service, launched by the brothers Ali and Hadi Partovi in 2006?

    (c) Created in 2005 by Michael and Xochi Birch, the name of the social networking site Bebo is an acronym representing which four words?

10. **Your starter for 10:**
    Having its origins in Moscow in the early twentieth century, *habimah*, meaning 'the stage', became, in the 1950s, the national theatre of which country?

Three bonus questions on North American place names:

(a) 200 miles north-east of Atlanta and the seat of Mecklenburg County, which city, the largest city of the Carolinas, takes its name from the wife of King George III?

(b) The small city of Charlottetown is the capital of which Canadian province, noted for its associations with the fictional character Anne of Green Gables?

(c) The estate of Monticello in Charlottesville, Virginia, was remodelled on neo-classical lines by which future president, following his term as Minister to France from 1785 to 1789?

11. Your starter for 10:

In the play *Henry VIII*, usually attributed to Shakespeare and Fletcher, which two of Henry's wives feature among the *dramatis personae*?

Three bonus questions on terms that begin with the prefix 'poly':

In each case, give the term from the definition:

(a) In chemistry, the combination of several molecules to form a more complex molecule, usually by a step- or chain-growth mechanism?

(b) Music in two or more parts, each having a melody of its own? The term is widely used of the ringtones of mobile telephones.

(c) In geometry, a solid figure with many faces?

12. Your starter for 10:

What two given names link the Danish physicist who gave his surname to the CGS unit of magnetic induction, and his close friend, a writer noted for his poetry and stories for children?

Three bonus questions on terms from a website:

The Anglish Moot is a website that proposes words coined from Germanic roots to replace those of Romance or Greek origin. For example, 'all-ken-book' is 'encyclopaedia' and 'learnhall' is 'university':

(a) The Anglish term 'mootsmanship' represents what social science subject on the 'learnplot', or curriculum, at many universities?

(b) Possibly after the 'mark one' of 1948, 'manchestercraft', along with 'reckonercraft', is an Anglish version of what subject?

(c) If 'yorelore' is history, what is 'wealthlore'?

13. **Your starter for 10:**

What three-letter abbreviation links: a political party co-founded in 1893 by Keir Hardie; a list of books that members of the Roman Catholic church were forbidden to read; and a student-specific programme of education that takes into consideration the student's strengths and weaknesses?

Three bonus questions on the River Moselle (or Mosel in German):

(a) Which city on the River Mosel in Germany is noted for the Porta Nigra, the largest Roman city gate north of the Alps?

(b) Noted for its yellow limestone architecture and taking its name from the Gallic tribe of the Medio-Matrici, which city on the River Moselle is the capital of the French region of Lorraine?

(c) Which village on the River Moselle in Luxembourg gives its name to EU conventions of 1985 and 1990 which abolished border controls between participating countries?

14. Your starter for 10:

Quote: 'Can you do division? Divide a loaf by a knife, what is the answer to that?' In which 1872 work of fiction are these words spoken by the White Queen?

Three bonus questions on operatic couples:
(a) Which couple, a queen and a Trojan prince, are the subject of an opera by Purcell, with a libretto by Nahum Tate based on his tragedy *Brutus of Alba, or The Enchanted Lovers*?
(b) In an opera by Wagner, set in Cornwall and Brittany, which couple unwittingly drink a love potion together?
(c) In a work that George Gershwin described as his 'folk opera', which two eponymous characters are a crippled beggar and his lover who live together on Catfish Row?

15. Your starter for 10:

After a French physicist born in 1841, what term denotes a dimensionless measure of gas density in terms of density at standard temperature and pressure?

Three bonus questions on an adjective:
(a) What name is given to the ghost ship which supposedly haunts the seas around the Cape of Good Hope, and inspired an opera by Wagner, first performed in 1843?
(b) What name for a flying fish has become a proprietary name for a form of rocket-propelled short-range guided missile used especially in sea warfare?
(c) 'Flying' and' hanging' are types of which architectural feature consisting of a projecting support built onto the outside of a wall?

16. Your starter for 10:

When playing golf, I hook my first shot, which lands 200 yards due north of the tee and 210 yards due west of the hole. How far is it from hole to tee?

Three bonus questions on religion:

(a) What word, from the Latin meaning a case or chest for books or papers, is given to a holy or sacred place that is dedicated to a specific deity or saint, and often becomes a place of pilgrimage?

(b) The 'Shrine of the Book', in the Israel Museum in Jerusalem, houses which collection of around 900 documents discovered between 1947 and 1956 in caves near the Wadi Qumran?

(c) The Shrine of the Three Kings, said to contain the bones of the Magi, is in which cathedral, the largest gothic church in Northern Europe, situated close to the River Rhine?

17. Your starter for 10:

In glaciology, what is the name given to the transition zone between the ice sheet and the ice shelf?

Three bonus questions on the Nobel Prize for Chemistry:
In each case, identify the winner from the words of the official citation:

(a) Who won the Prize in 1918 'for the synthesis of ammonia from its elements'?

(b) Which New Zealand-born physicist won the Chemistry Prize in 1908 for, in the words of the citation, 'his investigations into the disintegration of the elements and the chemistry of radioactive substances'?

(c) Who won the first of his Nobel Prizes in 1954 'for his research into the nature of the chemical bond and its application to the elucidation of the structure of complex substances'?

18. Your starter for 10:

From a comparative form of the Greek word for 'both', what adjective denotes a chemical capable of reacting both as a base and as an acid, for example amino acids and the oxides of zinc and aluminium?

Three bonus questions on Gilbert and Sullivan's modern Major-General:

(a) In *The Pirates of Penzance*, the Major-General says he can 'quote the fights historical, from Marathon to Waterloo, in order categorical.' How many years lie between those two battles? You can have 100 either way.

(b) He also claims he can 'quote in elegiacs all the crimes of Heliogabalus.' Now usually known as Eagabalus, one of this Roman Emperor's most notorious crimes, although probably invented, was that he attempted to smother guests at a dinner party by what unusual means?

(c) He also claims he can 'write a washing bill in Babylonic cuneiform', a type of inscription named after what precise shape?

19. **Your starter for 10:**
Give the single word that completes this statement by Leonardo da Vinci: 'Whoever in discussion adduces authority uses not intellect but rather...' what?

Three bonus questions on English words that have the same spelling but an entirely different pronunciation and meaning in a major Western European language:

(a) Which English word for 'bodily suffering' shares a spelling with a French noun denoting a staple food?

(b) A four-letter synonym for both 'sort' and 'benevolent' in English spells a common German noun meaning what?

(c) The Spanish word for the number 'eleven' and an English adverb meaning 'a single time' share the same four-letter spelling. What is it?

20. Your starter for 10:

An example being the creature made by the Maharal of Prague to defend the Ghetto from anti-Semitic attacks, what, in Jewish folklore, is the term for an animated being crafted from mud or other inanimate material?

Three bonus questions on poets in the Spanish Civil War:

(a) Having been given a diplomatic posting to Barcelona, which Chilean poet, a communist and supporter of the Republican forces, was the author of the collection *Espana en la Corazon*, or *Spain in My Heart*?

(b) Shortly before he left for Spain to join the International Brigade, which poet was told by the British Communist leader Harry Pollitt to, quote, 'Go and get killed – we need a Byron in the movement'?

(c) The poet Julian Bell, killed while driving an ambulance at the Battle of Brunete in 1937, was the nephew of which literary figure, who died in 1941?

21. Your starter for 10:

Which American writer, who committed suicide in February 2005, styled his unique brand of journalism 'Gonzo' and was associated with the trademark clenched fist on an upthrust forearm?

Three bonus questions on physics:

(a) In dynamics, what generic term can be defined as a device that applies or transmits force over a distance in order to perform work more easily?

(b) Also called the force ratio, what two-word term indicates the ratio of the force exerted by a simple machine to the force exerted on it by the operator?

(c) A machine for generating rotary mechanical power from the energy in a stream of fluid is given what name?

22. **Your starter for 10:**

What six-letter word is both an intransitive verb meaning 'to move or swerve about wildly, often downhill', and a noun denoting 'an individual's progression through a specific occupational sequence'?

Three bonus questions on viruses:
(a) Many animal viruses, including the herpes virus, have what regular shape, based on the optimum way of forming a closed shell from identical sub-units?
(b) The capsid is the protein coat of a virus; what is the name of the individual morphological sub-units from which it is built?
(c) Meaning 'bacteria-eating', what term is used for viruses which attack bacteria?

23. **Your starter for 10:**

The medical condition known as Hyponatremia denotes abnormally low levels of what substance in the body?

Three bonus questions on operatic divas:
(a) Which German-born composer wrote such roles as Rodelinda and Cleopatra in *Giulio Cesare* for Francesca Cuzzoni, who died in poverty in 1778?
(b) Nicknamed La Stupenda, which soprano made her concert debut in a performance of *Dido and Aeneas* in Sydney in 1947?
(c) The Romanian soprano Angela Gheorghiu topped the UK Classical music album chart in March 2009 singing the title role of which opera by Puccini?

24. **Your starter for 10:**

Formulated by atmospheric chemist James Lovelock, what controversial theory proposes that the Earth functions as a single organism that maintains conditions necessary for its survival?

Three bonus questions on photomontage:

(a) The technique of photomontage was popularised as a method for political propaganda and social criticism by which art movement, founded in Zurich in 1916?

(b) Often consisting of multiple images of a subject taken over time, or of Polaroid photographs arranged so that their white borders form a grid over the complete image, which British artist developed a form of photomontage he called 'joiners'?

(c) A photomontage called *People We Like* by the artist Peter Blake and his then-wife Jann Haworth achieved widespread recognition when it appeared in 1967 in what context?

25. Your starter for 10:

With production levels commonly over 12,000 tonnes per day making it the most produced chemical product in the UK, what is the chemical name for oil of vitriol?

Three bonus questions on the philosopher Francis Bacon:

(a) Speaking figuratively, of what did Bacon say, 'some … are to be tasted, others to be swallowed, and some few to be chewed and digested'?

(b) In an essay of the same name, what, according to Bacon, 'openeth the gate to good fame, and extinguisheth envy'?

(c) Give the single-word gerund that completes the opening statement of Bacon's essay 'Of Expense': 'Riches are for…' what?

26. Your starter for 10:

What term indicates literary works such as the 1969 French novel *La disparition* by Georges Perec, which are written without using one particular letter of the alphabet – in this case the letter 'e'?

Three bonus questions on Alexander the Great:
In each case, give the present-day country in which the
following took place:

(a) Alexander's journey to the oracle at Siwa Oasis in 332
BC, where he was acknowledged as the son of Zeus-
Ammon?

(b) The battle of the Hydaspes or Jhelum, at which
Alexander, in alliance with the King of Taxila, defeated
King Porus in 326 BC?

(c) The city of Susa, where, in 324 BC, Alexander held
marriages of himself and his Macedonian companions
with women of the local aristocracy?

27. **Your starter for 10:**
During the Second World War, three capitals of
belligerent European states were never occupied by
force: name any two of them.

Three bonus questions on Paris Metro stations:
(a) Which Metro station on the Left Bank is named after a
museum and a university in Paris?

(b) The French Prime Minister who presided over the
Paris Peace Conference is commemorated in the name
of a Metro station a third of the way up the Champs
Elysées. What was his name?

(c) What is the name of the Metro station at the Arc de
Triomphe which combines the name of a statesman
with the French word for 'star'?

28. **Your starter for 10:**
What can be classed as either 'duchenne', in which case
they involve the zygomaticus major and the orbicularis
oculi muscles and are generally viewed as sincere, or
as 'pan-American', in which case they use only the
zygomaticus major, and are often seen as insincere or
'professional'?

Three bonus questions on a literary theme:

(a) Which novel by Jane Austen is the story of Catherine Morland, an avid reader of gothic novels who is invited to stay at a friend's eponymous family home?

(b) The 1818 *Nightmare Abbey* was the third satirical novel by which author? It was preceded by *Headlong Hall* and *Melincourt*.

(c) Which abbey in Surrey inspired the name of Walter Scott's hero in a novel about the heir to an English estate who travels north and becomes involved in the 1745 Jacobite uprising?

29. Your starter for 10:

Which city between Milan and Bologna gives its name both to a delicate dry-cured ham and to a hard, dry cheese?

Three bonus questions on Edinburgh:

(a) The oldest surviving building in Edinburgh stands at the highest point of Castle Rock and is a chapel dedicated to which saint, the wife of eleventh-century monarch Malcolm III?

(b) Princes Street in Edinburgh was named after the Duke of Rothsay and Frederick, Duke of York, the sons of which king?

(c) Now an everyday word, what term was coined by the Irish painter Robert Barker in the 1790s to describe his views of Edinburgh, painted on the interior of a cylinder and designed to be viewed from the inside?

30. Your starter for 10:

Give the single word that completes this proverb, said to occur in various languages: 'Experience is a comb that nature gives to men when they are ...' what?

Three bonus questions on emigration:

(a) Which rock is known as 'Ireland's Teardrop' because it was the last sight of the country for emigrants sailing to America, and is found off Mizen Head, Ireland's most south-westerly point?

(b) 'True patriots we, for be it understood, / We left our country for our country's good.' These lines of 1796 by Henry Carter gave which American-born British playwright the title of her play *Our Country's Good*, first performed at the Royal Court in 1988?

(c) Often associated with the Pre-Raphaelite movement although never actually a member, which artist painted *The Last of England* in 1855, depicting the wistfulness of two emigrants aboard ship?

> 'Well, it's an embarrassing score, but, I'll tell you what: at least you laughed about it. The purpose of this competition is to find people who know things — and you don't know enough!'

Match Two

1. **Your starter for 10:**
Expressed as the negative logarithm of the hydrogen-ion concentration in a solution, how is the *pondus hydrogenii* or the power or potential of hydrogen more commonly known?

> **Three bonus questions on renewable energy projects:**
> (a) Between 1998 and 2001, the Power project aimed to assess the potential within the EU of what specific type of wind power?
> (b) In March 2007, Europe's first commercial concentrated solar power plant was opened near which city of southern Spain?
> (c) In autumn 2007, one of the world's largest tidal energy projects was unveiled when Alex Salmond opened the new testing facility at the European Marine Energy Centre on which group of Scottish islands?

2. **Your starter for 10:**
From two unconnected Greek words, what five-letter word links a punctuation mark used to separate clauses when the second expands or illustrates the first, and the main part of the large intestine, between the caecum and rectum?

> **Three bonus questions on a planet:**
> (a) The discovery of which planet's actual rotation rate

of 58.6 days was made in 1965 by bouncing radar off the planet's surface from the Arecibo Observatory in Puerto Rico?

(b) Which single-word term refers to the most favourable time to view Mercury when it achieves its greatest apparent distance east or west of the sun?

(c) How many Earth days does it take Mercury to orbit the sun? You can have ten days either way.

3. **Your starter for 10:**
Which old measure was used for various liquids, but chiefly for ale when it was originally the equivalent of a quarter of a barrel or nine gallons?

Three bonus questions on a Spanish city:
(a) Which Spanish city on the Guadalquivir river is the capital of Andalusia?

(b) Which old name for the River Guadalquivir is reflected in the name of one of Seville's football teams?

(c) Whose fleet of five ships set out from Seville on 10 August 1519, attempting to find a westward route to the Spice Islands of Indonesia?

4. **Your starter for 10:**
The case of the Huguenot merchant Jean Calas, executed by being broken on a wheel after he was falsely charged and convicted of killing his son, was taken up by which French writer who, in 1765, helped to secure a posthumous pardon for him from the Paris parliament?

Three bonus questions on book titles:
(a) *One Fat Englishman* is a 1963 work by which prolific novelist, author of *The Old Devils* and *Difficulties with Girls*?

(b) *The Last Englishman* by Byron Rogers is a biography of which novelist, noted for *A Month in the Country* and *How Steeple Sinderby Wanderers Won the F.A. Cup?*

(c) Which political figure does the historian Christopher Hill call 'God's Englishman' in the title of a work on the seventeenth-century English Revolution?

5. **Your starter for 10:**
Used generally to mean 'of that type or kind', what phrase is used specifically after the names of clan chiefs in Scotland to mean that they come from an estate or place of the same name as their family name?

Three bonus questions on geography:
(a) An area of rainforest and swampland uncrossed by any road and thus the missing link of the Pan-American Highway, the Darien Gap separates Colombia from which country?

(b) The Cumberland Gap is a pass through the Appalachians close to the meeting-point of Tennessee, Virginia and which other state?

(c) In which European country is the Fulda Gap, an area of relatively low land that assumed strategic significance during the cold war?

6. **Your starter for 10:**
In 1967, a British government minister said that a suffixed 'e' stood for 'excellence, England, Europe... and entente', when it was agreed to add it to the name of which aircraft?

Three bonus questions on literary terms from German:
In each case, give the term that corresponds to the following definition:
(a) A novel that follows the development of the protagonist from childhood or adolescence into adulthood, often involving a painful search for identity.

(b) A celebratory publication, commonly a collection of writings published in honour of a scholar or other eminent person.

(c) The earliest version of a text, or of a composer's original work; it often denotes a version that is lost and has to be reconstructed by textual criticism.

7. Your starter for 10:
What architectural term for a diagonal rib of a vault or a pointed arch or window is also used in statistics for a graph representing cumulative frequency?

Three bonus questions on nonsense:
(a) Meaning insincere or pretentious talk, what word derives from the slang name for an eighteenth-century theatrical device or gag employed to draw applause from the audience?

(b) Also used to describe illicitly distilled liquor, which term has a longer history as a description of romantic piffle, the word possibly derived from the illusory images produced upon the surface of water at night?

(c) Which synonym for empty drivel is a figurative use of a term dating probably from the fifteenth century and used originally to describe the swill from a brewery usually fed to pigs?

8. Your starter for 10:
In the words of John Stuart Mill, which ethical theory asserts that 'actions are right in proportion as they tend to promote happiness, wrong as they tend to produce the reverse of happiness'?

Three bonus questions on reference works:
(a) Since 1879, James Murray, C.T. Onions and Robert Burchfield have been three of the seven chief editors of which major work of reference?

(b) What was the name of the compiler of the rhyming dictionary first published in 1775, in which the headwords are listed in order of reverse spelling from the indefinite article and 'baa' through to the word 'fuzz'?

(c) The *Encyclopaedia Britannica*, now American-owned, was first published from 1768 in which city?

9. Your starter for 10:

What is the surname of the cricketing family whose members include father Walter, a New Zealand Test captain who died in 2006, and his sons Dayle, Barry and Sir Richard, who in 1988 became the first player to take 400 test wickets?

Three bonus questions on England cricket captains:

(a) Which England cricket captain was born in Ootacamund, India, in 1932?

(b) Which England cricket captain was born in Milan in 1935 and became first chairman of the England committee in 1989?

(c) Which England cricket captain of the 1970s was born in South Africa in 1946?

10. Your starter for 10:

What subfield of physics deals with plasmas, such as those in fusion reactors and interplanetary space, and more generally with the interactions between a conducting fluid and a magnetic field?

Three bonus questions on shopping:

(a) Which term for a large self-service shop is first recorded in the *New York Times* in 1933?

(b) Which Beat poet, who died in April 1997, wrote 'A Supermarket in California' about the death of his first hero, Walt Whitman?

(c) In the UK, who hosted the game show *Supermarket Sweep* on its inception in 1993?

11. Your starter for 10:
Fifty years after Cortina d'Ampezzo, which city became the second Italian venue of the Winter Olympics in February 2006?

Three bonus questions on Paul McCartney songs:
(a) Which duet did McCartney write after a tiff with his wife Linda, saying that he wondered: 'Why can't we get it together – our piano can'?
(b) Which track on the *Sgt Pepper* album was inspired by an advertisement for Kellogg's cornflakes?
(c) Which track on album *Band on the Run* was named after McCartney's land rover?

12. Your starter for 10:
Iain Macleod, Nigel Lawson, Charles Moore and Boris Johnson are among the former editors of which political periodical, founded in 1828?

Three bonus questions on tennis in films:
(a) Which Frenchman, played by Jacques Tati in a film of 1953, enjoys a game of tennis while on holiday in Brittany?
(b) Which Alfred Hitchcock film of 1951 features Farley Granger as tennis star Guy Haines, who finds himself involved in a murder plot?
(c) Which cult film of 1966 stars David Hemmings as Thomas, who wanders onto a tennis court to see mime-like hippies are playing tennis without a ball?

13. Your starter for 10:
What name is given to the outermost layer of a planet's atmosphere?

Three bonus questions linked by a word:

(a) Also known as risk capital, what term is used for money invested in a new or expanding business in exchange for shares?

(b) What is measured by a Venturi tube?

(c) Who first came to fame in the title role of the film *Ace Ventura, Pet Detective*?

14. Your starter for 10:

Which widespread phenomenon in animals and plants, that may be transient or balanced, is the functional or structural variation between two or more members of a species, determined by differences in either genetic constitution, environmental conditions, or both?

Three bonus questions on Britain:

(a) Which is the earliest known name for the island of Britain, being used by Greek geographers of the fourth century BC?

(b) The name Albion has been translated as 'White Land', and was explained by the Romans as referring to which geographic feature?

(c) Which pejorative adjective was used in connection with Albion in a poem of 1793 by the Marquis de Ximenes?

15. Your starter for 10:

Eleanor of Provence and Eleanor of Castile were the mothers of which two successive English kings?

Three bonus questions on American states:

(a) Which state of the southern USA has been known as the Volunteer State since 1812?

(b) Which state was admitted to the Union in 1876 and is hence known as the Centennial State?

(c) Which state has been nicknamed the Equality State

because in 1869 it granted voting rights to women as well as men?

16. Your starter for 10:
Occurring in various fruits and vegetables, the plant pigment carotene is converted by the liver into which vitamin?

Three bonus questions on variations of English:
(a) In which Scottish city is Kelvinside, which has given its name to an imitation of received pronunciation?
(b) Taken from a type of stew, what name is given to the variety of English spoken on Merseyside?
(c) The English spoken in which university city, as opposed to that spoken by the townspeople, was formerly considered 'the best' English usage?

17. Your starter for 10:
From the Swedish for 'speed' and 'play', what term denotes a method of training for distance runners in which the terrain and pace are varied to enhance psychological aspects of conditioning?

Three bonus questions on music used as deterrents:
(a) Which composer's incidental music to *Hassan* was played over the loudspeakers of the Tyneside Metro to keep vandals away?
(b) Which singer's version of 'Big Spender' was allegedly used to drive birds from the runway at Liverpool Airport?
(c) In the 1996 film *Mars Attacks!*, which singer's yodelling version of 'Indian Love Call' was used to wipe out the Martians?

18. Your starter for 10:
In 1971, Carolyn Davidson, a Graphic Design student at Portland State University, created the logo of which sports-shoe and clothing manufacturing company, founded by Bill Bowerman and Phil Knight?

Three bonus questions on viticulture in France:
(a) Midway between Paris and Geneva, the town of Beaune in the Cote d'Or département is a major centre of which broad French wine region?
(b) The town of Condom in the Gers département is a centre of production of which alcoholic spirit, named after a historical area of Gascony?
(c) The town of Epernay in the Marne département is a principal centre for the storage and trading of what wine, also named after a French region?

19. Your starter for 10:
Amundsen's expedition of 1903 to 1906 was the first to make a successful navigation of which sea route, previously sought by Frobisher, Drake, Henry Hudson and Sir John Franklin?

Three bonus questions on a Greek letter:
(a) Which Greek letter is the symbol of chemical potential and also of the coefficient of friction?
(b) Mu also denotes a multiplicative function in number theory, named after which German mathematician, who gives his name to the surface with only one side and only one boundary component?
(c) The same letter can also represent a muon which, along with the electron, the tauon and the three neutrinos, is classified as what type of fundamental particle?

20. Your starter for 10:
Etymologically unconnected, what short name links a

French département named after a tributary of the Loire with the US singer and actress whose films include *The Witches of Eastwick* and *Moonstruck*?

Three bonus questions on librarians:

(a) In 1955, 'with magnificent irony' as he himself put it in a poem, which Argentinian literary figure was named Director of his National Library just as he finally lost his sight?

(b) Of which country was Mohammad Khatami elected President in 1997, having spent the previous five years as head of the National Library?

(c) Nadezhda Krupskaya, who spearheaded the drive to create new libraries after the Russian Revolution, was the wife of which political figure?

21. Your starter for 10:

What two-word term did the poet Keats use in a letter to his brother in 1817 to mean the ability of a reader to accept, quote: 'uncertainties, mysteries, doubts, without any irritable reaching after fact and reason'?

Three bonus questions on French kings and their mistresses:

(a) Madame de Maintenon, widow of the poet Paul Scarron, secretly married which king a few months after the death of his queen? An ardent Catholic, she is said to have influenced the revocation of the edict of Nantes.

(b) Diane de Poitiers was a mistress of which French king, almost twenty years her junior? Noted for her political acumen, she was an influence behind his marriage to Catherine de' Medici in 1533.

(c) For twenty years a major influence on state policy, and blamed by many for French military defeats, Madame de Pompadour was the mistress of which king?

22. Your starter for 10:
In a poem entitled 'Cosmic Gall', what did John Updike describe as, quote: 'very small. / They have no charge and have no mass / and do not interact at all'? Their existence was first postulated by Wolfgang Pauli in 1930.

Three bonus questions on literary prizes:
(a) Established in 1999, the prize for the competition open to all works of non-fiction published in English is named in honour of which eighteenth-century literary figure?
(b) 'What I have most wanted to do ... is to make political writing into an art.' These are the words of which literary figure, who gives his name to prizes for political writing founded in 1993?
(c) Which annual award for fiction by a female author was established in response to the furore surrounding the absence of women on the 1991 Booker shortlist?

23. Your starter for 10:
What French term is used for the ancient Egyptian hierographical symbol consisting of an oval or oblong enclosure, which indicated that the name inscribed inside it was of royal status?

Three bonus questions on Benjamin Britten's librettists:
(a) Which poet, who became an American citizen in 1946, wrote the libretto for Britten's first opera *Paul Bunyan*?
(b) Working in conjunction with Eric Crozier, which English novelist wrote the libretto of *Billy Budd*?
(c) Myfanwy Piper based the libretto of Britten's last opera on which 1912 novella of the same name by Thomas Mann?

---

24. Your starter for 10:

Farmed for both meat and milk, the red and white breed of cattle called Simmental is named after a valley in which European country?

Three bonus questions on Einstein:

(a) Einstein received the 1921 Nobel Prize for his services to physics and especially for his discovery of which 'effect', an insight which forms the basis of modern quantum theory?

(b) 'The Lord God is subtle but he is not malicious.' The German original of this remark by Einstein is carved above a fireplace in the Mathematical Institute of which American university, where he was a professor?

(c) After realising that his work had made the atom bomb possible, Einstein was reported as saying, 'If only I had known. I should have become a...' what?

25. Your starter for 10:

The word 'lusophone' describes a speaker of the language of which country, now covering roughly the same area as the Roman province of Lusitania?

Three bonus questions on the Second World War:

(a) Officially designated Operation Chastise, what popular name was given to the RAF bombing raids of May 1943, carried out by 617 Squadron against the heavily industrialised Ruhr Valley?

(b) The Dambusters raids breached the Möhne and Eder dams by utilising the 'bouncing bombs' designed by which English scientist and engineer?

(c) Following the Dambusters raids, 617 adopted what motto for their squadron badge, the phrase usually being associated with the French king Louis XV? You may answer in French or English.

26. Your starter for 10:

What is the English name for the musical sign known as *dièse* in French, *diesis* in Italian, and *sostenido* in Spanish?

Three bonus questions on European languages:
(a) Branches of which large language family include Baltic, Slavonic and Celtic?
(b) Two languages of south-eastern Europe are 'isolates' within Indo-European, that is, they do not belong to any established branch. One is Albanian; which EU official language is the other?
(c) To which branch of the Indo-European family does English belong?

27. Your starter for 10:

What is the relative molecular mass of calcium carbonate, that is, $CaCO_3$?

Three bonus questions on Ancient Rome:
In each case, give the name of the second-century Emperor who gives his name to the following:
(a) A column in Rome commemorating the conquest of Dacia between 101 and 106?
(b) A defensive structure between the Clyde and the Forth?
(c) The exposition of stoic philosophy usually known in English as the *Meditations*?

28. Your starter for 10:

What name is given to an integer, k, with n digits that has the property that the last n digits of k squared added to the first n or $n-1$ digits of k^2 results in the original number, k?

Three bonus questions on Scottish and English monarchs:
(a) Quote: 'Young, lovely, learned and pious, she won the

heart of the Scottish king, Malcolm Canmore, who married her in 1069.' These words from *Chambers Biographical Dictionary* describe which queen, canonised in 1251?

(b) The granddaughter of Alexander III of Scotland, Margaret, the 'Maid of Norway', was betrothed to which future English king, but died in 1290 on a voyage from Norway to Orkney?

(c) Margaret Tudor, married in turn to James IV of Scotland, Archibald Douglas and Henry Stewart, was the eldest daughter of which English king?

29. Your starter for 10:
Give any of three etymologically unrelated homographs that denote, respectively: to recover confidence or vitality; an incidental benefit attached to one's employment or position; and an abbreviated form of the verb that denotes the action of repeatedly passing boiling water through ground coffee beans?

Three bonus questions on flags:

(a) The cross of St Piran, patron saint of tin miners, is a white cross on a black background and is displayed on the flag of which English county?

(b) Thought by some to be the source of the name 'Saxon', what is a *seaxe*, as depicted on the county flag of Essex?

(c) In his *Ecclesiastical History*, the Venerable Bede described the banner which hung over St Oswald's tomb, providing the inspiration for the council flag of which county, the site of Bede's monastery?

30. Your starter for 10:
Listed in a work by Alan Dawson and thought to be inspired by the forename of a 1950s actress, what name

is given to British hills of any height with a drop of 150 metres or more on all sides, in other words, 'relatively high hills'?

Three bonus questions on clauses:

(a) Which thirteenth-century document included clause number 39, 'No freeman shall be seized or imprisoned … except by the lawful judgement of his equals or by the law of the land'?

(b) In 1995, the controversially rewritten Clause IV of the Labour Party constitution was approved, having formerly affirmed the party's commitment to – what?

(c) Which act of 1701 still regulates the succession to the British throne, and includes a clause stating that anyone who 'shall profess the Popish religion, or shall marry a Papist' cannot be monarch?

> **'We shall look forward to seeing how close you want to take it to the wire next time, but thank you, and we'll see you in Round Two.'**

THE RULES

The rules are the same as ever: 10 points for starters, 15 for bonuses, 5-point penalties for incorrect interruptions to starter questions. Fingers on buzzers, here's your first starter for 10.

Match Three

1. Your starter for 10:

Rachel Johnson, sister of Boris, won the 2008 *Literary Review* Bad Sex in Fiction Award for her novel *Shire Hell*. Which US author won a lifetime achievement award at the same ceremony after he received his third nomination, on that occasion for *The Widows of Eastwick*?

> **Three bonus questions on UK geography:**
> (a) Which major city lies closest to the midpoint of a straight line drawn on the map from London to Edinburgh?
> (b) Which cathedral city lies closest to the midpoint of a straight line drawn on the map from Belfast to London?
> (c) The midpoint of a straight line drawn on the map from Land's End to John O'Groats lies on which island?

2. Your starter for 10:

What Latin term referred to a soldier added to a legion after it had reached its full complement and also denotes, in biology, structures occurring in addition to the normal ones, and, in genetics, an irregularly occurring chromosome that may be absent from normal individuals?

Three bonus questions on a shared term:

(a) Indicated by a lower case 'n', what measurement is used for the ratio of the velocity of light in air or a vacuum to its velocity in another medium?

(b) For what do the initials of the F.T.S.E. Index stand?

(c) What index existed in several versions from 1559, when it was promulgated by Pope Paul IV, to 1966, when it was abolished by the Roman Catholic Church?

3. Your starter for 10:

If a particle of mass 15 kilograms undergoes a constant force of 165 newtons, what is its acceleration?

Three bonus questions on primitive primates:

(a) 'Slender', 'slow' and 'lesser slow' are the three species of which primitive primate, native to forests in South and Southeast Asia and characterised by a pale face with dark rings around large eyes?

(b) Which primitive primate from Madagascar derives its name from a Latin term meaning 'spirit of the night' or 'ghost', supposedly on account of its highly reflective eyes, and its wailing cry?

(c) What name is given to the Madagascan primate distinguished by long and slender fingers, especially the third finger, which it uses for digging insects out of tree bark?

4. Your starter for 10:

Commonly known as a line segment in one dimension, an equilateral triangle in two dimensions and a tetrahedron in three dimensions, what name is given to a simplex in four dimensions?

Three bonus questions on eponymous awards:

(a) The Newbery Medal, named after an eighteenth-century publisher, and the Caldecott Medal, named after a nineteenth-century illustrator, are awards in which field of American literature?

(b) Presented by the British Academy of Songwriters, Composers and Authors, which annual awards are named after the composer of the song 'Keep The Home Fires Burning'?

(c) As yet unawarded, a prize established in 1980 for the first controlled flight of a human-powered helicopter is named after which engineer, who built the first successful helicopter in 1939?

5.   Your starter for 10:

The eleventh-century Saint Sophia Cathedral and a monument to St Vladimir the Great are landmarks in which European capital, situated on the River Dnieper around 800 kilometres south-west of Moscow?

Three bonus questions on adjectives:

(a) Which two adjectives from the same verb can both be used to describe a lamb that has had its fleece removed, while one has the additional meaning in physics of 'distorted by tangential stress'?

(b) Both ultimately derived from the same noun, which two adjectives are used to describe a musical instrument such as a violin or guitar, and anything threaded in the manner of a rope of pearls?

(c) The past participle and adjective meaning 'shown to be true' has two forms, one standard for a weak verb, and the other a Scottish variant favoured in the USA that is replacing it in normal usage in England. What are they?

6.   Your starter for 10:

In the second millennium AD, which century saw the fewest reigning monarchs on the throne of England or, after 1707, Great Britain?

Three bonus questions on an expression:

(a) What phrase, specifying the rudiments of an elementary education but manifesting a profound lack of it, is said to have its origins in a speech by a barely literate MP and businessman, Sir William Curtis, in about 1807?

(b) 'Relief, Recovery and Reform' were the so-called 'Three Rs' of which political programme initiated in 1932?

(c) Among IT support staff, which two words follow 'reboot' in a somewhat humorous 'R.R.R.' by which there are three simple steps to make almost any problem go away?

7. Your starter for 10:

Which US President held a special screening of D.W. Griffith's notoriously racist film *Birth of a Nation*, a film which repeatedly quoted the President's five-volume *History of the American People*?

Three bonus questions on a colour:

(a) Which term of literary criticism did the Roman poet Horace introduce in his *Ars Poetica* to refer to words 'tacked on ... to works of grave purpose ... to give an effect of colour'?

(b) Which very hard rock was quarried in Egypt from the first century onwards, was used particularly for ornamental purposes, and has a name derived from the Greek for 'purple'?

(c) In French academic dress, the colour purple is associated with graduates in which one of five traditional fields of study?

8. Your starter for 10:

Which adjective describes something having the property of reversibly changing its colour or molecular structure in response to exposure to light, as is often exhibited in a pair of glasses?

> **Three bonus questions on words containing all the five standard vowels only once:**
>
> (a) Which medical term means 'introduced into or within a vein' and contains all five vowels only once?
>
> (b) The word 'nugatoriness' contains the five standard vowels in the order 'u, a, o, i, e'. Which of its synonyms contains them in the order 'u, i, o, a, e'?
>
> (c) Which fifteen-letter word, with each of the five standard vowels occurring only once, means 'not playing the game'?

9. **Your starter for 10:**
At the 2005 British Academy Television Awards, Rhys Ifans was named best actor for his portrayal of which comedian in the Channel 4 drama *Not Only but Always*?

> **Three bonus questions on restorative beverages:**
>
> (a) Which word derives from a Greek term for a drink made from pearl barley, and now means any herbal infusion other than that of the leaves of the tea bush *Camellia sinensis*?
>
> (b) Which tisane is made from the flowers of *Anthemis nobilis* and is thought by some to have relaxing properties, leading to its use as an aid to alleviating insomnia?
>
> (c) Which South American beverage is made from the leaves of Ilex paraguariensis, a member of the holly family?

10. **Your starter for 10:**
In life sciences, what name is given to the phenomenon of a plant's involuntary response to an environmental

stimulus that has directional orientation?

Three bonus questions on twentieth-century philosophy:

(a) Which school of philosophy was associated in the 1930s with Max Horkheimer and Theodor Adorno, and was the first Marxist-oriented research centre affiliated with a major German university?

(b) Which German-born American philosopher of the Frankfurt School wrote *Soviet Marxism* in 1958, and looked to students as the alienated elite who would initiate revolutionary change?

(c) Its period of exile during the Nazi era saw the Frankfurt School operating outside of Europe in which city?

11. **Your starter for 10:**

What is the name of the point at which paired homologous chromosomes remain in contact forming a cross shape during the first phase of meiosis?

Three bonus questions on linguistic terminology:

The answer in each case begins with the prefix 'para-'

(a) What word means a set of the inflected forms of a noun or verb, especially when used as a model for words of the same type?

(b) What word means the arrangement of clauses without connecting words, as in the sentence 'I tell you, this answer is wrong!'

(c) What word means those elements of communication other than words, such as tone of voice, gestures and facial expressions?

12. **Your starter for 10:**

Found in egg white, blood serum and milk, what is the name of a class of simple, water-soluble proteins that can be coagulated by heat?

Three bonus questions on Asian rulers:

(a) In AD 301, Tiridates the Great proclaimed Christianity as the state religion of which country, thus making his kingdom the first in the world officially to embrace Christianity?

(b) Sejong the Great, noted for cultural achievements including the institution of Hangul, a highly phonetic native script, was king of which country from 1418?

(c) Taksin the Great is noted for reunifying which country after its capital, Ayutthaya, was destroyed by the Burmese in 1767?

13. Your starter for 10:

The Bordeaux wine *entre-deux-mers* is so called because it is grown between which two rivers?

Three bonus questions on international agreements:

In each case, give the decade during which the following took place:

(a) The Treaty of Paris, signed by France, Britain and Spain, which ended the Seven Years' War.

(b) The Pact of Paris, also known as the Kellogg-Briand pact, which formally condemned recourse to war as an instrument of national policy.

(c) Finally, the Congress of Paris, which ended the Crimean War.

14. Your starter for 10:

According to its manufacturers and distributors, which traditional commodity cost 7p in 1962, 54p in 1982 and £1.87 in 2002?

Three bonus questions on flags:

(a) Which country's flag, adopted in 1949, features one large yellow star and four smaller ones, said to represent the proletariat, the peasants, the petty bourgeoisie, and the 'patriotic capitalists'?

(b) The five points of the white star on which African country's flag represent its people's traditional homelands, some of which now lie in Djibouti, Ethiopia and Kenya?

(c) Which Asian country became fully independent in 1965 and has a crescent and five stars on its flag, the stars representing 'democracy, peace, progress, justice, and equality'?

15. Your starter for 10:

'Hypostasis of the Archons', discovered in Upper Egypt in 1945, is a scripture of which esoteric and unorthodox branch of Christianity, whose name derives from a Greek word meaning 'knowledge'?

Three bonus questions on disease:

(a) What is the specific cause of any disease in humans or animals that is called a mycosis?

(b) Which fungus that develops on rye grass, was the cause of a disease that was widespread in the Middle Ages and which was also known as St Anthony's Fire?

(c) Which acid derived from ergot is the active principle in the psychedelic drug LSD?

16. Your starter for 10:

What links: a battle outside Edinburgh in 1547; a young gang leader in Graham Greene's *Brighton Rock* and a colloquial word for the little finger?

Three bonus questions on a scientific award:

(a) Given annually for outstanding achievements in research in any branch of science, and first awarded in 1731, the Copley Medal is the oldest award of which learned institution?

(b) Winner of the Copley Medal in 1808, which

Manchester-born chemist gives his name to the law that the concentration of a solute gas in a solution is directly proportional to the partial pressure of that gas above the solution?

(c) Which naturalist was awarded the Copley Medal in 1908 for 'the part he took in working out the theory of the origin of species by natural selection'? He gives his name to the line dividing Asian and Australasian fauna.

17. Your starter for 10:
What surname is shared by Burton, a US physicist and pioneer in colliding beam technology, Sviatoslav, a Russian pianist; and Charles, a seismologist who gave his name to a scale of earthquake strength?

Three bonus questions on medicine:
(a) What is the chief characteristic of the medical condition Hyperlipidaemia, which underlies a group of metabolic disorders?

(b) Which group of lipid-lowering drugs, which act by inhibiting the enzyme HMG-CoA, are used to treat Hyperlipidaemia in which high-cholesterol concentration is the main feature?

(c) The two most important types of fat circulating in the blood are cholesterol and which other, whose name indicates its composition from glycerol and three fatty acid molecules?

18. Your starter for 10:
How many litres are there in a cubic metre?

Three bonus questions on space missions of 2007:
(a) In 2007, new data from the Cassini-Huygens project suggested that Tethys and Dione are geologically active. Which planet do they orbit?

(b) In May 2007, Corot, a French-led satellite mission to

search for extra-solar planets, identified a 'hot Jupiter' in which constellation, whose name translates as 'Unicorn'?

(c) Launched by NASA in 2007, Themis is a mission composed of five satellites to study the cause of what atmospheric phenomena, especially visible in polar latitudes?

19. Your starter for 10:

The acronym CITES denotes the convention on international trade in what?

Three bonus questions on communications:

(a) Which Irish broadcasting company has taken its title from the original name of the legendary hero Cúchulainn?

(b) Which electronic protocol takes its name from the nickname of Harald I, credited with uniting Denmark in the tenth century?

(c) Which communications company is named after an ancient settlement in Sardinia?

20. Your starter for 10:

Which musical instrument is a type of bugle, used in brass bands and occasionally in the orchestra, pitched in B Flat like the cornet and trumpet? It was developed in the early nineteenth century by fitting valves to the key bugle instead of the keys, and is used in Stravinsky's *Threni* and in Vaughan Williams's Ninth Symphony.

Three bonus questions on pairs of words whose spellings are identical but for the letters 'g' and 'h', for example 'fit' and 'fight':

In each case, give the two words that correspond to the definitions:

(a) An adverb indicating motion away from a place,

and an auxiliary verb expressing rightness, duty, advisability or strong probability.

(b) A second person singular personal pronoun used in the King James Bible and formerly associated with South Yorkshire, and a conjunction that introduces adverbial clauses of concession.

(c) The egg of a head louse, and the period between sunset and sunrise.

21. Your starter for 10:

According to Immanuel Kant, 'Rhetoric is the art of transacting a serious business of the understanding as if it were a free play of the imagination.' What literary form did Kant say was the art of 'conducting a free play of the imagination as if it were a serious business of the understanding'?

> **Three bonus questions on royalty according to J.L. Carr's 1977 Dictionary of English Queens, King's Wives, Celebrated Paramours, Handfast Spouses and Royal Changelings:**
>
> In each case, identify the personage described. To make it easier for you, all three have the same given name:
>
> (a) 'Only a male heir could have saved her from her abominable husband. On a trumped up charge of adultery she was beheaded without blindfold by a French swordsman.'
>
> (b) 'An attractive, empty-headed blonde who, at 15, married King James VI or I... who, although he preferred good-looking young men, fathered seven children.'
>
> (c) 'A dull person, usually unwell and often uncharitable. Her farming levy, much resented by non-Anglicans, made parsons rich for 200 years.'

22. Your starter for 10:
Characterised by massive strength and the use of round-headed arches, the style of architecture prevailing in most of Europe during the eleventh and twelfth centuries is known by which term?

> **Three bonus questions on rainbows:**
> (a) 'The rainbow comes and goes, / And lovely is the rose'. Who wrote these lines in 'Intimations of Immortality from Recollections of Early Childhood'?
> (b) What literary form did D.H Lawrence call 'a perfect medium for revealing to us the changing rainbow of our living relationships'?
> (c) The goddess Iris, who personified the rainbow and acted as Hera's messenger to the mortal world, is summoned to celebrate a betrothal in which play by Shakespeare?

23. Your starter for 10:
Which English king is often known as the last of the Angevin kings because he lost Anjou in 1204?

> **Three bonus questions on deaths in Shakespeare:**
> (a) Having stabbed himself with his own blade, which of Shakespeare's tragic heroes dies with the words, 'I kissed thee ere I killed thee: no way but this / Killing myself, to die upon a kiss'?
> (b) Having kissed 'the gashes / That bloodily did yawn' upon the face of his cousin's corpse, the Duke of York dies, according to the report of Exeter in the fourth act of *Henry V*, during which battle?
> (c) 'O true apothecary! / Thy drugs are quick. Thus with a kiss I die.' These are the last words spoken by which of Shakespeare's title characters?

24. Your starter for 10:
In 2005, which British landmark, already a world heritage site in its own right, was joined by the Upper German-Raetian Limes to form the first section of a trans-national world heritage site called Frontiers of the Roman Empire?

> **Three bonus questions on mythology:**
> (a) In Greek mythology, although they were formally called the Erinyes, the Furies were better known by what euphemistic name?
> (b) In the *Oresteia* of Aeschylus, the Eumenides hound Orestes to madness for which crime?
> (c) What was the title of T.S. Eliot's 1939 drawing-room comedy loosely based on the *Oresteia*?

25. Your starter for 10:
What is the opening line of the poem 'To the Virgins, to Make Much of Time', first published in 1648 in *Hesperides*, a collection by Robert Herrick?

> **Three bonus questions on temperature:**
> (a) Under standard conditions, at what Kelvin temperature does pure water freeze?
> (b) To the nearest degree, at what Celsius temperature does water have its maximum density?
> (c) What, in degrees Fahrenheit, is the difference between the boiling points and freezing points of water under standard conditions?

26. Your starter for 10:
Founded in 1987 as an offshoot of the Egyptian Muslim Brotherhood, which movement and political party is generally known by a five-letter acronym which means 'zeal'?

Three bonus questions on garden flowers:

(a) Which garden flower took its name from the Latin for 'wolf-like', in the mistaken belief that it 'wolfed' minerals from the soil?

(b) The name of which garden plant is a Latinised version of the Greek 'larkspur' or 'little dolphin'?

(c) Which flowering plant derives its popular English name from the French for 'thought'?

27. Your starter for 10:

The concept of 'élan vital' or 'vital principle' is associated with which philosopher, born in Paris in 1859?

Three bonus questions on a town:

(a) Which Yorkshire town gives its name to a double lamb or mutton chop?

(b) Which Barnsley-born playwright's best known work is 1959's *Sergeant Musgrave's Dance*?

(c) Born in Barnsley in 1964, which novelist's work includes *Chocolat* and *Gentlemen and Players*?

28. Your starter for 10:

Which planet is principally made of iron, but shares its name with that of a different metal?

Three bonus questions on an island:

(a) On which island in the Bay of Naples is the celebrated cave known as the Blue Grotto?

(b) Which Roman Emperor retired to Capri in the first century AD?

(c) Which Rochdale-born singer and comedienne followed his example and retired to the island in the 1950s?

29. Your starter for 10:

What optical phenomenon is the changing of colour when viewing from different angles, often caused by the interference of light from different layers of a material, examples being the semi-precious stone opal and some butterfly wings?

Three bonus questions on a shared name:
(a) What name is shared by three kings of Scotland and three tsars of Russia?
(b) What name did William Alexander, Earl of Stirling, give to that part of Canada granted to him by King James I in 1621?
(c) When Field Marshal Alexander was created a viscount in 1946, he took as his title the name of which North African country?

30. Your starter for 10:

In which city did Shannon Sickles and Grainne Close become the first same-sex couple in the UK to celebrate a civil partnership ceremony after the new law granting legal status to gay and lesbian couples came into force in December 2005?

Three bonus questions on place names:
(a) The official name of which of the United States of America is completed by the phrase '... and Providence Plantations'?
(b) The full name of which US city begins 'El Pueblo de la Reyna de...'?
(c) The full name of which capital city translates into English as 'Saint Mary of the Good Air'?

'Not terribly good, I have to say, but you were up against some very, very fearsome opposition today. So we shall have to say goodbye to you, I'm afraid, but thank you for taking part.'

Match Four

1. **Your starter for 10:**
White tin – which is metallic and stable above 13.2
Celsius – and grey tin – which is non-metallic and stable
below 13.2 Celsius – may be described by what term,
denoting the different forms an element can take, usually
because of variation in crystal structure?

> **Three bonus questions on the colours of horses:**
> (a) What name is given to a horse which is brown all over,
>   except for a black muzzle, mane, tail and extremities of
>   the legs?
> (b) A white horse is officially described as being what
>   colour?
> (c) What term is used for a horse with a combination of
>   red, white and yellow or black, white and yellow hairs?

2. **Your starter for 10:**
The 2005 Ang Lee film *Brokeback Mountain* is based
on a short story by which American writer, who won a
Pulitzer Prize for her second novel, *The Shipping News*?

> **Three bonus questions linked by a word:**
> (a) What term was coined by Charles Dickens to describe
>   men who carried advertising placards in the streets?
> (b) Which island group was originally named after the Earl
>   of Sandwich by Captain Cook, in recognition of his
>   interest in exploration?

(c) Who, in 1759, married Mary Lambert, an 'Orphan of Sandwich'? In 1791, he wrote *The Rights of Man*.

3. Your starter for 10:
What two-word Latin term links a coastal city in southern Texas, a Roman Catholic festival honouring the Eucharist, and colleges of Cambridge and Oxford Universities, founded in 1352 and 1517 respectively?

Three bonus questions on miracles:
(a) In which city on the shore of the Sea of Galilee did Jesus choose the disciples Peter, Andrew and Matthew?
(b) In which poem did Samuel Taylor Coleridge write 'It was a miracle of rare device / A sunny pleasure dome with caves of ice!'?
(c) According to the title of the one-act ballet with music by Sir Arthur Bliss, in which district of Glasgow did a miracle occur?

4. Your starter for 10:
Acaricides are pesticides used in the control of which organisms?

Three bonus questions on chemistry:
(a) The husband and wife team who won the 1935 Nobel Prize for Chemistry were, respectively, the son-in-law and daughter of which Nobel Prize winners?
(b) Reflected in its name, which element, atomic number 43, was the first element to be artificially produced?
(c) Produced by neutron-induced reactions in uranium ores, which was the first transuranic element to be artificially produced?

5. Your starter for 10:
Which word can mean all of the following: a woman's short hairstyle in which the hair tapers to the nape of

the neck, a rectangular wooden roof tile, and a mass of small rounded pebbles along a shoreline?

Three bonus questions on a name:
(a) Which Irish scientist derived the law which expresses the terminal velocity of a small sphere falling through a viscous fluid?
(b) In a parliamentary context, how are Stoke, Desborough and Burnham better known?
(c) The Chiltern Hills lie mainly within which county?

6. **Your starter for 10:**
An apologue is a type of moral fable, especially one where the characters are represented by what?

Three bonus questions on underworlds:
(a) Which son of the Titans Cronus and Rhea ruled the Underworld with his queen, Persephone?
(b) What collective name is given to Tisiphone, Megaera and Alecto, who would rise from the Underworld to pursue the wicked?
(c) Whose novel *Underworld* was first published in the UK in January 1998?

7. **Your starter for 10:**
San Andreas, Liberty City and Vice City are fictional cities that are among possible settings of which popular entertainment work?

Three bonus questions on nineteenth-century history:
In each case, name the British Prime Minister who was in office during the entire term or terms of the following US presidents:
(a) Abraham Lincoln.
(b) James Monroe.
(c) Chester A. Arthur.

8. **Your starter for 10:**
The mythological Chinese barbarian leader Houyi, the Hindu deity Arjuna, the Greek goddess Artemis, the centaur Sagittarius and the Roman god Cupid are frequently depicted carrying what items, originally used for hunting or warfare?

Three bonus questions on Welsh counties:
(a) Haverfordwest is the administrative centre of which Welsh county, which includes the most westerly point in Wales?
(b) One of the locations of the BBC comedy series *Gavin and Stacey*, Barry is the administrative centre of which Welsh county borough?
(c) Llandrindod Wells is the administrative centre of which county, the largest in Wales?

9. **Your starter for 10:**
Including the settlements of Dawley, Oakengates and Wellington, which town near the River Severn, north-west of Birmingham, was designated a new town in the 1960s?

Three bonus questions on tigers in literature:
(a) In the novel *The Life of Pi* by Yann Martel, the shipwrecked Pi shares a lifeboat with a zebra, a spotted hyena and a tiger with what full name?
(b) Set in Manchester in the 1930s, *Shabby Tiger* was the debut novel of which writer, a journalist on the *Manchester Guardian* under C.P. Scott? His most notable success was with *Fame Is the Spur* in 1940.
(c) Having been shortlisted on two previous occasions, which writer won the 1987 Booker Prize for the novel *Moon Tiger*?

10. Your starter for 10:

What term denotes the scientific description of nations or races of people, including their customs and points of difference, and is formed of Greek-derived components meaning 'people' and 'writing'?

Three bonus questions on medieval universities:

(a) Which city in southern Italy is the site of a medical school dating to the ninth century and regarded by some as the first university in Europe?

(b) The oldest university in Europe is more generally considered to be the University of Bologna, founded in 1088, which received its charter nearly 150 years later from which Holy Roman Emperor?

(c) Which university in north-east Italy was founded in 1222 by students and professors who left the University of Bologna in search of greater academic freedom?

11. Your starter for 10:

What surname is shared by Harriet in Jane Austen's *Emma*, Wayland in Sir Walter Scott's *Kenilworth*, and Winston in Orwell's *Nineteen Eighty-Four*?

Three bonus questions on Russian tsars:

(a) The subject of a tragedy by Pushkin and an opera by Mussorgsky, which chief adviser to Tsar Fyodor I became Tsar himself in 1598?

(b) An adversary of Napoleon I, which Tsar formed the Holy Alliance in 1815 and retreated into reactionary policies towards the end of his reign?

(c) The first Grand Prince to have himself officially crowned Tsar, which ruler ordered the construction of St Basil's Cathedral to celebrate victory against the Tatars?

12. **Your starter for 10:**
    In addition to London and Dublin, seven EU capitals have English names of six letters. For ten points, name three of them.

    Three bonus questions on engravings:
    (a) The work of which artist of the Northern Renaissance includes the engravings *Melancholia* in 1514, and *Saint Christopher* in 1521?
    (b) Which Italian artist issued the 'imaginary prisons' series of engravings in 1750?
    (c) *Industry and Idleness* is a series of twelve didactic engravings produced in 1747 by which British artist?

13. **Your starter for 10:**
    Peregrine, Elberta and Rochester are among about 2,000 varieties of which species of stone fruit, *prunus persica*, belonging to the rose family?

    Three bonus questions on physics:
    (a) What name is given to the physical law which states that the heat current due to radiation emitted from a surface is proportional to the temperature of the surface raised to the fourth power?
    (b) In terms of Boltzmann's constant k and temperature t, what is the average translational kinetic energy of a molecule of an ideal gas?
    (c) According to Boltzmann, what thermodynamic quantity is given by Boltzmann's constant times the natural logarithm of the number of microstates corresponding to a given macrostate?

14. **Your starter for 10:**
    What five-letter word links: an exclamation of glee or exultation; a member of a brutish race in Swift's land of the Houyhnhnms; and an internet enterprise set up by

David Filo and Jerry Yang in 1994?

Three bonus questions on clerical offices:

(a) In June 2009, Bishop David Chillingworth was elected to what office as head of the Scottish Episcopal Church?

(b) Which term for an honorary canon is derived from the word meaning that part of the revenues of a cathedral or collegiate church formerly granted to a canon as his stipend?

(c) The head of the chapter of a cathedral has what title?

15. Your starter for 10:

Named after the celebrated French surgeon who described it, Dupuytren's Contracture is a medical condition that usually affects which part of the body?

Three bonus questions on borrowed titles:

(a) Which novel of 1872 by Thomas Hardy takes its title from a song in Shakespeare's *As You Like It*?

(b) The Coen Brothers' film *No Country for Old Men* takes its title from the first line of a work first published in 1928 by which poet?

(c) The rock band Coldplay borrowed the title of their 2008 album *Viva la Vida* from a painting by which Mexican artist?

16. Your starter for 10:

Traditionally believed to have been a victim of the Diocletian Persecutions and sometimes depicted carrying a plate bearing her own eyes, which saint's feast day is celebrated on 13 December which, under the Julian calendar, was the shortest day of the year?

Three bonus questions on countries of the Americas:

Specifically, those that share borders with two and only

two others. In each case, name the country from its neighbours:

(a) Panama and Nicaragua.

(b) Mexico and Guatemala.

(c) Peru and Colombia.

17. Your starter for 10:

Which West African country is home to what is now claimed to be the world's second-largest film industry in terms of the number of films produced, ahead of the USA and slightly behind India, the industry being known colloquially as Nollywood?

Three bonus questions on castles and palaces in Germany:
In each case, give the present-day German state in which the following are located:

(a) Sanssouci, built for Frederick the Great, and the Orangery Palace, built in the mid nineteenth century.

(b) The Baroque Zwinger Palace, begun by King Augustus the Strong from around 1710, and Castle Colditz, which dates to the sixteenth century.

(c) Finally: the Nymphenburg, begun in the seventeenth century, and Neuschwanstein, built for King Ludwig II from 1869.

18. Your starter for 10:

Originally a Catholic priest, which Protestant reformer was a chaplain to Edward VI? He fled to Geneva during the reign of Mary Tudor and returned to found the Church of Scotland in 1560.

Three bonus questions on an artist:

(a) 'When Matisse dies, [he] will be the only painter left who understands what colour really is.' These words of Picasso refer to which Russian-born French artist, who died in 1985?

(b) What word did the poet and art critic Guillaume Apollinaire coin in around 1918, reportedly for Chagall's work, although it is now more often applied to artists such as Dalí and Magritte?

(c) In the 1920s, Chagall was commissioned to produce illustrated editions of La Fontaine's *Fables* and which novel by Nikolai Gogol?

19. Your starter for 10:
'Geometry is not true, it is advantageous.' These words are attributed to which French mathematician, who gives his name to a conjecture proved in the twenty-first century by Grigori Perelman?

Three bonus questions on ancient history:

(a) Which country, then under Persian control, was invaded and captured in 332 BC by Alexander the Great, who was told by an oracle that he was the son of the country's chief deity?

(b) Which dynasty ruled Egypt after Alexander's death, and was named after the Macedonian general who became satrap, or provincial governor, in 323 BC, adopting a royal title in 304 BC?

(c) Who became queen on the death of her father Ptolemy XII in 51 BC, and, reigning successively with her brothers and then her son, was the last of the Ptolemaic dynasty to rule Egypt?

20. Your starter for 10:
From the Latin meaning 'to bind', which word can mean both a horizontal line drawn above a group of mathematical terms and, in physiology, a ligament that limits the movement of an organ?

Three bonus questions on a fabric:

(a) Needle, bobbin, chain, pillow and Brussels are all

types of which open-work fabric formed by looping, interlacing, braiding or twisting threads?

(b) Which hand-made bobbin lace is named after the town to the north of Paris where it has been made since the seventeenth century?

(c) Lacecaps and mopheads, or hortensias, are the two main ornamental forms of which shrub that produces blue flowers on acid soils and pink on alkaline?

21. **Your starter for 10:**

The claim of Archduke Charles to the throne of which country was a *casus belli* of conflicts concluded by the treaties of Utrecht and Rastatt in 1713–1714?

Three bonus questions on siblings:

(a) Who was described by an editor of her journals as 'probably the most distinguished of English writers who never wrote a line for the general public'? A major influence on the poetry of her brother, she died at Rydal Mount in 1855.

(b) Which Welsh artist's work was, in her lifetime, overshadowed by that of her brother, also a painter, although since her death in 1939 critical opinion has tended to regard her as the more talented of the two?

(c) What was the surname of the nineteenth-century composer Fanny Cäcilie? Considered to be as talented as her brother, she was forbidden by their father from having a career in music and published some of her work under her brother's name.

22. **Your starter for 10:**

Identify the author of these lines: 'Music, when soft voices die, / Vibrates in the memory; / Odours, when sweet violets sicken, / Live within the sense they quicken.'

Three bonus questions on mathematics, as understood by Gilbert and Sullivan's modern Major-General:

(a) In *The Pirates of Penzance*, the Major-General boasts that 'about binomial theorem I am teeming with a lot of news'. Which scientist discovered the binomial theorem in 1676?

(b) He also claims to have 'many cheerful facts about the square on the hypotenuse'. What is the numerical value of that quantity if the lengths of the sides of a right-angled triangle are three successive integers?

(c) His final mathematical boast is that 'in conics I can floor peculiarities parabolous'. A parabola can be defined as a type of conic that has an eccentricity equal to what?

23. Your starter for 10:
An abridged version of which play was performed by a Norwegian Sami theatre group in 2003 in a replica of the Globe theatre made of ice and snow?

Three bonus questions on words which contain all five vowels only once:

(a) In botany, what is the collective term for the stamens of a flower in which the five vowels occur in the order 'a-e-o-i-u'?

(b) The fossil hominid discovered in Java in the 1890s was given what name, a fifteen-letter word with the five vowels in the order 'i-e-a-o-u'?

(c) In which common nine-letter word for a domestic servant do all five vowels appear once in the order o-u-e-a-i?

24. Your starter for 10:
Malachite, often used as a gemstone, is a minor ore of which metal?

Three bonus questions on a shared prefix:

(a) Which layer of the atmosphere lies from about fifty to eighty-five kilometres above the Earth's surface, its name referring to its position between the stratosphere below and the thermosphere above?

(b) Also called the Age of Reptiles, the Mesozoic era lies between the Cenozoic and the Palaeozoic, and itself comprises three periods: the Triassic, Jurassic and which other?

(c) Sharing the same prefix, what specific name is given to the cell tissue that forms the lining of the chest and the abdomen in vertebrates?

25. Your starter for 10:

Which lake is formed by a natural widening of the River Adda and lies in the foothills of the Bernese Alps in the Lombardy province of northern Italy?

Three bonus questions on early man-made plastics:

(a) What is generally considered to be the first man-made thermo-plastic? It was invented by Alexander Parkes in 1855 and is transparent, highly flammable, and made from cellulose nitrate with a camphor plasticiser.

(b) With a name derived from its Belgian inventor, which thermo-setting plastic is produced by the reaction under pressure of phenol and formaldehyde, combined with a filler such as wood flour?

(c) Which synthetic polyamide thermo-plastic was developed by the DuPont Company in 1935? It was first used for the bristles of toothbrushes, and later replaced silk in stockings.

26. Your starter for 10:

What verb of five letters can mean: to prepare an explosive for detonation; to fill a pump with its working liquid before starting; to supply a person with necessary facts in advance; to cover a surface with a preparatory coat or colour?

Three bonus questions on British fashion:
(a) Which shoe company was established in the Somerset village of Street in 1825 by its eponymous founder, a Quaker, and remains largely owned by his family?
(b) Famed for its jackets, which outdoor clothing company was established at Number 5, Market Place in South Shields in 1894?
(c) Which former draper's apprentice invented the breathable and waterproof gabardine fabric in 1880, and gave his name to a company known for its red, black and camel check?

27. **Your starter for 10:**
Prior to Matthew Dobson's discovery of sugar in the blood suggesting it affected the entire body, diabetes was considered a problem of what organ?

Three bonus questions on coal:
(a) Among the organic chemical constituents of coal tar is which aromatic hydrocarbon with the chemical symbol $C_6H_5CH_3$, alternatively known as methyl-benzene?
(b) The dark nebula called the Coal Sack, a relatively starless area detectable with the naked eye, is part of which constellation containing four chief stars?
(c) Which British politician said, in a speech of May 1945, 'This island is made mainly of coal and surrounded by fish. Only an organising genius could produce a shortage of coal and fish at the same time'?

28. **Your starter for 10:**
Launched in the UK in 1979, employing an audio cassette player for mass storage and a TV set as a

monitor, what was the first computer in the world to sell
for less than £100?

**Three bonus questions on the history of
telecommunications:**
In each case, give the decade in which the following
occurred:
(a) The invention of Morse code by Samuel Morse, and
the patenting of the electric telegraph by Cooke and
Wheatstone.
(b) The demonstration of radio transmission by Marconi,
and the invention of the cathode ray tube by K.F.
Braun.
(c) The establishment of regular public radio broadcasting
in Britain and the U.S.A., and the first demonstration
of television by Baird.

29. Your starter for 10:
Which game in fiction involved members of the
animal species 'Phoenicopterus ruber' and 'Erinaceus
europaeus'?

Three bonus questions on art in the Maritime Alps:
(a) The Museum of the Biblical Message in Nice is named
after which Russian-born artist, who died in 1985?
(b) The Chapel of the Rosary at Vence outside Nice is
often given the name of which artist? Its interior
decoration, begun in 1949, was his last major work.
(c) Les Collettes, a farm outside Nice, is now a museum
dedicated to which impressionist artist, a friend of
Monet and Cezanne, who spent the last twelve years of
his life there?

30. Your starter for 10:
Give the single word that completes this observation by
the American writer Eric Hoffer: 'Faith in a holy cause

is to a considerable extent a substitute for the lost faith in...' whom or what?

Three questions about Japan in western musical theatre:
(a) Puccini's *Madam Butterfly* is set in which Japanese city?
(b) Which 1976 musical with music and lyrics by Stephen Sondheim is about the opening up of Japan by the US commodore Matthew Perry in the mid nineteenth century?
(c) Who was the director of the 1999 film *Topsy-Turvy* about the creation of *The Mikado* by Gilbert and Sullivan?

'You were on fire – terrific. We shall look forward to seeing you in the next stage of the contest.'

THE RULES

You know all the guff about 10 points for starters, 15 for bonuses, 5-point penalties for incorrect interruptions to starter questions. Fingers on the buzzers, here's your first starter for 10.

Match Five

1. **Your starter for 10:**
    A former carpenter, which of Chaucer's Canterbury pilgrims tells the tale of Symkyn, a dishonest miller whose wife and daughter are seduced by two students?

    Three bonus questions on lawyers in Dickens:
    (a) In which novel by Dickens is the manipulative lawyer Mr Tulkinghorn murdered, with several of the characters having reasons for wanting him dead?
    (b) Which attorney tells the young boy Pip that he has a benefactor who wishes him 'to be removed from his present sphere of life ... and brought up as a gentleman – in a word, as a young fellow of great expectations'?
    (c) In *David Copperfield*, what is the name of Mr Wickfield's clerk, who, through manipulation and blackmail, succeeds in becoming his partner despite his protestation 'We are so very 'umble'?

2. **Your starter for 10:**
    What did H.L. Mencken describe as 'the delusion that one woman differs from another'?

    Three bonus questions on women:
    (a) What word for a quarrelsome and scolding woman derives from that of an imaginary Muslim deity, a stock character in medieval mystery plays?

(b) In modern English suggestive of loudness or ill-temper, what six-letter word is used by Virgil and Ovid to denote a strong, vigorous woman, and became the name of a publishing company founded in 1973?

(c) Both in Shakespeare and in modern times, the name of which insectivorous mammal indicates a troublesome, nagging woman?

3. Your starter for 10:

At about 0.93 per cent of dry air, what is the commonest inert gas in the atmosphere?

Three bonus questions on architects:

(a) Born in 1849, which architect was responsible for completing the V & A museum, giving a new façade to Buckingham Palace and building Admiralty Arch?

(b) Which landmark in Bath, designed by John Wood the Elder and completed by his son, features all three classical orders of architecture and resembles the exterior of the Colosseum in Rome?

(c) In 1856, architect Alfred Waterhouse set up a practice in which city, for which he designed the Gothic revival town hall in Albert Square?

4. Your starter for 10:

Which human diseases are caused by rhinoviruses?

Three bonus questions on Antarctica:

(a) Which British seafarer gives his name to the narrowest point of the Southern Ocean, lying between Cape Horn and the Antarctic Peninsula?

(b) Almost 4,900 metres high, what is Antarctica's highest peak, named after the first man to serve 50 years in the US Congress?

(c) Formerly a major centre of Antarctic exploration, the Bay of Whales was created by the uneven advancement of which ice shelf, the world's largest body of floating ice?

5.   Your starter for 10:
Lying between 'pebble' and 'boulder' on the Wentworth-Udden scale for measuring and describing the size of grains of minerals, which large round stone is a traditional road-paving material?

Three questions about larks:

(a) The song that begins 'Hark, hark! The lark at Heaven's gate sings' is used by Cloten in his attempts to woo Imogen in which play by Shakespeare?

(b) 'The music soars within the little lark, / And the lark soars'. Who wrote these words in the 1857 poem 'Aurora Leigh'?

(c) 'Hail to thee, blithe spirit! / Bird thou never wert'. Which Romantic poet addressed a skylark with these words?

6.   Your starter for 10:
In astronomy, what word describes the apparent or real motion of a satellite, such as the moon, which makes it appear to oscillate in such a way that the parts near the edge of the disk are alternately visible and invisible?

Three bonus questions on London theatres:

(a) Opening in 1905, which theatre is named after the crescent on which it stands, and became the London home of the RSC from 1960? Notable productions include *The Devils* by John Whiting in 1961, and several plays by Harold Pinter.

(b) Now owned by Cameron Mackintosh, which theatre near Leicester Square opened in 1884 and in the following year saw performances by Lily Langtree?

(c) Which theatre was founded in 1818 and saw notable performances by Edmund Kean in 1824? John Gielgud established a theatre company there in 1929, and in 2003 Kevin Spacey became its Artistic Director.

7. Your starter for 10:
In which decade of the nineteenth century was the first rugby international, in which Scotland beat England; the first cricket Test, in which Australia beat England; and the first FA Cup final, in which Wanderers beat Royal Engineers?

Three bonus questions on the expansion of the British Empire:
In each case, give the decade during which the following occurred:
(a) The Peace of Paris confirmed Britain's possession of Ontario, Quebec, Prince Edward Island, Dominica, Grenada and Florida.
(b) The Seychelles, Mauritius, Ceylon and the Ionian Islands were all ceded to Britain.
(c) Britain assumed direct control of India from the East India Company; Victoria and Queensland became colonies.

8. Your starter for 10:
Born in Versailles in 1766, which violinist became a friend of Beethoven, who dedicated to him the Violin Sonata (Op. 47) that bears his name?

Three bonus questions on the year 1985:
(a) At the Geneva summit of November 1985, the new de facto leader of the Soviet Union met the US President for the first time. For five points, name both.
(b) In July 1985, which Greenpeace ship was bombed and sunk by French agents in Auckland Harbour as

it prepared to sail in protest against French nuclear weapons tests?

(c) In July 1985, more than fifty of the world's top rock stars took part in the Live Aid concerts in London and which US city?

9. Your starter for 10:
Which English county lends its name to the rag-stone – a sandy, limestone used for masonry and road repairs and traditionally taken from the lower greensand there?

Three bonus questions on political defeats:

(a) In 1998, which European head of government lost power after sixteen years in office? He was defeated in his own constituency but returned to the National Assembly under the regional 'party list' vote.

(b) In 1993, which politician became the first Canadian Prime Minister to be voted out by her own constituents when Hedy Fry won Vancouver Centre for the Liberals?

(c) In 2007, which Prime Minister, defeated at a federal election, lost his own parliamentary seat when his Bennelong constituents elected the former TV journalist Maxine McKew to the House of Representatives?

10. Your starter for 10:
Used of fish such as dace and barbell and of insects such as mayflies, the term 'rheophilic' indicates that they thrive in what specific type of water?

Three questions linked by a French adjective:

(a) What is the title in the original French of *The Lost Domain*, the 1913 novel by Alain-Fournier about a young man's search for a girl he has seen only briefly?

(b) *La Grande Odalisque*, a painting of a nude concubine with an elongated back in the Mannerist style, is by which early nineteenth-century Neo-Classical French artist?

(c) *La Grande Jatte*, the large pointillist painting of a Sunday afternoon by the riverside, is by which French artist?

11. Your starter for 10:
By what initials is the Russian state security organisation, which is the domestic successor to the KGB, now known?

Three bonus questions linked by a word:
(a) In *All Creatures Great and Small*, what was the name of Mrs Pumphrey's pampered Pekinese?
(b) 'Tricky' Sam Nanton and 'Bubber' Miley were sidemen in whose jazz orchestra of the 1920s?
(c) Who was first called 'Tricky Dick' by Helen Gahagan Douglas, his opponent in the 1950 senatorial election in California?

12. Your starter for 10:
Which species of mycobacterium is the cause of a disease in which a growth of tubercles occurs on the lining of the lungs?

Three bonus questions on Caribbean literature:
(a) *The Final Passage* and *Dancing in the Dark* are works by which Caribbean-born author?
(b) Which poet, who refused an OBE in 2003, has made several records, including 'Free South Africa', which he made with the Wailers?
(c) Which poet and playwright, born in St Lucia in 1930, received the Nobel Prize for Literature in 1992?

13. Your starter for 10:
Ankara, Yerevan, Baku and which East Asian capital

city all lie within one degree of latitude 40 degrees
north?

Three bonus questions on a supernatural practitioner:
(a) Who is Frieda Haxby Palmer, in the title of the novel
by Margaret Drabble?
(b) Which Old Testament king consulted the Witch
of Endor, so learning of his coming defeat by the
Philistines and death the next day?
(c) In Englebert Humperdinck's opera *Hansel and Gretel*,
the witch turns the two children into what?

14. Your starter for 10:
'The curve formed by a chain or rope of uniform density
hanging freely from two fixed points not in the same
vertical line' is how the Oxford English Dictionary
defines what curve of the form $y = \cosh x$?

Three bonus questions on emeralds:
(a) The emerald is a bright green variety of which mineral?
(b) According to custom, how many years of marriage are
celebrated in an emerald wedding anniversary?
(c) Located in Chiang Rai until 1436, in which city in
Thailand is the so-called Emerald Buddha now to be
found?

15. Your starter for 10:
Which four-letter contraction, originally referring to
the name, no longer in technical usage, of a chemical
solution, is often used for sodium thiosulphate, the fixer
in photographic processing?

Three bonus questions on poetry:
(a) A song or poem known as an 'Epithalamion' would be
written to celebrate what rite of passage?

(b) Which Roman poet attempted to fuse the ribald Fescennine verse to the Greek form of the Epithalamion?

(c) Which poet's 'Epithalamion' was written on the occasion of his second marriage in 1595?

16. Your starter for 10:
In humans, the vestibular apparatus is part of the inner ear responsible for bodily orientation and which other faculty?

Three bonus questions on miracles:

(a) In the Roman Catholic Church, what is usually the minimum number of miracles attributed to a person before they can be declared a saint?

(b) Which French writer was the author in 1945 of *The Miracle of the Rose*, based on his own prison experiences?

(c) In a film of 1947, on which street in Manhattan did a miracle apparently occur, leading some New Yorkers to believe in Santa Claus?

17. Your starter for 10:
Herpestes edwardsi is the scientific name for which small carnivore known for its ability to kill venomous snakes? Rudyard Kipling wrote about such an animal's contest with king cobras in *The Jungle Book*.

Three bonus questions on a shared surname:

(a) Sir John Charnley developed an artificial replacement named after him for which major joint in the human body?

(b) In which Channel 4 comedy series did Neil Pearson play the office charmer, Dave Charnley?

(c) In which sport did another Dave Charnley retire as undefeated British champion in 1965?

18. **Your starter for 10:**
In the world of finance, what does the letter 'A' represent in the acronym AIM?

> **Three bonus questions on film-makers:**
> (a) By what name is the photographer and film-maker born Emmanuel Rudnitsky in Philadelphia in 1890 better known?
> (b) Which 1955 film by Satyajit Ray was primarily responsible for introducing Indian cinema to the West?
> (c) The director Nicholas Ray was nominated for an oscar for which 1955 film, the second major film to star James Dean?

19. **Your starter for 10:**
The given names of the wife of the Emperor Justinian I and of William Wordsworth's sister both derive from Greek elements meaning 'gift of the gods'. For ten points, give either name.

> **Three bonus questions on literature and film:**
> (a) 'Among ash-heaps and millionaires' and 'Trimalchio in West Egg' were among titles considered by the author for which novel of 1925?
> (b) The 1974 film version of *The Great Gatsby* starred Robert Redford in the title role. Which noted director wrote the screenplay?
> (c) In 1963, which actress changed her name to that of a minor character in *The Great Gatsby*? In 1988, she received two Academy Award nominations for *Gorillas in the Mist* and *Working Girl*.

20. **Your starter for 10:**
Edward Murdstone in Dickens's *David Copperfield* and Claudius in Shakespeare's *Hamlet* both stand in what relationship to the title character?

Three bonus questions on criticism:

(a) Of which of his contemporaries does Byron say in *Don Juan*, "Tis strange the mind, that very fiery particle / Should let itself be snuffed out by an article', referring to the poet's over-sensitivity to bad reviews?

(b) In *The Critic as Artist*, which nineteenth-century playwright and poet wrote 'Every great man nowadays has his disciples, and it is always Judas who writes the biography'?

(c) According to the playwright Christopher Hampton, 'asking a working writer what he thinks about critics is like asking a lamp-post what it feels about...' what?

21. Your starter for 10:

3 March 2009 was a so-called 'square root day', because when expressed as oh-three, oh-three, oh-nine the last two digits of the year form the square of both the month and the day. On what date was the last square root day of the twentieth century?

Three bonus questions on incendiary devices:

(a) Burning even on water and with an exact composition no longer known, what incendiary weapon was fired from pressurised containers on ships of the Byzantine Empire?

(b) What animals were to be utilised in the plan devised in 1942 by the American dental surgeon Lytle S. Adams and approved by Roosevelt? They were to be attached to small incendiary devices and dropped by parachute over Japanese cities.

(c) What incendiary device was given its familiar name by the Finnish army during the winter war of 1939 to 1940, who named it after the Soviet Commissar for Foreign Affairs?

22. Your starter for 10:
Which hypothesis proposed by the palaeontologist Peter Ward views life on Earth as inherently self-destructive? An alternative to the Gaia theory of James Lovelock, it is named after the woman of Greek myth who murdered the children she bore Jason.

Three bonus questions on twinned towns:
(a) The fact that each has around a million tourists a year is one reason given for the twinning of which two sites, one, in Yorkshire, best known for the former inhabitants of its parsonage, and the other, in Peru, for its 'lost' city?

(b) Hay-on-Wye, which calls itself 'the secondhand-book capital of the world', is twinned with which city on the same longitude, noted for a major collection of Islamic manuscripts dating from the fourteenth century onwards?

(c) Romsey in Hampshire, the home of the late Earl Mountbatten of Burma, is twinned with which village in Hesse in Germany?

23. Your starter for 10:
The foundation stone of which building is traditionally believed to have been laid in the presence of Pope Alexander III in 1163, its construction being supervised by Bishop Maurice de Sully until his death in 1196?

Three bonus questions on agencies of the United Nations:
In each case, give the words for which the following acronyms stand:
(a) UNCTAD
(b) UNEP
(c) UNESCO

24. Your starter for 10:

From the declaration of war in September 1939 to the surrender of Japan in August 1945, how many men were Prime Minister of the UK?

Three bonus questions on exhibits in the British Museum:
(a) Named after a river now known as the Amu Dar'ya, which so-called 'treasure' dates from the fifth and fourth centuries BC and is regarded as the most important extant collection of Achaemenid metalwork?
(b) Believed to have been executed in the early 1550s, the cartoon known as 'Epifania' is the work of which Italian artist?
(c) Displaying a decree issued by Ptolemy V in 196 BC, which granitoid slab was discovered by a detachment of French soldiers in 1799?

25. Your starter for 10:

A proposed system of semaphore, the first use of the biological term 'cell', and a law describing the extension of springs and other elastic objects are among the achievements of which scientist, born in the Isle of Wight in 1635?

Three bonus questions on power series in mathematics:
(a) Which fast-growing mathematical function has a power series expansion whose nth term equals x to the power of n over n factorial?
(b) Which periodic mathematical function, ubiquitous in trigonometry, has power series expansion beginning x, minus x cubed over three factorial, plus x to the power five over 5 factorial?
(c) Give a rational expression for the power series, valid when x has modulus less than one, whose nth term is equal to x raised to the power n?

26. **Your starter for 10:**
What common substance links: a proverbial happy or carefree character; a French novelist born in 1804; and a temporary defence against floodwaters?

Three bonus questions on Australian state capitals:
(a) Named after a Secretary of State for the Colonies, which state capital stands at the mouth of the Derwent river?
(b) Which port was founded in 1824 as a penal colony and is named after a Scottish soldier and astronomer who was Governor of New South Wales from 1821 until 1825?
(c) Which Australian state capital lies on the River Swan?

27. **Your starter for 10:**
Powdered calcium sulphate hemi-hydrate, obtained by heating gypsum, is commonly known by what three-word name, both in medicine and in building?

Three bonus questions on European history:
(a) The childless Charles II, who ruled Spain from 1665 to 1700, chose which grandson of Louis XIV of France as his successor, a decision which ultimately gave rise to the War of the Spanish Succession?
(b) Having no surviving male heirs, the Holy Roman Emperor Charles VI drafted which decree of 1713 in an attempt to ensure that his daughter Maria Theresa succeeded to the Habsburg Dominions?
(c) Which conflict of 1700 to 1721 saw Russia, Denmark and Poland in opposition to Sweden which, in spite of the victories of Charles XII, lost its empire?

28. **Your starter for 10:**
What insect links: a planetary nebula in the constellation Ophiuchus; a valve with hinged plates used for flow

regulation; a variety of wing-nut; a nervous sensation in the stomach; and an opera by Puccini?

Three bonus questions on paintings:

(a) Rediscovered in the Scottish borders in 2009, a painting of 1837 by Paul Delaroche depicts which seventeenth-century figure being insulted by his captors?

(b) In a painting of 1836 by Delaroche, which advocate of absolutism and adviser to Charles I is depicted shortly before his execution in 1641 being blessed by Archbishop Laud?

(c) The execution of which figure in 1554 is the subject of a large work by Delaroche in the National Gallery?

29. **Your starter for 10:**

Who is being described? Born in Hanover in 1738, he composed twenty-four symphonies and several concerti and was appointed Director of Public Concerts at Bath, but is usually remembered as the astronomer who discovered two moons of Saturn and, in 1781, the planet Uranus?

Three bonus questions on the Nobel Peace Prize:

In each case, give the decade during which the following received the Prize:

(a) Fridtjof Nansen and Frank B. Kellogg.

(b) Albert Schweitzer and George C. Marshall.

(c) Willy Brandt, Amnesty International and Mother Teresa?

30. **Your starter for 10:**

What three-letter name is given to the conical hills of the Auvergne in France, formed from extinct volcanoes, and also to the small green lentils produced in the area and awarded appellation contrôlée status?

Three bonus questions on wine:

(a) Malmsey, bual and sercial are among grape varieties used in the production of which fortified wine, named after an island in the Atlantic?

(b) Which seaport in western Sicily gives its name to a dark dessert wine popular in Britain since the 1790s?

(c) Sanlucar de Barrameda is a centre for the production of which generic fortified wine?

'You were just a bit slow, I thought. You got some great answers, but not good enough to beat a very impressive team.'

THE RULES

OK, you all know the rules. I'll just remind you of the key thing: incorrect interruptions to starter questions – a 5-point penalty. Fingers on the buzzers, here's your first starter for 10.

Match Six

1. Your starter for 10:

In spherical geometry, what is the area of a triangle on the surface of a unit sphere, if every angle on the triangle is 90 degrees?

Three bonus questions on a word:

(a) Equivalent to 1.85 kilometres per hour, what unit of speed derives its name from the piece of string originally used in the measurement of a ship's speed?

(b) The red knot and the great knot are, along with the curlew and snipe, members of which family of wading birds with relatively long legs and long, slender bills?

(c) Its name being a reference to a secret society operating during the period, the historical re-enactment society the Sealed Knot recreate battles from which conflict?

2. Your starter for 10:

Which metal with atomic number 24 is used to impart corrosion resistance as an alloy constituent in stainless steel?

Three bonus questions on an artistic philosophy:

(a) What four-word English phrase, translated from a motto adopted by a French philosopher, is used for the theory that the only 'true' art is that which has no moral or utilitarian function?

(b) A leader of the aesthetic movement, which American-born artist wrote that art 'should stand alone and appeal to the artistic sense of eye or ear, without confounding this with emotions entirely foreign to it'?

(c) Which film company uses a Latin version of this phrase, *Ars gratia artis*, as its slogan, with the words appearing around the roaring head of the lion in their logo?

3.   Your starter for 10:
Sponsored by British American Tobacco, a statue of which Elizabethan explorer and literary figure was unveiled in February 2006 at his birthplace of East Budleigh, Devon?

Three bonus questions on nicknames:

(a) Which king was nicknamed 'Old Coppernose' after he debased silver coinage in order to pay for wars against France and Scotland? The raised areas of his portrait on such coins would rub off, revealing the copper below.

(b) Which pre-conquest king was the son of 'Forkbeard' and the father of 'Harefoot'?

(c) Which Plantagenet king was known as 'Fitz-Empress', because his mother's first husband, his stepfather, had been Holy Roman Emperor?

4.   Your starter for 10:
An example being the *Volsunga*, recounting legends used by Wagner in his *Ring* cycle, what form of narrative dealing with family histories, kings or heroes, intertwined with myths, comes from Iceland and Norway in the Middle Ages?

Three bonus questions on girls' names invented by writers:

(a) Which girl's name, later made popular by Samuel Richardson, is said to have been invented by Sir Philip

Sidney in his 1581 romance *Arcadia*?

(b) Later popularised by Sir Walter Scott, the name Rowena was first recorded for the daughter of Hengist who married Vortigern, by which twelfth-century Welsh monk in his *Historia Regum Britanniae*?

(c) Which eighteenth-century Irish writer invented the name Vanessa to refer in verse to Esther Vanhomrigh, with whom he had some sort of romantic relationship for about fifteen years?

5. **Your starter for 10:**
In 2005, for the first time in 45 years, Wisden's five 'Cricketers of the Year' were all Englishmen. Name three of them.

Three bonus questions on terms coined by the Swedish chemist Jöns Jacob Berzelius:

(a) What term for the existence of a chemical element in two or more forms in one state of matter was coined by Berzelius in 1841?

(b) What general one-word term for the existence of molecules that have the same number of the same kind of atoms, and therefore the same chemical formula, but different chemical and physical properties, was defined by Berzelius in 1830?

(c) The decomposition of bodies and the 'formation of new compounds into the composition of which they do not enter' was given what name by Berzelius in 1836?

6. **Your starter for 10:**
'Of the monks' is a literal translation of the name of which US state capital, situated on a tributary of the Mississippi?

Three bonus questions on titles:

(a) Which title is shared by the 2009 English version of

Les Bienveillants by Jonathan Littell and, in some translations, the third part of the *Oresteia*?

(b) What title is shared by a novel of 1842 by Nikolai Gogol, and one of 1999 by Ian Rankin?

(c) What title is shared by a play by Ivan Turgenev first staged in 1872, and a novel by J.L. Carr nominated for the Booker Prize in 1980?

7. **Your starter for 10:**
What three words link the opening lines of Shakespeare's *Richard III* with industrial unrest from November 1978 to the spring of 1979?

Three bonus questions on biological tests:

(a) Named after the professor of biochemistry at Berkeley who described it in the early 1970s, which test is a system for assessing the mutagenicity of compounds?

(b) The term 'IMVIC test' is an acronym for Indole, Methyl red, Vosges proskaur and Citrate. It consists of a series of biochemical tests used for the differentiation of which group of organisms?

(c) Which reagent is used as a test for the presence of reducing sugars? In a positive reaction, soluble blue copper two ions are converted to red copper one oxide, and precipitated.

8. **Your starter for 10:**
Characterised by horizontal motion normal to the direction of travel, with no vertical motion, what type of earthquake surface wave occurs when the shear-body-wave velocity in the surface medium is lower than that in the underlying strata?

Three bonus questions on unfinished buildings:

(a) Uncompleted due to financial difficulties, the shell

of the 330-metre-tall Ryugyong Hotel dominates the skyline of which Asian capital?

(b) Sharing its name with that of a racecourse, which mansion in West Sussex was unfinished on the death of its owner, the 3rd Duke of Richmond, in 1806?

(c) The construction of which as-yet-unfinished Barcelona church, designed by Antoni Gaudi, began in 1882?

9. **Your starter for 10:**

Queen Elizabeth I appeared under the names of 'Britomart', 'Belphoebe', 'Mercilla' and 'Gloriana' in which poem by Edmund Spenser?

Three bonus questions on South America:

(a) Influenced by the stars and stripes, which country's flag was designed by the North American Charles Wood, who fought for the nation's independence in the army of General José de San Martin?

(b) Which country's coat of arms includes a vicuna to symbolise the animal kingdom, and a cinchona tree?

(c) The national symbol of Argentina, which first appeared on its flag in 1818, is known as the 'sun' of which month, referring to the revolution of 1810?

10. **Your starter for 10:**

In Britain and its colonies, September 1752 was the shortest month of the millennium for what reason?

Three bonus questions on German history:

(a) Around 50 kilometres south of Stuttgart, which castle gives its name to the German dynasty that ruled Brandenburg-Prussia from 1415, and Imperial Germany from 1871 to 1918?

(b) Which Hohenzollern ruler was the victor of the Battle of Hohenfriedberg in 1745, and is said to have composed the military march of the same name?

(c) Prince Chlodwig von Hohenlohe succeeded Count Caprivi in 1894 as Chancellor to which Hohenzollern ruler?

11.   Your starter for 10:
Used as street names in industrial towns from the mid nineteenth century, Alma, Inkerman and Sebastopol were actions during which war?

Three bonus questions on a letter of the alphabet:
a) What letter has around 140 entries in the current *Oxford English Dictionary*, despite being described by Samuel Johnson in 1755 as 'a letter which, though found in Saxon words, begins no word in the English language'?

(b) In his 1637 work *La Geometrie*, which mathematician coined the usage of the letter 'x' as the sign for an abscissa, or quantity measured along the principal axis of coordinates?

(c) In Roman numerals, 'X' denotes the number 10. What number is represented by an 'X' with a horizontal line drawn above it?

12.   Your starter for 10:
Name either of two countries, one a European microstate, the other in Central Asia, said to be 'double landlocked'. That is, they not only lack direct access to the open sea, but they are surrounded by other countries also lacking?

Three bonus questions on ski resorts:
(a) Including the resort of Courchevel, the ski region known as the Trois Vallees is located in which French département, named after a former duchy annexed by France in 1860?

(b) The venue for the annual Vitranc trophy in world

cup men's slalom races, Kranjska Gora is in which
European country?

(c) The Italian ski resort of Cortina (d'Ampezzo) is
situated in which range of the Alps?

13. Your starter for 10:
Noted for its dry white wine, which Italian wine
region takes its name from that of a town near ancient
Tusculum, south-east of Rome?

Three questions about things 'departed':

(a) 'Dead he is not, but departed, – for the artist never
dies.' These words by the poet Longfellow refer to
which German Renaissance artist, noted for several
self-portraits resembling depictions of Christ?

(b) Martin Scorsese's 2006 film *The Departed*, starring
Leonardo DiCaprio and Matt Damon, is a retelling of
which 2002 Hong Kong thriller?

(c) 'Glory has departed from Israel.' These words from the
First Book of Samuel allude partly to the capture of
what artefact by the Philistines?

14. Your starter for 10:
In chemistry, what is the maximum number of hydrogen
atoms which can combine with an atom of carbon?

Three questions on a country:

(a) The Gulf of Sidra is a broad inlet of the Mediterranean
on the coast of which African country?

(b) Which port is the commercial centre of eastern Libya
and the country's second largest city after Tripoli?

(c) Libya is bordered to the south by Niger and which
other country, with whom a peace settlement was
agreed in 1994 concerning the Aouzou Strip, which
Libya had seized in 1973?

15. **Your starter for 10:**
Meaning the degree of asymmetry about the central value of a distribution, $\gamma_1 = \mu_3/(\mu_2)^{3/2}$, where μ_2 and μ_3 are the second and third moments about the mean, is the coefficient of what?

> **Three bonus questions on Aldous Huxley:**
> (a) Huxley's novel of 1923, *Antic Hay* took its title from lines by which Elizabethan dramatist?
> (b) *The Doors of Perception*, in which Huxley detailed his experience of taking mescaline, took its title from a work by which English artist and poet?
> (c) Huxley's collection of short stories published in 1922 and entitled *Mortal Coils* took its title from which play by Shakespeare?

16. **Your starter for 10:**
What two-word term denotes the powers and immunities held by the Crown, which, although limited in practice, currently include the right of making treaties and of declaring war, the appointment and dismissal of ministers, and the summoning and dissolution of parliament, and which state that the Monarch 'can do no wrong', meaning that the Queen cannot be prosecuted in her own courts?

> **Three bonus questions on a composer:**
> (a) His works distinguished by their expressive melodies and rococo charm, which prolific composer, born in Italy in 1743, is noted for the minuet from his String Quartet in E, opus 13?
> (b) Boccherini was both influenced and admired by which composer, born in eastern Austria in 1732?
> (c) Boccherini was a virtuoso performer on which stringed

instrument, for which he wrote numerous concertos and sonatas?

17. Your starter for 10:
'And still they gazed, and still the wonder grew / That one small head could carry all he knew.' These lines describing a village teacher are from a work of 1770 by which poet?

> **Three bonus questions on poetry:**
> In each case, name the poet from the last lines of an early twentieth-century poem:
> (a) 'Stands the church clock at ten to three? / And is there honey still for tea?'
> (b) 'A poor life this if, full of care, / We have no time to stand and stare.'
> (c) 'I took the one less travelled by, / And that has made all the difference.'

18. Your starter for 10:
Honouring Queen Victoria, who died that year, which London borough was granted Royal status by Edward VII in 1901 as the place of his mother's birth?

> **Three bonus questions on Latin third-declension neuter nouns, specifically those incorporated into English unchanged in spelling:**
> (a) Which third-declension Latin noun meaning 'swelling' has become an English noun meaning the short, thick part of a stem or rhizome, an example being the potato?
> (b) The word 'acer' denotes a genus that includes which common trees?
> (c) From the Latin verb meaning 'to fall', which seven-letter word means 'corpse' or 'dead body' in both Latin and English?

19. **Your starter for 10:**
Often named as the third most expensive after saffron and vanilla, which spice consists of the seed capsules of certain plants of the ginger family? Used as a flavouring in desserts and coffee, it is traditionally chewed in Asia as a breath cleanser?

Three bonus questions on tree names:
(a) 'Of all the trees that grow so fair, / Old England to adorn, / Greater are none beneath the sun, / Than oak and ash and thorn.' Which British Nobel laureate wrote these lines?
(b) Ash is traditionally the name given to a ligature used mainly in Old English but residual in the modern spelling of some words. Of which two letters does it consist?
(c) Thorn, resembling a lower-case letter 'p' in which the vertical stroke has been extended upwards, is used in old English and which modern Nordic language?

20. **Your starter for 10:**
Which burgh in Central Scotland was the site of two battles, one in 1298, when Edward I defeated William Wallace, and the other in 1746, when Charles Edward Stuart defeated General Hawley?

Three bonus questions on fiction and the weather:
(a) *Snow*, a novel published in English translation in 2004, is by which Nobel Prize-winning writer?
(b) The title of which 1976 play by Michael Frayn is a direct translation of *Nephelai*, the title of a comedy by Aristophanes?
(c) 'Rain', a short story set in Samoa, tells of the conflict between a missionary and a prostitute and is the work of which author, born in 1874?

21. **Your starter for 10:**
What term, particularly used for the streamlined outer casing of an aircraft engine, is derived from the French for 'little ship'?

Three bonus questions on a letter of the alphabet:
(a) Rickettsial pneumonia or Balkan grippe is a fever usually known by which single letter?
(b) Known by the pseudonym 'Q', who was the editor of the first *Oxford Book of English Verse*?
(c) Which singer fronted the Q-Tips from 1978 to 1982 before success as a solo artist?

22. **Your starter for 10:**
The historical novels *Count Belisarius* and *Sergeant Lamb of the Ninth* are among the works of which literary figure, also noted for *The Greek Myths* and *I, Claudius*?

Three bonus questions on a lack of clothes:
(a) Which 1961 novel opens with a group of schoolgirls outside the school gates, all of them wearing their hats because 'hatlessness was an offence'?
(b) Who, during her husband's presidential campaign of 1945–1946, addressed the masses as 'los descamisados' or 'shirtless ones'?
(c) W.P. Kinsella's novel *Shoeless Joe*, about the disgraced Chicago White Sox player Joe Jackson, was the basis for which film of 1989?

23. **Your starter for 10:**
Born in 1546, who established an observatory at Uraniborg in Denmark and devised a compromise between the Copernican and Ptolemaic systems of the universe, in which five planets orbit the sun, but the sun in turn orbits a stationary Earth; in 1566, he lost his

nose in a duel and reportedly replaced it with a metal one?

What do the following proofreaders' marks represent:
(a) lc
(b) bf
(c) sc

24. **Your starter for 10:**
Also known as the Society of the Friends of the Rights of Man and of the Citizen, which extreme revolutionary group, founded in Paris in 1790 by Danton and Marat, organised the demonstration in the Champs-de-Mars that resulted in the deaths of fifty protesters at the hands of the National Guard?

Three bonus questions on a board game:
(a) In London in 1851, the German Adolf Anderssen won the world's first (unofficial) international tournament in which game?
(b) Who defeated Boris Spassky to become the first official American World Chess Champion in 1972?
(c) Which Briton, with Gary Kasparov, formed the Professional Chess Association in 1993?

25. **Your starter for 10:**
With which other government department was the Inland Revenue merged in 2005?

Three bonus questions on gardens in art:
(a) Which writer claimed the idea for her novel *The Secret Garden* came to her from her own rose garden at her home in Kent?
(b) Which early sixteenth-century Dutch artist created the triptych *The Garden of Earthly Delights*?
(c) Born in 1821, which explorer translated the erotic

work *The Perfumed Garden* from the French?

26. Your starter for 10:

The invention of which mathematical technique is now attributed to both Newton and Leibnitz?

Three bonus questions on anaesthetics:
(a) In 1799, the British scientist Sir Humphrey Davy investigated the anaesthetic properties of which gas?
(b) Which substance interrupts the conduction of impulses in nerves and has the chemical formula $C_{17}H_{21}NO_4$?
(c) Which anaesthetic was introduced in 1905 and is a derivative of benzoic acid, but has largely been replaced by lignocaine in dentistry?

27. Your starter for 10:

Used in the making of films such as the *Lord of the Rings* trilogy, for what do the letters CGI stand?

Three bonus questions on mosquito-borne diseases:
(a) Also known as breakbone fever, which viral disease is characterised by extreme pain in the joints and limbs?
(b) Which disease, characterised by jaundice, was a major scourge until the *Aedes aegypti* mosquito was controlled and a vaccine developed?
(c) Blackwater fever is one of the most dangerous complications of which disease, carried by mosquitoes?

28. Your starter for 10:

What five-letter prefix appears in words meaning 'mania for writing verse' and 'device that marks time by an inverted pendulum'? The same five letters form an etymologically unrelated word for an urban railway system.

Three bonus questions on musical catalogues:
(a) The Köchel Catalogue is a full chronological listing of

the compositions of which composer, whose works in the list are each assigned a unique 'K' number?

(b) K527 is the number of which of Mozart's operas? It contains the 'Catalogue Aria', in which the servant Leporello recounts a list of the eponymous hero's many sexual conquests.

(c) Which work is the last on Köchel's list? It has the number K626 and was written in 1791, which was also the year of Mozart's death.

29. Your starter for 10:

Established with a base value of 500 in January 1980, the 'All Ordinaries Index', or 'All Ords', is the major stock price index in which Commonwealth country?

Three bonus questions on designations:

(a) K1 was the designation given in 1921 to the UK's first standard version of which communication structure, designed for public use and originally made of concrete?

(b) K2 was the designation given to the first red telephone kiosk, its design being the result of a competition won in 1924 by which architect?

(c) K6 was the designation of a later version of the red kiosk, designed by Giles Gilbert Scott to celebrate which anniversary in 1935?

30. Your starter for 10:

Which 1973 novel by William Goldman tells of a farmhand named Westley who is supposedly murdered by the dread pirate Roberts, but returns to rescue Buttercup from the clutches of Prince Humperdinck?

Three bonus questions on Japanese history:

In each case, give the decade during which the following were acquired by Japan, and the country to which the territory passed after the Second World War:

(a) The island of Taiwan, by the Treaty of Shimonoseki.

(b) The Northern Mariana Islands, including Saipan and Tinian, by military seizure.

(c) South Sakhalin, by the Treaty of Portsmouth.

'You dozed off a bit towards the end, I thought, but nonetheless you won pretty convincingly and we shall look forward to seeing you in Round Two.'

THE RULES

You all know the rules, but I'll remind you: 10 points for starters, 15 for bonuses, no conferring on starters, and incorrect interruptions to starters – a 5-point penalty. So here's your first starter for 10.

Match Seven

1. Your starter for 10:

The *Paradiso*, noted for its colossal size, *The Finding of the Body of St Mark* and *The Origin of the Milky Way* are among the works of which Venetian painter, born in 1518?

Three bonus questions on the short novels of Henry James:

(a) Set in Venice, which story is based on an anecdote told to Henry James about an American admirer of Shelley who attempted to acquire valuable letters written by the deceased poet?

(b) In which of James's narratives does John Marcher spend his life believing he has a unique destiny, only to discover that his fate was to be '*the* man to whom nothing on Earth was to have happened'?

(c) Of which story did James say that his intent was to make the reader's 'general vision of evil intense enough [that] his own experience, his own imagination will supply him with all the particulars'?

2. Your starter for 10:

Reckoned to have walked more than 23,000 miles in his explorations, John Rae, born in Orkney in 1813, contributed greatly to the surveying of sparsely inhabited northern regions of which present-day country?

Three bonus questions on bodyguards:

(a) Originally formed as a club in 1676, which company functions as the sovereign's bodyguard in Scotland?

(b) Effectively the Roman Emperor's bodyguard, which elite military corps nominated Claudius as Emperor in AD 41, and murdered Galba in AD 69?

(c) 'I am between 19 and 30 years old'; 'I am not married' and 'I am a faithful Roman Catholic' are among the admission requirements for which corps, which also has a minimum height requirement of five feet nine inches (174 centimetres)?

3.   Your starter for 10:
Established in 1927 and said to have been modelled on Lenin's *Cheka*, OVRA was the secret police force of which European country?

Three bonus questions on nuclear physics:

(a) What model of the atomic nucleus, proposed in 1935 by Gamow, was based on the observation that nearly all nuclei have the same density?

(b) What formula, based upon the liquid drop model and derived by Carl von Weizsäcker partly from theory and partly from experiment, is used to predict the binding energies and masses of nuclei?

(c) Consider a decaying radioactive material. After two half-lives have passed, what amount of the original material has decayed?

4.   Your starter for 10:
The model for many subsequent establishments of the same kind, the laboratory founded in Leipzig by Wilhelm Wundt in 1879 was the first expressly dedicated to the advancement of which science?

Three bonus questions on the body's immune system:

(a) T-cells, the leukocytes which form an essential part of the immune system, mature in the thymus behind the sternum but originate in which specific body tissue?

(b) Part of the immune system of vertebrates, which cells are found in connective tissue and contain chemicals such as heparin and histamine, which are released during inflammation and allergic responses?

(c) Which organ, consisting of red pulp and white pulp and located, in humans, in the upper left quadrant of the abdomen, plays an important role in the formation and removal of red blood cells, and also in fighting infection by the production of certain immune cells?

5. Your starter for 10:

With the power of Kaiser Wilhelm greatly diminished, two generals assumed virtual control of the war effort in Germany from 1916 to 1918. For ten points, name either one.

Three bonus questions on opportunity:

(a) Quote: 'There is a tide in the affairs of men / Which, taken at the flood, leads on to fortune; / Omitted, all the voyage of their life / Is bound in shallows and in miseries.' In which play by Shakespeare do these words appear?

(b) What, according to George Bernard Shaw, 'is popular because it combines the maximum of temptation with the maximum of opportunity'?

(c) In an attributed remark, the American novelist Gore Vidal advised, 'Never miss a chance to have sex or...' do what?

6. Your starter for 10:

Based on research at Oxford University, a study

published in 2009 suggested that the treatment of post-traumatic stress disorder might be aided by the playing of which computer game?

Three bonus questions on nineteenth-century US Presidents:
In each case, give the given name and surname of the President whose first name corresponds to the following:
(a) The Roman name of the Greek hero whose wanderings and return to Ithaka are the subject of an epic poem.
(b) A city on the River Dee close to the Welsh border, which is the site of a Roman legionary fortress.
(c) The New Zealand-born physicist who became a professor at Manchester in 1907 and established the nature of alpha and beta particles.

7. **Your starter for 10:**
Filiform, fungiform, circumvallate and foliate are the four forms of papillae, or small bumpy projections, found on the upper part of which organ of the body?

Three bonus questions on European geography:
(a) Noted for its Baroque architecture, which German state capital lies roughly midway between Berlin and Prague?
(b) The site of Poland's oldest cathedral, which major city is around halfway between Berlin and Warsaw?
(c) Which former EU capital lies close to the midpoint of a straight line drawn on the map from Paris to Berlin?

8. **Your starter for 10:**
From a late Latin word meaning 'womb', what term denotes a rectangular array of elements, or the rock material in which fossils are embedded?

Three bonus questions on constellations:

(a) Merak and Dubhe, two stars known as 'the Pointers' because they point almost directly to the North Star, are part of which pattern of bright stars that lie within the constellation of Ursa Major?

(b) The fifth brightest star, Vega, and the Ring Nebula lie within which constellation, named after a musical instrument used since antiquity?

(c) Mira, the first recognised variable star, lies in the large constellation called Cetus, sometimes described as depicting a sea monster but generally referred to as which mammal?

9. **Your starter for 10:**

What is the radius of a sphere whose volume-to-surface area ratio is one unit?

Three bonus questions on amino acids:

(a) Human haemoglobin is one of the richest sources of which amino acid, first isolated in 1881 from lupin seedlings, and also found in the artificial sweetener aspartame?

(b) First isolated from the wheat protein gliadin and widely distributed in plants, which amino acid, important in cellular metabolism, is readily capable of crossing the barrier between blood and brain?

(c) Which chemical substance found in the blood and the brain is synthesised from the amino acid tryptophan, and is involved in sleep and mood patterns?

10. **Your starter for 10:**

From the Greek for 'thick-skinned', what term did the French zoologist Georges Cuvier use to classify large, non-ruminant ungulate mammals such as the rhinoceros, hippopotamus and elephant?

Three bonus questions on twinned towns and cities:

(a) In 1959, which city in the English Midlands was twinned with Dresden, then in the German Democratic Republic, as a gesture of peace after their similar experiences in the Second World War?

(b) In 2000, the London Borough of Greenwich decided to twin with a town in Africa and chose the port of Tema, near Accra in Ghana, for what reason?

(c) Bourg-en-Bresse in Burgundy is famous for its poultry, particularly a breed of chicken, and is appropriately twinned with which English town north-east of Oxford?

11. **Your starter for 10:**

What surname is shared by Daniel, an American politician who negotiated the Ashburton Treaty with Britain in 1842; John, a dramatist, author of *The White Devil*, and Noah, an American lexicographer, born in 1758?

Three bonus questions on a perennial protagonist:

(a) Which character from European myth was the subject of a 'légende dramatique' by Berlioz, a symphony by Liszt, a concert work by Schumann, an overture by Wagner and operas by Spohr, Busoni and Gounod?

(b) Which German writer's version of the Faust myth takes the form of the life of the composer Adrian Leverkühn?

(c) In Marlowe's *Dr Faustus*, the protagonist makes a compact with Lucifer to surrender his soul after how many years?

12. **Your starter for 10:**

In chess, what is the term for an opening in which a pawn is sacrificed in return for a favourable position?

Three bonus questions on seafood:

(a) 'Thermidor', 'à la Newburg' and 'à l'Americaine' are names of recipes that originated as methods of cooking which shellfish?

(b) The epithet 'à l'Americaine' sometimes appears on menus as 'à l'Armoricaine', after 'Armorique', an old name of which region of France in which lobsters are commonly eaten?

(c) 'Thermidor', the month of the French Revolutionary Calendar from which 'lobster thermidor' ultimately gets its name, began in which month of the Gregorian calendar?

13. **Your starter for 10:**
Born Françoise Quoirez and taking her pseudonym from a character in Marcel Proust's *A la recherche du temps perdu*, who died at the age of 69 in September 2004 having made headlines as a teenager with her precocious first novel *Bonjour Tristesse*?

Three bonus questions on precious stones:

(a) What name is given to gem-quality corundum of any colour other than red?

(b) Chromium is the impurity that imparts the green colour to emerald, which is essentially a silicate of aluminium and which very light metal?

(c) The purple colour of amethyst is due to trace quantities of iron in crystals of which very common mineral?

14. **Your starter for 10:**
Ohio, Arkansas and Missouri are among US states sharing their names with rivers that join which river, itself the name of a state?

Three bonus questions on disorders of the eye:

(a) What term means the disorder caused by an

abnormally high internal pressure in the eye, which leads to damage of the retina and loss of vision?

(b) 'Floaters' are seen as spots, threads and networks in front of the eyes when looking at uniformly bright surfaces, and are the result of deposits of various size and refractive index in which component of the eye?

(c) What name means the clouding of the lens, most commonly associated with old age, and resulting in blurred vision?

15. Your starter for 10:

'Someone who leaves no turn unstoned' was George Bernard Shaw's description of members of what profession?

Three bonus questions on terminology:

(a) Introduced into sociology by Herbert Spencer and Emile Durkheim in the nineteenth century, what term described their application of a biological metaphor to society?

(b) Author of *Argonauts of the Western Pacific* in 1922, which Polish anthropologist developed the functionalist perspective in social anthropology?

(c) Known for his experimental, functional constructions of skyscrapers, and for the maxim 'form follows function', which architect designed the Wainwright Building in St Louis, completed in 1891?

16. Your starter for 10:

In Tensor analysis, the D'Alembertian operator is represented by what geometric figure to the power of two?

Three bonus questions on languages of Asia:

In each case, give the island nation in which the following are official or principal languages:

(a) Portuguese and Tetum.

(b) Tamil and Sinhala.

(c) Mandarin Chinese, English, Malay and Tamil.

17. **Your starter for 10:**
Which stretch of water is known in French and Italian by their respective words for 'sleeve' and finally became less of a barrier in 1994 with the opening of a tunnel underneath it?

Three bonus questions on the Tropic of Capricorn:

(a) In Australia, the Tropic of Capricorn crosses the Northern Territory and two states. For five points, name both.

(b) The Tropic of Capricorn crosses Madagascar, Mozambique and three other African countries. For five points, name two of them.

(c) Excluding island territories, what is the only country through which both the Equator and the Tropic of Capricorn pass?

18. **Your starter for 10:**
What word of four letters can, in archaeology, precede 'barrow' or 'beaker', in mining, precede 'pit', and in statistics the word 'curve', to indicate normal distribution?

Three bonus questions on words that are easily confused:
You will be given definitions of two words that are similar in form. In each case, give both the words defined:

(a) Which two similar verbs mean 'deplore' and 'reduce the monetary value of'?

(b) 'Assess the value or quality of' and 'inform'.

(c) 'Forbid publication of' and 'express severe disapproval of'.

19. **Your starter for 10:**
A type of Magneto-Bremsstrahlung, what kind of radiation does a relativistic charge emit when its path is bent by a magnetic field?

Three bonus questions on happiness:
(a) Noted for measuring his country's wellbeing not by its GDP but by its GNH, or Gross National Happiness, King Jigme Singye Wangchuck was the former ruler of which country, which completed its transition to a constitutional monarchy in 2008?
(b) In 2007, which Dorset town was found to be the 'happiest' town in the UK, with eighty-two per cent of its residents saying they were happy; its beaches and 'cosmopolitan town centre' were cited as reasons?
(c) 'On True Happiness' is an essay by which eighteenth-century American statesman and scientist who said, 'The constitution only guarantees the American people the right to pursue happiness. You have to catch it yourself'?

20. **Your starter for 10:**
What combination of vowel letters begins words denoting: an unqualified past tense, especially in Greek; a Maori name for New Zealand; and the main artery of the body?

Three bonus questions on musicians and biography:
(a) Published in 1997, ten years after the subject's death, *A Genius in the Family* focuses on the life of which British musician and was written by her sister and brother?
(b) *A Life in Music* is the autobiography of which pianist and conductor, who married Jacqueline du Pré in 1967?

    (c) Du Pré attended the master class of which Catalan cellist, an account of whose life and sayings was compiled by Julian Lloyd Webber under the title *Song of the Birds*?

21. **Your starter for 10:**
As seen through a telescope as it rises or sets with the sun, what shape is the image of the planet Mercury?

Three questions about hybrid fruits:
    (a) A soft fruit produced by crossing a blackberry and a raspberry has what name, after that of the longest river in Scotland near to which it was introduced in the 1970s?
    (b) Which fruit, a cross between a raspberry, blackberry and loganberry, was named in the 1930s after the American horticulturalist who developed it?
    (c) A tangelo is the result of crossing a tangerine with which other citrus fruit?

22. **Your starter for 10:**
Bruxism, which usually occurs at night during sleep and may be due to nervous tension or stress, is commonly known as what?

Three bonus questions on German Expressionist cinema:
    (a) Released in 1922, which film by F.W. Murnau prompted a lawsuit for infringement of copyright to be issued on behalf of the estate of Bram Stoker?
    (b) Which creature of Jewish folklore was the subject of three films by the director Paul Wegener, the first of which appeared in 1915?
    (c) Directed by Robert Wiene, which film of 1920 concerned the somnambulist Cesare, presented as a carnival attraction by the eponymous doctor?

23. Your starter for 10:
Name two of the four founding members of Mercosur, the common market formed at the treaty of Asunción in 1991?

Three bonus questions on a German word:
(a) What is the English name for the day of the week known in German as 'Donnerstag'?
(b) In 1868, who composed the polka *Unter Donner und Blitz*, or *Thunder and Lightning*?
(c) Francesca Donner, born in Austria in 1900, was the wife of Syngman Rhee, the first President of which Asian state?

24. Your starter for 10:
'Malodorously flatulent' and 'an aggressive small dog' are among possible derivations of what adjective, meaning 'lively', 'spirited' or 'excitable' and applied especially to women?

Three bonus questions on lighting:
In each case, give the lighting system denoted by the following abbreviations:
(a) CFL, sometimes known as 'energy-saving lights'.
(b) HID, used for car headlights and street lighting.
(c) LED, used in spotlights, mobile phones and bicycle lamps.

25. Your starter for 10:
Give the three words that complete these couplets from Lewis Carroll's *Through the Looking-Glass*: 'The time has come, the Walrus said / To talk of many things: / Of shoes and ships – and sealing wax – / Of...' whom or what?

Three bonus questions on substance abuse in the nineteenth century:

(a) Elizabeth Barrett Browning and Thomas de Quincey were among literary users of what tincture of opium, thought to have been named by Paracelsus for its 'praiseworthy' properties?

(b) In which novel of 1868 is the eponymous treasure stolen by a character in a laudanum-induced stupor?

(c) Subtitled 'A Vision in a Dream', which 1797 fragment did the poet compose upon waking from a laudanum-induced dream?

26. Your starter for 10:

The orrery, invented around 1710 by George Graham and named in honour of Charles Boyle, 4th Earl of Orrery, and in use for several centuries despite its necessary inaccuracies in sizes and distances, was a mechanical model of what?

Three bonus questions on novels and film:

(a) Which 1936 novel by George Orwell was made into a 1997 film starring Helena Bonham Carter and Richard E. Grant?

(b) A film version of which 1936 novel by Noel Streatfeild starred Emma Watson and Yasmin Paige as aspiring dancers?

(c) Three years after publication, which 1936 first novel was filmed in a version starring Clark Gable and Vivien Leigh?

27. Your starter for 10:

What three letters precede the word 'tile' in the name of a kind of roof tile, curved to form an S-shape section so that the tiles overlap when laid?

Three bonus questions on chronology:

(a) Who was on the English throne when Leonardo painted the *St John the Baptist*, Copernicus published his heliocentric theory, and the Spanish conquered Peru?

(b) British involvement in which war between European powers began in the year that University College, Dublin was founded, and finished the year in which William Henry Perkin prepared the first aniline dye?

(c) Which planet was discovered the year Kant published the *Critique of Pure Reason*, and the British surrendered at Yorktown?

28. Your starter for 10:

Which country lost its sea coast and became landlocked as a result of territorial losses sustained in the War of the Pacific of 1879–1884 when it fought against Chile in an alliance with Peru?

Three bonus questions on popular songs in classical works:

(a) Which popular song did Stravinsky incorporate into *Greetings Prelude*, which he composed in 1955, unaware that he was in breach of copyright?

(b) Which national anthem features in Schumann's *Viennese Carnival Pranks*, and in Tchaikovsky's *1812 Overture*?

(c) Erno Dohnanyi used the nursery rhyme 'Ah, Vous Disai-Je Maman' for his *Variations on a Nursery Song*. How is this piece of nursery music known in English?

29. Your starter for 10:

What term is used for the upper harmonics of the fundamental note produced by a musical instrument, which greatly affect the timbre of that instrument?

Three bonus questions on a word:

(a) In Greek cosmology, what word signified the primeval emptiness of the universe before things came into being?

(b) In an application of Chaos Theory, what minor event did meteorologist Edward Lorenz suggest can change the weather?

(c) Oscar Wilde described the style of which Victorian poet as 'chaos, illuminated by flashes of lightning'?

30. Your starter for 10:

What name is given to the tides that are raised when the moon is full or new? In both cases they are the highest high tides and the lowest low tides?

Three bonus questions on a scientific term:

(a) Which nineteenth-century German chemist popularised the condenser used in laboratory distillations that is named after him?

(b) A condenser is an old name for which component of an electrical circuit?

(c) What term is used for the heat that is evolved when, for example, a vapour condenses into a liquid?

> 'Terrific performance, although you did seem to flag in the middle. But you came back strongly in the end. We shall look forward to seeing you in Round Two.'

THE RULES

The rules are absolutely unchanging in this contest: starter questions are worth 10 points, they're solo efforts; bonuses are team efforts, you can confer on those, they're worth 15 points; there's a 5-point penalty for incorrect interruptions to starter questions. Here's your first starter for 10.

Match Eight

1. Your starter for 10:

What term describes either of the ridges in the floors of the lateral ventricles of the brain that have an important role in memory processes? It is derived from the Greek for 'horse' and 'sea monster'.

> **Three bonus questions on the eponymous heroines of novels, usually referred to by their first names:**
> What are the surnames of the following:
> (a) Jane Austen's Emma.
> (b) Samuel Richardson's Pamela.
> (c) L.M. Montgomery's Anne of Green Gables.

2. Your starter for 10:

How is the number four expressed in Roman numerals on many clock faces? The clock faces of Westminster Tower, housing Big Ben, are exceptions, having four expressed as 'IV'?

> **Three bonus questions linked by a word:**
> (a) In which Japanese city is the Glover Mansion, reputedly the setting of Puccini's *Madam Butterfly*?
> (b) John, a sixteenth-century Warwickshire glover, alderman and bailiff, is remembered primarily as the father of whom?
> (c) Brian Glover played the P.E. teacher Sugden in the 1970 film version of which novel by Barry Hines?

3. Your starter for 10:

Awarded for the first time in 2003, which prize, named after the Norwegian mathematician Niels Henrick, recognises a lifetime's achievement in mathematics? It was introduced to complement the Nobel Prizes, which do not have an award for mathematics.

Three bonus questions on American place names:

(a) How do white Americans know Greasy Grass River, the scene of a Dakota Sioux victory in June 1876?

(b) The Bluegrass region, centred on Lexington, lies at the heart of which US state?

(c) In which song by Lennon and McCartney did Jojo leave his home in Tucson, Arizona, for some California grass?

4. Your starter for 10:

Designed by R.J. Mitchell, the supermarine S.6B, which won the Schneider Trophy in 1931, was a forerunner of which fighter aircraft?

Three bonus questions on a shared surname:

(a) Born in Vienna in 1882 and moving to London in 1926, which psychoanalyst is best known for her work with young children?

(b) The French painter Yves Klein usually worked in a distinctive shade of which colour, which he dubbed 'International Klein'?

(c) In topological space, a Möbius band has just one surface and one edge; what are the analogous properties of the so-called Klein Bottle?

5. Your starter for 10:

An agency founded in 1951 and based in Geneva, for what do the letters UNHCR stand?

Three bonus questions on an artistic method:

(a) 'The bridle and rudder of painting' was Leonardo da Vinci's description of what method of depicting three-dimensional objects on a two-dimensional plane?

(b) 'There is nothing ugly; I never saw an ugly thing in my life: for let the form of an object be what it may,—light, shade, and perspective will always make it beautiful'? Which English landscape painter born in 1776 wrote these words?

(c) 'Treat nature by the cylinder, the sphere, the cone, everything in proper perspective.' These are the words of which leading post-impressionist, born in Provence in 1839?

6. **Your starter for 10:**
What form of ileitis, a medical condition in which part of the intestine becomes inflamed, is named after the American who first identified it in the 1930s?

Three bonus questions on trees in Spenser:
In the first Canto of Book One of Spenser's *Faerie Queene*, the poet describes the Redcross Knight and a lady sheltering in a wood; identify each of the following trees from Spenser's description of them in that passage.

(a) Which tree is 'the builder', 'sole king of forests all'?

(b) Which tree is 'worn of forlorn paramours'?

(c) Which tree is 'obedient to the bender's will'?

7. **Your starter for 10:**
Derived from the Hebrew for 'fitness' or 'legitimacy', the term *kashrut* describes the religious restrictions governing which aspect of Jewish life?

Three bonus questions on animals named after places in Kent:

(a) Which of the Cinque Ports in Kent gives its name to a

species of tern?

(b) The flatfish *solea solea* is thought to have taken its usual English name from which of the other Cinque Ports?

(c) A small perching bird of which family gets its name from the town of Dartford in Kent where it was first seen in England?

8. **Your starter for 10:**
Canada in 1867, Australia in 1900 and New Zealand in 1907 were given what precise status, denoting a self-governing polity within the British Empire?

Three bonus questions on record labels:
In each case, identify the label from the description:

(a) Which label was created in 1984 by the hip-hop producer Russell Simmons and the New York student Rick Rubin in Rubin's dormitory room? One of its first singles was 'I Need A Beat' by the rapper LL Cool J.

(b) Founded in Hollywood in 1942, which label's past artists have included Frank Sinatra and Nat King Cole, while current acts include Coldplay, Katy Perry and Lily Allen?

(c) Founded in 1959 in Jamaica, which label's artists have included Bob Marley and the Wailers, Pulp, U2 and Grace Jones?

9. **Your starter for 10:**
Which French adjective links: essays, usually of criticism, written for aesthetic effect; the period from the late nineteenth century to the First World War, and a poem of 1819 by John Keats about a knight 'alone, and palely loitering'?

Three bonus questions on the Millennium Prize Problems:
Seven problems were identified in 2000 by the Clay

Mathematical Institute. In each case, name the problem from the description given:

(a) Conjecture: the rank of the group associated with an elliptic curve is equal to the order of the zero of its l-function at one.

(b) To determine whether every language accepted by some non-deterministic algorithm in polynomial time is also accepted by some deterministic algorithm in polynomial time.

(c) All non-trivial zeros of the zeta function have real part one-half.

10. Your starter for 10:

In 2009, which prominent US citizen travelled to Ennis in County Clare, the home town of his great-grandfather Abe Grady, and was made its first freeman?

Three bonus questions on an unofficial status:

(a) From 1992 to 2009, Sir Edward Heath, Tam Dalyell and Alan Williams successively held which unofficial title of honour in the House of Commons?

(b) Living in about the eighth century BC, who has been called 'the father of Greek didactic poetry'? His surviving works include the *Theogony* and *Works and Days*.

(c) Stephen Fuller Austin is known as the 'Father' of which US state, having been prominent in events leading to the revolution that secured its independence in 1836?

11. Your starter for 10:

Characters in which of Shakespeare's plays include the Welsh parson Sir Hugh Evans, the French physician Doctor Caius, Mistresses Ford, Page and Quickly, and Sir John Falstaff?

Three questions about body cells:

(a) Named after the nineteenth-century German physiologist who discovered them, Schwann cells produce which insulating layer, covering the axons of many neurons?

(b) Deriving their name from the Latin for 'fat', which cells are found in connective tissue and are specialised to synthesise large globules of fat?

(c) First described by the anatomist Vladimir Betz in the 1870s, Betz cells are found in which organ of the body?

12. **Your starter for 10:**

Depicted in Bernini's statue of 1642 in the Piazza Barberini in Rome, which Greek god was the son of Poseidon and the messenger of the sea, his attributes being a trident and a conch shell?

Three bonus questions on spices:

(a) With aromatic seeds that can be used both in cooking and to flavour tea and coffee, which spice of the ginger family gives its name to a range of hills in southern India?

(b) An ingredient of the Thai soup known as tom yam, what is the common name of the rhizome of the genus *alpinia*, also known as thai ginger or kha?

(c) Produced from the dried and ground rhizomes of *curcuma longa*, another plant of the ginger family, which spice is sometimes known as Indian saffron?

13. **Your starter for 10:**

The Toronto Maple Leafs, Montreal Canadiens and the Edmonton Oilers are among professional teams in which winter sport?

Three bonus questions on Erasmus:

(a) Although he lived there for only a few years, Erasmus

is principally associated with which Dutch city, where a statue of him was erected in 1622 outside St Laurence's Church?

(b) A satirical attack on theologians and church dignitaries, Erasmus's 1511 work *Encomium Moriae* is usually given what English title?

(c) *In Praise of Folly* is thought to have been written at the suggestion of which English scholar and statesman?

14. **Your starter for 10:**
Suslik and Shrew-Faced are among ground-dwelling species, and Oriental Giant and Red among tree-dwelling species of which animal, whose common name comes from the Greek for 'shade tail'?

Three bonus questions on mathematics:

(a) What is defined as 'the power x to which a fixed number b must be raised to equal another number n'?

(b) The logarithmic function is the inverse of which function, that can be expressed as y = ex, and which as a term is used more generally to refer to any process of runaway growth?

(c) Logarithms to the base e are called natural logarithms, but also have what alternative name after a Scottish mathematician?

15. **Your starter for 10:**
In chemistry, what term describes a substance in which the proportions of its constituent compounds or elements are such that it melts and solidifies at a lower temperature than any other combination of those constituents?

Three bonus questions on a name:

(a) In Greek mythology, which nymph of the mythical island of Ogygia entertained Odysseus for seven years, but could not overcome his longing for home even by promising him immortality?

(b) Calypso, a traditional ballad form in which topical comment is sung to a simple percussion accompaniment with a syncopated beat, is primarily associated with which Caribbean island?

(c) Calypso, discovered in 1980, is a natural satellite of which planet?

16. Your starter for 10:

What is 17.5 per cent as a fraction in its lowest terms?

Three bonus questions on a metallic element:

(a) In terms of structure, a molecule of chlorophyll resembles one of haemoglobin with the atom of iron replaced by one of which metal?

(b) Which compounds, named after their discoverer and widely used in organic chemistry, are produced by dissolving magnesium in an ethereal solution of an alkyl halide?

(c) A double carbonate with calcium, which mineral is an important source of magnesium, and is the origin of the name of a mountain range of southern Europe?

17. Your starter for 10:

The city of Exeter, the United States Marine Corps and Plymouth Argyle Football Club share what two-word Latin motto, meaning 'always faithful'?

Three bonus questions on Roman history:

(a) What term coined by Machiavelli describes the era from AD 96 to 180, described by Edward Gibbon as 'the period in the history of the world during which the condition of the human race was most happy and prosperous'?

(b) Arguably the most famous of the Five Good Emperors

was Hadrian. For five points, name two of the others.

(c) Marcus Aurelius, the last of the Five Good Emperors, writes: 'Does aught befall you? It is well; all that befalls was part of the great web,' in a work commonly known by what name?

18. Your starter for 10:
Preceding Beauchamp, Burnett, Turville and Trussel in the names of English villages, what locality name appears in the names of four underground and three railway stations in West London?

Three bonus questions on a natural material:
(a) Which decorative substance has been used in jewellery since the Palaeolithic age and is, chemically speaking, largely a complex mixture of various terpenoids?

(b) Having deduced that amber must have had a liquid state in order to trap insects, which Roman naturalist called it *succinum*, or 'gum-stone', in his *Naturalis Historia* of the first century AD?

(c) The 'Amber Coast', a source of European amber since the Roman Empire, is on which body of water?

19. Your starter for 10:
The term 'paparazzi' is derived from the name of a character in which film by Federico Fellini?

Three bonus questions on things seen by poets:
(a) Which eponymous character, in a poem first published in 1915, tells the reader he has seen his 'head (grown slightly bald) brought in upon a platter'?

(b) Which poem of 1956 has as its opening lines: 'I saw the best minds of my generation destroyed by madness, starving hysterical naked...'?

(c) In a work of 1807, which poet wrote: 'It is not now as it hath been of yore; – / Turn whereso'e'er I may, / By night or day, / The things which I have seen I now can see no more'?

20. **Your starter for 10:**
Calorimetry is the science of the measurement of what?

Three bonus questions on the moon:
(a) With respect to the moon's orbit around the Earth, what is the meaning of the term 'perigee'?
(b) The rotation of the moon on its axis takes 27.3 days. How long does the moon take to orbit the Earth?
(c) Which lunar maria was the site of the landing of the Apollo 11 mission in July 1969?

21. **Your starter for 10:**
Represented by Tam Dalyell from 1962 to 2005, which Scottish constituency gave its name to an anomaly whereby MPs for Scottish seats at Westminster may vote on purely English affairs, while being unable to influence legislation on matters devolved to the Scottish Parliament?

Three bonus questions on a word:
(a) Now meaning so lacking in originality as to be obvious and boring, what word first meant a feudal service which was compulsory for all, and therefore commonplace?
(b) 'The banal Eldorado of all the old boys' was which French poet's description of the island of Cythera in a collection of 1857?
(c) Hannah Arendt wrote of 'the fearsome word-and-thought-defying banality of evil' when referring to the revelations of whose trial in Jerusalem in 1961?

22. **Your starter for 10:**
Widely used for radio telescopes and television, what

type of aerial consists of one or two dipoles, a parallel reflector and a series of closely spaced directors in front of the dipole?

Three bonus questions on French cathedrals with UNESCO World Heritage Site status:

(a) Which Gothic cathedral is the tallest completed cathedral in France, and is situated in the Somme valley around 100 kilometres north of Paris?

(b) Located in the Champagne region around 130 kilometres north-east of Paris, which cathedral was the traditional site of the crowning of French kings?

(c) Eighty kilometres south-west of Paris, which Gothic cathedral is noted for its two contrasting spires and its thirteenth-century stained glass?

23. **Your starter for 10:**

Used mainly for viewing plant tissues in optic microscopy, what stain colours lignified and cutinized tissues and nuclei red and chloroplasts pink?

Three bonus questions on government:

(a) What Greek-derived single word denotes a system of government with two heads of state, as, for example, in the Roman Republic, or ancient Sparta?

(b) In what area under British rule did the Montagu-Chelmsford reforms of 1919 prescribe a diarchy of ministers who were individually responsible to the legislature?

(c) Which present-day European microstate has two 'co-princes' as its heads of state, one of whom is the Bishop of Urgell?

24. **Your starter for 10:**

'The city so nice they named it twice', 'the melting pot', 'Baghdad on the Hudson', 'Empire City', and 'Gotham' are all nicknames of which city?

Three bonus questions on anagrams:
The answer is a word of four letters in each case:
(a) Which German boy's name is an anagram of the names of a Pentecostal church, an imperial unit of length, and a citrus fruit?
(b) Which word meaning 'dreadful' is an anagram of a term for a road for horses especially through a wood, the surname of a recent Home Secretary, and a German numeral?
(c) Which word is a song title used by Queen, The Damned and the Sex Pistols, and is an anagram of terms for a form of transport, an animal's den, and the currency of Turkey?

25. Your starter for 10:
Born in 1516, the German humanist Hieronymus Wolf is credited with the introduction of what two-word term to describe the polity centred on Constantinople between the fourth century and 1453?

Three bonus questions on royal families:
(a) Edward the Black Prince, the son of Edward III, was the father of which English king?
(b) Who became king in 1399 after Richard II's forced abdication?
(c) Henry IV's sister, Philippa of Lancaster, became queen consort of which country through her marriage to John I?

26. Your starter for 10:
What five-letter word links a spiral-horned antelope, brown with vertical white stripes, and either of a pair of long-bodied drums, usually held between the knees and played with the fingers?

Three bonus questions on the openings of children's novels:

(a) 'This is a story about something that happened long ago when your grandfather was a child' is the opening sentence of which of the Narnia books, published in 1955?

(b) 'Nomes are small. On the whole, small creatures don't live for a long time. But perhaps they do live *fast*.' This is the start of which Terry Pratchett novel, the first in the trilogy *The Bromeliad*?

(c) Which book, the first in a series by the British author-illustrator Jill Murphy, begins, 'Miss Cackle's Academy for Witches stood at the top of a high mountain surrounded by a pine forest'?

27. **Your starter for 10:**

'Writing (such) a book… is like dropping a rose petal down the Grand Canyon and waiting for the echo.' To what literary form is the American humorist Don Marquis referring here?

Three bonus questions on sport:

(a) *Riding Through the Storm* is an account of which former England footballer's 2005 charity bike ride over the complete Tour de France course as an aid to his recovery from leukaemia?

(b) *Breaking Back: How I Lost Everything and Won Back My Life* was written by which American tennis player who, in 2004, broke his neck just weeks before the death of his father?

(c) Mark Law's book *The Pyjama Game* is subtitled *A Journey into…* which sport?

28. **Your starter for 10:**

What common name is given to the dietary component

which includes insoluble carbohydrate?

Three bonus questions on country houses:
(a) Which novella by Henry James is set in a country house called Bly?
(b) Which novel by Iris Murdoch is set around an abbey called Imber?
(c) Which play by Alan Bennett is set in a school called Cutlers' Grammar?

29. Your starter for 10:
Whirligig, bombardier and minotaur are all types of insects belonging to which order, the largest order in numbers of species in the animal and plant kingdoms?

Three bonus questions on British coins:
(a) 'So many irons in the fire' appears on the edge of a £2 coin of 2006. The reverse bears an image of the arches of which London terminus station?
(b) 'United into one kingdom' appears on the edge of a 2007 £2 coin. The reverse bears the images of a rose, a thistle and what other insignia?
(c) 'In victory magnanimity, in peace goodwill' appears on the edge of a £2 coin of 2005. Which building appears on the reverse?

30. Your starter for 10:
The town of Oltu in Eastern Turkey is often cited as the birthplace of which popular fast-food dish, similar versions of which are known in Arabic as *shawarma* and in Greek as *gyros*?

Three bonus questions on European cities:
(a) The city of Lyon in France lies at the confluence of the River Saone with which other river?
(b) Passau in Bavaria is situated at the confluence of the

Inn and the Ilz with which major river?

(c) Koblenz in Germany lies at the confluence of the Mosel with which river?

'Well, you started well, but you faded pretty quickly, and you woke up towards the end. Maybe you'll be more consistent next time...'

THE RULES

The rules are the same as ever: starter questions you answer on the buzzer, they're solo efforts, they're worth 10 points; bonuses are worth 15 points, they're team efforts; there's a 5-point penalty if you interrupt a starter question incorrectly.

Match Nine

1. Your starter for 10:
The expression 'Barra to the Butt' indicates a journey from the south to the north of which islands?

Three bonus questions on Scottish place names:
(a) The Gaelic name of which Hebridean island translates as 'Island of Mist', although some claim it comes from the Gaelic for 'winged isle' referring to its shape?
(b) The Gaelic name of which peak, mountain range and, since 2003, national park, translates as 'Blue rocky hill'?
(c) The Gaelic name for which highland town and outdoor sports centre on Loch Linnhe is An Gearasdan, meaning 'the garrison'?

2. Your starter for 10:
Celebrated on 28 December, which Christian festival commemorates Herod's massacre of the children of Bethlehem shortly after the birth of Christ?

Three bonus questions on adjectives from the names of planets:
In each case, you will be given a definition; give the adjective and the planet from which it is derived:
(a) Active, sprightly, ready-witted, quick and changeable in temperament.
(b) Grave, gloomy, dark, brooding and melancholy.

(c) Joyous, hearty, convivial and good-humoured.

3. **Your starter for 10:**
The work of which British writer and director includes the television dramas *Shooting the Past* and *The Lost Prince*, the latter being the true story of a British prince who was kept from public view because he suffered from epilepsy?

Three bonus questions on lips in poetry:

(a) 'Those lips that love's own hand did make / Breath'd forth the sound that said "I hate".' Who wrote the sonnet that begins with these lines?

(b) According to Shakespeare's Sonnet 130, what is 'far more red' than the lips of the poet's mistress?

(c) According to Sonnet 116, what is 'not time's fool, though rosy lips and cheeks / within his bending sickle's compass come'?

4. **Your starter for 10:**
'The Clowns' is the translation into English from Italian of the title of which 1892 opera by Leoncavallo?

Three questions linked by a word:

(a) Round, box (or square), curly (or braces) and angle are terms used to describe various forms of which punctuation marks?

(b) In architecture, what name derives from the Latin for raven in reference to its beaked shape, and is given to an ornamental bracket, particularly to one used to support a mantelpiece?

(c) A bracket turn, a movement performed on one foot with its direction of rotation opposite to the natural direction of motion, features in which Olympic sport?

5. Your starter for 10:

What reduplicated number denotes both normal visual acuity and a variety of truncated cricket introduced in the UK in 2003?

Three bonus questions on places of entertainment:
(a) What name is shared by a theatre in the Strand and the grove in Athens where Aristotle taught his pupils?
(b) Home of the English National Opera, which London theatre derives its name from that of a giant Roman amphitheatre?
(c) Which London building takes its name from a Greek stadium designed for racing horses and chariots?

6. Your starter for 10:

For what do the letters ERS stand, being the name of a pressure group founded in 1884 that campaigns for the introduction of the single transferable vote system?

Three bonus questions on America:
(a) The Bridge of the Americas, completed in 1962, crosses which major waterway?
(b) Playa de las Americas is a major beach resort on which of the Canary Islands?
(c) Captain America, otherwise known as Wyatt, is a character in which 1969 cult film?

7. Your starter for 10:

Used in optics for the curve or surface formed where rays of light intersect after being reflected or refracted, what word in everyday speech denotes language that is bitter, cutting or sarcastic?

Three bonus questions on cats under threat:
(a) Which physicist imagined a cat in a large box with a light source, polariser and detector, and a lethal device

which may or may not kill the cat?

(b) What, in a poem of 1842, 'fought the dogs and killed the cats'?

(c) In *A Midsummer Night's Dream*, who claims to be able to 'play Ercles rarely, or a part to tear a cat in, to make all split!'

8. **Your starter for 10:**
Mythology placing him in the seventh century BC, Jimmu Tenno is regarded as the founder and first Emperor of which Asian country?

Three bonus questions on electronics:
(a) What, in electronics, do the letters CRT stand for?

(b) The cathode rays in a cathode ray tube are actually a stream of which particles?

(c) The device that produces the electron stream in a cathode ray tube is known as an 'electron…' what?

9. **Your starter for 10:**
Which Manchester-born artist created the science fiction stories of Dan Dare in the *Eagle* comic, launched in 1950?

Three bonus questions on numbers:
(a) In *The Hitchhiker's Guide to the Galaxy*, which number was discovered to be the answer to life, the universe and everything?

(b) 'Number 45' came to be associated with which politician, after attempts to suppress issue 45 of his paper the *North Briton*?

(c) Which character in a popular song had size nine feet, and dwelt with her miner father, who was a 'Forty-niner'?

10. Your starter for 10:

The Baykonur Cosmodrome, the former Soviet Union's main space-launch facility, is located in which country of Central Asia?

Three bonus questions on the plots of well-known ballets:
(a) Clara's magical journey to the Land of Sweets is the story of which ballet of 1892 by Tchaikovsky?
(b) Which ballet, choreographed by Frederick Ashton, features clog dancers and a Shetland pony, despite being set in rural France?
(c) The last act of which ballet, with music by Tchaikovsky, is sometimes performed separately as 'Aurora's Wedding'?

11. Your starter for 10:

What British mammal links: the founder of the Society of Friends; the source of the drug digitalis, and a ballroom dance with slow and quick steps?

Three bonus questions on musical groupings:
Which outfits are sometimes known by the following initials:
(a) LSO.
(b) FSOL.
(c) ODJB.

12. Your starter for 10:

When the Danish astronomer Tycho Brahe died in 1601, his work became the possession of which German mathematician, his last assistant, who would give his name to laws of planetary motion?

Three bonus questions on European history:
(a) Which EU member state became independent on 6 December 1917, having previously been an

---

autonomous Grand Duchy of the Russian Empire?

(b) Which EU member state marks its independence day on 22 September, the day on which, in 1908, it became fully independent from the Ottoman Empire?

(c) Which EU member state declared its independence from the Netherlands on 21 July 1830? Its first king was Leopold of Saxe-Coburg.

13. Your starter for 10:
A chapel in Houston, Texas, dedicated in 1971, and a room in the Tate Modern containing murals commissioned for the Four Seasons restaurant in New York's Seagram building are named after which Latvian-born American painter, usually regarded as an abstract expressionist?

Three bonus questions on German novelists:

(a) Published in 1774 and an important novel of the *Sturm und Drang* period of German literature, *The Sorrows of Young Werther* was by which literary figure?

(b) Which Nobel laureate was the author of *Lotte in Weimar*, in which elderly Goethe is visited by one of the characters in *The Sorrows of Young Werther*?

(c) Awarded both the Nobel Prize and the Goethe Prize in 1946, which German-born writer's works include *The Glass Bead Game* and *Steppenwolf*?

14. Your starter for 10:
An architect who served as his country's last prime minister between 1981 and 1989 before the post was abolished, which reformist politician emerged as the leading opposition candidate in the election for President of the Islamic Republic of Iran in 2009?

Three bonus questions on band names:

(a) Which band formed in Canterbury in 1966 and took

its name from the title of a William Burroughs novel published immediately after *The Naked Lunch*?

(b) The Boomtown Rats took their name from that of a gang featured in *Bound for Glory*, a 1943 autobiographical novel by which US singer-songwriter?

(c) The band Shakespears Sister (sic) took their name from the Smiths' 1985 song of the same title. The Smiths had drawn that title from a reference in a feminist essay by which novelist?

15. **Your starter for 10:**
Words meaning 'joint between the femur and tibia', 'the anthropoid ape pan troglodytes' and 'unit of measurement for temperature, angles, or arcs' all end with what double letter?

> **Three bonus questions on shared names:**
> In each case, provide the given name and surname that the following pairs have in common:
> (a) A member of the Cabinets of both Tony Blair and Gordon Brown, and a ringleader of the Peasants' Revolt?
> (b) An Irish nationalist leader, and a member of the Apollo 11 crew?
> (c) A philosopher and politician born in 1561, and a painter who died in 1992?

16. **Your starter for 10:**
In the 1860s, which French scientist demonstrated the germ theory of disease by eliminating bacteria from silkworms? The institute he founded in 1887 is noted for its research into micro-organisms and vaccines.

> **Three bonus questions on philosophical notions of time:**
> (a) Winner of the 1927 Nobel Prize for Literature, which French philosopher stated that there were two possible

conceptions of time, one of which he compared to 'the notes of a tune, melting into one another'?

(b) Remembered for his doctrine of the 'flux' of all things, which pre-Socratic philosopher stated that one cannot step into the same river twice?

(c) Which religion states that all phenomena are in a state of flux or constant change, a doctrine known variously as 'Anicca', 'wu-chang' or 'mu-joh'?

17. Your starter for 10:

Which modern musical wind instrument is a development of the medieval and renaissance shawm?

Three bonus questions on elasticity:

(a) Consider a bar experiencing a small tensional force along its length. What name is given to the ratio of the force to the cross-sectional area of the bar?

(b) If the bar stretches under the force, what is the fractional change in its length called?

(c) Finally, which British scientist, born in 1773, gives his name to the quantity which is the ratio of the tensile stress to the tensile strain?

18. Your starter for 10:

Who, in 2009, at the age of 92, became the oldest living artist to enter the top 20 of the UK album chart? The album's release coincided with the seventieth anniversary of the declaration of the Second World War.

Three bonus questions on Shakespeare's sonnets:

(a) What concept or personification is variously described in Shakespeare's sonnets as 'sluttish', 'wasteful', 'never-resting', 'swift-footed', 'devouring' and a 'bloody tyrant'?

(b) What concept or personification is described by Shakespeare in Sonnet 116 as being 'Not time's fool,

though rosy lips and cheeks / Within his bending
sickle's compass come'?

(c) In the same sonnet, which begins 'Let me not to the
marriage of true minds / Admit impediments', how is
love described in relation to 'every wand'ring bark,
/ Whose worth's unknown, although his height be
taken'?

19. Your starter for 10:

What three-word phrase came into general use in
English after it was used as the title of an economic and
social study of 1958 by John Kenneth Galbraith?

Three bonus questions on happiness:
In each case, identify the person who said the following.
All three were born in the eighteenth century:

(a) 'The great end of all human industry is the attainment
of happiness. For this were arts invented, sciences
cultivated, laws ordained, and societies modelled.'

(b) 'Sir, that all who are happy, are equally happy, is not
true. A peasant and a philosopher may be equally
satisfied, but not equally happy. Happiness consists in
the multiplicity of agreeable consciousness.'

(c) 'The said truth is that it is the greatest happiness of
the greatest number that is the measure of right and
wrong.'

20. Your starter for 10:

What Greek-derived term denotes the scientific study
of humans in relation to their physical working
environment and, more broadly, to efficiency in the
workplace?

Three bonus questions on opera:
You will be given an English version of lines from a well-
known aria on the subject of love. In each case, identify the

opera in which it appears:

(a) From an opera of 1786: 'At the mere mention of love, of delight, / I become disturbed, my heartbeat changes'.

(b) From an opera of 1832: 'She loves me, that I see. / For just one moment the beating / of her hot pulse could be felt!'

(c) From an opera of 1875: 'Love is a rebellious bird / That nobody can tame.'

21. Your starter for 10:
Which figure in the book of Genesis has a name that, when read backwards, becomes a prefix denoting ten to the power of minus nine?

Three bonus questions on the international radio-telephony spelling alphabet, or NATO alphabet, which begins 'Alpha – Bravo – Charlie':

(a) In the NATO alphabet, a Greek letter and a nymph deprived of speech by the goddess Hera are followed by which dance?

(b) In the same context, which SI multiple comes between a Shakespearean character and a South American capital?

(c) Which alcoholic spirit precedes both a form of electromagnetic radiation and an inhabitant of New England?

22. Your starter for 10:
In a leap year, what other month begins on the same day of the week as February?

Three bonus questions on a geographical feature:

(a) What term, from an Old Norse word for a fjord, is used in Scotland for a river estuary?

(b) Dunnet Head, the northernmost point of the British mainland, lies eight miles north-east of Thurso at the western end of which firth?

(c) Cromarty Firth and the Beauly Firth extend inland from the inner reaches of which triangular-shaped inlet in north-eastern Scotland? The city of Inverness lies at its head.

23. Your starter for 10:

A concept developed by Canadian nutritionist David Jenkins, for what do the letters GI stand?

Three bonus questions on amphibious landings:

(a) In the First World War, on 6 August 1915, the British Ninth Corps began an amphibious landing at Suvla Bay, on the Aegean coast of which Turkish peninsula?

(b) On D-Day, 6 June 1944, Allied forces made landings on the Normandy coast at five codenamed beaches: Omaha, Gold, Juno, Sword and which other beach, named after a western US state?

(c) The landings of United Nations troops under General Douglas MacArthur at Inchon in September 1950 was a major strategic reversal in which conflict?

24. Your starter for 10:

In history, CE or the Common Era is an alternative to the use of what abbreviation or formula?

Three bonus questions on archaic place names:

(a) When writing in his journal, what name of Turkic origin did Marco Polo give to northern China?

(b) The author Peter Fleming used what name for the area of Eastern Europe and Northern Asia controlled by the Mongols in the thirteenth and fourteenth centuries in the title of a travel book of 1936?

(c) What former term for the coastal region of North Africa between Egypt and the Atlantic survives in the common name of a macaque monkey?

25. Your starter for 10:
Which word denotes the imitation or evocation of Chinese styles in western art and architecture, particularly in the eighteenth century when whimsical pseudo-Chinese designs accorded well with the rococo style?

Three bonus questions on the Commonwealth:
(a) Which founder member of the Commonwealth, when it was established in its present form in 1931, withdrew in 1949 on becoming a republic?
(b) Which British colony in Asia chose not to join the Commonwealth when it achieved independence in 1948?
(c) In 1995, which country became the first with no historical association with Britain or any other member state to join the Commonwealth?

26. Your starter for 10:
Its title a personal pronoun, which dystopic work by the Russian Yevgeny Zamyatin did George Orwell acknowledge as an influence on his *Nineteen Eighty-Four*?

Three bonus questions on Roman officials:
(a) The Roman official whose tasks included representing and defending the rights of the Plebeians gave his title to which British political weekly publication, founded in 1937?
(b) Which ancient Roman title was used by General Douglas MacArthur when he became Supreme Commander of the Allied occupation of Japan in 1945?
(c) Originally a Roman magistrate, governor or other official, the title 'Prefect' is used in France for the head

of what smaller administrative unit within a region?

27. Your starter for 10:
The chinotto, a small, bitter citrus fruit, is thought to be
a major flavouring component of which Italian aperitif,
introduced in 1860 and commonly drunk with soda?

> **Three bonus questions on different groups of lipids:**
> In each case, give the name of the group described:
> (a) What group of lipids are based on
>   perhydrocyclopentanophenanthrene, a molecule
>   consisting of four fused saturated rings? The group
>   includes bile acids, sex hormones and vitamin D.
> (b) Secondly, an ester of glycerol in which all of the
>   hydroxyl groups are esterified with a fatty acid? They
>   are a major energy store in living organisms.
> (c) Finally, also an ester of glycerol, but in which two of
>   the hydroxyl groups are esterified with a fatty acid, and
>   the third with a phosphorylated alcohol. They are a
>   major component of plasma membranes.

28. Your starter for 10:
'Improving' on Archbishop James Usher's 1654
calculation of 23 October 4004 BC, what Biblical scholar
declared that the Earth was created at 9 a.m. on that
date?

> **Three bonus questions on new worlds:**
> (a) Terrence Malick's 2005 film *The New World* is a
>   retelling of John Smith and John Rolfe's romantic
>   entanglement with which native American?
> (b) *We Are Making a New World* and *The Menin Road*
>   are among the works of which English painter, who
>   became an official war artist in 1917?
> (c) In the final scene of Shakespeare's *Tempest*, when
>   Miranda exclaims 'O brave new world / That has

such people in't!', what is her father's less enthusiastic response?

29. **Your starter for 10:**
Having all five vowel letters in *reverse* order, which word means 'pertaining to the land mass comprising India, Pakistan, Bangladesh and Sri Lanka'?

Three bonus questions on Juvenal's Satires:
(a) In 1692, the English publisher Jacob Tonson assembled a translation of Juvenal's *Satires* by various hands, five of them by which writer who was appointed Poet Laureate in 1668?
(b) In his sixth Satire, Juvenal asked '*Quis custodiet ipsos custodes?*' What is the English sense of these words?
(c) A reworking of Juvenal's tenth Satire, the 1749 didactic poem 'The Vanity of Human Wishes' is the work of which literary figure?

30. **Your starter for 10:**
A penniless research student goes to the races with a female companion, who gives him £10 with which to bet. He puts it all on 'Starter-for-Ten', which wins its race at odds of seven-to-one. He now wagers all his money on 'Answer-Me-Now', which proceeds to win the next race at odds of thirteen-to-eight. How much does he now have to buy a pair of nice new shoes for his companion?

Three bonus questions on waltzes in classical music:
In each case, name the composer of the following:
(a) The Waltz in D Flat Major, also called the 'Minute Waltz', composed in 1847.
(b) *Variations on a Waltz by Anton Diabelli*, composed between 1819 and 1823.
(c) 'Waltz of the Flowers', in a ballet of 1892.

'You like to live dangerously, don't you? We'll look forward to seeing you in the next stage of the competition.'

THE RULES

The rules are the same as ever – 10 points for starters, 15 for bonuses.

Match Ten

1.   Your starter for 10:

A response to the intrusions of dogma into science, what two-word term has the American satirical publication *The Onion* used for a 'theory' proposing that, as gravitational force cannot explain all aspects of the phenomenon, a supernatural power must necessarily be involved?

> **Three bonus questions on Greek mythology:**
> In each case, identify the figure from the description. To make it easier, all three have names that begin with the prefix 'poly':
> (a) The muse of sacred or choral poetry, and of the mimic art.
> (b) A son of Oedipus and Jocasta who became joint ruler of Thebes with his twin brother Eteocles after the banishment of their father.
> (c) In Ovid's *Metamorphoses*, which Cyclops killed Acis, his rival in his love for Galatea?

2.   Your starter for 10:

What links: an exclamation expressing surprise or delight; the upper member of a pillar or column; and money or assets with which an enterprise starts in business?

Three questions about methods of cooking:

(a) What is the English equivalent of the method of cooking known in North America as 'broiling'?

(b) Which specific verb means to grill a chicken or other bird after splitting it open down the back and spreading the two halves out flat?

(c) Which word, originally French, means to stew meat such as oxtail in a tightly closed vessel for a long time and over a low heat with only a small amount of liquid?

3. **Your starter for 10:**

In football, the local derby between Boca Juniors and River Plate takes place in which city?

Three bonus questions on French and Italian terms:

(a) In gardening, what French term meaning 'on the ground' is used for a level space occupied by an ornamental arrangement of flowerbeds?

(b) The Italian term 'terracotta' is used for a specific type of pottery. What is the literal meaning of the word?

(c) Terranova is the Italian name and Terre-neuve the French for which Canadian island?

4. **Your starter for 10:**

The meteorite ALH 84001, thought to have originated on the planet Mars, was discovered in 1984 on which continent?

Three bonus questions linked by a scientist:

(a) Who was responsible for the development of the Word and Excel applications for Microsoft, and funds the Chair of Public Understanding of Science at Oxford?

(b) Simonyi gave which two-word nickname to Professor Richard Dawkins, the Chair's first incumbent, because of his pugnacious defence of the Theory of Evolution?

(c) In which book of 2006 does Richard Dawkins argue that the dispute between Intelligent Design and Darwinism is 'seriously undermining and restricting the teaching of science'?

5. **Your starter for 10:**
Originally a surname, which girl's name became popular after its use by Charlotte Brontë in the title of an 1849 novel? The parents of the heroine Miss Keeldar had chosen it as a first name for their expected son but, when a girl was born, they gave the name to her anyway.

Three bonus questions on admirals:
(a) Which admiral took over command at Trafalgar following Nelson's death and came to be buried close by him in St Paul's Cathedral?
(b) The first Anglo-Dutch war of 1652–1654 involved a series of skirmishes between Admiral Robert Blake and which Dutch admiral, around whom has developed the possibly apocryphal story of him attaching a broom to his mast to signify that he had 'swept the seas clean' of his enemies?
(c) Which eighteenth-century Scottish-born American admiral lends his name to a ballroom dance of the 1920s, in which dancers change partners after circling in concentric rings?

6. **Your starter for 10:**
Which year saw the deaths of Salvador Dalí and the Emperor Hirohito, the US intervention in Panama, student demonstrations in Tiananmen Square and the fall of the Berlin Wall?

Three bonus questions on poetry and mirrors:
(a) In her poem 'Mirror', which poet wrote: 'I am sheer and exact. I have no preconceptions. / Whatever I see, I

swallow immediately. / Just as it is, unmisted by love or dislike'?

(b) 'Helen of Troy had a wondering glance, / Sappho's restriction was only the sky, / Ninon was ever the chatter of France; / But oh! What a good girl am I!' Which American writer's words are these, and, according to the title, are 'Words of Comfort to Be Scratched on a Mirror'?

(c) 'Through a mirror clear / That hangs before her all the year, / Shadows of the world appear.' In which poem does the eponymous heroine view the outside world in this fashion?

7. **Your starter for 10:**
Regulated by the Golden Bull of 1356, the Duke of Saxony, the King of Bohemia, the Count Palatine of the Rhine, the Margrave of Brandenburg and the Archbishops of Cologne, Mainz and Trier were members of which electoral body?

Three bonus questions on trees:

(a) Sometimes described as a 'living fossil', *Araucaria araucana*, also known as the monkey puzzle, is the national tree of which South American country?

(b) The sole remaining species of an order that existed in the Triassic period, which tree take its name from the Japanese for 'silver apricot', and is noted for the herbal extract derived from its leaves?

(c) Wollemia, thought to have become extinct at the end of the Cretaceous period, was discovered in 1994 in the Blue Mountains less than a hundred miles from which major city?

8. **Your starter for 10:**
Finca Vigia near Havana was the hilltop home where

which American writer spent the later years of his life, moving back to the USA in 1960, a year before he took his own life?

Three bonus questions on years whose three digits are identical, for example AD 999:
In each case, give the year in which the following occurred:
(a) According to the Annals of Ulster, in what year did St Patrick establish an archiepiscopal see at Armagh?
(b) In China, in what year did the state of Chin (Qin) overcome the state of Yen and thus pave the way for the unification of China under Chin rule?
(c) In what year did Alexander the Great defeat Darius III at the Battle of Issus?

9. **Your starter for 10:**
Meaning to flow back or return, what term denotes a process in which liquid is obtained from partial condensation of vapour, where the liquid is boiled in circumstances such that the vapour returns to the stock of liquid after condensing?

Three bonus questions on a letter of the alphabet:
(a) Which term was coined by Jane Deverson in 1964 for a study of British teenagers commissioned by *Woman's Own* magazine, her article concluding that they 'sleep together before they are married, don't believe in God, dislike the Queen and don't respect their parents'?
(b) 'L'Ex', or 'the Ex', was a nickname given to which French politician after he left the office of President in 1981 to be succeeded by François Mitterand?
(c) Built for the Royal Navy during the Second World War, the vessels codenamed X-craft were prominent in action against the German battleship *Tirpitz* in 1943, and were which particular type of submarine?

10. Your starter for 10:

Describing a type of structure in which the external skin is used to support most of its weight – as, for example, the fuselage of an aircraft – what term means, in French, 'single shell'?

Three bonus questions on Sir Isaac Newton:

(a) By what name do we now know the branch of mathematics that Newton, when he discovered it, called 'the science, or method, of fluxions'?

(b) According to Newton's law of cooling, the rate of loss of heat from a body is proportional to what?

(c) The first workable model of which astronomical instrument was constructed by Newton around 1668?

11. Your starter for 10:

If the numbers on a dartboard are replaced with the letters corresponding to each number, so that 1 is replaced by 'a', 2 by 'b' and so on, what three-letter word is spelt out anticlockwise starting from the 18 sector?

Three bonus questions on state capitals:

(a) Stephen Austin gave his name to the capital of which American state?

(b) The state capital of New York was named after the which dukedom held by the future James II?

(c) Which American state capital on the James river shares it name with a borough on the River Thames?

12. Your starter for 10:

Founded in 1845, the *Straits Times* is an English-language newspaper published in which Asian country?

Three bonus questions on sign language:

(a) In British sign language, what gesture means 'good'?

(b) The sign language Yerkish was chiefly devised by E.C. von Glaserfeld in 1973 to communicate with which animals?

(c) In which novel by Will Self do humans find themselves turned into primates and forced to communicate by sign language?

13. **Your starter for 10:**
In the cabinets of John Major, which post was successively held by Norman Lamont and Kenneth Clarke?

Three bonus questions on Spanish terms in geography:

(a) Which term derives from the Spanish for 'snow-capped', and is applied to mountain ranges in Spain and western North America?

(b) Which Spanish word is used for a chain of mountains and is especially applied to the Andes?

(c) What is the characteristic shape of a hill called a 'mesa', found particularly in the south-western USA?

14. **Your starter for 10:**
The nickname bestowed upon the character Ben Cooley, a barrister involved in radical politics, serves as the title for which D.H. Lawrence novel of 1923, set mainly in Sydney?

Three bonus questions on white:

(a) Which Moroccan city's name means 'White House' in Spanish?

(b) Which European capital city's name means 'White Fortress' in Serbian?

(c) 'Aotearoa', meaning 'Land of the Long White Cloud', is an alternative name of which Commonwealth country?

15. Your starter for 10:

For a flying object to attain hypersonic speeds, what mach number must be achieved?

Three bonus questions on a place name:

(a) The residents of which resort town to the east of Rome, included the poets Horace and Catullus?

(b) The Tivoli pleasure park is one of which capital city's attractions?

(c) One of London's most famous music halls, the Tivoli stood on which thoroughfare?

16. Your starter for 10:

An aumbry is a small recess or cupboard in the wall of what specific type of building?

Three bonus questions on mathematics:

(a) What name is given to a solid figure bounded by four triangular faces, with four vertices and six edges?

(b) A tetrahedral number is an integer of the form $n(n+1)(n+2)$ divided by 6, where 'n' is a positive integer. 1 is the lowest tetrahedral number; what is the next lowest?

(c) Also an ore of silver, the mineral tetrahedrite is a source of which metal?

17. Your starter for 10:

Give the three rhyming words that mean, respectively: a secondary, or non-mainstream, cultural festival, a period of unrestrained drinking, and a peevish or whining complaint?

Three bonus questions on events of the year 1547:

(a) Which conquistador died near Seville in December 1547; his remains were later moved to Mexico, in accordance with his wishes?

(b) In April 1547, which Holy Roman Emperor routed

the army of the Lutheran Schmalkaldic League at the Battle of Muhlberg?

(c) Which ruler acceded to the English throne in January 1547?

18. Your starter for 10:

Which overseas body is represented by the initials WGA? Its members took industrial action in November 2007 over issues including new-media royalties and DVD residuals.

Three bonus questions on former Italian colonies:

(a) The North African provinces of Tripolitania, Cyrenaica and Fezzan were unified under Italian rule to form a single colony that, in 1951, became which independent kingdom?

(b) Which group of Aegean islands was taken from Turkey by Italy in 1912? Italian became the official language until the islands were ceded to Greece in 1947.

(c) Existing from 1936 to 1941, Italian East Africa included Somaliland, Eritrea and which other state, annexed by Italy after a seven-month war and the exile of its emperor?

19. Your starter for 10:

The first states that a straight line segment can be drawn joining any two points; the fourth states that all right angles are congruent; the fifth and final cannot be proven as a theorem, although it has been attempted by many people. What two-word name is given to these five statements, the first four used for the first twenty-eight propositions in the *Elements* by the same author?

Three bonus questions on London fires:

(a) Scene of the execution of Charles I in 1649, which was the only part of the Palace of Whitehall to survive the fire of 1698?

(b) A belief that the Great Fire of 1666 was divine punishment for the sin of gluttony arose because it began in Pudding Lane and ended at which corner in Smithfield?

(c) The artist J.M.W. Turner made a series of watercolour sketches now in Tate Britain of the fire of 1834 that destroyed which London building?

20. Your starter for 10:

Which medical doctor, whose blog states that he 'works full time for the NHS in London', began debunking media myths in his weekly 'Bad Science' column in *The Guardian* in 2003?

Three bonus questions on literary feuds:

(a) A public feud began in the letters pages of *The Guardian* between John le Carré and which prize-winning novelist, who claimed that le Carré had tried to persuade him to stop paperback versions of his novel being sold?

(b) For nearly three decades the Peruvian writer Mario Vargas Llosa did not speak to which Colombian Nobel laureate, allegedly over an argument that began over Vargas Llosa's wife?

(c) Which American writer provoked a literary spat when he likened Norman Mailer, John Irving and John Updike to the Three Stooges in a debate over their criticism of his novel *A Man in Full*?

21. Your starter for 10:

The cities of Ruse in Bulgaria, Novi Sad in Serbia, Vukovar in Croatia, Esztergom in Hungary, Linz in Austria and Ulm in Germany are linked by which major river?

Three bonus questions on underground rail systems:
In each case, name the EU capital city from the list of its metro stations:
(a) Solna Centrum, Hornstull, Gamla Stan and Abrahamsberg.
(b) Oktogon, Astoria, Arpad Hid and Nepstadion.
(c) Pankow, Mendelssohn-Bartholdy-Park, Innsbrucker Platz and Rosa-Luxemburg-Platz.

22. **Your starter for 10:**
Who followed André Gide and preceded William Faulkner when he was awarded the 1948 Nobel Prize in Literature for, in the words of the official citation, 'his outstanding pioneer contribution to present-day poetry'?

Three bonus questions on medicine:
(a) In the early twentieth century, the French physiologist Charles Richet coined which term in the course of observing a serious allergic reaction in a sensitised animal upon a second exposure to an antigen?
(b) Introduced in the 1930s, what was the first synthetic drug used in the treatment of general bacterial infections in humans? Its use resulted from research on the anti-bacterial action of azo dyes.
(c) The early twentieth-century string galvanometer was a forerunner of which machine used to study the muscular contractions in the heart, thus allowing diagnosis of various cardiac diseases?

23. **Your starter for 10:**
Ashtanga, Anusara, Bikram and Iyengar are names given to various styles or schools of which form of physical and spiritual exercise?

Three bonus questions on the openings of children's novels:

(a) After stating the eponymous character's name, which book begins, 'I am 10 years 2 months old. My birthday is on the 8ᵗʰ of May. It's not fair, because that dopey Peter Ingham has his birthday then too, so we just got the one cake between us'?

(b) Which novel begins: 'It's a funny thing about mothers and fathers. Even when their own child is the most disgusting little blister you could ever imagine, they still think that he or she is wonderful'?

(c) First published in 1963, which novel has this opening? 'If you went too near the edge of the chalk pit the ground would give way. Barney had been told this often enough. Everybody had told him. His grandmother, every time he came to stay with her.'

24. Your starter for 10:

In molecular biology, what term describes an assembly of proteins and nucleic acids that acts as a means of forming amino acids into proteins according to a genetically specified sequence?

Three bonus questions on the Commonwealth:

(a) Which small African country joined the Commonwealth in November 2009? Although not a former British colony, two of its neighbours, Uganda and Tanzania, have been Commonwealth members since the early 1960s.

(b) In 1995, two African countries joined the Commonwealth for the first time. For five points, name both.

(c) Which African country joined the Commonwealth in 1931, left in 1961 and rejoined in 1994?

25. Your starter for 10:

What alpha-numerical designation is given to the twin-deck, twin-aisle airliner, nicknamed 'superjumbo', which made its first commercial flight, from Singapore to Sydney, in 2007?

> **Three bonus questions on Beatles albums:**
> In each case, give the album on which the following tracks appear:
> (a) 'Drive My Car', 'Nowhere Man' and 'Michelle'.
> (b) 'Taxman', 'Eleanor Rigby' and 'Yellow Submarine'.
> (c) 'When I'm Sixty-Four', 'Lovely Rita' and 'A Day In The Life'.

26. Your starter for 10:

'On old Olympus' towering tops, a friendly Viking grew vines and hops' is a mnemonic for the names of twelve nerves that include the olfactory, trochlear and vagus. How are they collectively known?

> **Three bonus questions on rivers in myth:**
> (a) According to Greek mythology, the rivers Acheron, Lethe, Phlegethon and Cocytus were to be found where?
> (b) In the poem by Coleridge, which sacred river ran through Xanadu, the summer residence of the Mongol emperor Kublai Khan?
> (c) According to German myth, which rock on the eastern bank of the River Rhine near St Goarshausen was home to, and shared its name with one of, the Rhine maidens?

27. Your starter for 10:

Independently studied by Leibniz and Newton, which branch of mathematics is concerned with rate of change of given quantities such as length, area and volume?

Three bonus questions on a biological term:

(a) What word, derived from a Latin term meaning 'the offspring of a tame sow and wild boar', is now more generally used for the offspring of two animals or plants of different species?

(b) What alphanumeric designation is usually given to a first-generation hybrid of two plant cultivars in which the yield or other desirable characteristics are greater than in either parent?

(c) What term, from the Greek for 'alteration', is used in addition to 'hybrid vigour' for the tendency of cross-breeding to produce plants that are hardier and more productive than either of the parents?

28. Your starter for 10:

What imperial measure is equivalent to 453.6 grams?

Three bonus questions on famous Belgians:

(a) Born in Liège in 1822, which composer is noted for works including his Symphony in D Minor, and the tone poem 'Le Chasseur Maudit'?

(b) Born in Ghent, which Belgian playwright, poet and essayist won the Nobel Prize for Literature in 1911, his works including the plays *The Intruder*, *The Blind* and *Pelléas et Mélisande*?

(c) Jozef de Veuster, born in Brabant in 1840, is better known as 'Father Damian' and is noted for his work on the Hawaiian island of Moloka'i with those suffering from which medical condition?

29. Your starter for 10:

The word 'cruciverbalist' denotes a person who compiles or solves what?

Three bonus questions on the structure of DNA:

(a) In 1953, a few months before Watson and Crick

published their double helix model, which American chemist and future Nobel laureate proposed a triple helix structure for DNA?

(b) An important contribution to Watson and Crick's discovery had been made in 1950 at Columbia University, when Erwin Chargaff showed that DNA contained equal numbers of which two groups of bases?

(c) Francis Crick's interest in biology had been inspired by the book *What Is Life? The Physical Aspects of the Living Cell* by which Nobel Prize-winning physicist, best known for his work in wave mechanics?

30. Your starter for 10:

To an Inuit, what is an *umiak*?

Three bonus questions on chemicals:

(a) Which compound with the formula $C_{13}H_{16}N_2O_2$ is a hormone produced by the pineal gland which helps regulate the body's sleep cycle, its production being affected by the exposure of the eyes to light?

(b) Which polymers produced by the oxidation of the amino acid tyrosine constitute a group of dark pigments responsible for the colour of the hair, skin and eyes?

(c) In China in 2008, thousands of babies fell ill after milk was contaminated with which chemical, a trimer of cyanamide, added to increase the apparent protein content by increasing the nitrogen level?

'Well, you were a damn good team, and you led for much of the match, but I'm afraid we're going to have to say goodbye to you.'

Match Eleven

1.   Your starter for 10:
Which city lies closest to the mid-point of a straight line drawn on the map from Bristol to Cambridge?

Three bonus questions on Canada:
(a) At 16.2 metres, the world's highest tide occurs in the Bay of Fundy which separates New Brunswick from which other province of eastern Canada?
(b) James Bay is a shallow southern extension of which Canadian bay, itself an inlet of the Arctic Ocean?
(c) Hudson Bay is surrounded by Nunavut Territory, Quebec, Ontario and which other province?

2.   Your starter for 10:
The Kipunji of Tanzania, the silky Sifaka of Madagascar, the Horton Plains Slender Loris of Sri Lanka and Miss Waldron's Red Colobus of West Africa are among the world's most endangered species of which order of mammals?

Three bonus questions on African football:
(a) What is the meaning of the word *bafana*, as in Bafana Bafana, the nickname of the national side of the 2010 World Cup hosts, South Africa?
(b) What is the nickname of the national team, first successful in qualifying for the World Cup finals in 2006, which includes Didier Drogba, Kolo Touré and Emmanuel Eboué?

(c) Mali's national side is nicknamed the Eagles. The team representing which other African nation is known as the Super Eagles?

3. Your starter for 10:

With over 800 surviving indigenous languages, which country has more linguistic diversity than any other, the most widely used being the Creole 'Tok Pisin' or 'Melanesian Pidgin'? Its two other official languages are English and Hiri Motu, spoken in the area around the capital Port Moresby.

Three bonus questions on the Greek prefix 'epi-':

(a) From the Greek meaning 'words spoken over a tomb', which noun now usually means a written inscription on a tomb or gravestone in memory of the deceased?

(b) From the Greek meaning 'intensification', which word is used in classical drama to describe the part of a play in which the main action develops?

(c) An epithalamium is a song or poem celebrating which rite of passage?

4. Your starter for 10:

What five-letter word links a political pamphlet of 1776 by Thomas Paine with an 1811 novel by Jane Austen?

Three bonus questions on whales:

(a) Known by the binomial *delphinapterus leucas*, which cetacean is sometimes called 'the canary of the sea' in reference to its high-pitched 'song'?

(b) The blue whale is the largest of any animal; what is the common name of *balaenoptera physalus*, the second largest?

(c) The eponymous white whale of Herman Melville's novel *Moby-Dick* is what species of cetacean, the largest of the toothed whales?

5. **Your starter for 10:**
Which US President rang the Liberty Bell in Philadelphia to mark his country's 200th year of independence from Britain?

   Three bonus questions on a contemporary writer:
   (a) *Status Anxiety* and *The Architecture of Happiness* are among the works of which writer, born in Zurich in 1969?
   (b) In 2009, de Botton became the first writer-in-residence at which transport facility, having been commissioned to produce a book about its inner workings?
   (c) In 2009, de Botton published a book entitled *The Pleasures and Sorrows of...* what?

6. **Your starter for 10:**
Born in 1806, which British philosopher expounded Von Humboldt's concept of the so-called 'harm principle', proposing it as a stringent limitation on the extent to which government might seek to control the lives of its citizens, in his essay 'on liberty'?

   Three bonus questions on US presidents:
   (a) Known as 'Old Rough and Ready', which military commander during the Mexican-American War became president in 1849, only to die in office just sixteen months into his term?
   (b) Benjamin Harrison, who held office from 1889 to 1893, was both preceded and succeeded by which president?
   (c) Having been vice-president to Warren Harding from 1921 to 1923, who succeeded as president on Harding's death and was re-elected in 1924?

7. **Your starter for 10:**
The Pythagorean philosopher and number theorist

Philolaus proposed a 59-year calendar based on how many months, the number in question being both the square of 27 and the cube of 9?

Three bonus questions on the G20 economies:
(a) In late 2009, the combined population of China and India, the most populous members of the G20, was around 2.5 billion. What percentage of the total world population is this? You can have five per cent either way.
(b) After China, India and the USA, the two most populous members of the G20 are both countries that straddle the Equator. For five points, name both.
(c) With an estimated population of 22 million in 2009, which member of the G20 has the smallest population?

8. Your starter for 10:
From the Latin for 'to dress', what term denotes the formal installation of an incumbent in public office, especially by taking possession of its insignia, and is most commonly used of formal offices of state, aristocracy and church?

Three bonus questions on memorable words of politicians:
The answer in each case is the father of a British Prime Minister:
(a) In a speech of 1904, who said, 'The day of small nations has long passed away. The day of empires has come'?
(b) In a public letter of 1886, who wrote, 'Ulster will fight; Ulster will be right'?
(c) In a speech in the House of Lords in 1777, who said, 'You cannot conquer America'?

9. Your starter for 10:
Concatenating the chemical symbols of iron, astatine,

hydrogen and erbium gives the name of which feature of avian anatomy?

Three bonus questions on twentieth-century Dutch art:
(a) Which movement in early twentieth-century Dutch art is defined by the Guggenheim Museum as being based on 'the geometry of the straight line, the square, and the rectangle, [and] the predominant use of pure primary colours with black and white'?
(b) A founder of the De Stijl movement, which Dutch artist's work includes his 1942 work now in the Tate collection *Composition with Yellow, Blue and Red*?
(c) *Ascending and Descending*, with its never-ending staircases, and the self-portrait *Hand with Reflecting Sphere* are among the works of which Dutch print-maker, famous for his spatial illusions?

10. Your starter for 10:
What is one-half plus one-third plus one-quarter minus one?

Three bonus questions on overseas territories:
(a) The islands of Wallis and Futuna in the Pacific Ocean and Mayotte in the Indian Ocean are overseas territories, or collectivities, of which European country?
(b) Which French overseas territory consists of islands including the Windward, Leeward, Marquesas and Gambier Islands?
(c) Saint Barthélemy and the northern part of the island of Saint Martin are French overseas collectivities in which body of water?

11. Your starter for 10:
What name is given to an angle formed by the intersection of two planes, an example being that of an

aircraft wing and the horizontal axis?

Three bonus questions on literature:
(a) What is the first line of the novel of 1851 whose epilogue begins with words from the Book of Job: 'And I only am escaped alone to tell thee'?
(b) Referring to both Melville's novel and the Biblical prophet, 'Call me Jonah' is the opening line of the 1963 novel *Cat's Cradle* by which American author?
(c) 'Perhaps it is because I was nearly born under water' is the opening line of which book by Philip Hoare, a meditation on Melville's *Moby-Dick*, among other things, which won the 2009 Samuel Johnson Prize for Non-Fiction?

12. **Your starter for 10:**
'Medical', 'Historical', 'Modern', 'Tender' and 'Blaze' are lines produced by which publishing company?

Three bonus questions on songs of the Second World War:
(a) Written by the American Frank Loesser in the immediate aftermath of the attack on Pearl Harbor, the title of a popular song of the Second World War demanded that one 'praise the Lord, and...' do what?
(b) Recorded by Arthur Askey and George Formby among others, a popular song of the Second World War demanded that a sergeant-major do what, before tucking the singer in his 'little wooden bed'?
(c) Written in 1915 but enormously popular with both Axis and Allied forces in the Second World War, which eponymous young lady, in the English-language version, stood 'underneath the lantern, / By the barrack gate'?

13. **Your starter for 10:**
The appeal of which TV series of the 1960s was

summed up by these lyrics from a 2004 UK number one:
'It always looks so cool / When spaceships come out of
the pool'?

**Three bonus questions on pairs of words that are
sometimes confused:**
In each case, give both the words defined:
(a) Which two similar words can have the individual
    meanings of 'extremely earnest or serious' and 'using
    large amounts of capital or other inputs to increase
    production'?
(b) 'Courteous, kind and pleasant' and 'showing beauty or
    elegance of movement'?
(c) 'The act of refraining from voting' and 'the practice of
    not drinking alcohol'?

14. **Your starter for 10:**
Supposedly martyred by the Danes for his adherence
to Christianity, which ninth-century Anglo-Saxon king
became the centre of a miracle cult centred on a shrine
in a Suffolk market town that still bears his name?

Three bonus questions on medical procedures:
(a) From the Latin for 'to listen', what term denotes those
    procedures based on listening to the internal sounds of
    the body, usually through a stethoscope?
(b) What is the lay term for laparoscopic surgery?
(c) Used to record the electrical activity of the heart, for
    what does the acronym ECG stand?

15. **Your starter for 10:**
Discredited by Lazzaro Spallanzani in 1765, what is the
common term for the belief that the decomposition of
plant or animal matter is able to create new life forms?

Three bonus questions on beef:
(a) What name of Yiddish origin is given to a cured meat, usually brisket, which has been brined, seasoned, and then smoked?
(b) Valtellina in Lombardy is the original source of which air-dried salted beef?
(c) What highly prized Japanese beef takes its name from a major seaport to the west of Osaka?

16. Your starter for 10:
In mobile phone technology, what does SIM, as in 'sim card', stand for?

Three bonus questions on webcomics:
(a) Its title a computer keyboard command, which webcomic created by Tim Buckley features Ethan and Lucas in 'a strip about two guys who sit around and play video games'?
(b) Describing itself as an 'ongoing chronicle of life (or the lack thereof) in grad school', for what do the letters 'P-H-D' of Jorge Cham's *PHD Comics* stand?
(c) Jeph Jacques says that *QC*, his webcomic, is, 'ostensibly about romance, indie rock, little robots, and the problems people have'. For what do the letters 'QC' stand?

17. Your starter for 10:
If '5' is Classical, '10' is Romanesque, '20' is Gothic, '50' is Renaissance and '100' is Baroque, which currency are we talking about?

Three bonus questions on the Devil's Dictionary of Ambrose Bierce:
In each case, give the specific word from the definition in these entries, which appear consecutively under the letter 'a':

(a) What noun is 'an overmastering desire to be vilified by enemies while living, and made ridiculous by friends when dead'?

(b) What noun is 'the state's magnanimity to those offenders whom it would be too expensive to punish'?

(c) What verb means 'to grease a king or other great functionary already sufficiently slippery'?

18. Your starter for 10:
Which three-letter verb means to compress one or more files, either for archival purposes or to speed their transfer over the internet?

Three bonus questions on adaptations of fairy tales:

(a) Which fairy tale, first recorded in print in the eighteenth century, was the basis for a film version directed by Jean Cocteau and released in 1946?

(b) Which fairy tale by Charles Perrault, supposedly based on an historical figure over two centuries earlier, was reworked by Angela Carter in her 1979 story 'The Bloody Chamber'?

(c) Which fairy tale, collected by the Brothers Grimm, was the subject of an opera of 1893 by Englebert Humperdinck?

19. Your starter for 10:
What surname is shared by the counsel for the defence at the Scopes 'Monkey Trial'; the patenter of the board game Monopoly; and the film character played by Fay Wray in 1933 and Naomi Watts in 2005?

Three bonus questions on car logos:

(a) Sharing its name with an eighteenth-century Native American leader, which marque of car was introduced by General Motors in 1926 and has a representation of an arrowhead as its logo?

(b) Maserati relocated to Modena in the 1930s, but the company's trident logo is the traditional symbol of which Italian city where the cars were originally made?

(c) In the late 1930s, which car manufacturer adopted a stylised dirigible airship as its emblem? This evolved into a stylised aeroplane in the 1950s, and in 1964 became a lightning bolt.

20. Your starter for 10:
What is the current name of the metallic element, atomic number 23 and chemical symbol V, that was originally named after the Greek for 'red' because of the colour of its salts?

Three questions on getting things wrong:

(a) From a Latin word strictly meaning 'ramble' or 'misconception', what word means an ignorant or imprudent deviation from the norms or expectations for behaviour or correctness?

(b) Dating to the early twentieth century and believed to derive from a French term meaning a boat hook, what word usually denotes a verbal mistake made in a social environment, and is now particularly associated with politicians?

(c) From a Middle English term meaning roughly to shut one's eyes or doze, what word means a mistake made through stupidity, ignorance or carelessness?

21. Your starter for 10:
In 1894, the Japanese Kita-Sato Shiba-Saburo and the Swiss-born Alexandre Yersin both independently discovered the infectious agent, now called *yersinia pestis*, responsible for which disease, which killed over 80,000 people in China that year and which two centuries earlier had killed a sixth of the population of London?

Three bonus questions on polyhedra:

(a) The D-angle is the angle, in degrees, between any pair of adjacent faces in a polyhedron. What word does this letter 'D' represent?

(b) Two spheres are associated with regular polyhedral. One, the in-sphere, fits inside so as to touch all the faces while the other fits around the outside to touch all the vertices and has what name?

(c) For any regular polyhedron, the number of vertices minus the number of edges plus the number of faces always equals what number?

22. Your starter for 10:

Which country was ruled from 987 by the Capetian dynasty, whose subsequent branches included the Valois and Bourbon?

Three bonus questions on historical figures:

(a) The composers George Frederick Handel and Domenico Scarlatti were almost exact contemporaries of which king of Great Britain?

(b) Anthony Van Dyck, Diego Velasquez and Francesco Borromini were all born in the year before which British king, himself a noted patron of the arts?

(c) Rudyard Kipling was born in the same year as which British king and died within a few days of him in 1936?

23. Your starter for 10:

Which legendary figure is the subject of these lines: 'She left the web, she left the loom / She made three paces through the room, / She saw the water-lily bloom, / She saw the helmet and the plume, / She looked down to Camelot'?

Three bonus questions on like-sounding place names:
In each case, give the European country in which the
following regions are located:
(a) Wallachia.
(b) Wallis, also known as Valais.
(c) Wallonia.

24. **Your starter for 10:**
Uniting the conservative Anglo-Catholic wing of the
Church of England with the evangelicals, the Cost of
Conscience movement developed as a reaction mainly
against the result of which vote at the General Synod of
1992?

Three bonus questions on religion:
(a) What religious term does the catechism of the Book of
Common Prayer define as 'an outward and visible sign
of an inward and spiritual grace'?
(b) According to the catechism, 'Christ [hath] ordained
two [sacraments] as generally necessary to salvation';
what are they?
(c) Sub-section 1113 of the Catechism of the Roman
Catholic Church recognises how many sacraments?

25. **Your starter for 10:**
Zygodactylous birds, such as parrots and woodpeckers,
have how many toes pointing backwards and how many
forwards?

Three questions about Edinburgh:
(a) Which novel by Sir Walter Scott was based in part on
the 1736 Porteous Riots in the centre of Edinburgh?
(b) In the eighteenth century, the Heart of Midlothian was
the nickname of the old Edinburgh 'Tolbooth'. What
was the function of this building?
(c) Today the Heart of Midlothian is a mosaic of granite

stones set in the pavement just outside the main entrance of which building?

26. Your starter for 10:
Which Swiss city gives its name to a widely used device for producing intermittent rotary motion, characterised by alternate periods of motion and rest with no reversal in direction, such as was used in early motion picture projectors?

> **Three bonus questions on a card game:**
> (a) Former Test cricketer Sir Everton Weekes has also represented Barbados at which card game?
> (b) Which world leader's only official post at the time of his death in 1997 was said to be president of his country's bridge association?
> (c) Born Michel Shalhoub in 1932, which actor led a successful professional bridge team?

27. Your starter for 10:
Parerga and Paralipomena and *The World as Will and Idea* are works by which German philosopher, born in Danzig in 1788?

> **Three bonus questions on ballerina brides:**
> (a) Which British economist married the ballerina Lydia Lopkova in 1925?
> (b) Which artist, while working on the ballet *Parade* in 1917, met his future wife, Olga Kokhlova, who was one of the production's dancers?
> (c) Which writer and broadcaster married the ballerina Moira Shearer in 1950?

28. Your starter for 10:
First detected in 1965 by Arno Penzias and Robert Wilson, what three-word term describes the radiation

field emitted when the universe was about 380,000 years old? Its dipole anisotropy reveals that our galaxy is travelling at 627 kilometres per second towards the constellation Hydra.

Three bonus questions on a word:
(a) Which word for a large sepulchre is derived from the name of a king of Caria whose monument stood at Halicarnassus?
(b) The palace and mausoleum of the Emperor Diocletian can be seen in which Croatian port?
(c) Whose mausoleum is surmounted by what is allegedly the largest Christian symbol ever erected and stands in the Valley of the Fallen near Madrid?

29. Your starter for 10:
'Gaul as a whole is divided into three parts.' These words begin an account by which politician and historian, born in 100 BC?

Three bonus questions on a musical instrument:
(a) The Serenade in Mozart's *Don Giovanni* was written for which musical instrument, related to the lute?
(b) 'Mandolin Wind' was a track on whose 1971 album *Every Picture Tells a Story*, which also contained the number one hit 'Maggie May'?
(c) Whose mandolin featured in the title of Louis de Bernière's novel, set in Cephalonia during the Second World War?

30. Your starter for 10:
In biology, the sliding filament model describes the way thick and thin filaments slide relative to each other in which tissue of the body?

Three bonus questions on a colour:

(a) What common name is given to infants born with heart defects known as the Tetralogy of Fallot?

(b) The Blueshirts, a fascist movement whose members fought in the Spanish Civil War, were formed in which country?

(c) What is the alternative name for blue vitriol?

> 'Oh dear, that was a bit of a whitewash, wasn't it? It's not the worst score we've ever had, but...'

THE RULES

Doubtless the rules are all etched on
your hearts, so I'll just remind you
there is a 5-point fine if you interrupt
a starter question incorrectly.

Match Twelve

1. Your starter for 10:

Its mountain building having occurred mainly during the tertiary period that began about 65 million years ago, what is the most recent orogeny, probably still continuing in some parts of the world?

Three bonus questions on Mediterranean islands that were once British possessions:

(a) Which of the Balearic Islands was, with Gibraltar, ceded to Britain by the Peace of Utrecht in 1713?

(b) Which Mediterranean island was ceded to Britain at the Treaty of Paris in 1814?

(c) Which island, taken from the Ottoman Empire in 1878, was annexed in 1914?

2. Your starter for 10:

Identify the poet who wrote these lines: 'Red lips are not so red / As the stained stones kissed by the English dead. / Kindness of wooed and wooer / Seems shame to their love pure.'

Three bonus questions on twentieth-century history:

In each case, name the US president who was in office when the following were prime minister of the UK:

(a) Clement Attlee.

(b) Neville Chamberlain.

(c) Anthony Eden.

3.   Your starter for 10:
Familiarised in the 1930s, which French word, from the Greek meaning 'lawless', means the lack of the usual social or ethical standards in an individual or group?

Three bonus questions on a human capacity:

(a) All born in the nineteenth century, Herbert Spencer, Francis Galton, Henry Goddard, Charles Spearman and Cyril Burt are among those considered to have contributed to the current understanding and assessment of which broad capacity in human beings?

(b) Working in collaboration with Theodore Simon, which psychologist, born in Nice in 1857, devised the first practical method of assessing intelligence?

(c) The English psychologist Charles Spearman represented his construct of general intelligence, the factor that controls performance in a whole range of cognitive tasks, by which lower-case letter of the alphabet?

4.   Your starter for 10:
Answer in German or English. Apparently aiming to demonstrate the possibilities of a then-new tuning system, what phrase did J.S. Bach use for the title of his 1722 collection of twenty-four preludes and fugues in all the major and minor keys?

Three bonus questions on the prefix 'para-':

(a) In 'parachute' and 'parasol', 'para' comes from an Italian word for 'shelter', as it does in which architectural term, literally meaning 'breast guard'?

(b) From the latin for 'little', 'parum' is the etymology of the prefix in the name of which substance, so called because of its low chemical reactivity?

(c) The Greek meaning 'alongside' is the origin of the prefix of which term for the Holy Spirit?

5. **Your starter for 10:**
   What term was coined in the 1950s by French commentators to distinguish the developing countries from the capitalist and communist blocs, defining a concept which the writer Shiva Naipaul has described as 'an artificial construction of the West – an ideological empire on which the sun is always setting'?

   Three bonus questions on grandiose titles:
   In each case, name the current or former national leader who held the titles listed:
   (a) 'The Eternal Bosom of Hot Love', 'Guardian Deity of the Planet' and 'Supreme Commander at the Forefront of the Struggle against Imperialism and the United States'.
   (b) 'The Titan of the World Revolution', 'the Greatest Genius of All Time' and 'the Best Disciple of Comrade Lenin'.
   (c) 'Lord of All the Beasts of the Earth and Fishes of the Sea', 'Conqueror of the British Empire' and 'the Last King of Scotland'.

6. **Your starter for 10:**
   Often referred to as 'road tax' although it has not been ring-fenced for road building since 1936, for what do the three letters V.E.D. stand?

   Three bonus questions on number systems in mathematics:
   In each case, give the name of the number system commonly denoted by the following bold letter:
   (a) The letter 'z' when written in bold.
   (b) Referring to the mathematician who first described them, the letter 'h' when written in bold.
   (c) Finally, the letter 'c' when written in bold.

7. **Your starter for 10:**
What word of three letters can be added to the beginning of bed, head, house, plate and pot to make five longer words?

Three bonus questions on a US state:
(a) Which present-day western state of the USA saw the development of a number of boom towns following the discovery of the Comstock Lode silver deposit in 1859?
(b) Derived from the Washoe Indian word meaning 'big water', which large freshwater lake occupies a fault basin on the California-Nevada border?
(c) Calling itself the Biggest Little City in the World, which Nevada settlement became synonymous from the 1930s onwards with easily obtainable divorces?

8. **Your starter for 10:**
The fifteenth person to hold the position, a senior post in the royal household, Baron Rees of Ludlow, appointed in 1995, has what prestigious scientific title?

Three bonus questions on scientific terms beginning with the letters 'Rh':
In each case, give the term from the definition:
(a) A chromo-protein known as 'visual purple' contained in light-sensitive cells in the retina.
(b) An instrument that controls a current by varying the resistance.
(c) *Macaca mulatta*, an old-world primate that gives its name to an antigen occurring on the red blood cells of most humans.

9. **Your starter for 10:**
In the aftermath of the Second World War, to which musical instrument did the Japanese educationalist Shin'ichi Suzuki first apply his innovative teaching method?

Three bonus questions on royal offspring:

In each case, name the queen or queen consort who gave birth to the following:

(a) Henry the Young King; Richard the Lionheart; and King John.

(b) Mary, Queen of France; Margaret, Queen of Scots; and Henry VIII of England.

(c) 'Empress Frederick' of Germany; Alice, Grand Duchess of Hesse; and Princess Henry of Battenberg.

10. Your starter for 10:

What word meaning to solicit votes or support before an election appears to come from a verb originally meaning 'to toss in a sheet', which later came to mean 'to discuss' or 'to criticise'?

Three bonus questions on a chemical compound:

(a) What word, probably derived from the German words for vinegar and ether, is given to a compound formed as the condensation product of an acid and an alcohol?

(b) The hydrolysis of an ester by an alkali, a reaction known as saponification, is utilised in the preparation of what household product from fats and oils?

(c) What term describes the reaction of a chemical compound with water, such as the reaction of water with esters to form alcohols and carboxylic acids?

11. Your starter for 10:

Archimedes' is Pi, Pythagoras' is the square root of 2, Boltzmann's is represented by a lower-case 'k', Planck's by 'h' and Avogadro's by 'n.a.'; to what word for an unvarying quantity are their names linked?

Three bonus questions on a shell:

(a) What name for a bivalve mollusc of the genus *pecten*, and for its distinctive shell, also denotes thin slices of meat or fish often dusted with flour and sautéed?

(b) The words 'I hear those voices that will not be drowned' are found on a sculpture called *The Scallop* by Maggi Hambling. Situated on the beach at Aldeburgh, it is dedicated to which composer, from whose opera the words are taken?

(c) The scallop shell is also a traditional symbol of pilgrimage, denoting that the wearer has visited the shrine of St James at which site in northern Spain?

12. Your starter for 10:

Austenite, martensite and pearlite are substances associated with the production and treatment of what common alloy?

Three bonus questions on named coasts:

(a) The Mosquito Coast, believed to have been named after the Miskito people rather than the insect, runs along the Caribbean shore of two countries: for five points, name one of them.

(b) What name is given to the coast of eastern South India, on which lies the city of Chennai, formerly Madras?

(c) What name is shared by a resort region south of Brisbane and a former British colony in West Africa, now called Ghana?

13. Your starter for 10:

In his 1962 book *Anatomy of Britain*, Anthony Sampson describes members of Civil Service orders as rising from CMG, 'Call Me God', to KCMG, 'Kindly Call Me God', to GCMG. What does he claim these four letters stand for?

Three bonus questions on Michelangelo's sculpture:

(a) One of Michelangelo's first major sculptures, now in the Bargello in Florence, is of which Roman god?

(b) There are three attributable sculptures by Michelangelo, in Milan, Florence and, most notably, in St Peter's in Rome, of which popular religious subject?

(c) In the UK, the Michelangelo sculpture called the *Taddei Tondo* is on public display in which institution?

14. Your starter for 10:
What is the lowest positive integer to contain the letter 'c' when it is spelled out as a word in English?

Three bonus questions on national flags:
(a) Which is the only country in the world to have a flag which is not a form of rectangle, but consists instead of two overlapping right-angled triangles?

(b) Which country's flag consists of a horizontal green pall fimbriated white against an upper red and a lower blue band, and gold against a black triangle at the hoist?

(c) Which country's flag is the only one to consist purely of one solid colour, with no additional designs or symbols?

15. Your starter for 10:
Which campaigner for socialism and women's rights once said of her experiences, 'I have visited sweatshops, factories, crowded slums. I could not see the squalor... but I could smell it'?

Three bonus questions on seaweeds:
(a) In Wales, what name is given to the traditional Welsh foodstuff made from the purple seaweed porphyra species?

(b) Which polysaccharide consisting of sulphated D-glactose residues, is obtained from Rhodophyta, and is used as a gelling and stabilising agent in foods, cosmetics and pharmaceuticals?

(c) What polymer is composed largely of galactose, and is

mainly obtained from seaweeds of the genera *Gelidium* and *Gracilaria*? It is used as a gelling agent in food and microbiological culture media.

16. Your starter for 10:

In March 2004, the European Commission fined Microsoft almost €500 million for abusing its dominant market position. What did the software giant have to offer its Windows operating system without due to the ruling?

Three bonus questions on fictional drinking establishments:

In each case, name the creator of the following:

(a) In a radio play of 1954: the Sailors Arms, where 'half past eleven is opening time. The hands of the clock have stayed still at half past eleven for fifty years'.

(b) The Midnight Bell in a trilogy published in 1935 as *20,000 Streets Under the Sky*.

(c) The Prancing Pony, in a work of 1954?

17. Your starter for 10:

Which term, first used by the French chef Vincent la Chapelle in 1733, acquired wide currency in the 1970s as the name of a style of cooking in which rich foods were avoided and the emphasis was on fresh ingredients elegantly presented?

Three bonus questions on geography:

(a) In the south-western United States, what term, the Spanish for 'table', indicates an isolated flat-topped hill with steep sides?

(b) A large flat-topped mountain whose sides rise to 400 metres, Mount Roraima marks the triple border point of Venezuela and which two other countries?

(c) A large mesa in Venezuela is the location of which

waterfall, the world's highest, named after an aviator who crash-landed nearby in 1935?

18. **Your starter for 10:**
Also known as the Tower of Bramah, which binary puzzle in mathematics involves the transfer of a given number of discs of different sizes between three rods?

Three bonus questions on Greek tragedy:
(a) In the tragedy by Sophocles, which Greek hero commits suicide after the armour of Achilles is awarded to Odysseus rather than to him?
(b) Which tragedy by Euripides concerns the former wife of Jason and her murder of their children in revenge for his remarriage?
(c) The tragedy *Agamemnon*, in which the title character is murdered on his return home at the end of the war by his wife and her lover, is by which ancient Greek playwright?

19. **Your starter for 10:**
Comprising the Chagos Islands, whose inhabitants were expelled in the 1960s to make way for an American airbase, for what do the letters BIOT stand?

Three bonus questions on toes:
(a) The *Megalonychidae* are the two-toed, and the *Bradypodidae* are the three-toed families of which tree-dwelling mammal?
(b) The *Perissodactyla* are the odd-toed ungulates such as the horse and the rhinoceros. What name is given to the even-toed ungulates, which includes pigs and antelopes?
(c) Which long-tailed leaping desert rodent has thirty-three species including the three, four, and five-toed, the comb-toed and the feather-footed?

20. Your starter for 10:
In music, which Italian words are used for the instruction 'repeat from the beginning until you come to the word *fine*, or the pause mark'?

Three bonus questions on first names:
(a) Hebrew in origin and meaning 'God beholds', an early use of which girl's name occurs in Shakespeare's *Merchant of Venice* as the daughter of Shylock?
(b) Which male given name owed much of its initial popularity to the surname of an English admiral who defeated the Spanish at Cape St Vincent in 1780?
(c) The Greek for 'young green shoot' is the derivation of which five-letter girl's name?

21. Your starter for 10:
A friend of Leonardo da Vinci, the mathematician Luca Pacioli was the author of an early written description of which basic accountancy procedure, under which every transaction is recorded in at least two accounts?

Three bonus questions on Shakespeare's History plays:
Give the title of the play that ends with these lines:
(a) 'I'll make a voyage to the Holy Land, / To wash this blood off from my guilty hand. / March sadly after; grace my mournings here / In weeping after this untimely bier.'
(b) 'Saint Albans' battle, won by famous York, / Shall be eterniz'd in all age to come. / Sound drum and trumpets and to London all; / And more such days as these to us befall.'
(c) 'Now civil wounds are stopp'd, peace lives again – / That she may long live here, God say amen!'

22. Your starter for 10:
In early plant classification systems, the *pteridophyta*

was the name given to the club mosses, horsetails and which other major group comprising some eleven thousand species?

Three bonus questions on Russia:
(a) Which linguistic family that includes the Finno-Ugric and Samoyedic language groups takes its name from a Russian mountain range?
(b) Which Russian archipelago, whose name means 'New Land', constitutes a continuation of the Ural mountains?
(c) Into which sea does the Ural river discharge?

23. Your starter for 10:
The last known case of which disease being contracted naturally occurred in 1977 in the village of Merka in Somalia?

Three bonus questions on medieval churchmen:
(a) *Gesta regum Anglorum* or *History of the English Kings* is a twelfth-century work by which monk, named after a Benedictine abbey in north Wiltshire?
(b) Named after a village in Surrey, which scholastic philosopher gives his name to the maxim expressed in Latin as *entia non sunt multiplicanda praeter necessitatem*?
(c) Which bishop of Winchester under Edward III founded both New College, Oxford and the school whose pupils bear his name?

24. Your starter for 10:
What five-letter name links: an isolated island of the South Atlantic; the 'naked rambler'; the singer Badly Drawn Boy; and an England cricketer and ballroom dancer?

Three bonus questions on theatre and film:

(a) Expressed as an imaginary barrier completing the enclosure of the stage, what two-word term denotes the space separating the audience from the action of a theatrical performance?

(b) Breaching the fourth wall is a common convention in which improvised popular theatrical form, developed in sixteenth-century Italy?

(c) Who wrote and directed the 1985 film *The Purple Rose of Cairo*, in which Tom, played by Jeff Daniels, leaves the black-and-white film-within-a-film and enters the real world of colour?

25. Your starter for 10:

Which Second World War operational codename was given to the British withdrawal from Dunkirk and the adjacent French coast in May and June of 1940?

Three bonus questions on Westminster parliamentary procedure:

(a) What term is used for the disciplinary procedure by which the Speaker excludes an MP from the House for a period of five days for 'disregarding the authority of the chair'?

(b) In the Commons, what is the precise qualification for being elected 'father of the house'?

(c) Traditionally, MPs, being commoners, are not permitted to undergo what process within the Palace of Westminster? As a result, if they should happen to undergo it, it is officially recorded to have taken place in St Thomas's Hospital over the river?

26. Your starter for 10:

What noun of five letters can mean deep silence or tranquillity, a print of one of the frames of a film and, by

a different etymology, an apparatus for the production
of spirituous liquors?

Three bonus questions linked by a tool:

(a) In the Lennon and McCartney song, what was used
to kill Joan who 'studied pataphysical science in the
home'?

(b) According to tradition, at whose official death
ceremony does his secretary tap his head with a silver
hammer?

(c) The only man from his country to achieve the papacy,
what nationality was the Pope who crowned Frederick
Barbarossa in 1155?

27. Your starter for 10:

Marking the centre of our local supercluster, which large
galaxy cluster is roughly 50 million light years away and
lies in the direction of the largest constellation of the
zodiac, after which it is named?

Three bonus questions on a homophone:

(a) In which country are the semi-arid plateaux known as
the Great Karoo and Little Karoo?

(b) 'A broken-hearted woman tends the grave of mad
Carew' in the opening lines of which poem of 1911 by
J. Milton Hayes?

(c) Thomas Carew was the first of which group of poets,
whose name derived from their loyalty to Charles I
during the Civil War?

28. Your starter for 10:

During the reign of which emperor, who ruled from
1867 to 1912, did Japan transform from an isolated
feudal society into a major industrial and military
power?

Three bonus questions on optical aids:

(a) What was developed in the 1880s by Adolph Fick to correct irregular astigmatism?

(b) From the French for 'to squint', what name is given to a pair of eye glasses held in the hand by a long handle?

(c) What French term is used for a pair of spectacles kept in position by a spring clip which grips the nose?

29. Your starter for 10:

The name of which nymph – transformed, in Greek mythology, into the reed bed from which Pan cut and fashioned his pipes – is used to describe the vocal organ of birds, located at the base of the windpipe?

Three bonus questions on a tree:

(a) Chips of which wood are added to wine to give a 'cask mature' flavour, although the wine is produced in stainless-steel vats?

(b) What substance used in wine production is obtained specifically from the bark of *Quercus suber*, an evergreen species of oak?

(c) In which park in Berkshire are the Watch oak and the King oak?

30. Your starter for 10:

On the MHO scale of hardness of minerals, which value is given to diamond?

Three bonus questions on the nervous system:

(a) What single word is used for a cell which has the specialised function of transmitting nerve impulses?

(b) Which neurones conduct information from the central nervous system to effectors such as muscles?

(c) In the USA, motor neurone disease is often given the name of which baseball player, who suffered from the illness from 1939?

'You were a bit diffident to start with, but you got going, and you had some very, very good interventions, so congratulations to you. We shall look forward to seeing you in the second round.'

THE RULES

Well, you shouldn't be here if you don't know the rules, but I'll remind you – there is a 5-point penalty for incorrect interruptions to starter questions.

Match Thirteen

1. Your starter for 10:

How many days are in the first three months of a leap year?

> **Three bonus questions on countries:**
> (a) In September 2009, Samoa adopted what practice, bringing it into line with other South Pacific countries, and also with Japan, India and the UK?
> (b) In most South American countries, cars are driven on the right, but in two they are driven on the left. One is Guyana; which of its neighbours, a former Dutch colony, is the other?
> (c) Driving on the left is the practice in which country, bordering Burma, Laos and Cambodia, all of whom drive on the right, so requiring a changeover at the border?

2. Your starter for 10:

The Fach System is a German method of categorising performers in what area of the arts, partly according to their physical appearance and acting ability but mainly according to the range, colour and character of a major attribute?

> **Three bonus questions on the names of wine grapes:**
> (a) The name of which white wine grape comes from the French for 'wild' on account of its vines' vigorous

growth patterns?

(b) Which black grape used to make red wine derives its name from the French for 'blackbird'?

(c) The name of which grape combines the German word for 'spice' with the name by which the Italian town of Termeno in the Alto Adige region was known when it was in the Austrian Südtirol?

3. Your starter for 10:
A Hellenic language, Charles Dickens's house in Broadstairs, and those who, according to the New Testament, will inherit the Earth, all rhyme with the common name of which vegetable, whose scientific name is *allium porrum*?

Three bonus questions on orchestras:

(a) Founded in 1832, which orchestra's principal conductors have included Herbert von Karajan, Claudio Abbado and Simon Rattle?

(b) Noted for its aim of addressing some of its country's social problems through musical education, the Simón Bolivar Youth Orchestra was formed in 1975 in which country?

(c) Which orchestra was founded in Manchester in 1858 by a German-born pianist and conductor, and has premiered works by Vaughan Williams and Elgar?

4. Your starter for 10:
The Act of Parliament passed in 1931 to establish a status of legislative equality between the self-governing dominions of the British Empire and the United Kingdom is known by what name, after the location of the body that passed it?

Three bonus questions on physics:

(a) From a Greek word meaning 'activity' or 'operation',

what is the common name in physics of an object's capacity to do work?

(b) A ball weighing one kilogram is held five metres above the ground. If the local acceleration due to gravity is ten metres per second squared, what is the potential energy of the ball?

(c) If the ball is then released, what is its speed when it hits the ground?

5. Your starter for 10:

From the Latin meaning 'desire' or 'lust', what Freudian term was used in early psychoanalytical theory to mean sexual energies, but later came to mean more generally those psychic energies employed in the service of the life instinct?

Three bonus questions on art and literature:

(a) *Modernista* was the Spanish name for which artistic style, also known as *Stile Liberty* in Italy, and *Sezession-Stil* in Austria?

(b) *Modern Love* is an innovative poetical work of 1862 by which author, whose novels include *The Egoist* and *Diana of the Crossways*?

(c) Published in five volumes between 1843 and 1860, *Modern Painters*, which began as a defence of Turner, is a work by which author and art critic?

6. Your starter for 10:

Which American writer, who died in 1982, was a prolific contributor of short stories to the *New Yorker* magazine as well as the author of full-length novels including *The Wapshot Chronicle* in 1958, and *Falconer* in 1977?

Three bonus questions on Soviet memorabilia:

(a) Sometimes known as Stalin's World, the controversial Grutas Park sculpture garden of Soviet-era statues and other memorabilia lies close to the borders of Belarus and Poland in which EU member state?

(b) Now home to a sixteen-foot statue of Lenin salvaged by an art lover from Slovakia after the fall of the communist government, Fremont is a noted centre of American counter-culture and forms part of which major city?

(c) In which EU capital is Memento Park? Situated close to the Danube, its exhibits include a pedestal topped by Stalin's boots, the rest of the statue having been torn down by a crowd in 1956.

7. **Your starter for 10:**
Hamlet said he saw a camel, then a weasel, then a whale. Joni Mitchell saw 'rows and flows of angel hair and ice-cream castles in the air'. They were both looking at what?

Three bonus questions on a shared surname:

(a) What was the surname of the American physicist who collaborated with A.A. Michelson in the 1887 experiment to detect the so-called 'ether drift'?

(b) Sylvanus Griswold Morley, born in 1883, is noted for his excavations and restoration work at Cichen Itza, a major pre-Columbian site built by which civilisation?

(c) A pupil of William Byrd, the composer Thomas Morley compiled *The Triumphs of Oriana*, a collection of madrigals thought to have been written in honour of which English monarch?

8. **Your starter for 10:**
What is the vector or cross-product of i + j and i − j, where i and j are unit vectors in the x and y directions respectively?

Three bonus questions on volcanic islands:

(a) Which Pacific island, the largest of a chain and also known as 'Big Island', is formed by five volcanoes, one of which is often claimed to be the world's most active?

(b) The US territory of Guam is part of which volcanic island arc in the Western Pacific, named after an Austrian-born Spanish queen?

(c) Which chain of volcanic islands are the westernmost part of the USA by longitude, and are in the northern end of the Pacific 'Ring of Fire'?

9. Your starter for 10:

Killed in a duel in 1832, which mathematician was expelled from school for failing to support the Revolution and is famous for his research on the origins of modern algebra?

Three bonus questions on keyboard symbols:

(a) Which non-letter symbol on a computer keyboard is derived from a capital 'L', standing for *librum*, the basic Roman unit of weight which is in turn derived from the Latin word for scales or a balance?

(b) Which character was originally a ligature of 'e' and 't' used in printing, and has a name that comes from 'and per se, and'?

(c) What word, probably derived from a term meaning to cut, or draw lines, is used in the UK for the character that designates a number?

10. Your starter for 10:

Popularised by Ian Buruma and Avishai Margalit in a book of the same name, what term, from the Latin for 'setting sun', denotes stereotyped and sometimes dehumanising views of the so-called 'western world'?

Three bonus questions on definitions from Johnson's Dictionary:

(a) Which word, now often used in broadcasting and social contexts, did Johnson define as 'anything reticulated or decussated at equal distances, with interstices between the intersections'?

(b) What was defined in the first edition of the Dictionary as 'pay given to a state hireling for treason to his country', but later amended to 'the allowance made as an acknowledgement for any eminent and distinguished services'?

(c) What form of address did Johnson define as 'a term of reproach for a Frenchman'?

11. Your starter for 10:

DVDs with region code 6 are designed to be played in which country?

Three bonus questions on title characters in Shakespeare:

(a) The first names of the title characters of which play are Alice and Meg?

(b) Valentine and Proteus are the title characters of which Shakespeare play?

(c) Of which play by Shakespeare are the title characters described in the *Dramatis Personae* as a son of Priam and a daughter of Calchas?

12. Your starter for 10:

Which unusual pastime was founded in 1973 at the Cricketers Arms in Wisborough Green, West Sussex with the rules requiring all entries to be propelled by an engine and to be designed for domestic use? They are divided into four categories: with and without a bonnet, those with a towed-seat design, and run-behind models.

Three bonus questions on love at first sight:

(a) 'Here is a deity stronger than I, who, coming, shall rule over me.' Which poet wrote these words, having fallen in love at first sight in May 1274?

(b) Name the Elizabethan playwright and poet who wrote the words 'Where both deliberate, the love is slight: / Who ever loved that loved not at first sight?'

(c) Who fell in love at first sight with a chaplain in the opening line of a novel first published in 1961?

13. Your starter for 10:

Which poet wrote the following lines: 'When I consider how my light is spent / Ere half my days in this dark world and wide / And that one talent which is death to hide / Lodged with me useless, though my soul more bent / To serve therewith my maker, and present / My true account'?

Three bonus questions on alloys:

(a) What name is given to the alloys of iron with carbon and metals such as chromium and nickel?

(b) Brass is an alloy of copper and which other metal?

(c) In chemistry, an amalgam is an alloy of which metal with another, or others?

14. Your starter for 10:

One example being acetone, what is the term for an organic molecule consisting of a carbonyl radical bonded to two other carbon radicals, wherein the two available carbonyl carbon bonds are used to attach the carbon atoms of the other radicals?

Three bonus questions on film directors:

(a) Early in his career, the Spanish director Luis Buñuel collaborated with which artist on the films *Un Chien Andalou* and *L'Age d'Or*?

(b) The Foreign Language Film Award at the 2005 Oscars went to which Alejandro Amenábar film about the struggle of Ramon Sampedro, played by Javier Bardem, to end his life with dignity after some thirty years as a quadriplegic?

(c) In 2006, Spain's prestigious Asturias Prize for the Arts was awarded to which director, whose films include *All About My Mother*, *Talk to Her* and *Volver*?

15. Your starter for 10:

Which farm animal was once known in Ireland as 'the gentleman who pays the rent' and was valuable because, in the words of the old country saying, every part could be used 'except the eyes and the squeak'?

Three bonus questions on binomial classification:

In each case, give the common names of the following plants and animals, each of which is a homophone of the name of a letter of the alphabet:

(a) *Pisum sativum*.

(b) *Garrulus glandarius*.

(c) *Camellia sinensis*.

16. Your starter for 10:

Identify the author of these lines: 'In the bleak mid-winter / Frosty wind made moan / Earth stood hard as iron, / Water like a stone'.

Three bonus questions on an Italian city:

(a) What is the full name of the city near Parma from which the second half of the official name for Parmesan cheese, Parmigiano-Reggiano, is derived?

(b) After the curds of the milk have been removed to make Parmesan cheese, the remaining whey is used indirectly in the manufacture of which foodstuff?

(c) Which traditional British confectionery item is named

after Parma, although its connection with that city is remote?

17. Your starter for 10:
Born in 1867, Dr Maximilian Bircher-Benner is generally credited with devising what breakfast food, whose name is a diminutive form of a Swiss-German word meaning 'puree', 'mix' or 'mush'?

Three bonus questions on cartoon captions:
(a) A cartoon in which a prosecuting counsel produces a kangaroo and says to a witness 'perhaps this will refresh your memory' is the work of which American humorist, particularly associated with the *New Yorker* magazine?
(b) Born in 1872, which English illustrator and cartoonist became particularly known for his drawings of overly elaborate and unlikely machines, such as a chair designed to remove warts and a device for resuscitating stale scones?
(c) What three words typically begin the captions of a series of cartoons by H.M. Bateman which first appeared in 1912 and depict an extreme reaction to social gaffes?

18. Your starter for 10:
Named after one of the Titans of Greek mythology, what name is given to the first cervical vertebra which articulates with the skull?

Three questions on Richard Dawkins:
(a) Richard Dawkins's 1998 book *Unweaving the Rainbow* takes its title from which work by John Keats, in which the poet claims that Newton had destroyed the beauty of the rainbow by explaining the origin of its colours?

(b) Which work of 1986 by Dawkins takes its title from the argument proposed by William Paley in the eighteenth century, that the complexity of living organisms is evidence of a divine creator?

(c) 'Isn't it enough to see that a garden is beautiful without having to believe there are fairies at the bottom of it?' These words by which British comic novelist, who died in 2001, were quoted by Dawkins in *The God Delusion*?

19. Your starter for 10:
Which character from the First Book of Samuel gives his name to: Englishman Karl Bushby's twelve-year expedition to walk around the world; a large brightly coloured beetle; and a species of West African frog, thought to be the largest in the world?

Three bonus questions on vaccines:

(a) The 1950s saw the development of a vaccine called Quadrigen which combined the DPT vaccine against diphtheria, pertussis and tetanus with a vaccine against which disease?

(b) A vaccine against Hib, or Haemophilus Influenza Type B, was introduced in the UK and Ireland in 1992, since when the incidence of the bacterial form of which disease has been substantially reduced?

(c) The term vaccine itself derives from which animal, used by Edward Jenner in his early work on smallpox?

20. Your starter for 10:
What architectural feature may be described as an arch that has been rotated around its vertical axis? Its name derives from the Italian for 'cathedral' and ultimately from the Latin for 'house', and its varieties include umbrella, saucer and onion.

Three bonus questions on Classical music and literature:

(a) Dedicated to Rudolph of Austria, the 'Archduke' Trio in B-Flat Major is an 1811 work by which composer?

(b) Beethoven's 'Archduke' trio plays a prominent part in *Kafka on the Shore*, a 2002 work by which Japanese novelist, also noted for *Norwegian Wood*?

(c) A standard piano trio consists of a piano and which two stringed instruments?

21. Your starter for 10:

Which former Soviet republic in the Caucasus remained outside the Commonwealth of Independent States when it was formed in 1991, later joining in 1993?

Three bonus questions on an African country:

(a) Holden Roberto, Jonas Savimbi and Agostinho Neto were leaders of armed groups in the independence struggles and subsequent protracted civil war of which African country?

(b) Agostinho Neto, the first President of Angola, was the founder of which political party, formerly supported by the Soviet Union and, as of May 2010, still the ruling party of Angola?

(c) Angola shares borders with Republic of the Congo, Democratic Republic of the Congo and two other countries. For five points, name either one.

22. Your starter for 10:

Which labour-saving device is often credited to the American Thomas Sullivan in about 1904, its original form being a hand-sewn muslin bag that he used to send samples of his product to his customers. This model was adapted by other companies, including Lipton, who patented a novelty four-sided variety called the flo-thru in the 1950s?

Three bonus questions on an English county:

(a) 'From Clee to Heaven the beacon burns, / The shires have seen it plain' are the opening lines of which literary work, a series of sixty-three nostalgic verses first published in 1896?

(b) The Shropshire towns of Ludlow and Much Wenlock lend their names to epochs of which geological period, extending from the end of the Ordovician to the beginning of the Devonian?

(c) Dubbed 'a Heaven-born general' by Pitt the Elder, which Shropshire-born soldier, created Baron Plassey in 1762, served as both Shrewsbury's MP and its mayor?

23. Your starter for 10:

Which revolutionary party was founded in California in 1966 by Huey P. Newton and Bobby Seale, one of its original aims being to protect residents of black ghettoes from police brutality?

Three bonus questions on a saint:

(a) Which saint, born in Egypt around 251, is identified with the series of temptations he endured during his fifteen-year solitary retreat?

(b) The condition known as St Anthony's Fire is caused by which fungal disease of cereal crops, especially rye?

(c) Who, in 1873, composed *Variations on a Theme of Haydn*, which is now often called the *St Anthony Variations*?

24. Your starter for 10:

Which scientist is regarded as the father of immunology?

Three bonus questions on Welsh geography:

(a) Which river rises in the Brecon Beacons National Park, and is the longest river entirely in Wales?

(b) Which town on the River Usk north of Newport was

the site of the camp of the Roman Second Legion?

(c) Lying to the east of the River Usk, between Abergavenny and Hay-on-Wye, what name is given to the easternmost highlands of the Brecon Beacons National Park?

25. Your starter for 10:

The fifth symphony of which composer is commonly subtitled 'A Soviet artist's reply to just criticism'?

Three bonus questions on celebrations:

(a) Which word meaning a riotous celebration derives from the Latin for 'removal of meat'?

(b) In which city on the Adriatic Coast was tradition of carnival revived in the 1980s as a boost to tourism?

(c) What is the literal meaning of the term 'Mardi Gras', referring to the festivities in New Orleans and elsewhere?

26. Your starter for 10:

A hybrid unit of imperial and metric measures, one foot per nanosecond is approximately equal to the speed of what?

Three bonus questions on a word:

(a) Recorded in a slang dictionary of 1891, what word has become widely used to mean someone who gives financial backing to a play or film?

(b) In which hilltop cathedral was the Angel Choir added at its eastern end to contain the Shrine of St Hugh?

(c) Which eponymous heroine, created by Thomas Hardy, was abandoned on her wedding night by Angel Clare?

27. Your starter for 10:

Supposedly killed by the same shot by which his fellow plotter Thomas Percy perished, which conspirator died in a siege at Holbeche House in Staffordshire in November 1605?

Three bonus questions on Greek prefixes:
(a) What is the meaning of the prefix 'peri', as used in words such as 'perihelion' and 'peripatetic'?
(b) Which four-letter prefix denotes 'among', 'with', 'later' or 'after'?
(c) Which three-letter prefix denotes 'through', 'across' or 'during'?

28. Your starter for 10:
Known to the French as 'la drôle de guerre', what enduring two-word term did American journalists give to the period of comparative inactivity from the start of the Second World War until the invasion of Norway in April 1940?

Three bonus questions on films of novels by Henry James:
(a) Which English actress played the spinster Olive Chancellor in the 1984 Merchant Ivory film of *The Bostonians*?
(b) Later known for comedy roles, which actress took the title role in Peter Bogdanovich's 1974 film of *Daisy Miller*?
(c) Which English actress starred as Kate Croy in the film of *The Wings of a Dove*, released early in 1998?

29. Your starter for 10:
The River Ganges enters the sea in which large inlet of the Indian Ocean, bounded by the Andaman and Nicobar islands to the east?

Three bonus questions on Latin America:
In each case, name the country of Latin America whose first three letters correspond to the following definition.

For example, 'state of equality' would be 'Par-aguay'.

(a) A depression or pass between two mountains.
(b) The twenty-second letter of the Greek alphabet.
(c) A long-leaved lettuce named after an Aegean island.

30. Your starter for 10:
A drama by Euripides of the fifth century BC, reworked by Goethe and adapted as an opera by Gluck in the eighteenth century, concerns which of the daughters of Agamemnon, a priestess in the temple of Artemis at Tauris?

Three bonus questions on shoes and literature:

(a) Telling of a girl who is made to dance perpetually as a punishment for having worn her dancing shoes to church, eventually asking an executioner to cut her feet off, 'The Red Shoes' is a story for children by which author and poet?

(b) Set in Montmartre and concerning Vianne Rocher and her family, *The Lollipop Shoes*, published in 2007, is the sequel to which novel by Joanne Harris?

(c) *Blue Shoes and Happiness* is the seventh in a series of books by which Zimbabwean-born Scottish author?

> **'Well, you rather nodded off in the middle of that, didn't you? You were absolutely lamentable on Beethoven, too.'**

THE RULES

You all know the rules by now, so
here's your first starter for 10.

Match Fourteen

1. **Your starter for 10:**

Answer as a percentage or as a fraction. In pre-decimal currency, what proportion of a pound was fifteen shillings?

Three bonus questions on recent additions to the Oxford Dictionary of Quotations:

(a) The principal author of the Declaration of Independence, which early President of the United States has a new entry in the Dictionary with his evergreen observation that 'Banking establishments are more dangerous than standing armies'?

(b) Which English theoretical physicist is quoted as saying 'Computer viruses should count as life. Maybe it says something about human nature, that the only form of life we have created so far is purely destructive'?

(c) Which socialite and heiress, born in 1981, entered the dictionary with the words: 'Dress cute wherever you go. Life is too short to blend in'?

2. **Your starter for 10:**

A theory propounded by John Locke in his 1690 work *An Essay Concerning Human Understanding*, what two-word Latin expression describes the concept of the human mind being a blank slate at birth?

Three bonus questions on milk:

(a) Milk is the primary natural source of which sugar, the only common sugar of animal origin?

(b) What is the name of the pituitary hormone which initiates human milk production?

(c) The distinctive golden-yellow colour of Guernsey milk is produced by the presence of which substance?

3. **Your starter for 10:**

Words meaning the thick, triangular muscle that covers the shoulder joint, a tree nymph, and a person who is habitually inebriated all begin and end with which letter of the alphabet?

Three bonus questions on architects:

(a) Regarded by some as a postmodernist although he rejected the label, which British architect's works include the Clore Gallery at Tate Britain and the Staatsgalerie in Stuttgart?

(b) Which Luxembourg-born architect worked for James Stirling from 1969 to 1972, and in the late 1980s developed the overall plan for the Duchy of Cornwall's development at Poundbury in Dorset?

(c) In 2004, which Iraq-born British architect became the first woman to win the prestigious Pritzker Prize for architecture? Her works include the Rosenthal Centre for Contemporary Art in Cincinnati, and the Bergisel ski-jump in Austria?

4. **Your starter for 10:**

In which of Shakespeare's plays does a period of sixteen years elapse between Act III and Act IV, during which time the abandoned baby daughter of the King of Sicilia grows up and falls in love with the Prince of Bohemia?

Three bonus questions on physics:

(a) Which law forbids the existence of a process whose sole result is the transfer of heat from a colder to a hotter body?

(b) What name is given to the hypothetical maximally efficient engine operating between two temperatures?

(c) Which temperature scale is based upon the efficiency of the Carnot cycle, and is independent of the physical properties of any specific material?

5. **Your starter for 10:**

First isolated from plants of the *Solanaceae* family at the University of Heidelberg in 1828, which alkaloid has the chemical formula $C_{10}H_{14}N_2$?

Three bonus questions on electronics:

(a) Which characteristic of an amplifier is defined as the ratio of the increased signal strength to the original strength?

(b) What term describes the amplitude of a radio-frequency carrier wave being varied in accordance with the amplitude of the input signal?

(c) Astable, monostable and bistable are types of which form of electronic oscillator, comprising two active devices coupled so that the input of each is derived from the output of the other?

6. **Your starter for 10:**

South Carolina is one of only two US states whose name contains six vowels. Name the other.

Three bonus questions on biography:

(a) 'A chance remark or a jest may reveal far more of a man's character than the mere feat of winning battles in which thousands fall.' These are the words of which ancient Greek biographer, noted for the *Moralia* and the *Parallel Lives*?

(b) According to Plutarch, which Roman leader, 'said that he had no fear of those fat and long-haired fellows, but rather of those pale and thin ones'?

(c) Which orator and statesman was, according to Plutarch, one of the first to discern the destructive force of Caesar's ambition, fearing it 'as one might fear the smiling surface of the sea'.

7. Your starter for 10:

In Christian theology, 'Thomism' is the name given to the doctrines of which thirteenth-century philosopher and theologian, also known as Doctor Angelicus? His best-known works are the *Summa contra Gentiles* and the incomplete *Summa Theologiae*.

Three bonus questions on the international radio-telephony spelling alphabet, or NATO alphabet, which begins 'Alpha – Bravo – Charlie':

(a) Which word of the international spelling alphabet follows 'Grand Babylon' and 'White' in the titles of novels by Arnold Bennett and D.M. Thomas respectively?

(b) Which word of the NATO alphabet is a title character of a 1988 Booker Prize-winning novel by Peter Carey?

(c) Finally, which word of the NATO alphabet appears in the title of a 1924 novel by E.M. Forster?

8. Your starter for 10:

A mathematical group is a finite or infinite set of elements together with a binary operation, and must satisfy the fundamental properties of closure, associativity, existence of an identity element, and which other property?

Three bonus questions on titles in Shakespeare:

(a) What title, from an Old English term meaning 'one who serves', was used in Anglo-Saxon England for a member of the noble class and is bestowed on Macbeth by King Duncan?

(b) The title conferred upon the warrior Caius Marcius in recognition of his defeat of a Volscian city gives which of Shakespeare's history plays its title?

(c) In *Twelfth Night*, whose desire to become a count is thwarted by a forged letter written by Maria, waiting woman to the Countess Olivia?

9. Your starter for 10:

Which word of four letters denotes: the decimal number 64,206 in hexadecimal; the visible part of a celestial body; each surface of a solid, and can be linked to the word 'off' to indicate the start of a game of ice hockey or lacrosse?

Three bonus questions on royal emblems:

(a) From his title as Earl of March, a white lion was a badge of which English king, born in 1442?

(b) Which of Edward IV's sons, who also became king, used the emblem of a white boar?

(c) A white hart was the personal emblem of which English king, who is depicted wearing it on the Wilton Diptych?

10. Your starter for 10:

In 1854, who started compiling the thirty-two volumes of *Deutsches Wörterbuch*, the German dictionary, but only managed to complete entries from 'a' to 'forsche' in their lifetime?

Three bonus questions on historical groups of three:

(a) The 'States-General', the assembly summoned by the

kings of France since the fourteenth century, usually to approve plans for higher taxes, was made up of deputies from the so-called 'Three Estates'. What were they?

(b) The 'Three Fs' – fair rent, free sale and fixity of tenure – were demands made in 1879 by the Land League, a political organisation in which territory then under British rule?

(c) Which battle of 1805 saw Napoleon decisively defeat the armies of the Tsar of Russia and Emperor Franz I of Austria, and was called the Battle of the Three Emperors?

11. Your starter for 10:

Mass, time and speed are examples of what type of quantity that is represented by magnitude only and, unlike a vector quantity, has no direction?

Three bonus questions on words that contain the first five letters of the alphabet only once:

(a) Which six-letter word contains the letters 'a', 'b', 'c', 'd' and 'e', and is the name given to a textile fabric woven with a pattern of raised figures?

(b) Which nine-letter word meaning a fugitive, especially from justice, contains within it the first five letters of the alphabet in alphabetical order?

(c) The ten-letter name of which piece of cricket equipment found off the field of play contains the first five letters of the alphabet in the order 'c, e, b, a, d'?

12. Your starter for 10:

From the Latin for 'ship', a name probably suggested by the keel shape of its vaulting, what term describes the main part of a church, flanked by the aisles and extending from the entrance to the chancel?

Three bonus questions on fungal diseases of plants:

(a) What is the common name for the group of diseases caused by members of the order *Ustilaginales*, characterised by black, soot-like spores on the leaves and stems of infected plants? They particularly affect grasses and cereals.

(b) What is the common name for the diseases caused by fungi of the family *Erysiphaceae*, appearing as white powdery patches on leaves, stems and other aerial parts of the infected plant?

(c) Wilts are diseases which invade and block the xylem and phloem of plants, such as that caused by the fungus *Ophiostoma novo-ulmi*, spread by a bark beetle to trees of the genus *Ulmus*, the disease having what common name?

13. Your starter for 10:

What igneous rock is the volcanic equivalent of granite?

Three bonus questions on English folklore:

(a) Commemorated in a poem by Sir Henry Newbolt and housed in Buckland Abbey, of what instrument is it said that it will beat at a time of war or national crisis to summon its owner to return to defend the country?

(b) Until the time when they come to the aid of Britain in crisis, King Arthur and his knights are, according to a local legend, sleeping inside a sandstone escarpment above the village of Alderley Edge in which English county?

(c) The legend of the slumbering King Arthur has been classified as a reversioning of the story of the Seven Sleepers of which ancient city in what is now Turkey?

14. Your starter for 10:

Name either of the two sisters who wrote the 1960s

novels *The Game* and *A Summer Birdcage*?

Three bonus questions on 21 September:

(a) As well as being the date on which, in 1962, *University Challenge* was first broadcast, it also saw the birth in 1934 of which Canadian poet, singer and songwriter, who performed on the Pyramid Stage at Glastonbury in 2008 at the age of 73?

(b) *Africa Must Unite* is among the works of which statesman, the first Prime Minister of Ghana, born on 21 September 1909?

(c) *Love and Mr Lewisham*, *When the Sleeper Awakes* and *The Shape of Things to Come* are works by which prolific writer and thinker, born on 21 September 1866?

15. **Your starter for 10:**

From what common English tree are cricket stumps traditionally made?

Three bonus questions on titles:

(a) *The Outsider* was the title of three major books of the 1940s and 1950s: a study of alienation by Colin Wilson, a novel by Richard Wright, and a translation of a 1953 work by which French novelist?

(b) Except for the definite article, which title of an 1897 fantasy by H.G. Wells was also used by the American Ralph Ellison for a novel about racism in the Deep South set in the 1930s?

(c) The title of which book by Iris Murdoch consists of the title of a play by Edward Bond followed by the identical title of a novel by John Banville?

16. **Your starter for 10:**

Which of the Great Lakes shares its name with Canada's most populous province?

Three bonus questions on the Alps:

(a) In which country are the Bernese Alps, whose peaks include the Jungfrau and the Mönch?

(b) Zugspitze is the highest mountain in Germany and lies in which Germany state that gives it and surrounding peaks their collective name?

(c) Which part of the Italian Alps, known for its saw-edged ridges and rocky pinnacles, includes the Marmolada, the southern face of which consists of a precipice 600 metres (2,000 feet) high?

17. Your starter for 10:

On the Beaufort wind scale, what number is allocated to a wind speed of between 55 and 63 kilometres per hour, regarded as storm force?

Three bonus questions on the European Union:

(a) The European Economic Community, formed in 1957, originally comprised six member states: the three Benelux countries, France and which two others?

(b) Along with the United Kingdom, two countries joined the EEC in 1973. For five points, name both.

(c) On 1 January 2007 which two Eastern European countries joined the EU?

18. Your starter for 10:

Which theatre critic, who took up the job after a devastating review of his own acting in a production of *Hamlet*, became literary manager of the National Theatre under Laurence Olivier, but is most often remembered for the erotic revue *Oh! Calcutta!*, which he devised and produced in 1969, and for being the first person to say a certain taboo word on British television?

Three bonus questions on banks:

(a) Who announced his resignation as President of the

World Bank in May 2007 following controversy over the lavish pay rise he had negotiated for his partner?

(b) Winner of the Nobel Peace Prize in 2006, the Grameen Bank was founded by Muhammad Yunus in 1976 to offer small, collateral-free loans to the rural poor in which country?

(c) In January 2008, preliminary charges were filed against Jérôme Kerviel, a 'rogue trader' blamed for huge losses at which French bank?

19. Your starter for 10:

In the Gregorian calendar, what is the hundredth day of a common, or non-leap, year?

Three bonus questions on the Second World War:

In each case, give the city that gives its name to the following conference:

(a) A meeting of Churchill and Roosevelt in January 1943 which endorsed the policy of unconditional surrender of the Axis powers?

(b) A meeting of Churchill, Roosevelt and Stalin in late 1943 that laid plans for the opening of a second front in coordination with Soviet offensives against the Nazis?

(c) A meeting of Churchill, Roosevelt and Stalin in February 1945 that acquiesced in post-war Soviet influence over much of Eastern Europe?

20. Your starter for 10:

The White Queen is a soubriquet that became attached to which monarch after she dressed in that colour to mourn the death of her French husband, Francis II?

Three bonus questions on wine-growing regions:

(a) Which wine-growing region shares its name with a Spanish autonomous region that borders Navarra, the

Basque country and Castile-Leon?

(b) Which wine-growing region shares its name with an Italian region that borders Liguria, Umbria and Lazio?

(c) Which wine-growing region shares its name with a French administrative region that borders Île-de-France, Champagne-Ardennes and Franche-Comté?

21. Your starter for 10:

Quote: 'She may still exist in undiminished vigour when some traveller from New Zealand shall, in the midst of a vast solitude, take his stand on a broken arch of London Bridge to sketch the ruins of St Paul's.' To what or whom is T.B. Macaulay referring in these words from a work of 1840?

Three bonus questions on honorary 'fathers':

(a) Robert Boyle, the youngest son of the seventeenth-century Earl of Cork, is known as the 'father' of which subject?

(b) Which sixteenth-century French writer was called the 'father of ridicule'?

(c) The Venerable Bede, often called the 'father of English history', spent almost all his life in which northern monastery?

22. Your starter for 10:

Which Australian physicist, who died in 2006, introduced the scatter plot in the 1950s often used in particle physics to represent the relative frequency of the various kinematically distinct manners in which the products of certain three-body decays may move apart?

Three bonus questions on a nation:

(a) According to historian Allan Bullock, who were 'the people Hitler never understood, and whose actions continued to exasperate him to the end of his life'?

(b) In an article in *The Times* in 1983, what did Margaret Thatcher say 'is totally alien to the British character'?

(c) In 1965, which field marshal said of toleration of homosexuality: 'We are not French, and we are not other nationals, we are British – thank God'?

23. Your starter for 10:

Aalborg, Aarhus and Odense are major cities of which EU member state?

Three bonus questions linked by a word:

(a) In Dirac notation, the second half of the symbol for an amplitude in quantum mechanics is known as a 'ket'; as what is the first part known?

(b) The Roman arena on the Piazza Bra is the venue for an opera festival every summer in which Italian city?

(c) Which anti-war novel of 1962 contains the line, 'an unhooked brassiere was as close as you ever hoped to get to paradise'?

24. Your starter for 10:

With a height of 25 kilometres, and a volume perhaps 100 times greater than that of its nearest rival on Earth, what is the solar system's tallest known volcano, located in the Tharsis region of Mars?

Three bonus questions on Indonesia:

(a) On which island is the Indonesian capital Jakarta?

(b) The Indonesian province of Irian Jaya principally comprises the western half of which island?

(c) Indonesian Kalimantan, which is divided into four provinces, covers the southern three-quarters of which island?

25. Your starter for 10:

The Volkskammer was from 1949 to 1990 the national

parliament of which European state?

Three bonus questions on Mystery Plays:
(a) In the York Cycle of Mystery Plays, which figure of the Old Testament traditionally had his story performed by the shipwrights?
(b) Which British composer used part of the text of one of the Chester Cycle of plays for his one-act piece *Noyes Fludde*?
(c) The Towneley Plays, named after the owners of the manuscript, were performed in which West Yorkshire city?

26. Your starter for 10:
In physics, what kind of activity is displayed by a molecule which is able to rotate the plane of polarisation of plane-polarised light?

Three bonus questions on a song:
(a) Used for the seventy-fifth anniversary of the BBC, the song 'Perfect Day' was written by which American performer?
(b) 'Perfect Day' featured on the soundtrack of which 1996 film, in a sequence depicting a drug overdose?
(c) Which book of the Bible contains the lines: 'The path of the just is as the shining light, that shineth more and more unto the perfect day'?

27. Your starter for 10:
Which decade saw the death of Leonardo da Vinci; the completion of Machiavelli's *The Prince*; the publication at Basel of Erasmus's Latin translation of the New Testament, and the posting of Martin Luther's 95 Theses on the church door at Wittenberg?

Three bonus questions on a pigment:

(a) Which pigment occurs in several different forms, 'A' and 'B' being the major types found in higher plants and green algae?

(b) Chlorophyll has a very similar molecular structure to which pigment, found in the blood cells of mammals and other vertebrates?

(c) An atom of which metal is found at the centre of the chlorophyll molecule and plays a part similar to that of iron in haemoglobin?

28. Your starter for 10:

What two-word term describes the policy adopted in early 2009 by the Bank of England in which money was created in order to buy up financial assets in an attempt to boost the economy?

Three bonus questions on Scottish monarchs:

(a) Reigning from 843 to 858, which king was the founder of the dynasty which ruled Scotland for much of the medieval period?

(b) Which queen was the last monarch of Scotland and concurrently the last monarch of England, and the first monarch of Great Britain?

(c) Which king of England, Scotland and Ireland was the last to be crowned in person in Scotland, at Scone in January 1651?

29. Your starter for 10:

Which Norwegian-American sociologist compared the conspicuous consumption of society's financially successful members with a so-called 'barbarian culture' in his 1899 work *The Theory of the Leisure Class*?

Three bonus questions linked by a foodstuff:

(a) Which cooking ingredient is called *pol kiri* in Sri

Lanka, *santan* in Malaysia and Indonesia, and *gati* or *kati* in Thailand?

(b) What two-word term describes the substance secreted by pigeons, doves, flamingos and penguins to feed their young?

(c) Milk of magnesia consists of a suspension of which compound in water?

30. Your starter for 10:

Situated at a height of more than 2,000 metres, with UNESCO 'world heritage site' status for its historic centre, Arequipa was the birthplace in 1936 of the author Mario Vargas Llosa and is the second-largest city of which country?

Three bonus questions on Swedish fiction:

(a) What is the English title of John Ajvide Lindquist's novel of 2004 which he adapted for the cinema in 2008, set in a suburb of Stockholm in which the bullied 12-year-old Oskar befriends the vampire child Eli?

(b) The novel *Roseanna* was the first in a series of ten books written by Maj Sjöwall and Per Wahlöö between 1965 and 1975 featuring which Stockholm-based detective inspector?

(c) Which diabetic police detective from Ystad was introduced in the Henning Mankell novel *Faceless Killers* in 1991, and was played on television by Kenneth Branagh in 2008 and 2010?

> **'Sorry... there's no way of sugaring the pill. You were up against very strong opposition, and you never found your stride.'**

THE RULES

Let's not waste time reciting the rules.

Match Fifteen

1.   Your starter for 10:
Which Czech-American physicist gives his name to the non-SI unit used in radio-astronomy to measure the flux density of radio signals from space? It is equal to a flux of 10^{-26} watts per square metre of receiving area per hertz of frequency band.

Three bonus questions on questions:
(a) Which Greek philosopher gives his name to a method of questioning which may be used to lead a student towards the truth without direct instruction?
(b) The question 'Who am I?' was posed by which Dadaist and surrealist in the first sentence of his 1928 novel *Nadja*?
(c) Which two words complete the title of the second collection of readers' answers to the questions in the 'Last Word' column of the *New Scientist*: 'Why don't penguins'...'?

2.   Your starter for 10:
Of which novel of 1929 is the protagonist a schoolboy with the surname Tischbein, robbed of his money whilst on a train from Neustadt to Berlin, and aided in its recovery by a group of local children?

Three bonus questions on 'men who...':
(a) Often depicting an overreaction to social gaffes, the

term 'the man who...' frequently appeared in the titles of cartoons by which British artist and humorist?

(b) The 1953 book *The Man Who Never Was* tells the story of Operation Mincemeat, in which bogus documents were planted on a dead body whose discovery deflected Axis attention away from which island as the target of an Allied invasion?

(c) *The Man Who Would Be King*, about the attempt by two adventurers to make themselves kings among mountain villagers of Afghanistan, is a story of 1888 by which writer?

3. **Your starter for 10:**
One joule, or the work done by a force of one newton acting over a distance of one metre, is equal to ten million of what CGS unit, defined as the work done by a force of one dyne acting through a distance of one centimetre?

Three bonus questions on composers:

(a) Born in 1858, which composer's works are performed at an annual summer opera festival in Torre del Lago, on the Tuscan Riviera?

(b) Performances of which Baroque composer's music take place regularly at the Church of La Pietà in Venice, where he taught music to orphans?

(c) The grounds of which composer's home at Troldhaugen, outside Bergen in Norway, include a small concert hall and the secluded cabin where he worked?

4. **Your starter for 10:**
What is the product of the complex numbers 4 plus 2i and 4 minus 2i, where i is the square root of minus one?

Three bonus questions on a group of elements:

(a) What name, derived from the Greek for 'to escape notice', is given to the rare earth elements that have the atomic numbers 57 to 71, and include erbium and samarium?

(b) Which lanthanide was the last to be discovered? It was produced artificially in a nuclear reactor and named after one of the Titans of Greek mythology because it symbolised the result of man's harnessing of the energy of nuclear fission?

(c) Which lanthanide has the atomic number 71 and is the densest and hardest in the group? Its name derives from a Roman name for Paris, although it was called *cassiopeium* in Germany until the 1950s.

5. Your starter for 10:

What was the first year in the Common Era to contain all possible letters when represented in Roman numerals?

Three bonus questions on an Italian city:

(a) Beginning with the Archbishop Ottone in 1277 and ending with the Duke Filippo Maria in 1447, the Visconti family were the rulers of which Italian city for 170 years?

(b) Based in Milan, which major Italian newspaper has a name that translates into English as 'Evening Courier'?

(c) Which sweet bread containing sultanas and candied peel originates in Milan, where it is traditionally associated with Christmas, and has become one of the symbols of the city?

6. Your starter for 10:

Azania was a word used by liberation movements and, formerly, by the People's Republic of China, to refer to which African country?

Three bonus questions on centenaries:

(a) The American Declaration of Independence took place on which centenary of the fall of the western Roman Empire?

(b) Which battle was the last on English soil and took place 200 years after the Battle of Bosworth, and 300 years before the Brixton riots?

(c) The enactment of the Bill of Rights in Britain, the adoption of the Declaration of the Rights of Man in France, the birth of Adolf Hitler and the fall of the Berlin Wall all took place in years ending with which two digits?

7. **Your starter for 10:**

Noted for his eloquence at the Council of Clermont, which Pope launched the First Crusade in 1095?

Three bonus questions on the Castel Sant'Angelo:

(a) The building now known as the Castel Sant'Angelo on the banks of the Tiber was built between AD 135 and 139 by which Roman emperor as a mausoleum for himself and his family?

(b) Regarded as the founder of medieval papacy, which pope claimed in 590 to have seen a vision of St Michael above the building, signifying that the city's plague was at an end?

(c) Which sculptor and goldsmith was present at the storming of the Castel Sant'Angelo in 1527, claiming in his somewhat fanciful autobiography that he shot one Spanish officer so accurately that his sword was struck by the bullet and cut him clean in two?

8. **Your starter for 10:**

Ostrava, an industrial city in the Moravian lowlands

of the Czech Republic, is situated in which coal-mining region?

Three bonus questions on shades of brown:
(a) If 'écru' is the colour of unbleached linen or raw silk, what shade of brown is defined as 'similar to the colour of undyed and unbleached wool'?
(b) The name of which brownish fabric comes ultimately from the Persian word for 'dust'?
(c) Which artist's pigment derives its red- or yellowish-brown colour from the presence of ferric oxides, and is named after a city and province in Tuscany?

9. **Your starter for 10:**
Of which fictional character are Gilles Triquet of Cogirep and Michael Scott of Dunder Mifflin, the French and American equivalents respectively?

Three bonus questions on Scottish islands:
(a) The Cuillin Hills and the Old Man of Storr can be found on which island?
(b) Located in the Orkney Islands, which sea stack is, at 137 metres (449 feet) high, the tallest of such features in Britain?
(c) Fingal's Cave on the uninhabited island of Staffa is named after which hero of Irish legend?

10. **Your starter for 10:**
In the title of *The Rubáiyát of Omar Khayyám*, the poem by Edward Fitzgerald, to what structure does the Rubáiyát refer?

Three bonus questions on English words of German origin:
In each case, give the word from the English sense given, for example 'time spirit' would be 'Zeitgeist':
(a) 'Education novel'.

(b) 'Bell play'.

(c) 'Harm joy'.

11. Your starter for 10:

The Greek expression *pathemata mathemata* gives what meaning to the tribulations of life?

Three bonus questions on exiled rulers:

(a) Exiled to Ratnagiri in Western India after his deposition by a British force in 1885, King Theebaw was the last king of which country?

(b) Bahadur Shah II, exiled to Rangoon in the late 1850s, was the last ruler of which dynasty?

(c) Which head of state made his home in Dharamshala in Northern India after fleeing his country in 1959?

12. Your starter for 10:

What is the English name for the body of water known in German as *ostsee*?

Three bonus questions on Greek mythology:

(a) Which of the Titans was associated with the sun and was the subject of an uncompleted poem by John Keats?

(b) Which of the second generation of Titans was the daughter of Hyperion and Theia, and associated with the moon?

(c) Which beautiful youth was the lover of Selene and was also the subject of a poem by Keats, although in that version Selene was named Cynthia?

13. Your starter for 10:

What phase is the moon entering when it is described as a waning crescent?

Three bonus questions on grasses:

(a) Construction began in 2005 on Britain's first totally

Miscanthus-fuelled power plant at Eccleshall in Staffordshire, *Miscanthus* being a non-native giant grass growing up to four metres high and commonly known by what two-word name?

(b) Grain, sweet, grassy and broomcorn are types of which tropical food crop? Their English name appears in the title of a 1987 film by the Chinese director Zhang Yimou.

(c) Which hardy perennial grass grows in cool regions, can withstand frequent grazing and trampling, and is particularly associated with the state of Kentucky?

14. Your starter for 10:

Which Norwegian county has given its name to a type of swing turn in skiing, developed by Sondre Nordheim? The county's name also appears in the title of a 1965 film about the raid on a heavy water plant in Nazi-occupied Norway?

Three bonus questions on fictional artists:

For each of the following, give the name of the author who created the fictional artist:

(a) Nat Tate, in a work of 1998.

(b) Lily Briscoe, in a novel of 1927.

(c) Basil Hallward, in a novel of 1890.

15. Your starter for 10:

In which EU member state are the provinces of Carinthia, Styria, Burgenland and Vorarlberg?

Three bonus questions on a film director:

(a) *The Interpreter, The Firm, Random Hearts* and *Tootsie* are among the films of which American director, who died in May 2008?

(b) Based on a 1935 novel of the same name, which Sydney Pollack film of 1969 stars Jane Fonda and

Michael Sarrazin attempting to win a Depression-era marathon dance?

(c) Mozart's Clarinet Concerto in A Major features prominently in which Sydney Pollack film of 1985, starring Meryl Streep and Robert Redford?

16. **Your starter for 10:**

According to an 1836 poem by Ralph Waldo Emerson, which war began with 'the shot heard round the world'?

Three bonus questions on queens of England:

In each case, name the king of England to whom the following were married:

(a) Eleanor of Castile.

(b) Eleanor of Provence.

(c) Eleanor of Aquitaine.

17. **Your starter for 10:**

The Apostolic Church, the Assemblies of God and the Elim Foursquare Gospel Alliance are all members of which church movement, inspired by the descent of the Holy Spirit upon the Apostles and characterised by baptism in the spirit, speaking in tongues and prophecy?

Three bonus questions on the periodic table:

(a) Which element is situated at the centre of the square of which the corners are boron, nitrogen, arsenic and gallium?

(b) If the top of the periodic table is north and each cell of the table is an exact square, the line from titanium to tungsten via niobium runs in which compass direction?

(c) If the periodic table were a giant chessboard, going from rubidium to magnesium or from nickel to gold would be a move for which piece?

18. Your starter for 10:

What, in signal processing, does the abbreviation QAM stand for?

> **Three bonus questions on religion:**
> (a) One of the five pillars of Islam, what is *Sawm*, practised by Muslims from sunrise to sunset during Ramadan?
> (b) In Sikhism, what is the symbol *Kesh*, which results in the wearing of a turban by Sikh males?
> (c) One of the Four Noble Truths of Buddhism, what is the name of the final liberation from desire and ignorance?

19. Your starter for 10:

'Paraffins' is another name for which group of hydrocarbons, having the general formula CnH_2n+2?

> **Three bonus questions on geographical features:**
> How are the following better known in English?
> (a) Pas de Calais.
> (b) Îles Normandes.
> (c) Golfe de Gascogne.

20. Your starter for 10:

Located 6,500 light years away in the constellation of Taurus, what nebula is the remnant of a supernova seen on Earth in the year 1054?

> **Three bonus questions on politics:**
> (a) Which political party was founded in 1902 by Arthur Griffith, with a policy of passive resistance, such as non-payment of taxes?
> (b) Which political party was formed in 1925, although it was not until 1966 that it won its first seat in the Commons?
> (c) Fielding its first candidates in the 1970 general election,

the party Mebyon Kernow seeks independence for which part of the UK?

21. **Your starter for 10:**
The atlas and the coccyx are found in which part of the human body?

> **Three bonus questions on fictional histories:**
> Who wrote the following novels:
> (a) *The History of Tom Jones, a Foundling.*
> (b) *The History of Henry Esmond, Esq.*
> (c) *The History of Mr Polly.*

22. **Your starter for 10:**
Originally referring to a knight's shield bearer and, in the later Middle Ages, a holder of a knight's estate who had not taken up his knighthood, what courtesy title is sometimes extended in Britain to professional men and appended to surnames in abbreviated form in place of the title 'Dr' or 'Mr'?

> **Three bonus questions on reluctant heroes of popular music:**
> (a) The hero of which song is said to be a music teacher who liked to stay out drinking? The song's popularity made his wife, Mrs Sarah Bailey Williams, divorce him.
> (b) James Taylor, Mick Jagger and Warren Beatty have all been suggested as the subject of which song by Carly Simon?
> (c) The Kim Carnes song 'Bette Davies Eyes' was reworked in the mid 1980s as 'Dickie Davies Eyes', by which band?

23. **Your starter for 10:**
Quote: 'That is the most beautiful overture in the whole world... but I had almost forgotten *The Magic Flute*.'

These words of Franz Schubert describe the overture to which opera, first performed on 1 May 1786?

Three bonus questions on the European Union:
In each case, name the EU member state whose first three letters correspond to the following definition. For example, 'flat appendage of a fish' would be 'Fin-land'. Got it?

(a) A unit of measurement of the intensity of sound.

(b) A title given to an Italian monk.

(c) The SI derived unit of illuminance.

24. Your starter for 10:
In 1790, Josiah Wedgewood displayed his copies of which Roman artefact of the first century AD, made of violet-blue glass decorated with a single continuous white glass cameo? Now known by the name of the family who purchased it in 1778, it is on display in the British Museum.

Three bonus questions on a word:

(a) In Norse mythology, Yggdrasil, the tree of the world whose branches extend to the heavens, is what common species of tree?

(b) The Anglo-Saxon letter known as 'ash' is a ligature of which two vowels?

(c) 'Ash on an old man's sleeve / Is all the ash the burnt roses leave.' These lines appear in a poem of 1942 by which poet and critic?

25. Your starter for 10:
Meaning 'inclusive of all elements', what polysyllabic adjective often precedes the words 'understanding', 'insurance' and 'education'?

Three bonus questions on Paris:
In each case, identify the *place* or public square from the

description:

(a) Once named after Louis XV, what is the name of the largest *place* in Paris? It has also been known as Place de la Revolution, and saw the execution of Marie Antoinette in 1793.

(b) Which *place* in the northern part of the city centre is the location of the Moulin Rouge cabaret?

(c) Which *place* is the site of the Arc de Triomphe and was known as the Place de l'Etoile from 1753 to 1970 in reference to the twelve avenues which radiate out from it?

26. Your starter for 10:

John Joseph Merlin, a Belgian maker of musical instruments, injured himself crashing into a mirror at a London soirée in 1760 when, having not yet learned how to stop or steer effectively, he offered the first public demonstration of what device?

Three bonus questions on mathematical problems solved in the last forty years:

In each case, give the name of the theorem that has the following statement:

(a) Every planar graph has chromatic number at most four.

(b) Every compact simply connected smooth n-dimensional manifold is homeomorphic to the n-sphere.

(c) For any integer n greater than 2, the equation $x^n + y^n = z^n$ is not solvable in integers.

27. Your starter for 10:

Dukkha is a term used in which religion to refer generally to suffering, particularly in the teaching known as the Four Noble Truths?

Three bonus questions on fictional Joes:

(a) Joe Christmas is the victim of violent racial prejudice in

the 1932 novel *Light in August* by which writer, who set it, as well as many other works, in the imaginary Mississippi county of Yoknapatawpha?
  (b) Joe Willet the publican's son is a one-armed soldier and suitor of Dolly Varden in which novel by Charles Dickens, set in the late eighteenth century?
  (c) Joe Kavalier, a Czech-born comic-book illustrator, and his Brooklyn-born cousin Sammy Klayman feature in a Pulitzer Prize-winning novel of 2000 by which American author?

28. **Your starter for 10:**
What surname links: a clergyman depicted skating on Duddingston loch, a Scottish chemist noted for his work on electrolysis, an art gallery in Liverpool, and the author of *The Color Purple*?

Three bonus questions on words that contain all five vowels once and once only, for example 'discourage':
In each case, give the word from the definition:
  (a) An adjective meaning 'waggish' or 'characterised by flippant or inopportune humour'.
  (b) An adjective meaning 'dependent on chance', 'insecure' or 'perilous'.
  (c) A noun meaning 'the imparting of intellectual, moral and social instruction, especially as a formal and prolonged process'?

29. **Your starter for 10:**
Built for King Philip II, which renaissance palace-monastery north-west of Madrid houses the tombs of many Spanish monarchs? Its name is derived from the scoria, or slag heaps, of the nearby quarries.

Three bonus questions on international agreements:
  (a) Which Nordic capital gives its name to a 1975

conference on security and cooperation in Europe; its objective was advancing the process of détente?

(b) Which Nordic capital gives its name to a Reagan-Gorbachev arms-control summit of 1986? Although inconclusive, the talks led to a series of advances in the years that followed.

(c) Which Nordic capital gives its name to an Israeli-PLO accord of 1993 which gave Palestinians limited self-rule in the Gaza Strip and parts of the West Bank?

30. Your starter for 10:
There are twelve edges or one-dimensional cubes on a three-dimensional cube. How many one-dimensional cubes are there on a four dimensional cube?

Three bonus questions on geology:
(a) Oolite, travertine and coquina are all types of which sedimentary rock?

(b) Which limestone region in Slovenia gives its name to a topography characterised by easily soluble rock, distinguished by numerous fissures, sink-holes, and caverns?

(c) Which mountains of southern Austria and northern Italy are named after the type of limestone, a carbonate of lime and magnesia, of which they are chiefly composed?

'Well, I'm afraid we're going to have to say goodbye to you... There was a lot of rather silent conferring on a number of questions, I thought, but you were coming back strongly in the end. Who knows what might have happened if we'd gone on for another half an hour.'

THE RULES

Too tedious to recite the rules, here's
your first starter for 10.

Match Sixteen

1. Your starter for 10:
What idea is expressed by the word 'deontic', used by linguists in the analysis of modal verbs and by philosophers when discussing ethics or logic?

Three bonus questions on the Greek prefix 'para-':
(a) What term denotes that part of the autonomic nervous system that is in control during periods of relaxation, as distinct from 'fight or flight' situations?
(b) What word, from the Greek meaning 'going aside', is the term used in classical Greek comedy for a speech in which the chorus comes forward and addresses the audience?
(c) What is the British name for the common analgesic whose molecule is a di-substituted benzene ring with hydroxyl and acetamide groups opposite each other?

2. Your starter for 10:
A schoolboy play on words between Latin and English, what jocular translation is usually given to the phrase *semper ubi sub ubi*?

Three bonus questions on the opening lines of novels:
(a) Which novel, first published in serial form from 1914 to 1915, begins 'Once upon a time and a very good time it was...'?
(b) 'It was a dark and stormy night' are the first words of

the 1830 novel *Paul Clifford* by which writer, whose other works include *Eugene Aram* and *The Last Days of Pompeii*?

(c) The novels *Midnight's Children*, *The Thirty-Nine Steps*, *Robinson Crusoe* and *Tristram Shandy* all open with which word?

3.   Your starter for 10:
'I am not going to take part in that process. I think that Mrs Thatcher will lead the Conservative Party into the next election and that she will win it.' Who voiced this support in October 1990, one month before announcing his own candidature for leadership?

Three bonus questions on a time of day:

(a) Which English term for a time of day is derived ultimately from the Latin phrase meaning the ninth hour after sunrise calculated according to the Roman method?

(b) Which Italian term meaning midday can also mean the southern portion of the Italian peninsula, including Sicily?

(c) Published in 1940, the novel *Darkness at Noon*, about a show trial in a Soviet-like regime, was originally written in German by which Hungarian-born author?

4.   Your starter for 10:
What is the term for a rock that is composed of fragments of minerals and rocks older than the rock itself?

Three bonus questions on an art form:

(a) Referring to a genre of Japanese woodblock prints popular between the seventeenth and twentieth centuries, the term *Ukiyo-e* is usually translated into English as what?

(b) Which exponent of *Ukiyo-e* produced the image of 'The Great Wave off Kanagawa', part of the picture set *Thirty-Six Views of Mount Fuji*?

(c) *An Artist of the Floating World* is the work of which British novelist, born in Nagasaki in 1954?

5. **Your starter for 10:**

In the plays of Chekhov, Chebutykin, Dorn and Astrov are members of which profession?

Three bonus questions on Oliver Cromwell:

(a) Which city in Lancashire gives its name to a battle of August 1648 in which Cromwell defeated a Scots force under Hamilton?

(b) Which burgh in East Lothian gives its name to Cromwell's decisive victory over David Leslie's Scots army, a surprise dawn attack on 3 September 1650?

(c) On 3 September 1651, at which city in the Severn Valley did Cromwell defeat Charles II's Scots army, after which Charles fled abroad?

6. **Your starter for 10:**

Of whom did Kenneth Clark say, 'he was the most relentlessly curious man in history. Everything he saw made him ask how and why. Why does one find sea-shells in the mountains?... How does a bird fly? ... What is the origin of winds and clouds? Find out; write it down; if you can see it, draw it'?

Three bonus questions on US presidential elections:

(a) Prior to 2008, who was the last sitting senator to be elected president?

(b) Who is the only man to have been elected twice to the office of president and twice to the office of vice-president?

(c) Who is the only elected president since Richard Nixon

not to have previously been a state governor?

7.   Your starter for 10:
What six-letter word can denote: a wheel that will automatically align itself to the direction from which it is pushed; an acrid-tasting oil used as a purgative and lubricant; and a finely granulated white sugar used in baking?

Three bonus questions on poetry:
(a) 'The fathers with broad belts under their suits / ... mothers loud and fat; / An uncle shouting smut; and then the perms, / The nylon gloves and jewellery-substitutes, / The lemons, mauves, and olive-ochres that / Marked off the girls unreally from the rest'. In which poem do these lines appear?

(b) Which word completes this verse by A.E. Housman: 'Loveliest of trees, the cherry now / Is hung with bloom along the bough, / And stands about the woodland ride / Wearing white for –'?

(c) 'Because I do not hope to turn again' is the opening line of *Ash-Wednesday*, a profession of faith by which poet who joined the Anglican Church in 1927?

8.   Your starter for 10:
The common names of members of the insect order orthoptera include grasshoppers, crickets and which other group of insects?

Three bonus questions on chemistry:
(a) Which nineteenth-century Scottish scientist gave his name to the law stating that the diffusion rate of a gas is inversely proportional to the square root of its density, a principle used in separating isotopes by the diffusion method?

(b) Thomas Graham discovered the properties of which

substances, their names derived in part from the Greek for 'glue' and composed of fine particles that are dispersed throughout a second substance?

(c) Colloids include gels, sols and which other type of substance, composed of minute droplets of one liquid dispersed in another?

9. Your starter for 10:
Used in geology for a composite rock consisting of rounded and water-worn fragments of previously existing rocks, united into a compact mass by some kind of cement, what word can also mean a business group or industrial corporation resulting from the merging of originally separate and diverse commercial enterprises?

Three bonus questions on ocean trenches:
(a) Which Pacific island group gives its name to the ocean trench that is the deepest known depression on the Earth's surface, at more than 10,000 metres?
(b) The basin that forms the deepest point in the Arctic Ocean shares its name with which ship used in the 1890s by Nansen in an expedition that saw him reach the highest latitude until then attained?
(c) At a depth of approximately 7,258 metres, the trench that forms the deepest point of the Indian Ocean shares its name with which Indonesian island?

10. Your starter for 10:
Which EU capital is known in Hungarian as Pozsony and in German as Pressburg?

Three bonus questions on wantonness in Shakespeare:
In each case, name the play in which the following words appear:
(a) 'As flies to wanton boys are we to th'gods – / They kill us for their sport.'

(b) 'A lover may bestride the gossamer / That idles in the wanton summer air, / And yet not fall; so light is vanity.'

(c) 'I, that am rudely stamped, and want love's majesty / To strut before a wanton ambling nymph'.

11. Your starter for 10:

How many radians are there in a semicircle?

Three bonus questions on Ireland:

(a) Associated with the rebellion of 1798, which bay lies between the Beara and Sheep's Head peninsulas in County Cork?

(b) Which bay has shorelines on Counties Sligo, Leitrim and the Ulster county with which it shares its name?

(c) The Aran islands are situated in which bay that shares its name with the Irish Republic's second largest county?

12. Your starter for 10:

'The Lord is my shepherd; I shall not want' is, in the King James version of the Bible, the opening to which psalm?

Three bonus questions on a type of pasta:

(a) The name of which type of almond or coconut biscuit is related etymologically to that of a variety of pasta?

(b) What is the meaning of the word 'macaroni' in the song 'Yankee Doodle'?

(c) Macaroni is the name of a species of which type of South Atlantic bird, probably on account of the golden crest on its head that was thought to resemble the headgear of an eighteenth-century fop?

13. Your starter for 10:

In anthropology, what term, from the Latin for

'threshold', is used for a temporary stage during a rite of passage, for example a graduation ceremony, when participants are separated from their former group and have not yet acquired the status of their new group?

Three bonus questions on first loves in literature:
(a) What was the name of the niece to Capulet, with whom Romeo was enamoured before he met Juliet?
(b) Which fictional heroine had an affair with a playwright named Michaelis before the passion for which she is better known?
(c) In Jane Austen's *Mansfield Park*, who was fascinated by the frivolous Mary Crawford, but later falls in love with Fanny Price?

14. Your starter for 10:
What five-letter word denotes: a rapid alternation of adjacent musical notes, also known as a shake; a fluttering or tremulous sound made by birds; and the pronunciation of the 'r' sound with a vibration of the tongue?

Three bonus questions linked by a name:
(a) In the 1950s, which tennis player entered the Wimbledon Ladies' singles championship three times, winning on each occasion?
(b) What was the name of Queen Victoria's Scottish servant, played by Billy Connolly in a 1997 film?
(c) What, according to the writer Cyril Connolly, is inside every fat man, wildly signalling to be let out?

15. Your starter for 10:
Recently discovered to be rotating slightly faster than the rest of the planet, what two-word term describes the solid part of the Earth mainly composed of iron?

Three bonus questions on an island:

(a) Separated from Turkey by the Strait of Marmaris, which is the largest of the Dodecanese Islands?

(b) Flourishing in Rhodes in the third century BC, in which of the arts were Lysippus and his pupil, Chares of Lyndus, noted exponents?

(c) What name is given to Chares' best-known work, the giant statue of the sun god Helios, which stood by Rhodes Harbour?

16. Your starter for 10:

Having returned to her homeland after a period of exile, the socialist Michelle Bachelet was, in January 2006, elected President of which South American republic, the first woman to hold such a position in that country?

Three bonus questions on theft:

(a) Which term comes from the Latin for 'a kidnapper', and means passing off someone else's ideas or writings as one's own?

(b) According to the playwright Wilson Mizner, 'If you steal from one author, it's plagiarism; if you steal from many, it's...' – what?

(c) In a 1953 song, which American entertainer wrote, 'Plagiarize! Let no one else's work evade your eyes'?

17. Your starter for 10:

A tribute to one of his most acclaimed sketches, Ronnie Barker's Westminster Abbey memorial service began with the clergy being led in by servers bearing how many of what item?

Three bonus questions on Russian art:

(a) Who produced, directed and wrote the screenplay for the classic Russian film *Ivan the Terrible*?

(b) Which author's first major work, published in 1962, was *One Day in the Life of Ivan Denisovich*?

(c) Which composer, born in 1804, wrote the music for the opera originally entitled *Ivan Susanin*, later changed to *Life for the Tsar*?

18. Your starter for 10:

A geo-political and economic organisation founded in 1967, the acronym ASEAN stands for what?

Three bonus questions on witches:
In each case, name the witch from the information given:

(a) According to the Old Testament, the witch ordered by Saul to summon the ghost of the prophet Samuel to foretell the outcome of Israel's battle against the Philistines?

(b) The witch named in the title of Shelley's poem, written after he climbed the Monte San Pellegrino in Italy in 1920, published in his *Posthumous Poems* in 1824?

(c) Finally, in mathematics, apparently arising from a mistranslation, the 'witch' associated with an eighteenth-century female mathematician?

19. Your starter for 10:

Canada is one of three Commonwealth countries to have an English name beginning with the letter 'C'; For ten points, name either of the other two.

Three bonus questions on terms used in both philosophy and aesthetics, but with different meanings in each:
For each one, supply the word that satisfies both of these two definitions:

(a) The philosophical doctrine that universals exist only in the mind with no external reality; and a form of abstraction that negates the importance of the art object, concentrating solely on the conveyance of the idea behind it?

(b) The belief that all phenomena can be explained in terms of material, as distinct from spiritual, causes and laws; and the practice of reproducing subjects as accurately as possible in the visual arts?

(c) The scholastic doctrine, opposed to nominalism, that universals exist independently of their being thought; and the representation in art of the world as it actually is, without idealisation?

20. Your starter for 10:

'Why do people gush over [him]? I'd rather visit a demented relative.' These words of Germaine Greer refer to which French novelist, whose major work was published in seven sections between 1913 and 1927, the first volume being *Swann's Way*?

Three bonus questions on travel writers:

(a) Which 1995 book chronicled the former *Times* sub-editor Bill Bryson's tour around Britain before his return to the USA?

(b) Bruce Chatwin is said to have left the *Sunday Times* after sending a telegram explaining that he had gone to which South American region 'for six months'? The account of his travels was published in 1977.

(c) Author of *The Old Patagonian Express*, which American wrote about his own journey around the UK in the 1983 work *The Kingdom by the Sea*?

21. Your starter for 10:

What single name links: the first Latin Emperor of Constantinople, from 1204; the author of novels including *Go Tell It on the Mountain* and *Another Country*, and the Prime Minister at the time of the General Strike and the abdication of King Edward VIII?

Three bonus questions on impressionist painters:

(a) Born to British parents in Paris in 1839, which artist spent most of his life around that city and mainly produced landscapes? The value of his work went largely unrecognised during his lifetime and he died in poverty.

(b) The sister-in-law of Manet, who painted several portraits of her, which impressionist artist's work frequently included domestic interiors and studies of children, as well as landscapes such as *The Grain Field* of 1875, now in the Musée d'Orsay?

(c) Born in the West Indies in 1830, who was the only artist to display his works at all eight impressionist exhibitions? He later experimented with pointillism.

22. Your starter for 10:

In Greek mythology, which king used the water of the River Pactolus to wash away the gift that had been reluctantly bestowed upon him by Dionysus?

Three bonus questions on people born in 1910:

(a) The US physicist William Shockley and his team at Bell Laboratories made a major technological breakthrough in 1947 when they produced the first working example of what general type of mechanism fundamental to the electronics industry?

(b) One of the first European jazz virtuosi, which Belgian-born guitarist formed the Quintette du Hot Club de France with Stéphane Grappelli in 1934, and later toured with Duke Ellington?

(c) Noted for contemporary reinterpretations of Greek myth, which French dramatist's works include *Médée*, *Antigone* and *La Machine Infernale*?

23. Your starter for 10:

Which novelist, born in 1811, used his own experiences at Charterhouse to create the Grey Friars School which appeared in several of his novels, notably *The Newcomes* in 1855?

> **Three bonus questions on European languages:**
> (a) The Finnish language is most closely related to which official language of the EU?
> (b) The Romanian language is practically identical with that of which neighbouring country, although for political reasons the two are often given different names?
> (c) To which official language of the EU is Latvian most closely related?

24. Your starter for 10:

What is the modulus of the complex number 8 plus 15i where i is the square root of minus 1?

> **Three bonus questions on insects:**
> (a) The term 'stridulation' refers to what characteristic behaviour of members of the insect order *orthoptera*, which includes the grasshoppers?
> (b) 'Migratory', 'desert' and 'red' are three species of which type of short-horned grasshopper, able to migrate long distances in destructive swarms?
> (c) 'Ant-loving', 'striped-ground' and 'leaf-rolling' are species of which *orthoptera*, known for the musical chirping of the male? In Britain, the 'dark' and 'speckled-bush' species are common.

25. Your starter for 10:

In physiology, the term peristalsis refers to the wavelike, involuntary muscular movement of which part of the body?

Three bonus questions on wine grapes:

(a) Which French grape exists in several varieties, including 'white' and 'grey', and derives its name from the supposed resemblance between a bunch of its grapes and a pine cone?

(b) As a consequence of the belief that it was brought to Europe by the Crusaders, Syrah, the red wine grape of the Rhône Valley, shares its English name with which city in Iran?

(c) 'Blood of Jupiter' is the meaning of the name of which Italian grape used to make Chianti?

26. Your starter for 10:

In 2003, scientists at the Laboratory of Reproductive Technology at Cremona in Italy announced their success in cloning what type of animal, the resultant creature being given the name Prometea?

Three bonus questions on words and their connotations:

(a) Although derived from the Greek for 'wisdom', what word now means the use of specious reasoning?

(b) Which word, now meaning 'over-theoretical and dogmatic', was first used in France after 1815 as a term for a member of a political party that desired constitutional government?

(c) Which term for a despot originally referred to the sole ruler in a Greek city-state and had few or no negative connotations beyond meaning that he had usurped his power?

27. Your starter for 10:

Born in Catalunya in 1893, which artist's work includes *The Harlequin's Carnival*, *The Tilled Field* and *Constellations*?

Three bonus questions on numbers:

(a) '352087' and '338171' were the service numbers assigned to T.E. Lawrence when he twice served as an aircraftsman in the RAF in the 1920s. Under what two surnames did he serve?

(b) Which of the Nazi war criminals was 'Prisoner Number Seven' during his time in Spandau Prison, where he died in 1987?

(c) In which novel of 1962 is the central character given the number '6655321' when he is sentenced to fourteen years in state jail, or Staja 84F?

28. Your starter for 10:

What is the term for the line on the visible disc of a planet that separates the sunlit and shaded regions, marking sunrise and sunset and enabling small geological details to become clearly visible due to the low angle of the sun?

Three bonus questions on British film documentaries:

(a) The winner of two awards at the 2009 Sundance film festival, Havana Marking's documentary followed contestants in an *X-Factor*-type singing competition in which Asian country?

(b) *Of Time and the City* is director Terence Davies's 2008 film about which city, in which he was born in 1945?

(c) Depicting Philippe Petit's 1974 wire-walk between the Twin Towers of the World Trade Center, which film won the 2009 Oscar for Documentary (Feature)?

29. Your starter for 10:

Which three-word legal term meaning 'obstruction' is a yoking together of two synonyms, one of Anglo-Saxon and the other of Norman-French origin?

Three bonus questions on the 1930s:

(a) Believed to have been instigated by the army of the aggressor, the Mukden Incident of 1931, in which railway lines were dynamited, was used as a pretext for aggression against which country?

(b) The Mukden Incident, in which Japan is generally regarded as having been the aggressor, was followed by the Marco Polo Bridge Incident, which marked the start of the Second Sino-Japanese War and took place on 7 July of what year?

(c) An attack on a radio station staged by Nazi troops, the Gleiwitz incident was used to justify the German invasion of which country?

30. Your starter for 10:

What name is given to the yellowish-gray powdery mixture of water-insoluble proteins in wheat and other cereals, which helps in the production of leavened baked goods?

Three bonus questions on the titles of novels:

(a) The market in *The Pilgrim's Progress*, in which all pleasures and delights are for sale, gives its name to which novel published in instalments from 1847 to 1848?

(b) Mr Standfast is a character in *The Pilgrim's Progress* and is also the title of a thriller featuring Richard Hannay by which writer?

(c) One translation of the name Beelzebub, a character in both *The Pilgrim's Progress* and *Paradise Lost*, was used as the title of which 1954 novel by William Golding?

'Well, we'll have to say goodbye to you. You were an entertaining team to watch — when you finally did buzz in, but... you were absolutely slaughtered, I'm afraid.'

Round
Two

'Hello. Once again, we're going to witness the calibre of the generation who will, before long, take over, God help us. But before that bright day dawns, they have to fight it out for a place in the quarter-finals.'

THE RULES

You could all recite the rules in your sleep, so … here's your first starter for 10.

Match One

1. Your starter for 10:

Mary, the wife of James V of Scotland and mother of Mary, Queen of Scots, belonged to which French noble family prominent during the sixteenth century?

Three bonus questions on scientific symbols:

(a) In scientific notation, an italic upper-case 'T' usually denotes which physical property of a system?

(b) An italic capital 'T' followed by a subscript lower case 'b' indicates what temperature?

(c) The symbol for the temperature at which DNA is half denatured is an italic upper-case 'T' followed by what lower-case subscript letter?

2. Your starter for 10:

In his 1959 work *The Presentation of Self in Everyday Life*, the Canadian sociologist Erving Goffman used the metaphor of which field of the arts to analyse the ways in which people play roles and manage the impressions they present to each other in different settings?

Three bonus questions on the Italian preacher Girolamo Savonarola:

(a) Which religious order, also known as the Black Friars, did Savonarola enter in 1474, later becoming its Vicar-General?

(b) The Arrabbiati, or 'Angry Ones', was the name of the

Florentine party formed in opposition to Savonarola. His followers were given what name, possibly indicating the penitence they professed?

(c) Viewing the event as God's means of ridding Florence of immorality, Savonarola welcomed the invasion of Italy in 1494 by which country?

3.   Your starter for 10:
Which noun, once used in English to refer either to a reformed prostitute or to a reformatory for prostitutes, derives from the name commonly used for the sinful woman in the seventh chapter of Luke's Gospel?

Three bonus questions on heat:

(a) The heat required to raise the temperature of one kilogram of a material by one Kelvin without a change of state is known as what?

(b) The quantity of heat required to change one kilogram of ice to water without a change in temperature is called what?

(c) What term describes the quantity of heat needed to change one kilogram of water to steam without a change in temperature?

4.   Your starter for 10:
In Islam, what is the *Sajjada*? Commonly used in *salat*, or formal prayer, they are often decorative and highly individual in style.

Three bonus questions on a prime minister:

(a) Sir Henry Campbell-Bannerman was succeeded as prime minister by which politician, of whom he said that he would offer a solution to a difficulty with the words 'send for the sledgehammer'?

(b) Before he became prime minister, Asquith held which cabinet position between 1905 and 1908, later telling

Philip Snowden that it was 'the easiest one in the Government'?

(c) The early years of Asquith's administration were marked by a prolonged clash with the Lords over the 'People's Budget' of 1909. This resulted in a restriction of their powers by which act of 1911?

5. Your starter for 10:

From the Greek meaning 'to lead the child', what term referred to a slave responsible for supervising the instruction of his master's sons, and now means a teacher, especially one who is pedantic or strict?

Three bonus questions on Irish history:

(a) Responsible, with Arthur Griffith, for negotiating the 1921 treaty, who became head of the Provisional Free State Government in 1922, but was killed in an IRA ambush soon after taking office?

(b) Who became head of the Free State Government in 1922 and was leader of the opposition from 1932 to 1944? His son, Liam, was Taoiseach in the 1970s.

(c) Born in New York, who broke with Sinn Fein to found Fianna Fail, initially an opposition party, in 1926? He was several times Prime Minister and Taoiseach between 1932 and 1959.

6. Your starter for 10:

Which integer completes this Pythagorean triple: 20, 21 and what?

Three bonus questions on the human body:

(a) Which major system of the body is divided broadly into two categories, the peripheral and the central, the latter including the spinal cord and the brain?

(b) Nerve fibres called axons conduct impulses away from each neuron; what name, meaning 'tree-like' or 'branching', is given to the filaments that receive impulses from other neurons?

(c) Which substance, consisting of a complex mixture of phospho-lipids and proteins, constitutes an insulating layer or sheath around many nerve fibres, and is responsible for the colour of the white matter of the central nervous system?

7.   Your starter for 10:
Launched in Europe in June 2004, what is represented by the initials ITMS, being Apple's digital download music service?

Three bonus questions on time periods:

(a) When used as a suffix after a date, the initials 'BCE' can stand for three slightly varying terms. For five points, name one of them.

(b) In geology and palaeontology, the symbol 'Ma' indicates what period of time?

(c) Beginning in 1954, metrologists established 1950 as the origin year for the BP timescale for use in the process of radiocarbon dating; for what does 'BP' stand?

8.   Your starter for 10:
Which poet wrote the following lines: 'Know then thyself, presume not God to scan; / The proper study of mankind is man. / Placed on this isthmus of a middle state, / A being darkly wise, and rudely great'.

Three bonus questions on traditional dyes:

(a) What is the common name of the plant in the *rubiaceae* family, from which was extracted the dye formerly used to colour the redcoats of the British army?

(b) A species of wild mignonette called 'weld' or 'dyer's rocket' was the source of a dyestuff of which colour, used since Neolithic times and popular for Roman wedding garments?

(c) Which Essex market town got its present name in part from a local product which, among other uses, provided a distinctive traditional dye?

9.   Your starter for 10:

The first to prove that pi^2 is irrational, which French mathematician is noted for his work on elliptic integrals that provide basic analytical tools for mathematical physics?

Three bonus questions on fiction in the 1950s:

(a) Sebastian Dangerfield is the hero of which 1955 novel by the American-born Irish writer J.P. Donleavy?

(b) Leo Colston is the name of the title character of which novel by L.P. Hartley, published in 1953?

(c) How is the vacuum-cleaner salesman James Wormold described in the title of Graham Greene's novel of 1958?

10.   Your starter for 10:

With scores ranging from three to fifteen and based on motor responsiveness, verbal performance and eye opening to appropriate stimuli, what scale was designed to assess the depth and duration of coma and impaired consciousness?

Three bonus questions on coastal footpaths:

(a) Which national trail in Wales runs along 186 miles of coast from Cardigan to Amroth?

(b) Named after a lowland area, which Scottish path runs for sixty-seven miles along the Firths of Forth and Tay, between North Queensferry and Newport-on-Tay?

(c) Which national trail runs from Minehead in Somerset along 630 miles of the coasts of Devon and Cornwall, finishing at Poole in Dorset?

11. Your starter for 10:

Which European national flag is composed of three horizontal bands that are the same colours, reading downwards, as the hoist band of the Belgian flag, the fly band of the French tricolour and the central section of the Spanish flag?

Three bonus questions on place names:

(a) Bandar Abbas is a major port in the south of which country?

(b) Bandar Seri Begawan is the capital of which Southeast Asian country?

(c) Bandaranaike was the surname of two prime ministers of which country, the first holding office from 1956 to 1959, the second for three terms from 1960 to 2000?

12. Your starter for 10:

The Strait of Bonifacio separates which two large Mediterranean islands?

Three bonus questions on the philosophy of religion:

(a) Which Archbishop of Canterbury proposed the ontological argument for the existence of God in his *Proslogion* of around 1077?

(b) In the 1802 work *Natural Theology*, which Christian apologist argued that the complexity of the natural world must indicate an almighty creator?

(c) In an essay of 1750, which British philosopher argued that human 'knavery and folly' was a better explanation of miracles than supernatural agency?

13. Your starter for 10:

If the twenty ordinal numbers from 'first' to 'twentieth' are written as words and arranged alphabetically, which comes first?

Three bonus questions on desserts:

(a) Which cooked dessert made with meringue and ice cream is known as an 'omelette norvégienne' or 'Norwegian omelette' in France, after both its appearance and contents?

(b) Which dough-based confections filled with an almond or marzipan cream are known as 'ein Kopenhagener' in Vienna and 'Wienerbrød' or 'Vienna bread' in the country after which they are usually named in Britain?

(c) 'Zuppa Inglese' or 'English soup' is the Italian name for which dessert?

14. Your starter for 10:

What four-letter word can mean: the spawn of oysters or other shellfish; a flat instrument used in playing ball-games; a quarrel or dispute; a short gaiter worn over the shoe; and the past participle of a verb meaning 'to eject saliva'?

Three bonus questions on music:

(a) Benjamin Britten's 1945 composition *A Young Person's Guide to the Orchestra* is based on a theme by which seventeenth-century composer?

(b) The theme by Purcell which Britten borrowed was originally part of the incidental music for the 1676 play *Abdelazar, or The Moor's Revenge* by which female dramatist?

(c) Purcell's 1692 composition *The Fairy-Queen* was an adaptation of which of Shakespeare's comedies?

15. Your starter for 10:

Vogul and Ostyak are two languages of the Ugrian family, spoken in northern Russia. What is the third language in the family, spoken by more than ten million in Central Europe?

Three bonus questions on a region of Italy:

(a) Which region, whose principal towns include Bari and Brindisi, is known as the 'heel' of the Italian boot?

(b) Now a major ferry port, which city in Apulia marked the end of the Roman road known as the Via Appia?

(c) Which city in Apulia gives its name to a type of poisonous spider and the frenzied dance thought to cure the symptoms of its bite?

16. Your starter for 10:

'I'll stay till the wind changes' is a promise made to the children of the Banks family in which collection of stories for children by the Australian-born writer Pamela Lyndon Travers?

Three bonus questions on Homer's Iliad:

(a) Book One of the *Iliad* recounts a quarrel between which two Greek leaders over the captive woman Briseis?

(b) In Book Three, the husband and the abductor of Helen fight an inconclusive duel in a vain attempt to bring the war to an end. For five points, give both their names.

(c) Book Six of the Iliad includes a poignant scene of a Trojan hero and his wife together with their child Astyanax. What are their names?

17. Your starter for 10:

What name, shared by several Latin American currencies, means 'weight' in Spanish?

Three bonus questions on mining:

(a) Some 60 kilometres from Athens, the hills at Laurium were deeply mined, particularly after the fifth century AD, for which precious metal, one of the chief sources of revenue for the Athenian state?

(b) At one time accounting for around a third of the

world's production, soma silver, named after a nearby village, was excavated extensively in the sixteenth and seventeenth centuries from the Iwami-Ginzan mine in which East Asian country?

(c) Which mineral, the chief ore of lead, was mined, notably from the fifth century AD at Melle in France, because its deposits often contain significant amounts of silver?

18. Your starter for 10:

In statistics, the capital of which Greek letter is used to denote the sum?

Three bonus questions on white suits:

(a) Known for his white suit, which former TV reporter stood against Neil Hamilton in the Tatton constituency in the 1997 general election?

(b) The 1951 film *The Man in the White Suit* starred which actor as Sidney Stratton, a scientist who creates a fabric that never wears out?

(c) In which film comedy of 1980 did actor Robert Hays parody John Travolta's white suit and dance routine from *Saturday Night Fever*?

19. Your starter for 10:

Born in 1932, what nationality is the dramatist Athol Fugard, whose works include *Blood Knot*, *Statements After an Arrest Under the Immorality Act* and *Sizwe Bansi Is Dead*?

Three bonus questions linked by a word:

(a) In Mozart's opera *The Magic Flute*, which character is the mother of the heroine, Pamina?

(b) Which Italian word describing a 'lady of the night' is given to a pasta sauce containing chillies, anchovies and capers?

(c) Which Bahamian-American actor starred as Virgil Tibbs in the 1967 film *In the Heat of the Night*?

20. **Your starter for 10:**
About 400 light years away, what young open star cluster is also known as M45 or the Seven Sisters?

   Three bonus questions on a term:
   (a) Referring to the movements and collisions of gas molecules, for what do the letters MFP stand?
   (b) In statistics, what is the alternative name for the mean squared deviation of a random variable or of a sample?
   (c) What is the geometric mean of the numbers 2, 4 and 8?

21. **Your starter for 10:**
On many domestic gas bills, what name is given to the unit of gas equal to 105.5 megajoules?

   Three bonus questions on a name:
   (a) Jones the cat, Bishop the android and Corporal Hicks have been among the companions of which screen heroine?
   (b) Robert Leroy Ripley devised a cartoon series in 1918 which depicted oddities from around the world under what title?
   (c) Alexandra Ripley's novel *Scarlett* was a sequel to which 1936 bestseller?

22. **Your starter for 10:**
Which two things are studied in the branch of botany known as carpology?

   Three bonus questions on the metallic element antimony:
   (a) Name the naturally occurring black sulphide of antimony, which has been used as an eye cosmetic since ancient times?
   (b) Sodium stibogluconate, a compound of antimony, is

used to treat which mainly tropical disease, spread by the sand fly?

(c) Which alloy has been used for making drinking vessels and consists of 91 per cent tin, 7.5 per cent antimony and 1.5 per cent copper?

23. Your starter for 10:
Part of Romania until 1940, the major part of the historical region of Bessarabia now falls within the territory of which modern-day European state?

Three bonus questions on pairs of words that differ only in their initial consonant, for example 'reed' and 'seed':
All three pairs contain a double 'e'. In each case, give both words from the definitions provided:

(a) Two nouns, one meaning 'one who is obsessively enthusiastic, for example about computers or quizzes', and the other 'vegetable appearing on pound coins'.

(b) Two verbs, one meaning 'to look keenly or with difficulty' and the other 'to look slyly or lasciviously'.

(c) Two verbs, meaning 'ooze' or 'percolate', and 'lament' or 'bewail'.

24. Your starter for 10:
Found on a Greek island in 1820, which marble statue is believed to be the work of the sculptor Alexandros of Antioch in the second century BC? It was presented by the Marquis de Rivière to Louis XVIII, who donated it to the Louvre.

Three bonus questions on the Nobel Prize in Physics:

(a) Who won the first Prize, awarded in 1901 and given, according to the citation, 'in recognition of the extraordinary services he has rendered by the discovery of the remarkable rays subsequently named after him'?

(b) Which Hungarian-born British scientist won the Prize

in 1971, quote, 'for his invention and development of the holographic method'?

(c) Although particularly associated with another advance in theoretical physics, which laureate was awarded the Prize in 1921, quote, 'especially for his discovery of the law of the photo-electric effect'?

25. **Your starter for 10:**
At 248 metres, Ditchling Beacon near Brighton is higher than the highest point in five US states. One of them is Rhode Island. For ten points, name two of the other four states.

Three bonus questions on art thefts:

(a) Stolen from Boston's Isabella Stewart Gardner Museum in 1990, *Storm on the Sea of Galilee* is the only seascape by which Dutch artist?

(b) Painted between 1812 and 1814, Goya's portrait of which public figure was stolen less than three weeks after its hanging in the National Gallery in August 1961?

(c) Along with a *Madonna* by the same artist, which expressionist painting was stolen from a museum in Oslo in 2004?

26. **Your starter for 10:**
Quote: 'We go about our daily lives understanding almost nothing of the world.' This is the opening sentence of the introduction to which work of 1988? Sometimes said to be the least read of all bestsellers, its subtitle is *From the Big Bang to Black Holes*.

Three bonus questions on the openings of plays by Shakespeare:

(a) Which play by Shakespeare begins with the words of Leonato, 'I learn in this letter that Don Pedro of

Aragon comes this night to Messina'?

(b) Spoken by the Prologue, what are the first two words of *Romeo and Juliet*, followed by '... both alike in dignity, in fair Verona, where we lay our scene'?

(c) Philo says, 'Nay, but this dotage of our general's o'erflows the measure' at the start of which play?

27. Your starter for 10:

What name is given to a refracting telescope with a split objective lens, used for finding the angular distance between two stars? The name suggests its original purpose for measuring the diameter of the sun.

Three bonus questions on people born in 1910:

In each case, identify the person from the works listed:

(a) The novels entitled, in translation, *Our Lady of the Flowers* and *The Miracle of the Rose*.

(b) The *Capricorn Concerto*, the ballet *Medea* and the *Adagio for Strings*.

(c) The films *Rashomon, Ran* and *Seven Samurai*.

28. Your starter for 10:

Lying between thallium and bismuth in the Periodic Table, which metal is the final stable product of the decay of uranium, and is a potent neurotoxin that accumulates in soft tissues and bone over time?

Three bonus questions on a South American city:

(a) The butter bean, native to tropical South America, has what alternative name, after a capital city in that region?

(b) The Peruvian capital Lima was founded in 1535 as 'the City of Kings' by which Spanish conquistador, as part of his conquest of the Incas?

(c) Lima syndrome, the psychological condition in which abductors begin to empathise with their hostages, is named after an incident at the Japanese embassy in Lima in 1996. Its opposite, when hostages empathise with their abductors, is named after which city?

29. Your starter for 10:
What is the sine of 30 plus the cosine of 60?

Three bonus questions on deposed kings:
(a) Which king of England reigned from April to June 1483 when he was deposed by his uncle, Richard, Duke of Gloucester, who succeeded him as Richard III?

(b) In 1792, what surname did the republican government give to the deposed Louis XVI? It was the nickname of a tenth-century French king, Hugh, and of the royal dynasty he founded.

(c) Enver Hoxha founded and led the Communist Party of which country in the fight for national independence and, in 1946, deposed its monarch, King Zog, to become head of state?

30. Your starter for 10:
What vegetable is the distinguishing feature of a dish described as 'Florentine'?

Three bonus questions on biochemistry:
(a) The 1934 Nobel Prize for Physiology or Medicine was awarded to three men who contributed to the discovery of which vitamin, then known as the 'anti-pernicious anaemia factor'?

(b) Who won the Nobel Prize for Chemistry thirty years later for elucidating the structure of vitamin B12 by X-ray crystallography?

(c) A molecule of vitamin B12 contains at its centre an atom of which metal?

'Well, I fear we'll have to say goodbye to you, but, you know, you were up against pretty strong opposition tonight. But thank you very much for joining us.'

THE RULES

You all know the rules, so here's
your first starter for 10.

Match Two

1. Your starter for 10:

'O mistress mine, where are you roaming?', 'Come away, death' and 'The rain it raineth every day' are among the songs of the clown Feste in which of Shakespeare's plays?

Three bonus questions on brain-imaging techniques:

(a) A PET scan detects pairs of gamma rays emitted indirectly by a radio-nuclide or tracer, which is introduced into the body on a biologically active molecule; what does 'PET' stand for in this context?

(b) Magneto-encephalography, or MEG, can be used to measure the magnetic fields produced by electrical activity in the brain via 'SQUIDs'. For what does the acronym 'SQUID' stand?

(c) NIRS is an optical technique for measuring blood oxygenation in the brain. For what does 'NIRS' stand?

2. Your starter for 10:

Born Armand Jean du Plessis, which nobleman was consecrated Bishop of Luçon at the age of 22, and was appointed Minister of State by Louis XIII in 1624?

Three bonus questions on sailing vessels:

In each case, identify the type of vessel from the description given:

(a) Developed from the carrack in the late sixteenth

century, which three-masted sailing ship was used as both a warship and a trading ship, and formed part of the Spanish Armada of 1588?

(b) Its name deriving from its association with piracy, which two-masted vessel was square-rigged on the foremast and fore-aft rigged on the mainmast?

(c) Built for the tea trade, the name of which type of mid-nineteenth-century vessel is believed to refer to its ability to beat the time of regular passage ships, a well-known example being the Cutty Sark?

3. Your starter for 10:

Which scientist gave his name to the effect in which a rapid rise in the temperature of a nuclear reactor pile results from particle bombardment of graphite and other materials, which then deform, swell and release energy? It was the cause of the fire in 1957 at what was then Windscale.

Three bonus questions on logic:

(a) What is the common name of the logical operator 'inclusive disjunction'?

(b) What is the common name of the logical operator 'joint denial'?

(c) What is the common name of the logical operator known as 'logical conjunction'?

4. Your starter for 10:

Born in Lancaster in 1792 and trained as a cabinet-maker, Thomas Edmondson gives his name to a system used continuously in the UK from 1837 to the 1980s in what service?

Three bonus questions on US state capitals:

(a) Usually cited as the smallest state capital in the USA, Montpelier is the capital of which state, whose largest city is Burlington?

(b) Its population around 20,000, Pierre is the capital of which state? Situated on the Missouri river close to the geographic centre of the state, it is around 300 miles from Sioux Falls, the largest city.

(c) The small city of Frankfort is capital of which state, whose largest city is Louisville, fifty miles to the west?

5.   Your starter for 10:

From the Greek meaning 'prophetess', what name was given to those female seers through whom the gods were supposedly able to speak and foretell the future, such as those at the sites of Erythrae, Delphi and Cumae?

Three bonus questions on pairs of words formed by the addition of an initial letter 's', for example 'hut' and 'shut':

In each case, give both words from the definitions provided:

(a) To make intensive preparations for an examination; and, colloquially, to decamp at speed.

(b) A freshwater fish of the family *cyprinidae*; and a steep slope.

(c) A Welsh national emblem; and an adjective meaning smooth and polished.

6.   Your starter for 10:

Meanings of what word include: in botany, a dense cluster of carpels or florets; in geology, a rock consisting of a mixture of minerals; and, in everyday speech, a sum or assemblage of many separate units?

Three bonus questions on a word:

(a) Originating in the reign of Henry III, what is the most ancient, but lowest, form of knighthood in the UK? It is known by the initials KB.

(b) The degrees of Bachelor of Arts, of Science and of Laws are often abbreviated to BA, BSc and LLB respectively: in these abbreviations what Latin word for 'bachelor' is sometimes said to be indicated by the letter 'B'?

(c) 'Beyond the obvious facts that you are a bachelor, a solicitor, a freemason and an asthmatic, I know nothing whatever about you.' Which character makes these observations in 'The Adventure of the Norwood Builder', first published in 1903?

7. Your starter for 10:

What has been variously defined as 'events where drugs are used to gain competitive advantage', 'anything you can't play in normal shoes', 'a contest in which a winner can be indisputably defined' and 'hunting, shooting and fishing: anything else is a game'?

Three bonus questions on Greek letters used as scientific symbols:

(a) Which Greek letter is the symbol for permeance when in the upper case, and for wavelength when in the lower case?

(b) In quantum mechanics, particularly in the Schrödinger Equation, what does the Greek letter 'psi' represent?

(c) The Greek-letter symbols for osmotic pressure, the brightest star in a constellation, and kinematic viscosity spell out the name of which Greek god?

8. Your starter for 10:

For what do the letters KLF stand, when signifying the name of an avant-garde music group?

Three bonus questions on a number:

(a) What is the first 'perfect number', that is, a positive integer that is the sum of all its divisors apart from itself?

(b) 'Les Six' was a group of six French composers formed in Paris in 1918 under the aegis of, but not including, Erik Satie and Jean Cocteau. For five points, name two of them.

(c) Six of the traditional nine counties that made up the historic province of Ulster are in Northern Ireland. For five points, name any one of the three in the Republic of Ireland.

9. Your starter for 10:
What single-digit number links: the so-called 'naked-eye planets'; the Pillars of Islam; the books of the Jewish Torah; and the classical 'elements', including aether?

Three bonus questions on the vertebrate nervous system:
(a) Composed of sympathetic and parasympathetic nerves, which part of the peripheral nervous system stimulates smooth and cardiac muscles?

(b) From the Latin for 'wandering', what name is given to the tenth cranial nerve, which supplies branches to many major internal organs?

(c) From the Greek meaning 'connection', what word means the junction between two adjacent neurones?

10. Your starter for 10:
Devised by Christopher Monckton and first solved by Alex Selby and Oliver Riordan in 2000, bagging them the £1 million award offered, what is the name of the puzzle made up of 209 twelve polydrafter pieces arranged in the shape of a slightly non-regular dodecagon?

Three bonus questions linked by a surname:
(a) *Consider Phlebas* and *The Player of Games* are among the science fiction works of which Scottish novelist?

(b) In what scientific capacity did Joseph Banks accompany

Captain Cook in his round-the-world voyage of 1768 to 1771?

(c) Gordon Banks, the goalkeeper at the time of England's 1966 World Cup win, is noted for a spectacular save against which player in the 1970 World Cup?

11. **Your starter for 10:**

'When you've got your back to the wall you must turn round and fight' is an aphorism attributed to which prime minister?

Three bonus questions on the Caribbean:

In each case, name the island or islands that complete the following full names of countries:

(a) St Vincent and the...?

(b) Antigua and...?

(c) St Kitts and...?

12. **Your starter for 10:**

Graves is an appellation from which large French wine-producing region?

Three bonus questions on fictional buildings:

(a) The opening paragraphs of which nineteenth-century novel inform the reader that Thrushcross Grange has been rented out to a Mr Lockwood?

(b) Which fictional house in Essex lends its name to the first of a series of novels for teenagers by K.M. Peyton, the books having been adapted for television in the late 1970s?

(c) Lancre Castle, described as having been built 'by an architect who had heard of Gormenghast, but hadn't got the budget', is the creation of which writer?

13. **Your starter for 10:**

What does a potamologist study?

Three questions on clowns:

(a) Which Shakespeare play features the song that begins, 'Come away, come away, death', sung by the clown Feste at the request of Duke Orsino?

(b) Annually, on the first Sunday in February, a service is held at Holy Trinity Church in East London for all UK clowns to remember which artist, who died in 1837 and was dubbed 'the father of modern clowning'?

(c) Images of clowns, acrobats and harlequins are typical of works from the 'Rose' period of which artist, between about 1904 and 1906?

14. Your starter for 10:

What was the highest official title of honour in the Ottoman Empire? The name, possibly of Persian origin, continued to be used for soldiers in the Turkish republic until 1934, when all Ottoman titles were abolished, and it is still used in conversation as a mark of respect to a social superior.

Three bonus questions on towers:

(a) In which of Edward I's Welsh castles, situated on the River Seiont, is the Eagle Tower to be found?

(b) Which fictional detective and poet is the hero of *The Black Tower*, first published in 1975?

(c) The Martello Tower at Sandycove near Dun Laoghaire houses a museum to which writer who briefly lived in it?

15. Your starter for 10:

Identify the poet who wrote these lines: 'The blessed damozel leaned out / From the gold bar of heaven; / Her eyes were deeper than the depth / Of waters stilled at even; / She had three lilies in her hand, / And the stars in her hair were seven'?

Three bonus questions on a place name:

(a) Lancaster House in London gives its name to an agreement of 1979 that paved the way for the independence in 1980 of which southern African state?

(b) Lancaster County in Pennsylvania is noted for settlements of which Anabaptist denomination, an offshoot of the Swiss Mennonites?

(c) 'Lancaster Gate' was formerly used metonymically to indicate which sporting organisation, based since 2000 in Soho Square?

16. **Your starter for 10:**

Which word can precede 'number', 'sin', 'virtue' or 'wind', is the name of a species of songbird, and also means a deep scarlet colour, with reference to its ecclesiastical definition of one of the members of the Sacred College of the Roman Catholic Church?

Three bonus questions on stars:

(a) 'I'll love you till the ocean / Is folded and hung up to dry / And the seven stars go squawking / Like geese about the sky.' These lines appear in 'As I Walked Out One Evening', a 1940 ballad by which poet, during his relationship with the American writer Chester Kallman?

(b) 'Three lilies in her hand, / And the stars in her hair were seven.' How was this woman described in the title of Dante Gabriel Rossetti's poem of 1847? He later represented the same subject in a painting.

(c) The 1903 work *The Jewel of the Seven Stars* is an early example of a horror novel describing the regeneration of an Egyptian mummy, and is by which Irish author?

17. **Your starter for 10:**

Which term, the first part of which is derived from the

German for 'rag', did Karl Marx coin for the lowest stratum of the industrial working class, including tramps and criminals?

Three bonus questions on politicians:
(a) Which senator for Arkansas gave his name to a 1946 programme to enable study abroad?
(b) Born Maria Jane Korbel in 1937, whom did Bill Clinton appoint as Secretary of State in 1996?
(c) What structure did Walter Ulbricht cause to be erected virtually overnight in August 1961?

18. Your starter for 10:
The equation 's = k log w' is carved on the gravestone of which Austrian physicist, born in 1844, who showed that much of thermodynamics could be explained by applying ideas of probability to atoms?

Three bonus questions on nineteenth-century French poets:
(a) Which French poet and adventurer wrote very little verse after the age of 19 and became a trader and adventurer in Africa?
(b) Imprisoned for shooting Rimbaud, who had been his lover, which poet first publicised his work in *Les Poètes maudits*?
(c) Which poet, noted for the collection *Les Fleurs du mal*, was inspired by the works of Edgar Allan Poe?

19. Your starter for 10:
Producing the fine pink colour in morganite when embedded in beryl and sometimes thought to give amethyst its depth of violet when trapped within quartz, which metallic element, atomic number 25, is used to toughen and harden steel without making it brittle?

Three bonus questions on surnames:
(a) What would have been the occupation of an ancestor of an Italian with the surname Sartori?
(b) A German named Bauer is a descendant of someone in what occupation?
(c) The French 'Lefevreand' and the Ukrainian 'Kowalsky' are the equivalents of which common English surname?

20. Your starter for 10:
Which sessile coelenterate shares its name with the many-headed Greek monster slain by Heracles?

Three bonus questions on Lancashire resorts which have changed their names:
(a) Which resort was known as Poulton-le-Sands but later became known by the name of the bay on which it stands?
(b) Which resort is built on the site of South Hawes, apparently being given its present name in the 1790s?
(c) Which Lancashire resort was originally known as Pool, but was given an addition to its name to distinguish it from nearby places also called Pool?

21. Your starter for 10:
Which EU member state is bounded by the River Prut to the north-east, the River Danube to the south, and the Black Sea to the east?

Three bonus questions on flour:
(a) What name is given to the unleavened crispbreads ground to make flour for use during the Jewish Passover?
(b) Flour from which cereal is used to make the variety of Chinese noodles called *fun*?
(c) Sometimes known as *kasha*, which flour is used

in North America and Eastern Europe for making
pancakes?

22. Your starter for 10:
In classical history, what number was indicated by the
word 'myriad'?

Three bonus questions on sea water:
(a) Which gulf is the northernmost arm of the Baltic Sea
and, as a result of the number of rivers flowing into
it, has such a low salinity that it is a habitat for many
freshwater fish?
(b) Dissolved salts account, on average, for what
percentage of the composition of sea water? You can
have two per cent either way.
(c) At 3.5 per cent salinity, what is the freezing point of sea
water, to the nearest degree Celsius?

23. Your starter for 10:
Defined by Brewer's *Phrase and Fable* as meaning
'persons of no note', what term might also refer jointly
to the title character of a novel of 1876 and friend of
Huckleberry Finn, George W. Bush's vice-president, and
the US president at the end of the Second World War?

Three bonus questions on the Medici family:
(a) Designed and begun by Giorgio Vasari in 1560, what
is the name of the building commissioned by the
Grand Duke of Tuscany, Cosimo I, to house the state's
government?
(b) Which member of the Medici family married the future
Henry II of France in 1533 and became the mother to
three future French kings, Francis II, Charles IX and
Henry III?
(c) In 1589, whom did the Grand Duke Ferdinand I
appoint as Professor of Mathematics at the University

of Pisa?

24. Your starter for 10:
What class of the phylum Chordata links the titles of works by Haruki Murakami, Maya Angelou, Daphne du Maurier and Harper Lee?

> **Three bonus questions on particle physics:**
> (a) What word, derived from the Greek for 'delicate', collectively denotes the fundamental particles of half integer spin that do not participate in the strong interaction?
> (b) The existence of which of the leptons was predicted as a result of the Dirac Equation, leading to the Nobel Prize for Physics being awarded to its discoverer Carl Anderson?
> (c) When a positron and an electron collide, what kind of particles are most likely to be produced as a result?

25. Your starter for 10:
'A virtual company with virtual profits' was how, in 2002, the *Financial Times* summed up which collapsed corporation, based in Houston, Texas and founded by Kenneth Lay.

> **Three bonus questions on Canada:**
> (a) A major business concern at the start of the twenty-first century, which trading company chartered in 1670 was once the de facto government of much of the land between the Arctic and the Great Lakes?
> (b) The first Governor of the Hudson's Bay Company, which nephew of Charles I gives his name to the territory that formerly comprised the Hudson Bay watershed, around forty per cent of present-day Canada?
> (c) Named after John, 1st Duke of Marlborough, and

used chiefly for grain exports, what is Canada's main seaport on Hudson Bay?

26. Your starter for 10:

Erythro-cytes, which are manufactured in bone marrow and whose primary function is the transport of oxygen and carbon dioxide in the blood, are also known by what common three-word name?

Three bonus questions on politics in the year 1910:

(a) Which Chancellor of the Exchequer was behind the 'People's Budget', which became law in April 1910 only after the King had threatened to create sufficient peers to carry it?

(b) In the same month a bill was introduced to abolish the House of Lords' veto on legislation. How was this known when it finally became law the following year?

(c) In November 1910, in an event known as Black Friday, campaigners clashed with police following the rejection of the first Conciliation Bill. What had the bill attempted to introduce?

27. Your starter for 10:

Said to be 'the largest number which has ever served a definite purpose in mathematics', which number is equal to 10^10^10^34 (i.e. 10 to the 10 to the 10 to the 34)?

Three bonus questions on an American river:

(a) Which major North American river has its source in Lake Itasca in Minnesota?

(b) Which city on the Mississippi river shares its name with the capital of the Egyptian Old Kingdom?

(c) *Life on the Mississippi* is an autobiographical work of 1883 by which writer, recalling his time as a steamboat pilot on the river?

28. **Your starter for 10:**

Derived from a word meaning 'servitude' or 'forced labour', what term was introduced into English in 1923 when the Czech writer Karel Capek's play *R.U.R.* was translated?

Three bonus questions on monarchs and their nicknames:

(a) Which British king reigned between 'the wisest fool in Christendom' and 'the Merry Monarch'?

(b) The English king who was the son of 'Curtmantle' and the grandfather of 'Longshanks' is usually known by what nickname?

(c) What was the blood relationship of 'the Grandmother of Europe' to 'the First Gentleman of Europe'?

29. **Your starter for 10:**

Dubbed 'the Big Dig', the Whitefriars project of 1999–2004 explored a large slice of the south-eastern part of which city, leading to speculation that the settlement originally developed around a religious sanctuary beside a ford over the River Stour?

Three bonus questions on characters who have appeared in different art forms:

(a) Which fictional character has been the subject of a ballet with music by Minkus which has been staged by Petipa, Nureyev and Baryshnikov, an opera by Massenet, and an ink drawing by Picasso?

(b) Which of Shakespeare's tragic heroes is the title character of operas by Verdi, Bloch and Sciarrino, and of a symphonic poem by Richard Strauss?

(c) Which fictional character has been the protagonist, in various languages, of a play by Molière, a poem by Byron, a novella by Hoffmann and an opera by Mozart?

30. Your starter for 10:

Keraunothnetophobia is the fear of what?

Three bonus questions on European universities:

(a) Its name meaning 'wisdom', which university in Rome was founded by Pope Boniface VIII in 1303 as Studium Urbis?

(b) What name links Spain's oldest existing university, dating to 1218, with an 1812 battle in which the Duke of Wellington reputedly defeated '40,000 Frenchmen in 40 minutes'?

(c) Founded by King Dinis and confirmed by a Papal Bull of Nicholas IV in 1290, the University of Coimbra is in which country?

> **'You live – for the questionable pleasure of the Quarter-Finals.'**

THE RULES

You all know the rules, so let's get
on with it.

Match Three

1. **Your starter for 10:**
Take any whole number greater than zero. If even, divide by two. If odd, multiply by three and add one, and repeat these operations on the resulting numbers. The as-yet unproven Collatz Conjecture of 1937 proposes that for all numbers this process converges at which number?

Three bonus questions on thousands:
(a) 'In questions of science, the authority of a thousand is not worth the humble reasoning of a single individual' is a remark attributed in Arago's *Eulogy* to which astronomer, born in Pisa in 1564?
(b) One of the five 'classics' in the flat racing calendar, the Thousand Guinea Stakes is run in April or May at which English racecourse?
(c) A line in the poem 'Kabul' by the seventeenth-century poet Sa'ib-e-Tabrizi gave which Afghan-born author the title of his novel *A Thousand Splendid Suns*?

2. **Your starter for 10:**
The gothic St Martin's Cathedral and the rococo Grassal-Kovich Palace are among the major buildings of which EU capital city? Situated on the River Danube, 60 kilometres from Vienna, it lies close to its country's borders with Austria and Hungary.

Three bonus questions on Roman poets:

(a) Which poet fought with Brutus and Cassius at Philippi in 42 BC, and is noted for the *Odes* and *Epodes*, which extol the virtues of friendship, love, good wine and a quiet life?

(b) The autobiographical poem 'Tristia' is a work of which poet, banished by Augustus, perhaps for having an affair with the emperor's granddaughter Julia? He is particularly known for his retelling of Greek and Roman myths.

(c) Perhaps best known for his poems addressed to a married woman known as 'Lesbia', which Roman poet's work also expresses a loathing for Julius Caesar?

3. **Your starter for 10:**

In his satirical essay of 1729, the 'Modest Proposal' of Jonathan Swift is that the poverty of the Irish be alleviated by the consumption of what?

Three bonus questions on a name:

(a) The nineteenth-century chemist James Marsh gives his name to the standard test for which toxic semi-metallic element with three allotropes: white, black and yellow?

(b) In 1871, Othniel Marsh led the party that discovered the first example found in the USA of which extinct reptile, characterised by an elongated fourth finger supporting a flight membrane?

(c) Born in 1877, the American metallurgist Albert Marsh was the first to devise a metal alloy for use as a durable and safe heating element, made of around ten per cent chromium and ninety per cent which metal?

4. **Your starter for 10:**

The name of which visible body part is contained in words meaning: the omission from a sentence of a word or phrase; a conic section in the form of a closed curve, and the obscuring of light from one celestial body by the presence of another?

Three bonus questions on Baroque composers:

(a) Born in 1659, the father is recognised as the founder of the Neapolitan school of opera. Born in 1685, the son is widely considered to be the father of modern keyboard technique. What is their surname?

(b) The suite known as *Water Music* or *Hamburg Ebb and Flow* is the work of which prolific composer, a friend of Handel, born in Magdeburg in 1681?

(c) *La Notte* and *La Tempesta di Mare* are among the concerti of which Venetian composer, ordained in 1703 and known as the Red Priest from the colour of his hair?

5.   Your starter for 10:

'If there is a god then he is a great mathematician.' These words are attributed to which British physicist, who shared the Nobel Prize for Physics in 1933 with Erwin Schrodinger?

Three bonus questions on quotations about work:

(a) In which novel does Jane Austen say 'There is nothing like employment, active indispensable employment, for relieving sorrow', and so her heroine Fanny Price 'had not time to be miserable'?

(b) 'I like work. It fascinates me. I can sit and look at it for hours.' These are the words of the narrator of which comic novel, first published in 1889?

(c) In a 1984 song by The Smiths, what follows the line 'I was looking for a job, and then I found a job...'?

6.   Your starter for 10:

In statistics, which goodness of fit test for any statistical distribution relies on the fact that the value of the sample cumulative density function is asymptotically normally distributed?

Three bonus questions on Europe:

(a) 'An iron curtain has descended across the continent,' said Winston Churchill of Europe in 1946, citing two seaports as its endpoints. One was Stettin, on the Baltic; which Adriatic seaport was the other?

(b) In his 'iron curtain' speech, which capital city did Churchill place 'behind' the Stettin-Trieste line, when geographically it lies around 60 kilometres to the west?

(c) A straight line drawn on the present-day map from Stettin to Trieste passes through Poland, Germany, the Czech Republic and three other EU member states. For five points, name two of them.

7. **Your starter for 10:**
Yangon, formerly Rangoon, is the capital of which country, officially renamed in 1989?

Three bonus questions on shared names:

(a) Although spelled differently, what forename and surname are shared by a former Director of the National Gallery and author of *Civilisation*, and a former Conservative Chancellor of the Exchequer?

(b) Again spelled differently, what forename and surname are shared by a nineteenth-century German composer, and the French statesman who in 1950 proposed a plan to pool the coal and steel resources of Western Europe?

(c) And finally, the thirteenth-century historian and author of *Chronica Majora*, and a columnist and former Conservative MP?

8. **Your starter for 10:**
An early defeat for US forces in the Mediterranean

theatre in the Second World War, in what present-day country did the Battle of Kasserine Pass take place?

Three bonus questions on smoked fish:
In each case give the name of the fish used in each product:
(a) Which fish is salted and hot-smoked to produce Arbroath Smokies?
(b) The fish used to produce lox may be simply salt-cured with spices, but in Scandinavia and Scotland it is more generally salted and then cold-smoked. What fish is used?
(c) Regarded by some as the best example of this type of smoked fish, what fish is lightly salted and cold-smoked to produce Manx kippers?

9. **Your starter for 10:**
An example being a noble gas, a substance that does not undergo chemical reactions is said to be what?

Three bonus questions on A Midsummer Night's Dream by William Shakespeare:
Among those performing the play-within-the-play, what are the first names of the following Mechanicals?
(a) Bottom the Weaver.
(b) Starveling the Tailor.
(c) Quince the Carpenter.

10. **Your starter for 10:**
What were the location and date of the last Olympic Games when the UK came top of the medals table?

Three bonus questions on the Beijing Olympics:
(a) The 2008 Olympics in Beijing was the third time that the summer games had been held in Asia, after Seoul in South Korea in 1988 and which city in 1964?
(b) The new events added to the games in Beijing included

the women's competition in which 3,000-metre race?

(c) At the Beijing games, there were two sports open only to men. One was boxing; what team event was the other?

11.   Your starter for 10:

Which novel was first published in part in *The Russian Messenger* in 1865 under the title 'The Year 1805' and later in six volumes between 1868 and 1869?

Three bonus questions on a northern city:

(a) Which northern city was the site of a victory for Oliver Cromwell and his forces in a battle of 1648, and of a defeat for the Jacobites in 1715?

(b) In the 1850s, Charles Dickens visited Preston during a strike by cotton workers. Which of his novels published in 1854 is set in Coketown, which he partly based on Preston?

(c) Preston was, until the 1980s, home to the largest factory in Europe, producing which man-made textile fibre, made from cellulose and originally called 'artificial silk'?

12.   Your starter for 10:

What is the common name of the insect which is the disease vector transmitting *plasmodium vivax*, the causative organism of malaria?

Three questions on religion:

(a) Which term describes Jews who are descendants of those who lived in Spain and Portugal until their expulsion in 1492, and who preserve the Babylonian Jewish traditions rather than the Palestinian ones?

(b) Born into a Jewish family that had fled from Portugal, which Dutch philosopher was expelled from the Jewish community for heresy in the 1650s?

(c) A Sephardim and a champion of oppressed Jews, the nineteenth-century American poet Emma Lazarus is noted for her sonnet 'The New Colossus', inscribed on the base of which landmark?

13. Your starter for 10:
Now implying a scene of chaos or disorder, what word, in the singular, referred originally to a special kind of table or stall on which meat was placed for sale, and in the plural to a meat market, later coming to mean a slaughterhouse and then a scene of carnage, the word remaining still in the names of buildings and streets in Nottingham, Chesterfield and York?

Three bonus questions on European football:
(a) Which European country's premier league is known as the 'Eredivisie'?
(b) By what name is France's premier league known?
(c) In Italian football, what name is given to the trophy won by the club that tops Serie A?

14. Your starter for 10:
The yellowhammer belongs to which group of long-tailed songbirds, less variable in appearance than the finches, and whose other species include the corn, reed and snow?

Three bonus questions on Carolingian architecture:
(a) Consecrated in 805, the Palatine Chapel forms part of the cathedral of which German city, and is the reason for the city's French name?
(b) Reichenau Island, noted for examples of Carolingian architecture, is a World Heritage Site in which large lake, part of the River Rhine?
(c) An innovation of Carolingian builders, a monumental entrance to a church consisting of porches and towers,

often with a chapel above, is named after the direction it faces. What direction is this?

15. Your starter for 10:

Thought by some to be laughably pretentious, what Italian word has come to be used in the UK for a person who makes and serves espresso and similar beverages?

Three bonus questions on letters of the alphabet:

(a) In printing, which two successive letters of the alphabet are used as the standard units of measurement for spaces?

(b) Which two words, differing only in the positions of the letters 'm' and 'n', are the English term for a Kantian contradiction in cosmology and the name of chemical element number 51?

(c) The name of which town in the Central Lowlands of Scotland differs from that of its historic county by being spelt with an 'm' rather than an 'n'?

16. Your starter for 10:

What office of state links Plantagenet Palliser, in the title of an Anthony Trollope novel of 1876, and Jim Hacker, in a television series of 1986?

Three bonus questions on room numbers:

(a) In George Orwell's *Nineteen Eighty-Four*, which room held the worst thing in the world for whomever was confined there?

(b) Who first presented BBC Two's *Room 101*, on which guests had to explain their pet hates for consignment to Room 101?

(c) Room 101 of the Crown Hotel in Amersham made an appearance as Room 12 of The Boatman in which film comedy, released in 1994?

17. **Your starter for 10:**
Examples including Sudbury in Canada and Popigai in Russia, what term for an eroded impact crater can be translated as 'star wound'?

Three bonus questions on buildings in Italian cities:
(a) In an Italian city, which building is frequently called *il Duomo*?
(b) Which building is the *municipio* or *palazzo communale*?
(c) What name is given to a bell tower, usually detached from the church?

18. **Your starter for 10:**
The Galapagos islands fall under the jurisdiction of which country?

Three bonus questions on edible legumes:
(a) Which tinned staple food was first test-marketed in the North of England in 1901 by H.J. Heinz of Pittsburgh?
(b) Which member of the bean family is grown in Britain for its red flowers and its pods, which are eaten green and immature?
(c) Which Greek mathematician supposedly said, 'Eating beans is a crime equal to eating the heads of one's parents'?

19. **Your starter for 10:**
What precedes the word 'Crimes' in the title of a 1996 set of stories by E. Annie Proulx in which various immigrants to America are linked together by the musical instrument in question?

Three bonus questions on eyes:
(a) Which author's third novel was set in Cornwall and was published in 1873 with the title *A Pair of Blue*

Eyes?

(b) Who wrote *The Lonely Girl*, the second in her *Country Girls* trilogy? It was renamed *The Girl with Green Eyes* in 1963.

(c) Which group was formed in 1989 by Paul Heaton, and had a minor hit in 1992 with 'Old Red Eyes Is Back'?

20. Your starter for 10:

Quote: 'The Soviet troops are assisting the… people to retain their independence from imperialism.' These words from the London *Daily Worker* refer to an uprising in which European country in November 1956?

Three bonus questions on the Nobel Peace Prize:

(a) Which British Foreign Secretary received the Nobel Peace Prize for negotiating the 1925 Locarno pact? His younger brother later became Prime Minister.

(b) Arthur Henderson, a campaigner for disarmament who was awarded the prize in 1934, served as Home Secretary in 1924 and as Foreign Secretary from 1929 to 1931 in the administrations of which Prime Minister?

(c) A founder and president of the international peace campaign awarded the Nobel Prize in 1937, Robert Cecil was the son of a Prime Minister usually known by what title of nobility?

21. Your starter for 10:

Fludd and *Beyond Black* are works by which British writer, whose novel *Wolf Hall*, an account of Thomas Cromwell's rise to power in the court of Henry VIII, was published in 2009?

Three bonus questions on political poets:

(a) Which poet became secretary to the Lord Deputy of Ireland in 1580, and acquired Kilcolman Castle in

. Cork where he worked on the epic poem for which he is best known?

(b) Which post in the Commonwealth Council of State was held by John Milton from shortly after the execution of Charles I until the Restoration?

(c) In 1586, while serving as Governor of Flushing in the Netherlands, Sir Philip Sidney was mortally wounded in a skirmish at the walls of which Spanish-held city?

22. Your starter for 10:

Probably born in Devon in about 675 and originally named Winfrid or Wynfrith, which missionary became the patron saint of Germany, where he preached to non-Christian peoples before his martyrdom in what is now the Netherlands?

Three bonus questions on basic concepts of mathematics:

(a) What short mathematical term denotes a collection of objects such as numbers or points in space, two such collections being equal if and only if they have precisely the same members?

(b) 'Greater than' in arithmetic, 'adjacent to' in graph theory and 'congruent to' in geometry are all examples of which mathematical concept, defined formally as a set of ordered pairs?

(c) What name is given to a binary relation in which the first element of each ordered pair is unique, and is more commonly thought of as a map or transformation between sets?

23. Your starter for 10:

In the early twentieth century, the Swedish oceanographer Walfrid Ekman recognised the importance of which effect, caused by the Earth's rotation, on ocean currents? He showed that it can be responsible for surface water moving at an angle to the prevailing wind direction.

Three bonus questions on an author:

(a) Sometimes used as a university text, *Ways of Seeing* is a 1972 work on western cultural aesthetics by which British-born art critic and novelist, a resident of France since the mid 1970s?

(b) Subtitled *A Story in Letters* and set in an unnamed country, which 2008 novel by John Berger was long-listed for the Booker Prize and tells of the pharmacist A'ida and her lover, the imprisoned insurgent Xavier?

(c) Its title consisting of a single letter, which novel by John Berger won the Booker Prize in 1972?

24. Your starter for 10:
The name of which class of organic compounds is contained within the names of two cathedral cities on the River Severn, one on the River Dee, and one on the River Itchen in Hampshire?

Three bonus questions on Latin expressions beginning with the preposition 'ex':

(a) Meaning 'from favour', what Latin expression refers to the paying of money out of a sense of moral obligation, rather than as a legal requirement?

(b) Meaning 'from the teacher's chair', what two-word expression means 'with the full authority of office', and is particularly used of Papal pronouncements?

(c) What two words appear on bookplate inscriptions showing the owner of the book?

25. Your starter for 10:
Which Russian mathematician is best known for his work on the theory of stochastic processes, especially those in which the previous states are irrelevant for

predicting the subsequent states, given knowledge of the current state?

Three bonus questions on US national historic landmarks:
In each case, name the state in which the following are located:
(a) The Bunker Hill Monument, and Lexington Green.
(b) The Martin Luther King Historic District, and the Dixie Coca-Cola Bottling Company Plant.
(c) The Lowell Observatory, and the Navajo Nation Council Chamber.

26. Your starter for 10:
Founded by Walter Gropius in Weimar in 1919, which school of applied art and architecture focused on design that took into account the nature of materials employed and the functionality of the object?

Three bonus questions on a contemporary artist and his models:
(a) Kathleen – or Kitty – Garman was the daughter of the sculptor Jacob Epstein and the first wife of which British artist? She sat for his portrait of her, *Girl with a White Dog*, in 1951.
(b) According to the title of Lucian Freud's painting of her which sold for over £17 million in 2008, Sue Tilley has what specific job title?
(c) Which Australian-born performance artist was the subject of many paintings by Lucian Freud in the early 1990s?

27. Your starter for 10:
What links the giving of Maundy money, Ladies' Day at Ascot and UK general elections since 1935?

Three bonus questions on the dramatist Caryl Churchill:

(a) What title did Caryl Churchill give to her play of 1987, satirising the excesses of those involved in the British stock market?

(b) What phrase, meaning a state of ecstasy, was the title of Churchill's play set first in Victorian colonial Africa and then in London in 1979, by which time the characters have aged only twenty-five years?

(c) Which play of 1982 concerned an eponymous employment agency for women, its characters including the ninth-century Pope Joan, the Victorian traveller Isabella Bird, and Chaucer's 'Patient Griselda'?

28. Your starter for 10:

Conductive keratoplasty costs about $1,500, lasts three minutes and uses radio waves to correct for types of what?

Three bonus questions on SI prefixes:

In each case, give the power of ten represented by the following:

(a) Exa-.

(b) Pico-.

(c) Giga-.

29. Your starter for 10:

What word follows 'International', in the title of a 1926 work by Goldsworthy Lowes Dickinson; 'Culture', in a volume of essays by Matthew Arnold; 'Mask' in a poem by Shelley and appears before 'UK' in a 1976 single by the Sex Pistols?

Three bonus questions on Canada:

(a) Excluding the five Great Lakes, three lakes in Canada have an area greater than that of Wales. For five points, name two of them.

(b) Flowing around 1,800 kilometres from the Great Slave Lake to the Arctic Ocean, which is Canada's longest river?

(c) For five points, name every country in the world that has a land area greater than that of Canada.

30. Your starter for 10:
In zoology, the term 'prehensile' indicates that a limb or tail is capable of doing what?

Three bonus questions on game birds:
(a) *Coturnix coturnix* is not legal quarry in the UK but is our only migratory game bird and has what common name?

(b) *Perdix perdix* is often described as the English or 'grey' variety of which game bird, to distinguish it from its red-legged French counterpart?

(c) *Gallinago gallinago* is which game bird, its zigzagging flight making it a challenging target and so giving rise to a term for one skilled in shooting?

'Well, bad luck – we're going to be saying goodbye to you. But you've been an entertaining team to watch, even if you've always seemed astonished that you're still in the competition!'

THE RULES

Right, let's get on with it, here's your
first starter for 10.

Match Four

1. Your starter for 10:
Fort Sumter, scene of the first action of the American
Civil War, is in which historic city of South Carolina?
The setting of the opera *Porgy and Bess*, it also gives its
name to a social jazz dance of the 1920s.

> **Three bonus questions on a film-maker:**
> (a) Said to be loosely autobiographical and concerning
>   two unemployed actors in the 1960s, the 1987 film
>   *Withnail and I* was written and directed by which
>   British film-maker?
> (b) Bruce Robinson made his debut as a screenplay writer
>   with which Oscar-winning movie of 1984, set in
>   Cambodia?
> (c) After a hiatus of over fifteen years, Robinson returned
>   to directing with an adaptation of *The Rum Diary*, a
>   novel about expat journalists in 1950s Puerto Rico by
>   which American author?

2. Your starter for 10:
Whose career with the British merchant navy began in
1878 at the age of 21, and ended in 1894, by which time
he had received British citizenship and embarked on a
literary career, his first novel, *Almayer's Folly*, appearing
in 1895?

Three bonus questions on raw cuisine:

(a) What two-word term describes a dish of raw minced beef, onion and seasoning, sometimes served with a raw egg yolk?

(b) Literally meaning 'pierce flesh', which Japanese dish consists of raw fish cut into very thin slices?

(c) What name is given to the South American dish of raw fish marinated in citrus juices?

3. **Your starter for 10:**
Quote: 'As valorous as Hector of Troy, worth five of Agamemnon and ten times better than the Nine Worthies.' In Shakespeare's *Henry IV Part Two*, this is Doll Tearsheet's somewhat generous assessment of which character?

Three bonus questions on contemporary photographers:

(a) Born in 1935 and perhaps best known for his work in war zones, which British photographer's portraits of impoverished urban Britain were exhibited at Bradford's National Media Museum during 2009?

(b) Having worked as a freelancer for the *Sunday Times* and *Time* magazine, which photojournalist was given exclusive access to Tony Blair's election campaign in 1997? His more recent work on Africa's AIDS pandemic has been widely published and exhibited.

(c) In July 2009, as part of the global 'Hear the World' initiative, the Saatchi Gallery exhibited photos of celebrities taken by which Canadian singer-songwriter and photographer?

4. **Your starter for 10:**
Near the modern port of Bodrum in Turkey, which city of ancient Caria was the birthplace of the historian Herodotus and the site of the tomb of King Mausolus?

Three bonus questions on place names:

(a) Its capital Kohima, the state of Nagaland is in which country?

(b) The disputed region of Nagorno-Karabakh is *de jure* part of, and is entirely surrounded by, which post-Soviet state?

(c) Nagoya is the third-largest incorporated city in which country?

5. **Your starter for 10:**
Born in 1749, which French scientist's achievements include a five-volume work on celestial mechanics, an elaborated probability theory, and the first publication of the value of the Gaussian integral?

Three bonus questions on an adjective:

(a) Colonel Percy Fawcett's description of the Serra Ricardo Franco in Brazil inspired which novel of 1912 by Arthur Conan Doyle, about an imaginary range of mountains in which dinosaurs survived into the twentieth century?

(b) The so-called 'Lost Colony', an early British settlement whose inhabitants mysteriously disappeared between its founding in 1587 and the return of the expedition's leader in 1590, was located on which island in North Carolina?

(c) Which female writer coined the term 'the Lost Generation' for the US expats, including Hemingway and Scott Fitzgerald, who gathered at her salon in Paris in the 1920s?

6. **Your starter for 10:**
At a similar latitude to that of New York City, which city on the River Douro gives its name both to a European country and to a variety of rich fortified wine?

Three bonus questions on biochemistry:

(a) What name is given to the protein found in vertebrates typically consisting of four polypeptide chains each bound to a prosthetic group called porphyrin containing an iron atom?

(b) Haemocyanin, which performs a similar function to haemoglobin in many molluscs, is blue rather than red as a consequence of the presence of which metal instead of iron?

(c) Which vitamin is an organo-metallic compound containing an atom of cobalt at its centre?

7.   Your starter for 10:

The Ishihara test is used to detect what, being made up of eight test plates where numbers are made up of variously coloured dots?

Three bonus questions on long walks:

(a) *A Time of Gifts* is Patrick Leigh Fermor's account of the first part of a journey he undertook on foot, starting out in 1933 from the Hook of Holland with which city as his final destination?

(b) Which Welsh poet wrote *The Autobiography of a Supertramp*, published in 1908, an account of six years on the road in North America?

(c) What is the title of Laurie Lee's volume of autobiography, published in 1969, recounting his journey on foot from Gloucestershire to London and then through Spain on the eve of the Civil War?

8.   Your starter for 10:

Identify the author of these lines: 'Twas brillig, and the slithy toves / Did gyre and gimble in the wabe: / All mimsy were the borogoves, / And the mome raths outgrabe.'

Three bonus questions on Shakespeare:
For each of the following, identify the play from the characters listed in its *Dramatis Personae*:
(a) The Lords Ross, Willoughby and Fitzwalter; the Bishop of Carlisle; and Bushy, Bagot and Green, described as 'favourites' of the title character?
(b) Caphis, Philotus, Titus and Hortensius who are servants to the title character's creditors; and an old Athenian, three strangers, a page and a fool?
(c) Frederick, the usurper of the Duke's dominions; Celia, Frederick's daughter; Charles, his wrestler; and Audrey, a country wench?

9. Your starter for 10:
What is the name for the streamline flow of a fluid in which the fluid moves in layers without fluctuations or turbulence so that successive particles passing the same point have the same velocity?

Three bonus questions on Commonwealth capitals:
(a) Which Commonwealth country's capital is a federal territory known as the National Capital Territory or NCT, which is thought to have around 16 million residents?
(b) The capital of which Commonwealth country is the centre of a federal territory known as ICT, the letter 'I' being the capital's initial letter?
(c) Australian Capital Territory, which includes the federal capital of Canberra, is completely surrounded by which state?

10. Your starter for 10:
Using their stinging tentacles to catch prey, the actinaria, rockpool animals closely related to jellyfish and coral, are known by what common two-word name?

Three questions on a sporting event:

(a) In July 2007, the newspaper *France Soir* carried a death notice claiming that which sporting event had 'died on 25 July 2007, at the age of 104, after a long illness...'?

(b) Following several expulsions for doping irregularities, which Spaniard emerged as the winner of the 2007 Tour de France?

(c) What name is given to the individual time trial that immediately precedes Stage One of the Tour de France, the winner wearing the yellow jersey for the first stage?

11. Your starter for 10:

Born in Alabama in 1966, which internet entrepreneur was the original creator of the free internet encyclopaedia Wikipedia?

Three bonus questions on seaports:

(a) Which port, the largest on Mexico's east coast, was occupied for seven months in 1914 by US forces during the Mexican revolution?

(b) Sfax is a major port on the Gulf of Gabes and the second-largest city in which North African country?

(c) Founded by Greeks in the seventh century BC, Durres is the principal port of which country on the Adriatic?

12. Your starter for 10:

Boyle's Law relates the volume of a gas to what other property of that gas?

Three bonus questions on a historian:

(a) 'Human beings are not efficiently designed for a capitalist system of production.' Which historian wrote these words in the 1994 work *The Age of Extremes*?

(b) What three words does Hobsbawm use to describe the time span of 'the age of extremes', namely the years

1914 to 1991?

(c) Give the single word, descriptive of a broad political philosophy, that completes this observation by Hobsbawm: 'The paradox of communism in power was that it was...' what?

13. Your starter for 10:

In which English county are the non-metropolitan districts of Rushcliffe, Broxtowe, Bassetlaw and Gedling?

Three bonus questions on a quotation:

(a) 'If I have seen further [than certain other men] it is by standing upon the shoulders of giants.' Who said this in a letter of 1675 to the scientist Robert Hooke?

(b) 'A dwarf standing on the shoulders of a giant may see farther than a giant himself.' These are the words of which author, in the 1621 work *The Anatomy of Melancholy*?

(c) 'Standing on the shoulders of giants' is an inscription found on which everyday object?

14. Your starter for 10:

Its name derived from the Latin for 'sausage', what severe form of food poisoning affects the central nervous system and is often contracted from spoiled meat?

Three bonus questions on artists:

(a) Thomas Girtin, John Sell Cotman and John Robert Cozens were leading English painters at the turn of the nineteenth century in which medium?

(b) A group of landscape painters in the early nineteenth century including John Crome and John Sell Cotman formed the nucleus of a celebrated school named after which English city?

(c) The English watercolourist, Thomas Girtin, who died

aged 27 in 1802, inspired the remark 'If Tom Girtin had lived, I should have starved' from which leading artist?

15. **Your starter for 10:**
A strategic route controlling ocean traffic to the oil terminals of the Gulf, which sea passage between Iran and the Musandam Peninsula of Oman links the Arabian Gulf to the Arabian Sea?

> **Three bonus questions on fishing:**
> (a) Which city between Mansfield and Leicester has given its name to both a style of fishing and a reel?
> (b) Which ecclesiastical term, also applied to a type of artificial fly, is used for the short, wooden mallet used to kill a fish when it has been landed?
> (c) What term is used for a fishing line with hooks or groups of hooks attached at intervals, because of its assumed resemblance to a rosary?

16. **Your starter for 10:**
Used to add tensile strength to steel, which silver-white metallic element, atomic number 23, was given its present name by Nils Sefstrom after the Norse goddess of love and beauty, more often called Freya?

> **Three bonus questions on a number:**
> (a) In music, what two-word term is used for the interval from A up to G Flat?
> (b) Which battle of 25 June 1876 resulted in a catastrophic defeat for the US Seventh Cavalry?
> (c) Which group topped the album charts in April 1988 with *Seventh Son of a Seventh Son*?

17. **Your starter for 10:**
What is the former institutional name for the thirty-

three British universities founded in 1992?

Three bonus questions on the edge:

(a) Which poet is the author of 'Come to the Edge', a copy of which the Irish President Mary McAleese had hand-painted onto the outfit she wore for her inauguration?

(b) *Postcards from the Edge* was the semi-autobiographical novel by which actress, about her relationship with her mother, Debbie Reynolds?

(c) Known as 'The Edge', what is the real name of U2's guitarist?

18. **Your starter for 10:**
Originally appointed in the sixteenth century to take over the military duties of the sheriff, holders of what honorary office serve as the representatives of the Crown for each county of the United Kingdom, their duties nowadays being largely ceremonial?

Three bonus questions on controversial photographs:

(a) What did the cousins Elsie Wright and Frances Griffiths claim to have photographed in their garden in Cottingley in 1917?

(b) What did the London surgeon George Spicer claim to have photographed on 1 April 1933?

(c) A photograph taken by Roger Patterson at Bluff Creek, California, in 1967, purports to depict which creature?

19. **Your starter for 10:**
Author of the books *Silence* and *A Year from Monday*, which American composer's musical works include *Living Room Music*, *Imaginary Landscapes*, *Number Pieces*, and the 1952 piece *4'33"*?

Three bonus questions on symbols:

(a) In the international code of signals used in maritime

communication and revised in 1969, the letter 'i' is
represented as a black dot on a field of which colour?

(b) What is the name of the symbol introduced in Germany
in 1991 and later adopted by other countries, which
tells consumers that the manufacturers of a product
contribute to the cost of recovery and recycling?

(c) Which British-based anti-television organisation claims
that watching TV causes lethargy and unhappiness
in viewers, and organises events in which people are
encouraged to turn off and talk to their neighbours
instead?

20. Your starter for 10:
Named after its crescent shape, the lunate bone forms
part of which joint of the human body?

Three bonus questions on the song 'Bohemian Rhapsody' by Queen:
In each case, identify the word featured in the lyrics from
its definition:

(a) A lively Spanish or Spanish-American dance in triple
time, performed by a pair of dancers accompanied by
guitars and castanets.

(b) A French name denoting a stock character of the
Commedia dell'arte who is an easily frightened,
cowardly braggart.

(c) An Arabic expression meaning 'in the name of God'.

21. Your starter for 10:
Often meeting in pubs to read aloud their own work,
C.S. Lewis, J.R.R. Tolkien and Nevill Coghill were
among the writers who were part of which informal
literary group?

Three bonus questions on a shared prefix:
(a) What is the term for a light, such as one in a lighthouse

or buoy, which shines for a longer period than that for which it is cut off?

(b) In dentistry, occlusion refers to the way that surfaces of the teeth do what?

(c) Occlumency, the ability to compartmentalise one's mental processes in order to avoid unwelcome psychic intrusion, is an extra-curricular skill taught in which fictional world?

22. Your starter for 10:

What three-letter adjective links: Georges Lemaître's 'hypothesis of the primeval atom'; the part of the connecting rod that is attached to the crankshaft in a car; and the North American name for the constellation also known as the Plough?

Three bonus questions on the cold war:

(a) Which world leader was described by Harold Macmillan in 1959 as 'a sort of mixture between Peter the Great and Lord Beaverbrook'?

(b) In 1958, of which city did Khrushchev say, 'When I want to make the West scream, [that's where] I squeeze'?

(c) 'Whether you like it or not, history is on our side. We will bury you.' Khrushchev said these words in the aftermath of which crisis of 1956?

23. Your starter for 10:

Which regular polyhedron has twenty vertices, thirty edges and twelve faces?

Three bonus questions on a saint:

(a) Of the national patron saints of the British isles, which is the only one generally regarded as having been born in the country with which he is associated?

(b) In which Welsh county, of which he is also the patron

saint, is St David buried in the city named after him?

(c) Now much disputed, a claim in a hagiography of the late eleventh century attributes to St David the founding of which abbey in Somerset?

24. Your starter for 10:

Which Romantic poet is the subject of biographies by Walter Jackson Bate, Robert Gittings and Andrew Motion?

Three bonus questions on food plants:

(a) Which basic foodstuff is obtained from two completely unrelated sources, a tall tropical grass native to Asia and, in temperate regions, a root crop in the same family as spinach?

(b) What is the name given to the eight-pointed dried fruit of the Chinese tree *illicium verum*? It has a flavour of liquorice despite not being closely related either to it, or to similar-tasting plants such as fennel?

(c) A coarse, dark type of flour often used for making pancakes comes from which plant that, despite its name, is not a true cereal but is related to rhubarb?

25. Your starter for 10:

An enneagram has how many points?

Three bonus questions on measurements:

(a) What is measured by the scale named after Frederick Mohs, who devised it in the early nineteenth century?

(b) What is measured by the derived SI unit katal, which is expressed in moles per second?

(c) A temperature of 212 degrees Fahrenheit corresponds to what on the Kelvin scale?

26. Your starter for 10:

Which major work of twentieth-century poetry has

sections named after a house in the Cotswolds, a Somerset village, a religious community and a small group of rocks off the north-east coast of Cape Ann in Massachusetts?

Three bonus questions on post-Reformation English prelates:
In each case, give the name of the monarch during whose reign the following were Archbishop of Canterbury:
(a) Matthew Parker, Edmund Grindal and John Whitgift.
(b) Archibald Campbell Tait, Edward White Benson and Frederick Temple.
(c) George Abbot and William Laud.

27. Your starter for 10:
According to the international weather-observing codes, what is defined as a cloud of small water droplets near ground level and sufficiently dense to reduce visibility to less than 1,000 metres?

Three bonus questions on taxation:
(a) What was the name of the tax to support the Navy levied by the English Crown on coastal districts until it was abolished by Parliament in 1641?
(b) Income tax was first introduced in Britain during the administration of which Prime Minister?
(c) During which decade was Value Added Tax introduced in the UK in place of Purchase Tax?

28. Your starter for 10:
Which fairground attraction takes its name from its inventor, a Pittsburgh bridge engineer, who introduced it at the Columbia World Fair in 1893 as a means of getting an elevated view over the grounds?

Three bonus questions on political memoirs:

(a) Published in 2004, *An Honourable Deception?* is the title of the memoirs of which politician who resigned from the Cabinet in 2003?

(b) Evoking the title of a novel by Jane Austen, which three words form the main title of the memoirs of the former Conservative minister Jonathan Aitken, published in 2000?

(c) Which Labour Cabinet minister, who died in 2005, is the subject of the book *Momentum: The Struggle for Peace, Politics and the People*?

29. **Your starter for 10:**

In biology, what is the common name for *oligochaetes* of the genus *lumbricus*, which inhabit the soil?

Three bonus questions linked by a place:

(a) Which present-day administrative region of France is the only one to share its border with Belgium, Luxembourg and Germany?

(b) Which city was, from the twelfth century to 1766, the capital of the independent Duchy of Lorraine?

(c) The Cross of Lorraine, with a double bar, is also known by what name, after the French general who adopted it as a symbol during the Second World War?

30. **Your starter for 10:**

'Few thought he was even a starter, there were many who thought themselves smarter. / But he ended P.M. / C.H. and O.M. / An Earl and a Knight of the Garter.' Which contemporary of Churchill is said to have penned this verse about himself?

Three bonus questions on wildernesses:

(a) 'They make a wilderness and call it peace.' Which Roman historian ascribed these words to the

Caledonian leader Calgacus before battle against Agricola's army?
(b) '... the enclosing a wilderness of idea within a wall of words.' What is the author Samuel Butler describing here?
(c) 'As I walked through the wilderness of this world'; which much-reprinted work of 1678 begins with these words?

'When you got going, you really got going, so we shall look forward to seeing you in the Quarter-Finals.'

THE RULES

OK, let's get on with it … here's your first starter for 10.

Match Five

1. Your starter for 10:
From an Arabic term meaning 'dry land', what name is given to the arid, fertile plateau around 2,000 feet above sea level, lying to the south of Madrid between the region of La Alcarria and the Sierra Morena? In Cervantes' novel, it is home to Don Quixote.

Three bonus questions on fictional pigs:
(a) Which fictional pig was credited as the author on the cover of an encyclopaedia of food published in 1932, the actual author being Hugh Lofting, who had featured the animal in several of the Doctor Doolittle stories?
(b) In the novels of P.G. Wodehouse, Lord Emsworth's prize-winning sow, the Empress of Blandings, is a remarkably plump specimen of which breed of pig?
(c) Which prize boar, described in *Animal Farm* as a purebred Middle White, is exhibited by the Joneses under the show name of 'Willingdon Beauty'?

2. Your starter for 10:
What regnal name is shared by kings of France nicknamed 'the simple', 'the bald', 'the wise', 'the mad' and 'the victorious'?

Three bonus questions on a field of science:
(a) A tutor of Richard Dawkins, the Dutch academic

Niko Tinbergen helped pioneer the application of which evolutionary theory to early animal and human behaviour?

(b) Which Austrian, who shared the 1973 Nobel Prize in Medicine with Tinbergen and Karl von Frisch, is usually credited with laying the foundations of modern ethology in the early 1930s? His works include *On Aggression* in 1966.

(c) Which English zoologist helped popularise ethology in the 1960s with his book *The Naked Ape*?

3. Your starter for 10:
Sometimes known as Tironian writing, the codified system devised by Marcus Tullius Tiro around 63 BC and widely used for over a thousand years was a script of a type now known as what?

Three bonus questions on baseball:
(a) Quote: 'A ball player has to be kept hungry to become a big leaguer. That's why no boy from a rich family has ever made the big leagues.' To which American sports star is this observation attributed?

(b) In baseball, the tactic of hitting a ball short to the infield to enable the runner on third base to break for the home plate is known by what two-word term?

(c) Which Canadian team defeated the Atlanta Braves in 1992 to become the first non-US team to win baseball's world series?

4. Your starter for 10:
Giving your answer in radians, what is the argument of the complex number one plus i square root 3, where i is the square root of minus one?

Three bonus questions on oceanic ridges:
(a) The Ninety East Ridge, which, as its name suggests, lies

on the ninety degrees east meridian, is in which ocean?

(b) Having an area of over 100,000 square kilometres, which island straddling the Mid-Atlantic Ridge was formed by volcanic outpourings, and is slowly getting wider as a result of plate tectonic activity?

(c) The Nazca Ridge and the Cocos Ridge both lie in which ocean?

5. **Your starter for 10:**
From the Latin for 'white', what name is given to the measure of reflectivity of a surface or body, i.e. the ratio of total electromagnetic radiation reflected to the total amount incident upon it?

> **Three bonus questions on national museums:**
>
> (a) In which city is Deepdale Stadium, the oldest continuously used professional football league ground in the world and the site of the National Football Museum?
>
> (b) In which northern city is the National Media Museum, formerly the National Museum of Photography, Film and Television?
>
> (c) Which museum is the oldest in the UK and is split across three sites, a museum in Leeds, Fort Nelson in Portsmouth, and the Tower of London?

6. **Your starter for 10:**
One of the world's major private art collections, the J. Paul Getty Museum is located in which resort to the west of Los Angeles, noted for its surf and secluded beaches?

> **Three bonus questions on a Greek prefix:**
>
> (a) In chemistry, which prefix, derived from the Greek for 'straight', is used to indicate that substituted atoms or groups on a benzene ring are adjacent?

(b) In entomology, *orthoptera*, meaning 'straight wings', is the name of the order which in the UK consists predominantly of two groups of insects. For five points, name either.

(c) In medicine, orthopaedics was originally the process of straightening out deformities caused by injury or disease in which group of people?

7.   Your starter for 10:
In terms of the letters they contain, what feature is shared by six-letter words including 'chintz', 'almost', 'abhors' 'ghosty', 'effort' and 'billow'?

Three bonus questions on war photographers:
(a) The Englishman Roger Fenton covered which nineteenth-century conflict as the world's first accredited war photographer?

(b) Born Andrei Friedmann in Budapest, which photojournalist was killed by a landmine in Indochina in 1954?

(c) Robert Capa and Henri Cartier-Bresson were among the war photographers who founded which photographic co-operative in 1947?

8.   Your starter for 10:
'Always use a small saucepan', 'always use a kitchen timer' and 'never have the water fast boiling' are three of the rules for cooking what on Delia Smith's website?

Three bonus questions on linguistics:
In each case, give the term from its definition, and the answer in each case contains the Greek-derived component 'gloss' or 'glott':
(a) The geographical boundary or delineation of a certain linguistic feature.

(b) The use of two or more varieties of language for

different purposes in the same community, for example classical Arabic and local colloquial Arabic in North Africa.

(c) Represented in the International Phonetic Alphabet by a dotless question mark, the consonant sound which is made by bringing the vocal cords tightly together and releasing them suddenly?

9. Your starter for 10:

What adjective meaning 'faithful', 'unchanging' or 'dependable' is used in mathematics as a noun to indicate a component of a relationship between variables that does not change its value?

Three bonus questions on conflicts:

(a) The war between Austria and Prussia in 1866, which culminated in the Prussian victory at the Battle of Sadowa, is usually known by what name, because of its approximate duration?

(b) At the end of the Seven Years War in 1763, which territory, now a US state, did Spain cede to Britain in exchange for Cuba?

(c) The Seven Day War, so called because of the length of time it took for Israeli forces to take possession of the Sinai Peninsula, was part of which larger conflict of 1956?

10. Your starter for 10:

Which part of the eye is affected by macular degeneration?

Three questions about bacteria:

(a) Which term means 'disease-causing' and is applied to bacteria capable of causing disease?

(b) Including monocytes in the blood and macrophages in the tissues, what term is used for cells that envelop and digest bacteria cells?

(c) The bacteria *Staphylococcus aureus* has developed a resistance to the antibiotic methicillin, giving rise to which 'superbug' infection?

11. **Your starter for 10:**

Noted for his roles in *The Hustler* and *Dr Strangelove*, who became the first actor to refuse an Oscar, as best actor in the 1971 film *Patton*?

Three bonus questions on English words from the French, all of which begin with an 'é':

In each case give the word from its definition:

(a) A word of four letters meaning enthusiastic vigour, distinctive style, flair, impetuosity or dash?

(b) A short musical composition or exercise, usually for one instrument, designed to train or test a player's technique?

(c) A political exile, in particular those aristocrats who fled as a result of the French or Russian revolutions?

12. **Your starter for 10:**

According to the Old Testament, which place is the source of the river that divides into four heads – the Pishon, Gihon, Tigris and Euphrates?

Three bonus questions on an adjective:

(a) The Land of Take-What-You-Want, the Land of Treats and the less pleasant Land of Dame Slap are to be found at the top of which eponymous tree, the creation of Enid Blyton?

(b) 'A quarrel in a faraway country between people of whom we know nothing'. These words of Neville Chamberlain refer to which state, declared independent in October 1918?

(c) *Faraway Hill*, first broadcast on US television in 1946, is often claimed to have been the first of what pervasive genre of TV programme?

13. **Your starter for 10:**
Choudhary Rahmat Ali, a law student at Emmanuel College, Cambridge during the 1930s, is generally credited with having invented the name of which modern state?

Three bonus questions on kings' reigns:
(a) Of the six British kings called George, which one had the longest reign?
(b) Of the eight English or British kings called Edward, which one had the longest reign?
(c) Of the eight kings of England called Henry, which one had the longest reign?

14. **Your starter for 10:**
Sagittarius A* is a source of X-rays and other radiation in the centre of our galaxy, and is thought to harbour what kind of object, which in this case has a mass between two and five million times that of the sun?

Three bonus questions on duelling:
(a) Which French mathematician, noted for his contribution to the part of higher algebra known as group theory, was killed in a duel in Paris in 1832?
(b) Later prime minister, which statesman fought a duel with Viscount Castlereagh in 1809?
(c) In which Russian novel does Pierre Bezuhov fight a duel which both participants survive?

15. **Your starter for 10:**
Yang Kaihui, executed by nationalist forces in 1930, He Zizhen, divorced in 1939, and Jiang Qing, who outlived him, were wives of which political figure?

Three bonus questions on a name:

(a) Under what pseudonym did composer Robert Bruce Montgomery write detective stories featuring Gervase Fen?

(b) Which battle was fought on St Crispin's Day, 25 October 1415?

(c) Sir Crispin Tickell was British Permanent Representative to which body from 1987 to 1990?

16. **Your starter for 10:**
Committed to the overthrow of 'bourgeois' society, which terrorist group was formed in Italy in 1969 and nine years later kidnapped and murdered the former Italian Prime Minister Aldo Moro?

Three staggering bonus questions:

(a) Which is the shortest Olympic distance run from a staggered start?

(b) 'Blind staggers' affects animals who have eaten grasses, especially rye, blighted by which fungal disease?

(c) In the 1994 film *Staggered*, who plays a character abandoned naked on a remote Scottish beach after his stag night?

17. **Your starter for 10:**
Which Nordic capital gives its name to an interpretation of quantum mechanics that had strong acceptance among physicists for much of the twentieth century?

Three bonus questions on Africa, specifically those countries that share land frontiers with two and only two others:
In each case, name the country from its two neighbours:

(a) South Africa and Mozambique.

(b) Liberia and Guinea.

(c) Algeria and Libya.

18. **Your starter for 10:**
    Quote: 'If happiness, then, is activity expressing virtue, it is reasonable for it to express the supreme virtue, which will be the virtue of the best thing.' These are the words of which Greek philosopher, in his *Nichomachean Ethics*?

    Three bonus questions on the plays of Tom Stoppard:
    (a) Which play begins with the election victory of the Radical Liberal Party? Its characters include the moral philosopher George Moore, and his wife Dotty, a former musical comedy actress?
    (b) Switching between Prague and Cambridge between 1968 and 1990, which play centres around a Czech PhD student and a British Marxist philosophy don? It also features a band called the Plastic People of the Universe.
    (c) Set in the country house of Sidley Park in both the present day and in 1809, which play touches upon subjects such as landscape gardening and Fermat's Last Theorem?

19. **Your starter for 10:**
    In 1945, which Chairman of the Labour Party lost a libel suit against the *Newark Advertiser* when it reported that he had advocated the use of violence to promote the political aims of socialism?

    Three bonus questions on alloys:
    (a) Britannia metal is an alloy composed primarily of tin with about two per cent copper and approximately seven per cent of which toxic element, commonly found in the ore stibnite?
    (b) Which German chemist, born in 1866, gives his name to magnetic alloys composed of metals that, in their pure state, are not magnetic?

(c) Brass is an alloy of copper and which blue-white metal?

20. Your starter for 10:
Which sixteenth-century English composer's works include 'Gaude gloriosa Dei mater', the Christmas Mass 'Puer natus est nobis', and the melody which inspired Vaughan Williams's *Fantasia* of 1910?

Three bonus questions on terms in 'Anglish':
This is a form of linguistic purism in which words are coined from Germanic roots to replace those of Romance or Greek origin. So, 'question' becomes 'ask-thing', and 'television' is 'sightcasting':
(a) In 'worldken' – that is, 'science' – 'sourstuff' and 'waterstuff' are among 'firststuffs'. For what basic scientific term is 'firststuff' an Anglish equivalent?
(b) 'Firststuffs' or elements figure largely in 'Uncleftish Beholding', an Anglish text by the US author Poul Anderson. Of what branch of physics is 'uncleftish beholding' an Anglish rendering?
(c) Poul Anderson names 'ymirstuff' as the heaviest 'firststuff'. How is it better known?

21. Your starter for 10:
Studied and named by Galileo in 1599, which curve is the locus of a point on the rim of a circle of radius *a* if the circle is rolled along a straight line?

Three bonus questions on a shared surname:
(a) Which American-born chess player took the world title from Boris Spassky in 1972 and defeated him again twenty years later in a much publicised rematch?
(b) The German baritone Dietrich Fischer-Dieskau performed in the premiere in 1962 of the *War Requiem* by which British composer, who wrote *The Songs and*

Proverbs of William Blake for him three years later?

(c) The Fischer-Tropsch Process is a method of obtaining which organic chemical compounds that are the principal constituents of petroleum and natural gas?

22. Your starter for 10:

Which member of the fictional band Gorillaz was delivered in a freight container after the other members advertised for a guitarist in the *New Musical Express*?

Three bonus questions on geological periods:

(a) Which geological period is the oldest to contain easily recognisable fossils, and derives its name from a Latin term for the part of Britain in which its rocks were first identified?

(b) The period from about 290 to 250 million years ago, which saw a mass extinction of marine life, is given what name, after a province in imperial Russia?

(c) Which range of mountains in France and Switzerland gives its name to the middle period of the Mesozoic era?

23. Your starter for 10:

In metallurgy, the coating process known as anodising is associated with which metal?

Three bonus questions on the cardiovascular system of mammals:

(a) What is the name of the vessel that carries de-oxygenated blood from the right ventricle of the heart to the lungs?

(b) Which vessel carries the absorbed products of digestion from the intestines directly to the liver?

(c) What is the largest blood vessel through which oxygenated blood leaves the left ventricle of the heart, and which branches to form supply arteries?

24. Your starter for 10:

Had he been known by his initials, as were JFK and LBJ, which post-war American president would have been JEC?

Three bonus questions on Tolstoy:

(a) What did Tolstoy describe as 'a human activity having for its purpose the transmission to others of the highest and best feelings to which men have risen'?

(b) In *War and Peace*, General Kutuzov says, 'The strongest of all warriors are these two: time and...' what quality?

(c) In a letter of 1871, what general category of writing did Tolstoy describe as 'an intellectual brothel from which there is no retreat'?

25. Your starter for 10:

What name links: Natty Bumppo in the novels of James Fenimore Cooper; Benjamin Pierce in the TV series *M*A*S*H*; and a virtual-reality tracking device used in cricket and tennis?

Three bonus questions on protests against death:

(a) Which Russian composer, who died in 1975, said of his fourteenth symphony, composed in 1969, 'The entire symphony is my protest against death'?

(b) Which poet wrote the lines 'Do not go gentle into that good night, / Old age should burn and rave at close of day; / Rage, rage against the dying of the light'?

(c) 'Death and taxes and childbirth! There's never any convenient time for any of them!' In which novel of 1936 does the heroine offer this observation?

26. Your starter for 10:

In biology, what name, from the Latin meaning wheel bearing, is given to the phylum of microscopic multi-cellular organisms characterised by the presence of a wheel-like ciliated organ used in swimming and feeding?

Three bonus questions on soil:

(a) Any soil high in calcium and magnesium carbonates, where leaching is slight, is called pedocal. What term describes a soil high in aluminium and iron oxides and from which bases have been leached?

(b) Often red in colour, what name is given to soils of the humid tropics characterised by a leaching of silica, a lack of humus, and an accumulation of iron and aluminium sesquioxides?

(c) The structure of soil can be determined when the proportion of three constituents is plotted on a triangular graph. For five points, name any one of them.

27. **Your starter for 10:**
In the USA, NASCAR is the sanctioning body of what branch of motorsports?

Three bonus questions on an artist:

(a) Described in one headline as 'Sex and Bling', the first major UK exhibition of works of which artist, born in Vienna in 1862, opened at Tate Liverpool in May 2008?

(b) Klimt was a leading figure in which artistic movement of the 1890s? It separated itself from academic art and developed decorative and opulent styles.

(c) 'Sezessionstil', or 'Secession style', is the name often used in Austria for what movement, usually denoted in Britain by what two-word French expression?

28. **Your starter for 10:**
What type of vessel are *Vanguard*, *Vengeance*, *Trenchant* and *Turbulent*, all successors to the Royal Navy's first

such vessel, *Holland I*, launched in 1901?

Three bonus questions on a German city:
(a) The *Almanach de Gotha*, first published in the city of that name in 1763, was a directory of the members and histories of what?
(b) The British royal house of Saxe-Coburg-Gotha dates from the accession of which king, the name of the house being that of the duchy of which his father was a prince?
(c) 'Critique of the Gotha Programme' is a document of 1875 by which German political thinker and activist?

29. Your starter for 10:
Associated in particular with rodents and ungulate mammals, the diastema is a prominent gap or space between which parts of the body?

Three bonus questions on a word:
(a) 'The One with the Monkey' and 'The One where Rachel Finds out' are episode titles of which American television series?
(b) The Society of Friends is more generally known by what name?
(c) In Act III, Scene ii of Shakespeare's *Julius Caesar*, which line follows 'Friends, Romans, countrymen, lend me your ears'?

30. Your starter for 10:
What shape are so-called 'early type' galaxies, formerly thought to be at an early stage of evolution?

Three bonus questions on the bull:
(a) A slat of wood on the end of a thong known as a bull-roarer is used in the religious ceremonies of which indigenous people?

(b) The first outside Europe to issue adhesive postage stamps, which South American country issued a series of stamps in 1843 known as 'bullseyes'?

(c) The red wine known in English as Bull's Blood is produced in which country?

'Another very, very powerful performance from you – you'll be some team to beat later on in the competition.'

THE RULES

Well, we could all recite the rules in
our sleep, so let's get on with it.

Match Six

1. Your starter for 10:
Which ellipsoidal granules form in chloroplats and
stain black, blue or purple when treated with potassium
iodide solution?

Three bonus questions on royal families:
(a) Which English king was deposed by his first cousin,
who became Henry IV?
(b) Which French king, whose father's sister was the wife
of Charles I, was the first cousin of Charles II and
James II?
(c) Which German monarch was the first cousin of King
George V?

2. Your starter for 10:
Examples in English being indicative, subjunctive and
imperative, what grammatical term indicates a form of
the verb that affects the general meaning of the sentence
or clause in which it occurs? In everyday speech the
same word means 'feeling' or 'disposition'.

Three bonus questions on children's literature:
(a) In the story by Oscar Wilde, which giant prohibited
children from playing in his garden?
(b) Created by Roald Dahl, which giant is known by the
initials B.F.G.?
(c) Who illustrated and wrote *Jim and the Beanstalk*, his

sequel to the famous folk tale?

3.   Your starter for 10:
What five-letter Germanic word describes a general
dread, arising especially from a perceived lack of
purpose or meaning in the universe? The concept is
particularly associated with Kierkegaard.

Three bonus questions on a painting:
(a) Commissioned in the early 1500s, perhaps to celebrate
their new home and the birth of their second son,
which painting depicts the wife of the wealthy
Florentine silk merchant Franceso del Giocondo?
(b) Which Dadaist created *L.H.O.O.Q.*, a parody of the
Mona Lisa made in 1919, in which a moustache and
goatee beard were added to a reproduction of the
painting?
(c) *Five Grins or Mona Lisa's Moustache* is a work by
which French composer, best known for his three piano
compositions known as the *Gymnopédies*?

4.   Your starter for 10:
A marble monument marks the spot where, in 1837, the
French nobleman Georges d'Anthes fatally wounded
which Russian poet in a duel fought with pistols?

Three bonus questions on Lord Chancellors and Lord Keepers of England:
Identify the holder of the office:
(a) Succeeding Simon Langham, Bishop of Ely, which Lord
Chancellor was appointed in 1367 and was himself
succeeded by Robert Thorpe?
(b) Succeeding Sir Thomas Egerton, which Lord
Chancellor was appointed in 1617 and was succeeded
by John Williams, Bishop of Lincoln?
(c) Succeeding Thomas Wolsey, Archbishop of York,

which Lord Chancellor was appointed in 1529, and was succeeded by Sir Thomas Audley?

5. Your starter for 10:
The Italian resort of Sorrento lies on a peninsula separating the Gulf of Salerno from which body of water?

> **Three bonus questions on secretaries-general of the United Nations:**
> (a) After serving as UN secretary-general from 1972 to 1981, who became president of his native country in 1986, when he was criticised for his record during the Second World War?
> (b) Waldheim's successor as UN secretary-general, Perez de Cuellar, became prime minister of which country in 2000 following the resignation of Alberto Fujimori?
> (c) Which former Korean diplomat succeeded Kofi Annan as UN secretary-general in 2007?

6. Your starter for 10:
Which planet in our solar system has moons called Atlas, Calypso, Helene, Prometheus and Titan?

> **Three bonus questions on an African country:**
> (a) Bamako on the Niger river is the capital of which large landlocked country of Western Africa?
> (b) Shortly before it became an independent state in 1960, Mali, then called the French Sudan, merged with which of its neighbours to form the Mali Federation?
> (c) The name of which town in central Mali, at the end of a trans-Saharan caravan route, is sometimes used figuratively to imply a distant and exotic destination?

7. Your starter for 10:
Which unorthodox American poet exhibited paintings

alongside Duchamp's readymade porcelain urinal and wrote a prose account of his First World War imprisonment in France entitled *The Enormous Room*?

Three bonus questions on patrons of the arts:

(a) The patrons of many painters including Mantegna, Rubens and Van Dyck, the Gonzaga family ruled which northern Italian city from the fourteenth to the eighteenth centuries?

(b) The humanist and diplomat Gian Giorgio Trissino was an early patron of which Venetian architect, born Andrea di Pietro della Gondola in 1508, but later known by the surname Trissino bestowed on him?

(c) In 1874, which of Richard Wagner's patrons made a substantial loan to rescue his Bayreuth Festspielhaus from bankruptcy?

8. **Your starter for 10:**

Its installations featuring in ceremonies to mark the ninetieth anniversary of the start of the Battle of the Somme in 2006, for what do the letters CWGC stand?

Three bonus questions on pre-revolutionary French provinces:

(a) Which medieval Duchy merged with Guyenne after the Hundred Years War to create one of the largest provinces in pre-revolutionary France, and has a name derived from *Vasco*, the Spanish word for 'Basque'?

(b) Which American state was the site of a French colony established in 1604, and is thought by some to be named after a province that lay between Bretagne and Orléanais?

(c) Centred on Paris, the name of which province is thought by some to refer to its position surrounded by the Rivers Seine, Marne, Oise and Beuvronne?

9. Your starter for 10:
Which eighteenth-century figure was a writer, a scientist, a printer, an inventor, a statesman, an ambassador and the oldest signer of the American Declaration of Independence?

Three bonus questions on a Greek historian:
(a) Born around 200 BC and detained in Rome from 168, which statesman's *Histories*, not all extant, chronicle the rise of Rome from 220 to the destruction of Carthage in 146 BC?

(b) Polybius's work on government was an influence on which French philosopher, whose 1748 work *The Spirit of the Laws* advocates the separation of powers?

(c) Polybius is also thought to have been an influence on the *Discorsi*, a 1518 work by which Florentine political philosopher?

10. Your starter for 10:
Midway between Nashville and Atlanta, which city on the Tennessee river gives its name to a decisive Union victory of November 1863 and to a popular song about a locomotive that featured in the 1941 film *Sun Valley Serenade*?

Three bonus questions on music censorship:
(a) In 1986, the American PMRC committee put an 'explicit lyrics' warning sticker on which musician's *Jazz from Hell* album, despite it being instrumental? He had previously protested against music censorship and called the committee the 'Mothers of Prevention'.

(b) In May 1977, Rod Stewart was number one in the UK singles charts with 'The First Cut Is The Deepest', but it was widely believed that which banned song outsold his that week?

(c) Which track from Pink Floyd's album of 1979 was
adopted by a national schools boycott in South Africa
and was banned by the apartheid government?

11. Your starter for 10:

The forces acting upon a powered aeroplane in flight are
thrust, drag and what other force?

Three bonus questions on Florence:

(a) Still fulfilling its original role as Florence's town hall,
which palace was completed in the early fourteenth
century although much of the interior was remodelled
for Duke Cosimo I in the mid sixteenth century?

(b) Named after a title given to the chief of police who was
based in the building, which palace was a prison until
the mid nineteenth century and now houses a collection
of sculpture, including Donatello's statue of St George
and his free-standing bronze *David*?

(c) The Giardino di Bóboli, opened to the public in the
1760s, is the only truly extensive area of greenery in
the centre of Florence and is recognised as the formal
gardens of which palace?

12. Your starter for 10:

Two major figures of English literature died on the same
day as John F. Kennedy in 1963. Name either of them.

Three bonus questions on scientific terms:

(a) Also used in the game of bridge, what term in
mathematics and logic denotes a set that contains
exactly one element?

(b) In physics and mathematics, what name denotes a
point at which a function takes an infinite value; it is
especially used to denote a point in space-time where
matter is infinitely dense such as at the centre of a
black hole?

(c) In mathematics, a singular matrix is a square matrix whose determinant has what value?

13. **Your starter for 10:**
The full titles of the Royal Army Nursing Corps and the Royal Naval Nursing Service both include the name of which royal figure, the wife of King Edward VII, who was president of both bodies until her death in 1925?

Three bonus questions on houseplants:
(a) What is the common name of *Monstera deliciosa*, distinguished by its large, irregular-shaped leaves with natural holes?
(b) Grown commercially in the tropics, which houseplant with large, oblong, glossy, leathery leaves has the scientific name *Ficus elastica*?
(c) After the sharpness of its leaves, what common name is often given to *Sansevieria trifasciata*, native to tropical West Africa?

14. **Your starter for 10:**
Taking its name from that of an English county, which period of the geological timescale follows the Silurian and precedes the Carboniferous?

Three bonus questions on names:
(a) Which mountain, sometimes called the Holy Mountain, is theoretically an independent state under the Greek constitution?
(b) Who, with Athos and Porthos, made up the Three Musketeers?
(c) Who founded a cosmetics company in 1946 which, in 1965, began to market products for men under the brand name Aramis?

15. Your starter for 10:

In the 1948 paper 'A Mathematical Theory of Communication', who defined the bit as a quantity of information?

Three bonus questions on the musical careers of Hollywood stars:

(a) Which actor had a top ten hit with 'Respect Yourself', after achieving fame in the TV series *Moonlighting* with Cybill Shepherd?

(b) Which Hollywood actor has been a member of the band Dogstar, with Robert Mailhouse and Bret Domrose?

(c) Which actor played lead guitar with The Kids before his first feature role as a short-lived character in *Nightmare on Elm Street*?

16. Your starter for 10:

Which fibre comprising tough flexible protein, rich in residues of the amino acid serine, is secreted by spiders for webs and some insects for cocoons and egg cases?

Three bonus questions on nicknames:

(a) A reference to his preferred means of executing his enemies, what nickname was given to the fifteenth-century Romanian prince Vlad Tepes?

(b) What was the gruesome nickname of Erik I, a tenth-century King of Norway who later ruled York?

(c) What was the nickname of Richard Fitzgilbert, whose invasion of Ireland in 1170 began the English conquest?

17. Your starter for 10:

In a speech to the House of Commons in 1940, what did Winston Churchill describe as 'one who feeds a crocodile hoping it will eat him last'?

Three bonus questions on emotional origins:

(a) From the Greek definition of the word, hysteria was thought to be connected with which part of the body?

(b) Which part of the body was once thought to be the seat of anger and melancholy?

(c) Rather than the heart, which part of the body was regarded as the seat of love and courage?

18. Your starter for 10:

Said to have been introduced to English colonists at the first Thanksgiving in Plymouth by the native American chief Quadequina, which foodstuff was believed to contain spirits of the dead who escaped when it burst on exposure to heat?

Three bonus questions on island groups:

(a) Gimsøya and Moskenesøya belong to which group of islands lying within the Arctic Circle?

(b) The South Sandwich Islands in the Atlantic were designated 'South' to distinguish them from which archipelago in the Pacific, formerly also known as the Sandwich Islands?

(c) The Archipelago Sea contains, by some definitions, the most extensive island group in the world, and is part of the territory of which EU country?

19. Your starter for 10:

The establishment in 1915 of the Ordnance Survey tidal observatory led to the heights above sea-level recorded on maps of the UK being calculated from the mean sea level at which town in Cornwall?

Three bonus questions on complex numbers:

(a) If the letter 'i' denotes a square root of −1, what name is given to the set of numbers which are real multiples of i?

(b) Apart from i, what is the other purely imaginary fourth root of 1?

(c) 'Even death is unreliable: instead of zero it may be some ghastly hallucination, such as the square root of minus one.' These are the words of which twentieth-century Irish playwright?

20. Your starter for 10:
The aromatic herb dittany, which gives off an inflammable volatile oil, and the summer cypress, which has russet leaves in the autumn, are both also known by what two-word name which, in the Old Testament, refers to the shrub by which God revealed himself to Moses?

Three bonus questions on twentieth-century history:
In each case, give the decade during which the following treaty was signed:

(a) The Anglo-Japanese Alliance, which arose out of the Russian challenge to British influence in China and marked the end of the policy known as 'splendid isolation'.

(b) The Anglo-Egyptian Treaty, which ended British occupation of Egypt, except for the Suez Canal, although its provisions legitimised military use of Egypt during the Second World War.

(c) The Anglo-Irish Treaty, which ended the Irish War of Independence and resulted in the creation of the Irish Free State.

21. Your starter for 10:
Creating a polity known in Polish as the 'Republic of the Two Nations', with which state did Poland combine in the Union of Lublin of 1569?

Three bonus questions on a shared prefix:

(a) A recording of the electrical activity of the brain using electrodes applied to the scalp, and usually presented as a tracing on paper, is known as an EEG; for what does EEG stand?

(b) Sometimes called 'electric shock therapy', what is the medical name for the treatment for patients with severe psychiatric problems, in which a seizure is produced by passing a low-level electric current through the brain?

(c) What is recorded by electro-laryngography?

22. Your starter for 10:

Sendal, chiefly used to make ceremonial robes and banners, is what type of material?

Three bonus questions on George Orwell:

(a) In which novel does the central character go hop-picking in Kent, as Orwell himself had done in summer 1931?

(b) Gordon Comstock, an aspiring writer who works in a bookshop as Orwell himself once did, is the protagonist of which novel?

(c) The architecture of which ministry in *Nineteen Eighty-Four* is said to be based on BBC Broadcasting House, where Orwell had worked during the Second World War?

23. Your starter for 10:

Determined outside thermodynamics, what is defined as the temperature at which the switch is made between equilibrium and non-equilibrium chemistry?

Three bonus questions on Scottish artists:

(a) The House for an Art Lover, situated in Bellahouston Park in Glasgow, opened to the public in 1996 and is based on a design of 1901 by which Scottist artist and architect, working in conjunction with his wife Margaret MacDonald?

(b) Noted for his portraits of David Hume and Jean-Jacques Rousseau, Allan Ramsay was appointed painter to which British monarch?

(c) Depicting a couple dancing on a beach, which Jack Vettriano painting sold for nearly £750,000 at auction in 2004?

24. Your starter for 10:
Using data provided by the Met Office and special traps, a website developed by entomologists at Edinburgh University gives a daily forecast, for locations in Scotland, of the nuisance level, on a one to five scale, of what members of the order *diptera*, believed to number up to 50 million per hectare in places?

Three bonus questions on books published during the 1620s:

(a) *On the Movement of the Heart and Blood in Animals* was published in Latin in 1628 by which English physician?

(b) Published in 1629, the first English translation of Thucydides' *History of the Peloponnesian War* was an early work by which political philosopher?

(c) Detailing a new system of logic, the 1620 *Novum Organum* is a work by which philosopher and statesman?

25. Your starter for 10:
From the Latin meaning key, what name is given to the collarbone?

Three bonus questions linked by a surname:

(a) Which 2005 film starring Judi Dench carries the tagline, 'The show must go on, but the clothes must come off'?

(b) Which track on The Beatles' *Sgt Pepper* album includes the lyrics 'The Hendersons will all be there' and 'The Hendersons will dance and sing'?

(c) The American composer Luther Henderson, who died in 2003, adapted whose music for the 1978 Broadway revival of *Ain't Misbehavin'*?

26. Your starter for 10:
With which branch of applied science are the Charpy and Izod tests associated?

Three bonus questions on endangered species:

(a) Bearing distinctive leopard-like spots, the Spanish or Iberian species of which critically endangered mammal is thought to have only two isolated breeding populations in Spain?

(b) Living in Southeast Asia, Sumatra and Borneo, what is the world's smallest species of bear? It was included on the Red List of Threatened Species for the first time in 2007.

(c) Thought to be 'functionally extinct', the Bai-ji is a dolphin unique to which Asian river?

27. Your starter for 10:
'Your Majesty, I am returning this in protest against Britain's involvement in the Nigeria-Biafra thing, against our support of America in Vietnam and against "Cold Turkey" slipping down the charts.' Who returned his MBE with this note to the Queen in November 1969?

Three bonus questions on a European dynasty:

(a) Which European dynasty takes its name from the Latin form of the name of the Frankish ruler who defeated the Moors somewhere between Tours and Poitiers in 732?

(b) Which grandson of Charles Martel was crowned Emperor at Aachen in 800?

(c) What uncomplimentary nickname was given to Charles II, a grandson of Charlemagne who was Emperor of the West from 875 to 877?

28. Your starter for 10:

What is the common name of the primarily sedentary marine animals of the invertebrate order *actiniaria*, which resemble flowers?

Three bonus questions on vandalised works of art:

(a) The *Rokeby Venus* by Velázquez in the National Gallery was attacked with a meat cleaver in March 1914 by a woman called Mary Richardson, a member of which organisation?

(b) Which work by Michelangelo was seriously damaged with fifteen blows of a hammer in 1972 and is now exhibited behind bullet-proof glass?

(c) In 2002, a statue of Margaret Thatcher in the Guildhall in London was decapitated by a protester using what piece of sporting equipment?

29. Your starter for 10:

In astronomy, what alphanumeric designation is given to neutral hydrogen gas, whose characteristic radio emission line has a wavelength of 21 centimetres?

Three bonus questions on particle physics:

(a) Born in 1902, which physicist's work on the energy states of the electron led to the concept of antimatter?

(b) What name was given to the first anti-particles to be discovered, by Carl Anderson in 1932?

(c) A collision between an electron and a positron results in their masses being converted into what form of energy?

30. Your starter for 10:

The Isle of Anglesey gives its name to anglesite, a naturally occurring sulphate of which metal?

Three bonus questions on shipping forecast areas:

(a) The sea area now known as German Bight was originally named after which island, ceded by Britain to Germany in 1890?

(b) Portland and which area formerly comprised the area known as 'Channel'?

(c) 'North' and 'South' precede the name of which Norwegian island?

> 'I'm afraid you were outplayed, and I kept wanting to cry every time you buzzed in incorrectly. You were doing exactly the right thing, but you were just a bit unlucky with the questions.'

THE RULES

Let's take the rules as read.

Match Seven

1. **Your starter for 10:**
Calcium sulphate and magnesium chloride are among
the coagulating agents used in the production of which
soft, cream-coloured foodstuff made from soya beans
and usually known in English by its Japanese name?

> **Three bonus questions on writers:**
> (a) Which Harvard graduate was the author of *Naked
> Lunch*, first published in Paris in 1959?
> (b) Which of Tennessee Williams's characters said, 'I can't
> stand a naked light bulb, any more than I can a rude
> remark or a vulgar action'?
> (c) Which poet is said to have told New York journalists
> that he came to America in search of naked women in
> wet mackintoshes?

2. **Your starter for 10:**
Identify the poet who wrote these lines: 'When you are
old and grey and full of sleep / and nodding by the fire,
take down this book, / and slowly read, and dream of
the soft look / your eyes had once, and of their shadows
deep.'

> **Three bonus questions on salad ingredients in literature:**
> (a) In Swift's *Gulliver's Travels*, the Academy of Lagado
> conducts experiments in which sunbeams are
> supposedly extracted from which vegetable?

(b) In Shakespeare's *Henry IV Part Two*, Falstaff says of Justice Shallow that when he was naked he was like a forked form of which salad ingredient, 'with a head fantastically carved upon it with a knife'?

(c) In Beatrix Potter's *Tale of the Flopsy Bunnies*, of what does she write: 'It is said that the effect of eating too much is soporific. I have never felt sleepy after eating [them]; but then I am not a rabbit'?

3. **Your starter for 10:**
The largest number whose factorial is less than 10^{100}, what two-digit number links 'the Year of the Four Emperors' in Roman history, the Carlisle to Tyneside trunk road and the age at which Ronald Reagan was first elected President?

Three bonus questions on high-tech swimsuits:
(a) Which three letters denote the speedo 'racer suit' worn by Rebecca Adlington when she won the 400 metres and 800 metres freestyle Olympic titles in 2008?

(b) Worn by many record-breakers at the 2009 Fina World Swimming Championships, the Arena X-Glide suit is made entirely of what thermoplastic polymer?

(c) Who suffered his first major defeat in several years at the 2009 World Championships when he was beaten in the 200 metres freestyle by Germany's Paul Biedermann, who was wearing an Arena X-Glide?

4. **Your starter for 10:**
As well as full-length novels and short stories, the writer Elizabeth Gaskell also produced a biography of which writer in 1857, two years after the death of the subject whom she describes as 'my dear friend'?

Three bonus questions on Chaucer's Canterbury Tales:
In each case, name the pilgrim from the lines of description

given in the 'General Prologue':
(a) 'It snewed in his hous of mete and drinke / Of alle deyntees that men coude thinke.'
(b) 'This noble ensample to his sheep he yaf, / That first he wroghte, and afterward he taughte.'
(c) 'He loved chivalrie, / Trouthe and honour, fredom and curteisie.'

5. **Your starter for 10:**
If all the numbers on a dartboard are replaced with the letters corresponding to each number, so '1' is replaced by 'a', '2' by 'b' and so on, what four letter word is spelt out anticlockwise from the 12 sector?

Three bonus questions on lines of longitude:
(a) The larger part of the UK lies between 0 degrees and 10 degrees west. Which other two European countries lie on the 0 degrees meridian?
(b) The 20 degrees east meridian passes through Norway, Sweden, the Aland Islands and the eastern Baltic Sea. In which country's territory does it make landfall again?
(c) Which country, usually considered to be part of Europe, lies at 20 degrees west?

6. **Your starter for 10:**
Italian chemist Stanislao Cannizzaro gave his name to a reaction he discovered whereby what type of substance is converted into an acid and an alcohol in the presence of a strong alkali?

Three bonus questions on literary initials:
(a) Which twentieth-century English poet was given his first name after a ninth-century prince of Mercia and Anglo-Saxon saint, whose bones were deposited in the church in the village of Repton where the poet's father had been at school?

(b) One of the leading contenders for the identity of Shakespeare's 'Mr W.H.' is the Earl of Pembroke, to whom the First Folio was dedicated in 1623. If the identification is correct, for what do the two letters stand?

(c) W.H. were also the initials of which poet, whose poem 'Leisure' begins 'What is this life, if, full of care, / We have no time to stand and stare'?

7.   Your starter for 10:

The naked torso of a woman, an inverted tuba and a cane-bottomed chair – all made to resemble clouds – loom ominously against a clear blue sky in *Threatening Weather*, a painting by which Belgian surrealist?

Three bonus questions on sacred minimalism in music:

(a) An example of the sacred minimalist style is the 1976 Third Symphony of which composer, born in Czernica in Poland in 1933?

(b) Which British composer's works include *The Protecting Veil* and 'Song for Athene', which was performed at Princess Diana's funeral?

(c) The Estonian Arvo Pärt wrote a Cantus to mourn which English composer, who died in 1976?

8.   Your starter for 10:

The word 'smaragdine' refers to which precious stone that has a chemical formula of $Al_2Be_3Si_6O_{18,}$ crystallises in hexagonal prismatic forms and is coloured bright green?

Three questions about libraries:

(a) What term denotes those libraries that, by law, are entitled to receive a free copy of every book published in the UK, for example the university libraries of Oxford and Cambridge?

(b) The National Library of Scotland is in Edinburgh. In which town is the National Library of Wales?

(c) The architect Colin St John Wilson designed which library building, completed in 1997?

9. Your starter for 10:

Who effectively became ruler of England in 1658 but clashed with Parliament, which he dissolved the following year, shortly before being forced to abdicate?

Three bonus questions on steam railways:

(a) What was the UK's first preserved standard-gauge passenger railway, set up in the late 1950s to reopen part of the old London, Brighton and South Coast Line?

(b) The Poppy Line runs for approximately five miles from the coastal resort of Sheringham to the Georgian market town of Holt in the north of which county?

(c) Which railway was revived by enthusiasts to begin operations in 1970 from Bridgnorth to Hampton Loade, before gradually extending southwards?

10. Your starter for 10:

What word for an organism that promotes the growth of microorganisms is often applied to food products, such as yoghurts, that contain so-called 'healthy bacteria' such as lactobacilli and bifido-bacteria species that can help to overcome disease-causing gut infections?

Three bonus questions on literary fakes:

(a) Whom did James Macpherson claim was the author of *Temora*, which appeared in print in 1763?

(b) The supposed 'autobiography' of which US aviator and industrialist was in reality a 1972 hoax perpetrated by Clifford Irving?

(c) Which British historian vouched for the authenticity of the bogus 'Hitler Diaries' in 1983?

11. **Your starter for 10:**

What name is shared by a small dark goose that breeds in the Arctic and migrates southwards, a Greater London borough, one of the founders of the internet company last-minute.com, and the gauche manager of a fictional company?

Three bonus questions on European monarchs:

(a) Forced to abdicate and flee the country in 1918, who was the last Emperor of Germany?

(b) Overthrown by a military coup in 1967 and formally deposed in 1973, Constantine II was the last monarch of which European country?

(c) Shot with his entire family in 1918, who was the last Tsar of Russia?

12. **Your starter for 10:**

The Light Programme was the forerunner of which BBC radio channel, to which it changed its name on 30 September 1967?

Three bonus questions linked by a name:

(a) Which fictional village lies just off the B3980, six miles south of Borchester?

(b) Isabel Archer is the title character of which novel by Henry James?

(c) The Archers film production company was based on the collaboration between Emeric Pressburger and which British director?

13. **Your starter for 10:**

From 2003, images from NASA's Hubble telescope revealed the existence of two previously undiscovered moons, named Mab and Cupid, orbiting which planet, now known to have at least twenty-five satellites?

Three bonus questions on mathematics:
(a) Which scientist referred in 1665 to the derivative or differential co-efficient of a function as a 'fluxion'?
(b) With which German philosopher and mathematician did Sir Isaac Newton have a long dispute as to who invented differential calculus?
(c) What is the numerical value of the derivative with respect to 'x' of the function 'y' equals 3'x' squared at the point 'x' equals 2?

14. **Your starter for 10:**
For what do the letters EHIC stand, being a document that in 2005 replaced the E111 form in guaranteeing medical treatment to UK citizens visiting certain countries?

Three bonus questions on quotations about the morning:
(a) In which of his plays did Shakespeare write: 'But look, the morn, in russet mantle clad / Walks o'er the dew of yon high eastern hill'?
(b) Which poet wrote of 'the brown fog of a winter dawn' in a work first published in 1922?
(c) Which Greek poet described the dawn as being 'rosy-fingered'?

15. **Your starter for 10:**
The term 'radical chic' was coined in 1970 by Tom Wolfe specifically to describe a fundraiser organised by Leonard Bernstein for which militant group, founded by Bobby Seale and Huey Newton?

Three bonus questions on nineteenth-century foreign secretaries:
(a) Who was foreign secretary from 1807 until 1809, when he fought a duel with Castlereagh, and later from 1820 until he became prime minister in 1827, dying

after only four months in office?

(b) Lord Bathurst, who followed Canning as foreign secretary in 1809, gave his name to the capital of the British colony of the Gambia. By what name is this city now known?

(c) Richard Wellesley, Bathurst's successor as foreign secretary, was an older brother of which military commander, who later became prime minister?

16. Your starter for 10:

Meanings of which short word include: the male of the Merlin hawk; a portable machine for levering weights from below; a device for pulling off boots, and a small white ball in the game of bowls?

Three bonus questions on administrative regions of France:

(a) Its capital Strasbourg, which region of France lies along the west bank of the Rhine adjacent to Germany and Switzerland?

(b) Besançon is the capital of which French region to the south of Alsace? Formerly part of the Duchy of Burgundy, it finally became part of France in 1678.

(c) To the west of Alsace and bordering Luxembourg and Belgium, which region in northern France includes the cites of Metz and Nancy?

17. Your starter for 10:

What common two-word name is often given to a flowering plant of the genus *saintpaulia*, referring both to its native habitat of Tanzania and Kenya, and the distinctive colour of its petals?

Three bonus questions on cricket:

(a) Quote: 'Once in my heyday of cricket / Oh, day I shall ever recall! / I captured that glorious wicket, / The greatest, the grandest of all.' These lines by Sir Arthur Conan Doyle describe his only first-class wicket, taken in 1900. Who was his victim?

(b) Which future Prime Minister played first-class cricket for Middlesex, Oxford University and the MCC during the 1920s under the name Lord Dunglass?

(c) Having played for Dublin University in two matches against Northants in the mid 1920s, who became the first cricketer from the first-class game to win a Nobel Prize, doing so for Literature in 1969?

18. **Your starter for 10:**

Which year saw the first Winter Olympics, in Chamonix, France; the deaths of Lenin and Franz Kafka; the birth of Doris Day; the disappearance of Mallory and Irvine on Mount Everest; and Britain's first Labour government, under Ramsay MacDonald?

Three bonus questions on definitions of poetry:

In each case, give the poet who provided the definitions:

(a) Which poet, in words attributed to him in 1827, described prose as 'words in their best order', and poetry as 'the best words in their best order'?

(b) 'Poetry is not a turning loose of emotion, but an escape from emotion; it is not the expression of personality, but an escape from personality.' Which poet wrote this in the essay 'Tradition and the Individual Talent'?

(c) Which American poet, who died in 1963, described poetry as 'what gets lost in translation'?

19. **Your starter for 10:**

Which 2003 film features the appropriately named characters of Bubbles, Gurgle, Bloat and Gill?

Three bonus questions on loanwords:

(a) 'Golf' means 'sweater', 'slip' means 'underpants',

'montgomery' means 'duffel coat' and 'tight' means 'morning dress' in what European language?

(b) In French, the word 'basket' can mean either 'basketball' or what item of clothing?

(c) In German, a 'handy' denotes what everyday appliance?

20. Your starter for 10:

The father of Robert Louis Stevenson invented a white box known as a 'screen' used in which branch of science?

Three bonus questions on the outbreak of diseases:

(a) Working as a cook for a number of families in New York in the early 1900s, Mary Mallon carried and spread what disease, characterised by diarrhoea and fever, although she herself remained healthy?

(b) Broad Street in Soho in 1854 saw an outbreak of which acute disease, causing severe vomiting and diarrhoea? The physician John Snow traced the source to contaminated water taken from a common pump.

(c) In 1665, William Mompesson, the Rector of Eyam in Derbyshire, persuaded his villagers to stay in their homes rather than flee to nearby towns, thus restricting the spread of which disease?

21. Your starter for 10:

Used in sunglasses, what trade name did the American inventor Edwin Land give in 1932 to a process of aligning crystals of quinine iodo-sulphate embedded in a clear plastic sheet?

Three bonus questions on twentieth-century symphonies:

(a) *Kaddish*, *The Age of Anxiety* and *Jeremiah* are symphonies by which American composer?

(b) The *Copernican* and the *Symphony of Sorrowful Songs*

are symphonies by which Polish composer?

(c) *To October*, *Leningrad* and *Babi Yar* are symphonies by which Russian composer?

22. Your starter for 10:
What is the meaning of the Latin word *lorica*, used for the hard external covering that functions as an exoskeleton in some invertebrates and forms part of the names of the *lorica segmentata* and *lorica squamata*, items worn by Roman legionaries?

Three bonus questions on a gemstone:

(a) Which gemstone is a fluorine aluminium silicate, most commonly found in a yellow form, as, for example, at the Schneckenstein cliff in Saxony?

(b) Topaz is the second Mrs Mortmain and stepmother to the narrator in which 1948 novel by Dodie Smith about an eccentric and impoverished family?

(c) Topaz was the middle name of which poet, born around 1830, whose works are described as 'uniformly bad, but possess a disarming naiveté and a calypso-like disregard for metre [that] never fail to entertain'?

23. Your starter for 10:
Which word of Arabic origin describes the craft – used in making decorative fringed borders, wall hangings and jewellery – of knotting and plaiting cords into a variety of patterns?

Three bonus questions on a writer and critic:

(a) Who is best remembered for *Eminent Victorians*, a series of short sketches of people such as Florence Nightingale, General Gordon and Cardinal Manning?

(b) What quality – or failing – did Strachey describe as 'the first requisite of the historian', that which 'simplifies and clarifies, which selects and omits, with a placid perfection unattainable by the highest art'?

(c) According to his biographer Michael Holroyd, what reply did Strachey give to the military tribunal in 1914 which, in assessing his claim of conscientious objection, asked him what he would do if he saw a German soldier attempting to violate his sister?

24. Your starter for 10:

Members of the Discovery Institute, a conservative think-tank based in Seattle, are among the chief proponents of which idea of the origin of species, sometimes described as 'creationism dressed in a lab coat'?

Three bonus questions on Latin grammar:

(a) What two-word alliterative term denotes a grammatical form described as 'the Rolls-Royce of Latin constructions: elegant, powerful and classy', and usually indicating the time or cause of an event?

(b) What alliterative ablative absolute expression means 'the necessary changes having been made'?

(c) What alliterative ablative absolute expression has the literal translation 'the position having been reversed'?

25. Your starter for 10:

6.626068×10^{-34} joule seconds and 5×10^{-44} seconds are quantities named after which German physicist born in 1858, a pioneer of quantum theory?

Three bonus questions on extinct species:

(a) What was the third species of the family *Raphidae*, which was extinct by 1681?

(b) A monument in Wisconsin to which species of pigeon declares that it 'became extinct through the avarice and thoughtlessness of man'?

(c) Of which mammal have the Bali, Caspian and Javan

species all become extinct?

26. Your starter for 10:
Which cold ocean current flows north along the west coast of South America, cooling the coastal regions as far as the Equator?

Three bonus questions on petrology:
(a) The three major types of rock formation are igneous, metamorphic and which other?
(b) Which sedimentary rock is mainly composed of calcium carbonate, usually in the form of calcite or aragonite?
(c) Which form of limestone makes up the Cotswolds, and gets its name because it is composed of grains like the eggs of a fish?

27. Your starter for 10:
Of the G20 major economies, three lie entirely within the southern hemisphere. One is Australia. For ten points, name either of the other two.

Three bonus questions on the internet:
In the context of the world wide web, what do the following initials stand for?
(a) ISDN.
(b) ISP.
(c) URL.

28. Your starter for 10:
What short adjective links 'Riot', 'Rabbit' and 'Christmas' in the titles of songs recorded by The Clash, Jefferson Airplane and Bing Crosby, respectively?

Three bonus questions on acronyms:
(a) What short adjective is also an acronym for the diameter of a person's waist, the CIA's special

operations force, and a mood disorder with depressive symptoms in the winter?

(b) What name is that of a thirteenth-century theologian nicknamed 'the Subtle Doctor', and is also an acronym for the highest US judiciary?

(c) What abbreviation for a semi-conducting material is also the regional code for an Italian island, an acronym for the venue of the Malaysian round of Formula 1, and is a Latin word meaning 'thus'?

29. Your starter for 10:

Now marked by a battlefield heritage centre, which site near Sutton Cheney in Leicestershire saw Richard III fall in battle against an army commanded by Henry Tudor?

Three bonus questions on paradoxes:

(a) Author of the 1903 work *Principia Ethica*, which British philosopher gives his name to the paradox exemplified by the line: 'It is raining, but I do not believe that it is'?

(b) Called 'the inventor of dialectic' by Aristotle, which Greek philosopher gave his name to a series of arguments purporting to demonstrate that motion is an illusion?

(c) 'A paradox, a most ingenious paradox / We've quips and quibbles heard in flocks, / But none to beat this paradox'. In which Gilbert and Sullivan operetta do these lines appear?

30. Your starter for 10:

In group theory, what term denotes the 26 finite simple groups that do not fit into any of the 18 infinite families of finite simple groups?

Three bonus questions on world population:

(a) Excluding microstates and island nations, which

sovereign state has the greatest population density in the world, with more than 1,000 people per square kilometre?

(b) What is the population density of the UK, in persons per square kilometre? You can have twenty-five either way.

(c) Three EU member states have a population density greater than that of the UK. For five points, name two of them.

'Well, I'm surprised – I expected you to do a bit better than that, but thank you for joining us.'

THE RULES

You all know the rules – too boring
to recite them – so here's your first
starter for 10.

Match Eight

1. **Your starter for 10:**
With work featured on a series of Wedgwood tea sets in 2004, which designer was linked to the Sex Pistols through her partnership with their manager?

Three bonus questions on English dukedoms:
(a) Which dukedom was held by Edmund Beaufort, who led the Lancastrians at the Battle of Tewkesbury in 1471, and by Edward Seymour, Lord Protector of England from 1547 to 1549 and brother of Henry VIII's wife Jane?
(b) Which dukedom was held by Humphrey Stafford, a major supporter of the House of Lancaster in the Wars of the Roses, and by George Villiers, a favourite of James I?
(c) Which dukedom, traditionally awarded to junior members of the British royal family, was held by George Plantagenet, the brother of Edward IV, who allegedly drowned in a butt of malmsey?

2. **Your starter for 10:**
What is the name for the splitting of lines in a spectrum when the source of the spectrum is exposed to a magnetic field?

Three bonus questions on royal titles:
(a) In ancient Egypt, the title 'Pharaoh' had what literal

meaning, related to architecture?

(b) Which two-word term of French origin meaning 'high gate' came into general use in the eighteenth century for the court of the Sultan at Istanbul, and thence metonymically for the Ottoman Empire?

(c) Which historic title, used mainly in English to describe an East Asian monarch, literally meant 'exalted gate'?

3. **Your starter for 10:**
What name is shared by a Provençal and a Chilean poet, awarded the Nobel Prize for Literature in 1904 and 1945 respectively, and a dry, cold northerly wind that affects the Rhône valley, particularly south of Valence?

Three bonus questions on the letter 'a':

(a) The capital letter 'A' with a small circle at the letter's apex (Å) can be a single-letter place-name in Scandinavian countries, and refers to what geographical feature?

(b) The anarchist symbol of the capital letter 'A' within the capital letter 'O' is usually regarded to derive from the phrase 'Anarchy is order', taken from the 1849 *Confessions of a Revolutionary* by which French political philosopher?

(c) In 2008, a *Times* sub-editor's removal of the indefinite article 'a', changing the words 'go for a nosh' to 'go for nosh', prompted a lively and much-reproduced email from which broadcaster and food critic, the author of the piece in question?

4. **Your starter for 10:**
In the periodic classification of elements, what is the name of the group of elements also called the rare earth metals, which includes element number 58, chemical symbol Ce, and element number 71, chemical symbol Yb?

Three bonus questions on writing about food:
(a) Credited with introducing regional Italian and French cooking to Britain in the post-war austerity years, which cookery writer's first volume was *Mediterranean Food* in 1950?
(b) Having published a successful volume of poetry in 1826, who produced her *Modern Cookery* in 1845, introducing the practice of listing ingredients and specifying cooking times, and serving as a model for the later works of Mrs Beeton?
(c) What ubiquitous foodstuff did the writer Nigel Slater use for the title of his autobiographical book of 2004, subtitled *The Story of a Boy's Hunger*?

5. Your starter for 10:
The flag of which European country has two equal horizontal bands, blue over yellow?

Three bonus questions on legendary sevens:
(a) Concerning the conflict between the brothers Polynices and Eteocles for the throne of Thebes, the play *Seven Against Thebes* is by which Greek dramatist?
(b) According to folklore, seven years was the time endured in the fairy realm by which thirteenth-century Scottish soothsayer?
(c) The Seven Sleepers, who supposedly survived decades of incarceration for their Christian faith, are usually associated with which ancient Anatolian city?

6. Your starter for 10:
Stinking gum and devil's dung are alternative names for which resin, obtained from a plant of the genus *ferula*, which is used as a flavouring in Indian and Iranian food?

Three bonus questions on trembling:
(a) 'I tremble for my country when I reflect that God is

just'. These words appear in a work of 1781 by which Governor of Virginia, later the third President of the USA?

(b) 'I only hope that when the enemy reads the list of their names he trembles as I do.' Quoting Lord Chesterfield, which military commander wrote these words of his own generals in a letter of 1810?

(c) 'Let the ruling classes tremble at a Communist revolution. The proletarians have nothing to lose but their chains.' These words appear near the end of what work of 1848?

7. Your starter for 10:
Which English physicist built air pumps for Robert Boyle, argued with Isaac Newton over who had devised the inverse square law of gravitation, and gives his name to a law describing the extension of springs and other elastic objects?

Three bonus questions on plant reproduction:

(a) What name do botanists give to the structure that develops in the ovary from the fertilised ovule of a flowering plant?

(b) The structure enclosed in the pericarp that develops from the wall of the ovary and may be either dehiscent or indehiscent, is known by what name?

(c) A fruit with a lignified indehiscent pericarp that is the product of more than one ovary but has only a single seed because the others have aborted is known as a what?

8. Your starter for 10:
Which EU capital city is situated on the River Tagus close to where it flows into the Atlantic Ocean?

Three bonus questions on long-distance footpaths:

(a) Which long-distance footpath runs from Sedbury Cliffs on the banks of the Severn Estuary to Prestatyn in North Wales?

(b) Which long-distance footpath runs from Milngavie, near Glasgow, to Fort William?

(c) Which village in Derbyshire is at the southern end of the Pennine Way?

9. Your starter for 10:

The 'Dunlap Broadside' and the 'Goddard Broadside' were early published versions of which political document, approved by the Second Continental Congress in July 1776?

Three questions on classical themes used in pop songs:

(a) 'Words', a 1983 hit for F.R. David, is based on the last movement of which French composer's Symphony No. 3 with Organ?

(b) 'A Lover's Concerto' was a hit for The Toys in 1965, and was adapted from which eighteenth-century composer's Minuet in G?

(c) Which song was based on Chopin's Piano Prelude in C Minor No. 20, and was a hit for Barry Manilow in 1978 and Take That in 1992?

10. Your starter for 10:

Which elemental gas takes its name from the Greek for 'strange'?

Three bonus questions on island states:

In each case, name the Pacific island nation whose first three letters correspond to the given definition. For example, 'colloquial world for "friend" would be 'Pal-au'.

(a) A drink made of white wine and blackcurrant syrup or crème de cassis.

(b) The fifth note of the diatonic scale.

(c) A covered vehicle for transporting goods.

11. Your starter for 10:
Which unit of power is equal to 1,000 gigawatts or one million megawatts, and is abbreviated as TW?

Three bonus questions on Henry VII's relatives:
(a) What was the name of Henry VII's mother, who was married in 1455 to Edmund Tudor, in 1462 to Henry Stafford, and in 1472 to Thomas Stanley?

(b) Henry's wife Elizabeth of York was the daughter of which English monarch?

(c) What relation was Mary, Queen of Scots to Henry VII?

12. Your starter for 10:
'Rise above oneself and grasp the world' is the English translation of words inscribed on the Fields Medal and attributed to which scientist of antiquity, whose head also appears on the medal?

Three bonus questions on scientific terms beginning with the letters 'Rh':
In each case, give the term from the definition:

(a) An underground root-like stem which produces both roots and shoots, as in for example the common iris.

(b) A fine-grained volcanic rock of granitic composition.

(c) Inflammation of the mucous membrane of the nose.

13. Your starter for 10:
Which word may be followed by 'up' when used in an agricultural sense, by 'on' when describing steady but laborious progress, by 'into' when talking of a crash at speed, and by 'back' when referring to the re-investment of profits in a business?

Three bonus questions on a shared word:

(a) What short two-word term denotes both a location on the Earth's surface that has experienced prolonged volcanic activity, and a public place where a wireless internet signal is available?

(b) A hot key on a computer keyboard is one that operates a short-cut function; under the Windows operating system, what function is performed when the F11 key is pressed?

(c) 'Hotspur' was first applied as a nickname to Sir Henry Percy, son of the Earl of Northumberland, who was killed in the rebellion against which king in 1403?

14. Your starter for 10:
Developed at Edinburgh University, southern blotting is a technique for transferring denatured what from a gel used for electrophoresis to a nitrocellulose filter?

Three bonus questions on unfinished literary works:

(a) Britomart and Belphoebe are two characters in which sixteenth-century poem, only half of whose twelve projected books were ever published?

(b) 'The English in Spain', 'The Pathology of Social Life' and 'The Plain of Wagram' were three of the many unfinished novels in a series of over one hundred and thirty interconnected works planned by which nineteenth-century French author?

(c) *John Jasper's Secret* by Henry Morford was an early attempt to complete and solve the central mystery of which novel, left unfinished at its author's death in 1870?

15. Your starter for 10:
'Both led military rebellions against English monarchs... each took local militia and forged professional armies on a national scale. Each infused a new ethos in his troops.'

Which two national leaders is historian Garry Wills comparing here?

> **Three bonus questions on the history of the English language:**
> In each case, give the decade in which the following occurred:
> (a) The publication of Dr Johnson's *Dictionary of the English Language*.
> (b) The first edition of *The Chambers Dictionary* and the publication of *The King's English* by the Fowler brothers?
> (c) The publication of *The Oxford English Dictionary*, after more than 70 years of preparation, and the establishment of the BBC?

16. **Your starter for 10:**
Applied in medieval times to a young noble awaiting knighthood, what appellation is given to Roland, in the title of a poem by Robert Browning, and to Byron's hero Harold?

> **Three bonus questions on the novels of the Brontë sisters:**
> (a) The term 'gytrash' for an apparition, usually in the form of a large dog or other animal, is first recorded in which novel by Charlotte Brontë, when it is the subject of stories told by the nursemaid Bessie?
> (b) What is the name of the narrator of *Wuthering Heights*, who sees the ghost of Catherine Linton when he is sleeping in her room and refuses to open the window to her?
> (c) In which Brontë novel does the heroine Lucy encounter a shadowy figure in the attic of a school, who may be the ghost of a nun buried alive for breaking her vows of chastity?

17. Your starter for 10:

Mathis der Maler is the title of both an opera and a symphony by Paul Hindemith based on the life of which sixteenth-century German painter, whose expressionistic depiction of the crucifixion is on the Isenheim Altarpiece at Colmar in Alsace?

> **Three bonus questions on a state of the USA:**
>
> (a) Acadia National Park and the northernmost section of the Appalachian National Scenic Trail are situated in which US state?
>
> (b) 'Goodnight you princes of Maine, you kings of New England' is said each night by Dr Larch as he turns out the dormitory lights at his orphanage in which novel by John Irving?
>
> (c) When the battleship USS *Maine* blew up and sank in Havana Harbor in 1898, which country was blamed as a *casus belli*?

18. Your starter for 10:

The Dutch New Yorker who was the fictional author of Washington Irving's *History of New York*, is said to have given his name to which knee-length breeches supposedly worn by Dutch men?

> **Three bonus questions on French overseas territories:**
>
> (a) With a population of around 400,000 each, the French overseas départements of Martinique and Guadeloupe consist of islands in which body of water?
>
> (b) The French territorial collectivity of St Pierre and Miquelon consists of several small islands off the coast of which Canadian province?
>
> (c) The islands of Wallis and Futuna comprise a French territory in which ocean?

19. Your starter for 10:
Flags used in the semaphore alphabet signalling system are conventionally squares divided diagonally, with yellow at the lower fly and which other colour at the upper hoist?

Three bonus questions on film:
(a) Which Anthony Minghella film won five Oscars in 1997?
(b) Michael Ondaatje, author of the *The English Patient*, was born in Sri Lanka but settled in which Commonwealth country in 1962?
(c) Which Greek writer's history was carried by the Hungarian count, protagonist of *The English Patient*?

20. Your starter for 10:
In chemistry, what adjective describes an atom able to combine with two atoms of hydrogen?

Three bonus questions on verbal confections:
(a) Originally meaning a hoax, which word is now used to mean hypocrisy and is also applied to a kind of peppermint-flavoured toffee?
(b) Also used to mean a compromise that solves little, which word denotes a soft-grained sweet, made by boiling together milk, sugar and butter?
(c) Which word, often used for the centre of a target, can also mean a round, hard peppermint, sometimes striped?

21. Your starter for 10:
What name for a house of worship and religious instruction is derived, via Old French and Latin, from the Greek words for 'meeting' and 'bring together'?

Three bonus questions on the use of scientific propositions

in literature:

(a) In Jeanette Winterson's work *Gut Symmetries*, the term 'gut' refers in part to which scientific proposition?

(b) Who wrote the play *I Have Been Here Before*, based on P.D. Ouspensky's theory that time moves in a spiral, not a straight line?

(c) Which Alan Garner novel of 1973 represented several different historical perspectives, the title being a phenomenon attributed to the Doppler effect?

22. Your starter for 10:

Which Northumberland-born artist illustrated editions of Goldsmith's *The Deserted Village* and Aesop's *Fables*, but is better known as the illustrator of the 1797 *History of British Birds*?

Three bonus questions on Shakespeare's collaborators:

(a) Thomas Middleton, author of *The Changeling*, *A Game at Chess* and *The Witch*, is thought to have contributed to both *Timon of Athens* and which of Shakespeare's tragedies?

(b) *The Two Noble Kinsmen* is a tragicomedy published in quarto in 1634, where it is attributed on its title page to Shakespeare and which other playwright?

(c) Fletcher is also believed to have collaborated with Shakespeare on which play, during a performance of which in 1613 a fire started, resulting in the Globe theatre burning down?

23. Your starter for 10:

If a ball bounces onto a floor with an angle of incidence 45 degrees and off with a reflected angle of 60 degrees, what is the coefficient of restitution of the ball on the floor?

Three bonus questions on the US Declaration of

Independence:

(a) Three 'unalienable rights' are listed in the preamble to the declaration. 'The pursuit of happiness' is the third; what are the other two?

(b) Two future US Presidents were among the 56 signatories to the Declaration of Independence. One was Thomas Jefferson; who was the other?

(c) The political philosophy of which English thinker, born in 1632, was a major influence on the principles outlined in the Declaration of Independence?

24. Your starter for 10:

What animal in Punxsutawney, Pennsylvania has been forecasting the weather on 2 February for around 120 years?

Three bonus questions on a region of France:

(a) The name of which region and former province of France is the origin of a term for a type of motor car, because in early models the driver sat outside under a canopy which somewhat resembled the traditional hooded cloak of the region?

(b) Which city, the capital of the Limousin region, is known for porcelain ware which has been manufactured there since the eighteenth century, when its factory was acquired as an adjunct of the royal factory at Sèvres?

(c) Whose marriage in 1152 to the future Henry II brought the province of Limousin under English control, where it remained until the early thirteenth century?

25. Your starter for 10:

'S E & C' constructions, such as tessellations, are created using only geometrical operations that can be performed using what?

Three bonus questions on initials:

(a) What initials were shared by the popular novelist who created Dr Finlay and a logical positivist who was usually known as Freddie?

(b) What initials were shared by the children's author of the Bobby Brewster stories from the 1950s onwards, and the novelist who wrote *Fair Stood the Wind for France* in 1944?

(c) What initials were shared by the poet born in Alexandria who wrote 'Waiting for the Barbarians', and the novelist who wrote *The Two Cultures and the Scientific Revolution*?

26. **Your starter for 10:**

In the early 1670s, Danish astronomer Ole Römer was offered a post at the Paris Observatory, where he became the first to obtain a reasonable approximation for the value of what?

Three bonus questions on castles in Wales:

(a) Designed by Edward I's military architect James of St George, work on which castle on Anglesey started in 1295?

(b) Which future King of England was born at Pembroke Castle in 1457, and spent part of his childhood there?

(c) Built by Gilbert de Clare during the thirteenth century, which castle is approximately seven miles north of Cardiff and is the largest in Wales?

27. **Your starter for 10:**

Albert Pierrepoint, played by Timothy Spall in a 2006 film, held what position from the 1940s to 1956, following in the footsteps of both his father and his uncle?

Three bonus questions on a prefix:

(a) In the mid 1980s, which new oestrogen-like chemicals, derived from plants, were discovered in human urine? Soya bean products and some other tropical legumes were found to be particularly rich sources.

(b) Plant life that is classified as 'phytobenthos' would be found where?

(c) 'Late blight' is a disease caused by the fungus *Phytophthora infestans*, which attacks tomato vines and which other plant? It was particularly virulent in the mid nineteenth century.

28. Your starter for 10:

Austerlitz, Iena, Alma, Bir-Hakeim and Carrousel are among the names of bridges crossing which European river?

Three bonus questions on a British car company:

(a) Which British car company's green and yellow logo carries the initials A.C.B.C., those of the company's founder?

(b) What name did Lotus give to the suspension system introduced in 1983 that uses computers to control a hydraulic system for keeping a car's body level at all times?

(c) In 1992 which cyclist won Olympic gold in the 4,000 metres pursuit, riding Lotus's revolutionary carbon-composite Monocoque 'Superbike'?

29. Your starter for 10:

In snooker and billiards, which French word is used for a shot played with the cue nearly vertical so as to achieve a sharp swerve in the cue ball?

Three bonus questions on the 1930s:

In each case, give the year of the 1930s during which the

following occurred:

(a) George VI was crowned King; the German Condor legion bombed Guernica; Japan invaded China and occupied the capital, Nanjing?

(b) Stanley Baldwin's National Government was re-elected; Italy invaded Abyssinia; Mao Zedong's communist armies completed the 10,000 kilometre 'Long March'?

(c) Prohibition ended in the USA; the Bodyline Test series soured relations between Britain and Australia; Adolf Hitler became German Chancellor?

30. Your starter for 10:

The state capital of Wisconsin, the Manhattan street associated with the American advertising industry, and the mermaid played by Daryl Hannah in the 1984 film *Splash* all take their names from that of which politician, the fourth US president?

Three bonus questions on painters:

(a) Which painter who worked mostly in Spain and died there in 1614 is best known for his Mannerist religious works in which elongated flame-like figures are painted in bright, acid colours?

(b) Which French painter born in 1877 is known for his light-hearted, brightly coloured views of racecourses, regattas and seascapes, for example, *The Bay of Angels, Nice*?

(c) Which English painter born in 1891 is famous for his large canvases of soldiers and shipbuilders and, particularly, of biblical scenes set in his home village in Berkshire, all executed in a faux-naïf linear style?

'Well, we shall have to say goodbye to you. I suppose it might have made some small difference if you'd known more about castles in Wales. I can't think it really matters, though. But thank you very much for playing.'

Quarter-Finals

'Once again, as John Keats
mistakenly put it, we stand, like
stout Cortez, silent upon a peak
in Darien, as we gaze at the vast
expanse of the student mind. Or so
we hope.'

THE RULES

OK, you all know the rules so let's perpetrate a quarter-final. Ten points for this...

Match One

1. **Your starter for 10:**

Montepulciano is a red wine from which region of west central Italy, on the Ligurian Sea?

Three bonus questions linked by a verb:

(a) In computing, what term is used for the system in which numbers are denoted by means of a decimal point and an exponent?

(b) Used in the construction of model aircraft, which wood gets its name from the Spanish for 'raft' or 'float'?

(c) Who claimed that he 'floated like a butterfly and stung like a bee'?

2. **Your starter for 10:**

Popularised by the work of the fifteenth-century Franciscan friar Luca Pacioli, which accounting system has every business transaction give rise to a debit and a corresponding credit, with each traditionally placed on opposite pages of a ledger?

Three bonus questions on peace treaties:

Which wars were ended by the following treaties?

(a) The Treaty of Paris in 1763.

(b) The Treaty of Westphalia in 1648.

(c) The Treaty of Prague in 1866.

3. Your starter for 10:

For what do the initials J.P.L. stand? Established in Pasadena by the California Institute of Technology, since 1958 it has been a NASA centre for the development and control of unmanned spacecraft.

Three bonus questions on a drink:

(a) In 1943, Winston Churchill declared that there was no finer investment for any community than providing which citizens with what beverage?

(b) 'For he on honey-dew hath fed, / And drunk the milk of paradise.' In which poem of 1816 do these lines appear?

(c) Which of Shakespeare's title characters is said by his wife to be 'too full o' the milk of human kindness'?

4. Your starter for 10:

Which number is the third perfect number, the thirty-first triangular number and would be used in predictive text to spell the word gym?

Three bonus questions on a shared surname:

(a) Which financier and statesman was Prime Minister of Cape Colony from 1890 to 1896?

(b) The seventeenth-century Jesuit missionary Alexandre de Rhodes was the first Frenchman to visit which Asian country?

(c) On which subject has Gary Rhodes written and presented TV programmes?

5. Your starter for 10:

At the 2004 Athens Olympics, Zhang Jun and Gao Ling of China defeated Nathan Robertson and Gail Emms, leaving the latter to take silver for Great Britain in which sport?

Three bonus questions on a sports ground:

(a) The oldest fixture at which sports ground is an annual match between Eton and Harrow schools, the first of which was played there in 1805 when Lord Byron played for Harrow?

(b) In addition to cricket, Lord's has hosted lacrosse and hockey matches. Which sport will it host for the London 2012 Olympics?

(c) The International Cricket Council, cricket's global governing body, was based in the Clock Tower at Lord's from its formation in 1909 until 2006, when it moved its offices to which of the Arab Emirates?

6. Your starter for 10:

Which tradition, inaugurated in Plymouth colony in 1621 when men of the Wampanoag tribe sat down to eat a meal with the pilgrims, became an official American national holiday in 1863?

Three bonus questions on British history:

(a) Of which seventeenth-century event did a spectator say 'The blow I saw given and, I remember well, there was such a groan by the thousands then present as I never heard before and desire I may never hear again'?

(b) Charles I was 'a mild and gracious prince who knew not how to be, or how to be made, great,' in the words of which Archbishop of Canterbury, whose support for the King led him to be beheaded in 1645?

(c) Although he later became Cromwell's unofficial laureate, which English poet wrote of Charles I on the scaffold: 'He nothing common did or mean, upon that memorable scene'?

7. Your starter for 10:

Which Romantic poet wrote these lines: 'I had a dove

and the sweet dove died; / And I have thought it died of grieving: / O what could it grieve for? Its feet were tied, / With a silken thread of my own hand's weaving'?

Three bonus questions on Classical music:
In each case, give the composer of the following:
(a) *Hungarian Rhapsodies*, composed from 1846.
(b) The 1934 work *Rhapsody on a Theme by Paganini*.
(c) The 1924 work *Rhapsody in Blue*.

8. **Your starter for 10:**
Composed of lipid and protein, what name denotes the structure that forms the outer boundary of a cell?

Three bonus questions on an expression:
(a) Which poet, who had fought at Philippi in 42 BC, wrote the words '*Dulce et decorum est pro patria mori*'?
(b) What three words precede '*Dulce et decorum est*' in the final couplet of Wilfred Owen's poem of the same name?
(c) Owen wrote the first draft of '*Dulce et decorum est*' in 1917 at which military psychiatric hospital for victims of shell-shock?

9. **Your starter for 10:**
Which sailor aboard HMS *Bellipotent*, who inadvertently kills the treacherous master-at-arms John Claggart, is the hero of a posthumously published novel by Herman Melville, which was made into an opera by Benjamin Britten and a film directed by Peter Ustinov?

Three bonus questions on fictional detectives:
(a) Which hard-drinking detective's wife Rhona leaves him in the first novel to feature him? He then begins a liaison with the woman who is to become his boss.
(b) The terminally ill wife of which lugubrious detective

dies in the first television episode to feature him, 'Care
and Protection', originally screened in December 1992?

(c) Which overweight detective was left a note by his wife
before she left him saying his dinner was in the oven
on the low burner; when he opened the oven door he
found a gently crisping ham salad?

10. Your starter for 10:
Used as a specification for internet access for radio
transceivers and cellular phones, what do the letters
'WAP' stand for?

Three bonus questions on a fruit:

(a) Which type of large, hard pear, now usually identified
as the Black Worcester and most often used in pies
and for roasting, probably takes its name from
the Cistercian abbey overlooking the Ivel valley in
Bedfordshire?

(b) Baked Warden pears in red wine is a pudding
traditionally served on 28 October, the feast day of
which saint, an apostle also known as Thaddaeus or
Lebbaeus?

(c) In which of Shakespeare's plays does Autolycus pick
the pocket of a clown sent to buy saffron for the
Warden pies being prepared for a sheep-shearing feast?

11. Your starter for 10:
In the animal phylum *Cnidaria*, what name is given to
the body form that consists of a tubular body with a
mouth surrounded by tentacles, as in a sea anemone?

Three bonus questions on a name:

(a) Which Austrian-born psychiatrist introduced the
concept of 'inferiority feeling', leading to his falling out
with Sigmund Freud?

(b) Which fictional detective was almost ensnared by Irene

Adler, whom he always referred to as 'the woman'?

(c) *Adlertag*, or 'Eagle Day', was the German codename for the first day of which air assault of the Second World War?

12. Your starter for 10:

Which American state takes its name from Choctaw words meaning 'red people', is nicknamed the 'sooner' state after those white settlers who pre-empted the terms of the Indian Appropriation Act of 1889, and is the original home of the Joad family in Steinbeck's *The Grapes of Wrath*?

Three bonus questions on American universities:

(a) Which university was founded as the College of New Jersey in 1746, making it the fourth oldest in the USA?

(b) Which term for the grounds of a college or university was first used at Princeton in about 1774?

(c) Eight universities in America are called 'Ivy League'. Princeton, Harvard, Yale and Columbia are four – name one of the others.

13. Your starter for 10:

The Mannerheim line was a defensive fortification constructed from 1920 onwards, and was of particular significance from 1939 to 1940 during the Soviet Union's offensive against which country?

Three bonus questions on falling stars:

(a) Which of the metaphysical poets wrote the verse on the inconstancy of women which begins: 'Go, and catch a falling star, / Get with child a mandrake root'?

(b) According to the book of Revelation in the King James Bible, what was the name of the star which, quote: 'fell... from heaven, burning as it were a lamp and it fell upon the third part of the rivers, and upon the fountains of waters'?

(c) 'The Falling Star' is the title of the second chapter of which novel by H.G. Wells, in which what is briefly believed to be a meteor lands on Horsell Common near Woking?

14. Your starter for 10:

When ordered alphabetically by chemical symbol, which element follows the lightest of the noble gases and a transition metal named after the Latin for Copenhagen?

Three bonus questions on France:

In each case, give the administrative region in which the following départements are located:

(a) Aisne, Oise and Somme.

(b) Creuse, Haute-Vienne and Corrèze.

(c) Dordogne, Gironde and Landes.

15. Your starter for 10:

In 1992, Pope John Paul II beatified the Spanish priest Josemaria Escrivá de Balaguer who founded which controversial and authoritarian organisation in 1928?

Three bonus questions on post-war prime ministers:

In each case, name the prime minister who was born in the same year as the following:

(a) The authors Somerset Maugham and G.K. Chesterton, and the US President Herbert Hoover.

(b) The novelists Roald Dahl and Harold Robbins, and the French President François Mitterand.

(c) The actor Pierce Brosnan, and the politicians Jeb Bush and Michael Portillo.

16. Your starter for 10:

What two-word French-derived term indicates a complete and annotated list of the works of a particular artist?

Three bonus questions on intelligence agencies:
(a) The *Securitate*, dissolved in January 1990, was the intelligence service of which country?
(b) Which security service was established in 1969 but wound up in 1980 after it was implicated in the so-called 'information' scandal, nicknamed 'Muldergate'?
(c) In which country of Eastern Europe was the official secret police known by the abbreviation 'Stasi'?

17. **Your starter for 10:**
Of uncertain etymology, what word denotes a period of low spirits or unhappy listlessness and a region of the ocean near the Equator, characterised by calms, sudden storms and unpredictable winds?

Three bonus questions on the rainbow in mythology:
(a) In Greek mythology, which messenger-goddess was the personification of the rainbow, and the means by which the gods communicated with mortals?
(b) Bifrost, meaning 'tremulous way', was the rainbow bridge between the realm of the mortals and the realm of the gods in which mythology?
(c) Which South American people believed that rainbows were the feather crown of Illapa, the god of thunder and rain?

18. **Your starter for 10:**
Birthplace of Cesar Franck and Georges Simenon, which city on the River Meuse was at the centre of a prince-bishopric until 1792 and is now the cultural centre of eastern Belgium?

Three bonus questions on bestselling books:
(a) *The Kite Runner* and *A Thousand Splendid Suns* are

novels by Khaled Hosseini set mainly in which country, the author's birthplace in 1965?

(b) According to the title of a 2002 work by the Norwegian Asne Seierstad, what is the occupation of Sultan Khan, who invites her to live with him and his family in Kabul?

(c) Which book by George Crile about a US congressman's involvement in a covert CIA operation to support the Afghan rebels in the 1980s was released as a film starring Tom Hanks in 2007?

19. Your starter for 10:

Which title bestowed upon the sorceress Ayesha by the tribe she has enslaved in H. Rider Haggard's novel has since passed into popular culture as the name by which Horace Rumpole refers to his wife?

Three bonus questions on a philosopher:

(a) Which nineteenth-century philosopher maintained that hope was 'the worst of all evils, because it protracts the torment of men'?

(b) What did Nietzsche describe as 'the herd-instinct in the individual'?

(c) Who or what did Nietzsche describe as 'God's second blunder'?

20. Your starter for 10:

Born in Belfast in 1824, which inventor, physicist and mathematician entered Glasgow University at the age of 10 and went on to propose the absolute temperature scale which was named after him?

Three bonus questions on a poet and his critics:

(a) 'Let him never come back to us! / There would be doubt, hesitation and pain, / Forced praise on our part – the glimmer of twilight, / Never glad confident morning again!' Robert Browning wrote these lines on which poet's acceptance of the laureateship and his perceived abandonment of liberalism?

(b) Antagonised by what he considered to be the provinciality of the Lake Poets, Byron wrote the preface to which of his poems as a rebuke to Wordsworth's own introduction to 'The Thorn'?

(c) 'In honoured poverty thy voice did weave / Songs consecrate to truth and liberty, – / Deserting these thou leavest me to grieve' are lines from 'To Wordsworth', an ode by which of his contemporaries?

21. **Your starter for 10:**
Which isotope of hydrogen with mass number 3 can be made in nuclear reactors, has a half-life of 12.3 years, decaying to helium-3, and is mainly used as a tracer in radioactive labelling?

Three bonus questions on film angels:
(a) In the film *The Preacher's Wife*, who plays the angel, Dudley?

(b) What is the name of the scruffy, cigarette-smoking angel played by John Travolta in the film of the same name?

(c) In which science fiction film was the blind angel Pygar, played by John Philip Law, rescued by Jane Fonda?

22. **Your starter for 10:**
Founded in 1934 by Ronald Kidd, which human rights group appointed Shami Chakrabarti as its director in September 2003?

Three bonus questions on a country:
(a) Which country of former Soviet Central Asia moved its capital from Almaty to Aqmola in 1997?

(b) On the border of Kazakhstan and Uzbekistan, which

saltwater lake was formerly the world's fourth-largest body of inland water?

(c) Which sea meets the southern section of Kazakhstan's western extremity?

23. Your starter for 10:

What single word links a 1912 document signed in Ulster to protest against the third Home Rule bill with political and religious agreements made in Scotland in 1638 and 1643?

Three bonus questions on Italian architects:

(a) Which Roman architect of the first century BC described the human figure as the main source of proportion in the classical orders of architecture?

(b) Designer of the colonnade and piazza in front of St Peter's in Rome, which seventeenth-century sculptor and architect was also responsible for several fountains in Rome, including the Triton Fountain and the Fountain of the Four Rivers?

(c) Winner of the Pritzker Architecture Prize, which Italian architect designed the auditorium Parco della Musica in Rome and the 'Shard of Glass' or London Bridge Tower currently under construction?

24. Your starter for 10:

What is nine-sixteenths of four-thirds?

Three bonus questions on verse forms:

(a) Which fourteenth-century poet was the first to use rhyme royal, a verse form consisting of stanzas of seven 10-syllable lines rhyming a, b, a, b, b, c, c?

(b) Which two-word Italian term is applied to a verse form using stanzas of eight lines, each with 10 or 11 syllables? It was employed by Byron, most notably in *Don Juan*.

(c) Monorhyme uses the same rhyme for every line of a verse or part of a work and is common to Welsh, Latin and Arabic literature including, in the latter case, sections of which collection of stories, translated into English in the 1880s by Richard Burton?

25. Your starter for 10:
Described in heraldic terms as 'or, four bars gules', the Senyera is the flag of which autonomous community of Spain?

Three bonus questions on American football in film:
(a) The eponymous hero of which 1994 film discards the leg braces he has worn for many years, discovers he can run at lightning speeds, and gets into university on a football scholarship?
(b) Which director's films include *The Fortune Cookie*, starring Jack Lemmon and Walter Matthau, in which a photographer is persuaded to file a claim against the Cleveland Browns when one of their players knocks him to the ground?
(c) Which comedy team wins a football game for Huxley College by taking the ball into the end zone in a horse-drawn garbage wagon in the 1932 film *Horse Feathers*?

26. Your starter for 10:
'A vast, lonely, forbidding expanse of nothing … rather like clouds and clouds of pumice stone'. To what do these words, broadcast by astronaut Frank Borman in 1968, refer?

Three bonus questions on boundaries in the natural world:
(a) In geology, what name is taken from that of a German geophysicist and is given to the discontinuity between the lower mantle and outer core of the Earth?

(b) Around the end of the second century, Alexander of Aphrodisias observed and later gave his name to the dark band forming part of which optical phenomenon?

(c) In meteorology, what suffix is used to indicate the topmost sections of the troposphere, stratosphere, mesosphere and thermosphere, where they border the layer above?

27. Your starter for 10:
What substance, a mixture of graphite and clay, is designated by number in the USA and by the letters 'f', 'b' and 'h' in the UK?

Three bonus questions on terms that begin with the prefix 'poly':
In each case, give the term from the definition:

(a) The art of painting in several colours, particularly when applied to ancient pottery or architecture.

(b) In linguistics, the propensity of words to have two or more senses from the same etymology, for example 'crane' meaning 'long-legged bird' and 'machine for moving heavy objects'.

(c) Practised in some Himalayan and Polynesian societies and regarded as a means of limiting births, what term specifically denotes a form of plural marriage where a woman has more than one husband?

28. Your starter for 10:
Calcaneus is the anatomical term for which bone of the human body?

Three bonus questions on Italian cookery terms:

(a) Born in 1460 and noted for his use of red pigments said to resemble raw meat, which Italian painter gives his name to an hors d'oeuvre consisting of thin slices of raw beef or fish served with a sauce or dressing?

(b) From the Italian for 'to fry gently', which term describes vegetables that are softened slowly and used as a condiment and flavouring?

(c) Of Tuscan origin and derived from the Italian for 'crust', which close relative of bruschetta consists of toasted bread with various toppings?

29. Your starter for 10:
Often seen as a symbol of connubial fidelity, which character in Homer's *Odyssey* is the narrator of a 2006 novel by Margaret Atwood?

Three bonus questions on a Roman legend:
(a) According to Livy's *History of Rome*, Romulus used the Consualia, the games in honour of Equestrian Neptune, to gain possession of whom or what?

(b) In the 1630s, which French artist executed two versions of the legend of the Sabine women, now in the Louvre and the Metropolitan Museum of Art?

(c) An adaptation of the legend of the Sabine women, Stephen Vincent Benet's short story 'The Sobbin' Women' was the basis for which 1954 Oscar-winning Hollywood musical?

30. Your starter for 10:
The concerto for flute, violins and bassoon entitled *La Notte* is a work by which prolific Italian composer, who died in 1741?

Three bonus questions on a place name:
(a) Which German electorate was joined to the British Crown from 1714 until 1837?

(b) The modern city of Hanover is the capital of which German Land, or state?

(c) What is the German spelling of Hanover?

'Umm... I'm rather at a loss
for words, because anything I
say is going to seem beastly and
it shouldn't be, because actually
going out in the quarter-finals is
absolutely fine, and if you get any
stick about it, I'd arrange to be out
of the bar the night this goes out.
Anyway – don't worry about it. You
played the game, and you were
thrashed by a very, very strong
team..'

THE RULES

The rules are constant as the
Northern Star, so let's crack on with
it...

Match Two

1. Your starter for 10:

In 1910, the Austrian-born violinist Fritz Kreisler gave the first performance of a Violin Concerto in B Minor dedicated to him by its composer. Who was that composer?

Three bonus questions on a country:

(a) The etymology of the name of which East African state is sometimes given as the Greek words for 'burnt' and 'face'?

(b) Which country invaded Ethiopia on 3 October 1935?

(c) Which operatic heroine is the daughter of Amonasro, King of Ethiopia?

2. Your starter for 10:

In physiology, the *foramen magnum* is a large, almost circular opening in the centre of the base of which part of the body's skeletal structure?

Three bonus questions on football in South America:

(a) Thought to have been named after its namesake toured the country in the early twentieth century, Everton de Viña del Mar has historically been of the most successful teams in which South American country?

(b) Liverpool FC, playing in black and blue striped jerseys, is a top-flight club in which South American country?

(c) SC Corinthians is one of the most successful football

clubs in which South American country?

3. **Your starter for 10:**
What name is given to a positive whose factors excluding itself sum to a number greater than it, for example 12, whose factors 1, 2, 3, 4 and 6 sum to 16?

Three bonus questions on the eight auspicious symbols of Buddhism:
(a) Known in Sanskrit as *padma* and in Japanese as *ren-ge*, which aquatic plant is used in Buddhism to symbolise spiritual purity and the oneness of cause and effect?
(b) A traditional Indian symbol of both protection and royalty, which device has the Sanskrit name *chattra* and symbolises spiritual power?
(c) Which 'right-turning' object stands for the fame of Buddha's teaching and the Dharma?

4. **Your starter for 10:**
Towards the end of 2004 which theatrical knight played a Lancastrian Widow Twanky in the Old Vic's production of *Aladdin*, a production conceived by the person in question and commissioned by Kevin Spacey?

Three bonus questions on a poem:
(a) 'Down by the Salley Gardens' was written by which Irish poet, who called it 'an attempt to reconstruct an old song from three lines imperfectly remembered by an old peasant woman'?
(b) Yeats's source for the poem lived in Ballisodare, a village in which traditional county of Ireland, where Yeats spent his childhood and from where he drew much of his inspiration?
(c) The Salley Gardens of the title refer to what trees, the name being an anglicised version of the Irish for trees of the genus *salix*?

5.   Your starter for 10:
An important modernist novel, *The Man without Qualities* is an unfinished work by which Austrian author, born in 1880?

> **Three bonus questions on Italian Renaissance art:**
> For each of the following lists of artists, give the Italian city of the school of art to which they principally belonged:
> (a) Domenichino, and the Carracci family of Annibale, Agostino and Ludovico.
> (b) Duccio, Martini, and Martino di Bartolomeo.
> (c) Finally, Donatello, Botticelli, and Masolino.

6.   Your starter for 10:
In biology, the myelin sheath surrounds which part of a nerve cell?

> **Three bonus questions on Machiavelli:**
> (a) Machiavelli says that the prince must 'play the animal well' and choose two beasts, one 'to recognise the traps', the other 'to frighten the wolves'. Which two animals does he recommend?
> (b) What, according to Machiavelli, 'begin when you will, but they do not end when you please'?
> (c) Machiavelli is credited with popularising what three-word dictum, meaning the imposition of authority by forestalling unity amongst subject peoples? You may answer in Latin or in English.

7.   Your starter for 10:
Which word, derived from the Latin for 'to fly', was originally applied to a simultaneous discharge of firearms or artillery, but is also now used more widely and is applied in tennis to a return stroke or hit at a ball before it has touched the ground?

Three bonus questions on the colour yellow:

(a) The scene of a Russo-Japanese naval battle in 1904, Inchon, on the Yellow Sea, is a major port for which city?

(b) *Half of a Yellow Sun* by Chimamanda Ngozi Adichie won the Orange Prize for Fiction in 2007. It is set amidst the upheaval of the civil war in which country in the 1960s?

(c) In Shakespeare, which conscientious but humourless steward is tricked into wearing yellow cross-gartered stockings in order to return his mistress Olivia's supposed love for him?

8. Your starter for 10:

Which decade saw the outbreak of the Second Opium War against China; the Treaty of Kanagawa, which forced Japan to open to foreign ships; and the rebellion in India which led to the transfer of the government of India to the British Crown?

Three bonus questions on Scotland:

(a) Campbeltown is the main town of which Scottish peninsula, whose southernmost promontory, or mull, is less than twenty miles from the Irish coast?

(b) Only accessible on foot or by boat, Inverie is the main settlement of which peninsula in Lochaber, sometimes known as 'the Rough Bounds'?

(c) Noted for spectacular rock formations such as the Quiraing, Trotternish is the northernmost peninsula of which Scottish island?

9. Your starter for 10:

From the Greek for 'down' and 'running', *catadromus* is a term used to describe the behaviour of freshwater fish, such as eels, swimming in which direction to spawn?

Three bonus questions on a name:

(a) Prodigy Lisa, baby Maggie and underachiever Bart are members of which fictional family?

(b) The Scottish physician Sir James Simpson was, in 1847, the first person to use which substance as an anaesthetic?

(c) What do the initials of the disgraced American football player O.J. Simpson stand for?

10. Your starter for 10:

The Shinto goddess Ama-Terasu, the Hindu god Surya, the Inca deity Inti, and the Egyptian god Ra are linked by which celestial body?

Three bonus questions on novelists:

(a) Which Russian-born novelist is best remembered for *Lolita*, published in 1958?

(b) Which American novelist, who attended Nabokov's course at Cornell, is best remembered for *Gravity's Rainbow*?

(c) Since the 1970s, rumours have surfaced that Thomas Pynchon is actually which other notoriously reclusive American novelist?

11. Your starter for 10:

According to a pronouncement attributed to both Leonhard Euler and Karl Gauss, what 'is the queen of the sciences'?

Three bonus questions on the states of Mexico:

In each case, give the name of the Mexican state from the English translation of its name:

(a) A Spanish word meaning 'nobleman', in this case the surname of a leader in the Mexican War of Independence.

(b) The Spanish for 'hot water' or 'hot springs'.

(c) The Spanish for 'true cross'.

12. **Your starter for 10:**
Which pair of antonyms appear in the titles of a 1970s television documentary series presented by Jacob Bronowski, and an 1871 work by Charles Darwin?

Three bonus questions on mathematical constants:
(a) Equal to one plus root-five, all divided by 2, and usually denoted by the Greek letter phi, what name is given to the ratio 'phi-to-one', which gives the proportions of a rectangle such that when a square is removed, the remaining rectangle has sides that are in the same proportion?
(b) Which Greek letter is used to denote the Euler-Mascheroni constant, defined as the limiting difference between the harmonic series and the natural logarithm?
(c) Which mathematical constant, approximately equal to 2.718, is the unique positive real number which, when raised to the power x, gives a function of x which is its own derivative?

13. **Your starter for 10:**
The residence of Froben, Erasmus, Holbein the Younger, Calvin, Nietzsche and the Bernoulli family have all resided in which city on the River Rhine, home to Switzerland's oldest university?

Three bonus questions on marine fauna:
(a) 'Sea pie' is an alternative name for which large, plover-like coastal bird with black and white plumage and a long reddish bill? It feeds chiefly on bivalve shellfish.
(b) 'Sea canary' and 'white whale' are alternative names for which small-toothed whale native to shallow arctic seas, and characterised by its white skin and lack of a dorsal fin?

(c) The term 'sea cow', formerly used for both walruses and hippos, is now applied to mammals of the order *sirenia*, comprising the dugong and which other?

14. Your starter for 10:

What comes next in this sequence, being the countries that border Germany, in clockwise order: Poland, Czech Republic, Austria, Switzerland and... which country?

Three bonus questions on abbreviations:

The answer for each question is a pair of abbreviations, each of which is the reverse of the other.

(a) What abbreviations denote 'of guaranteed quality in the Italian wine trade' and 'only paid for when it arrives'?

(b) 'The highest of the three classes of the order of the bath' and 'a vaccine against tuberculosis'?

(c) 'A mild oath used in online chat' and a product of biotechnology?

15. Your starter for 10:

What links 'MALAYA', 'EGYPT', 'HOLLAND', 'ITALY', 'BURMA' and 'POLAND', all of them acronyms associated particularly with the Second World War?

Three bonus questions on cities ancient and modern:

(a) Founded during the Macedonian campaign against the satrap of Bactria, how is the ancient city of Alexandria in Arachosia known today? The second city of its country, its modern name derives from a local version of the name Alexander.

(b) Alexandria Eschate, or 'furthest', located in the Fergana Valley, is today the city of Khujand, the second city of which Central Asian republic?

(c) Founded near the site of Alexander's victory at the

Battle of Issus, the modern city of Iskenderun is in which modern country?

16. Your starter for 10:
Derived from a Latin term meaning 'Persian apple', the name of which fruit links the titles of a 1961 work by Roald Dahl and a 1977 single by The Stranglers?

Three bonus questions on composers:
(a) 2008 marked the 150th anniversary of the birth in Lucca in Italy of which composer, considered by some to have been the last great representative of the Italian operatic tradition?

(b) 2008 marked the 200th anniversary of a concert at the Theater an den Wein which saw the first performances of which two symphonies by Beethoven?

(c) 2008 was the 180th anniversary of the untimely death from typhus of which composer, who established the art of the German lieder and was buried close to Beethoven, whom he greatly admired?

17. Your starter for 10:
The first international convention for the safety of life at sea was called in London in 1913 in the wake of which disaster?

Three bonus questions on gentlemen:
(a) 'The last gentleman in Europe' was the novelist Ada Leverson's tribute to which writer who died in Paris in 1900, having bestowed upon her the nickname 'Sphinx'?

(b) 'Gentleman' is how which character is described in the title of the novel of 1856 by Dinah Craik?

(c) 'Hereabouts died a very gallant gentleman' are the opening words of an epitaph on a cairn and cross erected in the Antarctic in November 1912 in memory of which British explorer?

18. Your starter for 10:
What name is given to the broad sash or belt, often heavily ornamented, worn around one shoulder to support a sword or bugle carried on the opposite hip?

> **Three bonus questions on contemporary Latin:**
> How do the following Latin phrases translate into English?
> (a) *Res inexplicata volans.*
> (b) Which recording medium is an '*instrumentum telehornamentis exceptorium*'?
> (c) What would be the occupation of someone described as *sui ipsius nudator*?

19. Your starter for 10:
What surname links: a bagpipe-playing Canterbury pilgrim in Chaucer; a Henry James novella of 1878; the author of the trilogy *Sexus*, *Plexus* and *Nexus*, and the playwright husband of Marilyn Monroe?

> **Three bonus questions on French scientists:**
> (a) The postulation of the existence of black holes and an exposition of celestial mechanics are among the achievements of which French scientist? Born in 1749, he gives his name to a differential equation in physics.
> (b) Born in 1736, which French scientist gives his name to that point at which a small body, under the gravitational influence of two large ones, will remain approximately at rest relative to them?
> (c) Which French chemist refuted the phlogiston theory of combustion by identifying and naming oxygen? He was guillotined in 1794 as a farmer of taxes, despite having helped reform the taxation system.

20. Your starter for 10:

'The Doctrine and Discipline of Divorce' was the first of four tracts on that subject by which English writer, the first being published in 1643 shortly after his first wife, Marie Powell, left him to return to live with her mother?

> **Three bonus questions linked by a word:**
> (a) What term is applied to drinks made from wine or ale which have been heated, spiced and sweetened?
> (b) What is the largest settlement on the Hebridean island of Mull?
> (c) Mullion Cove is a well-known beauty spot in which English county?

21. Your starter for 10:

In mathematics, what curve is formed when the inverse curve of a parabola is calculated using the focus of the parabola as the inversion centre? Its name derives from the Latin for 'heart'.

> **Three bonus questions on ancient Greek names:**
> In each case the answer is a pair of names that in English differ by only one letter:
> (a) A priestess of Aphrodite who killed herself when her lover drowned, and the queen of the Olympian gods?
> (b) A king of the city-state of Sikyon described by Aeschylus as the son of Apollo, and the son of Faunus who, according to Ovid, was the lover of Galatea?
> (c) The goddess of strife, who gives her name to a dwarf planet, and the goddess of the rainbow?

22. Your starter for 10:

Identify the prominent poet who is the addressee of the following couplets by W.H. Auden: 'I'm also glad I've your authority / For finding Wordsworth a most bleak old bore, / Though I'm afraid we're in a sad minority /

For every year his followers get more.'

Three bonus questions on the endings of novels:

(a) Which eighteenth-century novel appears to be summed up in its final line as a 'cock and a bull – and one of the best of its kind, I ever heard'?

(b) Which nineteenth-century Russian novel ends its first epilogue with these words: 'And my father? Oh father, father! Yes, I will do something with which even he would be satisfied'?

(c) Which twentieth-century American novel ends with the words 'So we beat on, boats against the current, borne back ceaselessly into the past'?

23. Your starter for 10:

In use from the mid seventeenth century, which firearm took its name from the Dutch 'thunder-box', and had a flared muzzle that was designed in the erroneous belief that it would spread the shot?

Three bonus questions on military history:

For each of the following sets of three battles, name the war during which they occurred:

(a) Fontenoy, Cartagena and Dettingen.

(b) The White Mountain, Breitenfeld and Luetzen.

(c) Formigny, Herrings and La Rochelle.

24. Your starter for 10:

What term, derived from the Greek for 'to interpret', is that branch of learning that deals with the interpretation of texts, especially the scriptures?

Three bonus questions on cricket in fiction:

(a) The Butley Flower Show match is a memorable evocation of village cricket in which Siegfried Sassoon novel, the first volume of his George Sherston trilogy?

(b) The annual match between Brandham Hall and the village sees schoolboy Leo Colston come on as twelfth man to take the crucial catch that dismisses farmer Ted Burgess in which 1953 novel?

(c) In Douglas Adams's *Life, the Universe and Everything*, Arthur Dent and Ford Prefect rescue which piece of cricket memorabilia that has been stolen from Lord's by robber robots from the planet Krikkit?

25. Your starter for 10:

The five Béjart siblings provided the nucleus of the company of actors associated with which French dramatist, born in 1622?

Three bonus questions on internet country codes:

(a) Two countries have top-level domain country codes comprising letters at the extremes of the alphabet. One is Azerbaijan, that is '.az'. What is the other country?

(b) Which two EU member states have top-level domain codes that are the reverse of one another?

(c) Which Eastern European country's top-level domain code is the reverse of that of Australia?

26. Your starter for 10:

The archaeological sites of Las Medulas in north-west Spain and Dolaucothi in South Wales were, in Roman times, major sources of what metal?

Three bonus questions on a shared name:

(a) Which Irish-born physicist proposed that, when in motion, a body is shorter along its line of motion than when at rest?

(b) Which US president had the middle name Fitzgerald?

(c) How was Monroe Stahr described in the title of F. Scott Fitzgerald's novel?

27. **Your starter for 10:**
In astronomy denoting the point at which a heavenly body in the Earth's orbit is furthest from the Earth, what six-letter word is used in a general sense to mean the highest or culminating point, e.g. of power or success?

Three bonus questions on Notting Hill:
(a) In 1963, Notting Hill was revealed to have suffered from the unscrupulous business practices of which 'slum landlord'?
(b) *The Napoleon of Notting Hill*, published in 1904, was the first novel by which writer, who created the clerical detective, Father Brown?
(c) Which rock guitarist formed the Notting Hillbillies in 1990, in an attempt to return to a more low-key style of performance?

28. **Your starter for 10:**
Officially opened in 1943, which building stands on a site previously occupied by the old Hoover Airport, a pickle factory, a race track and a residential estate in a district of Washington known as Hell's Bottom?

Three bonus questions on Hebrew and Yiddish words:
(a) What is the name of the prayer shawl worn by male Jews during the daily morning service?
(b) Which Yiddish word derives from the German *stadt*, and refers to small towns in Eastern Europe?
(c) What word of Yiddish origin means cheap, shoddy or defective goods, and is now applied to inferior forms of entertainment?

29. **Your starter for 10:**
To the nearest integer, what is E to the power of pi?

Three bonus questions on medieval universities:

(a) The Jagiellonian University, founded in 1364, is the second-oldest in Central Europe and the oldest in which country?

(b) The oldest university in Germany, founded in 1386, is in which city on the River Neckar?

(c) The college of the University of Paris founded in 1257 by Robert de Sorbon was for students of which subject?

30. Your starter for 10:

Taking into account differences between GMT and BST, what is the longest month of the year in the UK?

Three bonus questions on ancient Anatolia:

(a) Lydia, whose last king was Croesus, was a powerful state in the seventh and sixth centuries BC and is usually credited with which financial innovation in the western world?

(b) Which kingdom achieved great prosperity in the eighth century BC, and gave its name to the style of cap worn by its mythical king Midas to hide his asses' ears, and later came to symbolise liberty during the French Revolution?

(c) The original 'Mausoleum', one of the Seven Wonders of the Ancient World, was built for King Mausolus in which city in south-eastern Asia Minor, now known as Bodrum?

> **'I'm afraid we're going to have to say goodbye to you. You never recovered from a really terrible start.'**

Match Three

1.   Your starter for 10:
Identify the author of these lines: 'I leant upon a coppice gate / When frost was spectre-gray, / And winter's dregs made desolate / The weakening eye of day'?

> **Three bonus questions on pairs of homophones, that is, words pronounced alike but spelled differently:**
> In each case, spell both words from the definitions given. To make it a little easier, all answers begin with the letter 'm':
> (a) A goddess such as Thalia, Clio or Erato, and an area of stabling converted into dwellings or garages?
> (b) The hereditary rank of an eighteenth-century French author of licentious novels, and a large tent used for social or commercial functions?
> (c) A speck or particle of dust, and a deep defensive ditch around a fortification or country house, for example, that of the politician Douglas Hogg?

2.   Your starter for 10:
Etymologically unrelated, what four-letter homograph can denote: the SI base unit of amount of substance; a mammal of family *talpidae*; a massive breakwater or berthing facility; and a small, often slightly raised dark blemish on the skin?

Three bonus questions on the solar system:

(a) Jupiter's four largest moons are collectively known as the Galilean Satellites, after Galileo Galilei, who observed them in 1610. For five points, name two of them.

(b) Which of Saturn's moons is the only moon in our solar system to possess a dense atmosphere?

(c) In June 2006, the International Astronomical Union approved the names Nix and Hydra for two newly discovered satellites of Pluto, orbiting in the same plane as which much larger satellite?

3. Your starter for 10:

In biology, DNA contains the elements carbon, oxygen, hydrogen, phosphorus and which other element?

Three bonus questions on a French town:

(a) The site of an early German armoured breakthrough in May 1940, which town in the Ardennes département gives its name to a decisive French defeat in the war of 1870?

(b) Which French ruler surrendered with his army after the Battle of Sedan in 1870?

(c) The Battle of Sedan is described in detail in *The Debacle*, a work of 1892 by which French novelist?

4. Your starter for 10:

The French word for 'rocking horse', supposedly chosen at random out of a dictionary, is thought by some to be the origin of the name of which early twentieth-century cultural movement?

Three bonus questions on a shared name:

(a) Generally referred to by his initials and surname, what were the forenames of the English novelist E.M. Forster?

(b) Thomas Hunt Morgan established the chromosome theory of heredity as a result of his experimental work on which insects?

(c) The Welsh pirate, Sir Henry Morgan, was knighted by King Charles II and appointed Deputy Governor of which Caribbean island?

5. **Your starter for 10:**
In *The Waste Land*, to which play by Shakespeare is T.S. Eliot referring in the opening lines of Part II: 'The chair she sat in, like a burnished throne, / Glowed on the marble'?

Three abbreviated bonus questions:
(a) What is the chemical symbol for the element thallium?
(b) In electronics, what does the abbreviation TTL stand for?
(c) Similarly, the abbreviation TTL stands for what in a photographic context?

6. **Your starter for 10:**
Associated with the rise of the 'dot-com' industry, which ergonomic chair was designed by Chadwick and Stumpf in 1994?

Three bonus questions on counting and probability:
(a) A restaurant menu has five starters, five quite different main courses and four desserts. What is the total number of distinct three-course meals that may be served?
(b) Suppose that the five starters consist of smaller portions of the five mains. How many possible three-course meals are there that avoid having the same dish for starter and main?
(c) And in the same circumstances, given a random allocation of starter, main and dessert, what is the

probability that you will have the same dish for starter and main?

7. Your starter for 10:
'Do you want a dukedom or anything like that?' is reputed to have been said by the Queen in 1955 to which retiring statesman?

Three bonus questions on pigments:
(a) Orpiment, a bright yellow pigment used from ancient Egyptian times until the nineteenth century, is in chemical terms the tri-sulphide of which metalloid?
(b) Often used in medieval manuscripts, which blue pigment was made from lapis lazuli mined in Afghanistan, and derived its name from its overseas origin?
(c) Which greenish-blue pigment was prepared by treating copper sheets with vinegar and scraping the crust off the resulting corrosion?

8. Your starter for 10:
The Schengen Agreement on the relaxation of border controls was initially signed in 1985 by France, Germany, Belgium, the Netherlands and which other country, in which the town of Schengen lies?

Three bonus questions on a disease:
(a) If left untreated, which chronic disease is characterised by three distinct stages developing over a number of years, and is caused by the bacterium *Treponema pallidum*?
(b) Paul Ehrlich, who developed Salvarsan as a treatment for syphilis in the early years of the twentieth century, coined what two-word term for the selective targeting of a disease bacterium without affecting other cells or organisms?

(c) Considered scandalous on its first production in 1882, which play by Henrik Ibsen concerns the effects of syphilis, even though the name of the disease is never mentioned?

9. Your starter for 10:
Which archaic letter of the Greek alphabet, originally the sixth letter of that alphabet, had a phonetic sound like a 'w' and was also known as 'wau'?

Three bonus questions on a music producer:
(a) Born in 1923, which Turkish-American record producer was a co-founder of Atlantic records, whose early roster of artistes included Joe Turner, The Drifters and Ray Charles?

(b) At a tribute concert to Ahmet Ertegun in December 2007, which rock band performed in public together for the first time in over twenty-seven years?

(c) Described by Ahmet Ertegun as 'a declaration of war … the beginning of the Civil Rights Movement', who, in 1939, recorded the song 'Strange Fruit' about the victims of Southern lynch mobs?

10. Your starter for 10:
Which unit of weight for precious stones is now equivalent to 200 milligrams?

Three bonus questions on a prime minister:
(a) 'Most of our people have never had it so good.' These words are principally associated with which prime minister, born in 1894?

(b) 'First of all the Georgian silver goes, and then all that nice furniture that used to be in the saloon. Then the Canalettos go.' Of what government policy did Macmillan say these words in a speech of 1985, one year before his death?

(c) 'The wind of change is blowing through this continent.' Of which continent did Macmillan say these words in a speech of 1960?

11.   **Your starter for 10:**
The practice of dragging a smoked fish across the trail of a fox to throw hounds off the latter's scent is one possible derivation of which expression for a distraction that initially appears significant?

Three bonus questions on a colour:
(a) Which rock group performed *Concerto for Group and Orchestra* with the Royal Philharmonic Orchestra in 1969?
(b) First instituted in the United States of America in 1782 and revived in 1932, the Purple Heart is awarded in what circumstances?
(c) Also known as 'visual purple', which protein is contained in the retinal rods in the eye, and functions in the eye's adaptation to dim light?

12.   **Your starter for 10:**
Excluding one, what is the lowest number that is equal to the sum of the digits of its cube?

Three bonus questions on Latin terms:
(a) Which two-word Latin term means 'bounteous mother' and has been used in English to mean one's old school?
(b) The dura mater is the outer membranous envelope of the spinal cord and which organ of the human body?
(c) Born in 1732, which Austrian composer's works include the *Stabat Mater*?

13.   **Your starter for 10:**
Originally a work of Sophocles, which story was reworked by Jean Anouilh in 1944 to mirror the

French Resistance and those who collaborated with the Germans?

Three bonus questions on British theatres:

(a) Designed as an Elizabethan playhouse, which RSC theatre in Stratford-upon-Avon was opened in 1986 in part of the shell of the Shakespeare Memorial Theatre which had survived a fire sixty years previously?

(b) Founded initially in a public library in Scarborough and now housed in a former cinema, what is the present name of the theatre of which Sir Alan Ayckbourn was artistic director from 1972 to 2009?

(c) Of which London theatre was Sam Mendes appointed artistic director in 1990? He was succeeded in 2002 by Michael Grandage.

14. Your starter for 10:

What is the name of the site in Suffolk where, in 1939, archaeologists discovered the outline of a wooden ship and a burial chamber containing silver, gold, tableware and weapons, which are now in the British Museum?

Three bonus questions on disputed territories:

(a) Scene of an armed conflict in 2008, the de facto independent state of South Ossetia is viewed by most members of the United Nations as being part of which country?

(b) Also *de jure* a part of Georgia, which breakaway republic on the Black Sea has Sukhumi as its capital?

(c) Bordered by Ukraine to the east, the unrecognised breakaway republic of Transnistria is *de jure* part of which country?

15. Your starter for 10:

Coined by the music historian A.W. Ambros in the mid 1860s to describe a musical motto or theme which recurs in a piece of music to represent a character, object, emotion or idea, what term is particularly associated with the later operas of Wagner, though he did not use it himself?

Three bonus questions on the vertebrate kidney:

(a) What is the name of the functional excretory unit of the kidney, responsible for the filtration of blood, eliminating wastes and re-adsorption of non-waste substances, and the production of urine? There are approximately one million such units in the human kidney.

(b) Filtration of blood occurs in the portion of the nephron called the renal or malpighian corpus. What name is given to the tangled mass of capilliaries found in this body?

(c) What name is given to the hair-pin shaped structure situated between the proximal and distal renal tubules of the nephron? It is responsible for concentration of urine.

16. Your starter for 10:

What term means, in electronics, a phase difference of 90 degrees between two waves of the same frequency, as in television colour difference signals; in astronomy, the position of the moon or a planet when it is 90 degrees from the sun when viewed from Earth; and, in mathematics, the process of constructing a square with an area equal to that of a circle or other closed curve?

Three bonus questions on a dukedom:

(a) Running from Worsley to Liverpool, which canal was named after the title of Francis Egerton, the name now being shared with a concert hall that opened in Manchester in 1996?

(b) Which country park and stately home in Cheshire, now owned by the National Trust, was formerly home to the Dukes and Earls of Bridgewater?

(c) In which American novel of 1885 does the eponymous hero meet a conman who claims to be the long-lost 'rightful Duke of Bridgewater'?

17. Your starter for 10:

Which country's northern border with Russia runs roughly along the crest of the Greater Caucasus mountains, and is divided into its eastern and western halves by the Likhi range, which joins the Greater Caucasus to the Lesser?

Three bonus questions on love in Shakespeare:

In each case, name the play in which the following words appear:

(a) 'The course of true love never did run smooth.'

(b) 'I love you with so much of my heart that none is left to protest.'

(c) 'You are a lover; borrow Cupid's wings, and soar with them above a common bound.'

18. Your starter for 10:

In a botanical description of leaves, what does 'glabrous' mean?

Three bonus questions on a word:

(a) Which four-letter colloquial term is used in jazz and rock music for a phrase or figure played repeatedly?

(b) The Rif mountains are in which North African country?

(c) The Rif War of 1919–1926 was fought by the Moroccan Rif and Jibala tribes primarily against which European power?

19. **Your starter for 10:**

Killed in 1935, the Welsh journalist Gareth Jones was posthumously awarded which country's 'medal of freedom' in 2008 for his efforts in publicising the 'Holodomor', a famine of 1932 and 1933 during which several millions died as a result of policies instituted by Stalin?

Three bonus questions on a name:

(a) In Jane Austen's *Emma*, which old maid enjoys 'a most uncommon degree of popularity for a woman neither young, handsome, rich nor married'?

(b) Who played Norman Bates's victim in the shower scene in Alfred Hitchcock's *Psycho*?

(c) Created by H.E. Bates, the adventures of the Larkin family were televised under what title from 1991?

20. **Your starter for 10:**

Which century, according to George Bernard Shaw, 'crowned the idolatry of art with the deification of love, so that every poet is supposed to have pierced to the holy of holies when he has announced that love is the supreme, or the enough, or the all'?

Three bonus questions on Venetian islands:

(a) Sergei Diaghilev, Igor Stravinsky and Ezra Pound are all buried on Venice's cemetery island, named after which saint?

(b) The phrase 'the Garden of Venice' is used of La Vignole and which other island, named after the saint also known as St Elmo?

(c) Since the thirteenth century, the Venetian island of Murano has been a centre for the production of what material?

21. Your starter for 10:

Who comes next in this sequence of World Cup-winning football captains: Fritz Walter, Hilderaldo Bellini, Mauro Ramos de Oliveira and… who?

Three bonus questions on a religious order:

(a) What is the common name for the Order of the Reformed Cistercians of the Strict Observance, noted for its austere rule which includes abstention from meat, fish and eggs?

(b) Which mild, semi-soft cow's milk cheese with a distinctive orange crust is named after the abbey in the Loire Valley where it was first made by Trappist monks in the early nineteenth century?

(c) In addition to cheese, the Trappist monasteries of Chimay, Orval and Westmalle in Belgium are noted for what product?

22. Your starter for 10:

From which Semitic language do the English words 'syrup', 'cotton', 'sofa', 'giraffe' and 'algebra' ultimately derive?

Three bonus questions on an Italian thinker:

(a) Author of the *Prison Notebooks*, which political philosopher led the Communist Party in the Italian parliament until his arrest in 1926?

(b) From the Greek for 'deed', what term did Gramsci use for that which needs to be combined with theory to bring about change in the world?

(c) What term did Gramsci use for the ideological means by which the dominating class gains the spontaneous and consensual adherence of other classes to its rule?

23. Your starter for 10:

What cosmological theory developed by Alexei

Starobinsky and Alan Guth states that the universe underwent exponential expansion during its first fraction of a second? Its name is widely used in economics to describe the rate of increase in prices.

Three bonus questions on South America:

(a) Its name meaning 'Great Hunting Ground', which alluvial plain extends from southern Bolivia through Paraguay to northern Argentina?

(b) Which country's principal river is the Magdalena? It rises in the Andes and flows northwards for about a thousand miles to enter the Caribbean Sea at Barranquilla.

(c) Oil slicks regularly occur on which lake in Venezuela that provides the bulk of the country's oil production?

24. Your starter for 10:

What term denotes the rank or status of Chaucer's Canterbury pilgrim who tells of the story of Arveragus and Dorigen, and is also the first name of a thrice re-elected US President?

Three bonus questions on comets:

(a) The Great Comet of 1680 is also known by the name of which English scientist who used the observational data to show that comets are guided in their movements by the same principle that controls the orbits of planets?

(b) The Great Comet of 1997 or, more prosaically, C/1995 01, is also known by the names of which US astronomers, who independently observed and first reported it while studying the star cluster Messier 70?

(c) At the midpoint of which major novel is Pierre Bezukhov described watching the Great Comet of 1811?

25. Your starter for 10:

Which US legislator gives his name to the act of 1910 which banned the transportation of women across state borders for so-called 'immoral purposes'? Intended to prevent the trafficking of prostitutes, it led to many selective and unjust prosecutions.

> **Three bonus questions linked by a word:**
> (a) What name is given to the three remote second-magnitude stars Alnilam, Alnitak and Mintaka, in the constellation of Orion?
> (b) A 1997 rail tunnel and bridge across the 'Great Belt' linked the east and west of which European country?
> (c) Freddie Welsh, the British lightweight boxing champion, became the first recipient of which sporting belt in 1909?

26. Your starter for 10:

Give the three words that complete the title of this work of 1776: *An Inquiry into the Nature and Causes of the...* what?

> **Three bonus questions on foreign words, specifically those that may be made with the seven letters of the word 'sojourn' – for example, the French word 'nous', meaning 'we':**
> In each case, identify and spell the word from the definition:
> (a) A French word meaning 'bear' (the large mammal, that is).
> (b) A German word meaning 'only'.
> (c) A Latin word meaning 'load', 'cargo' or 'burden'.

27. Your starter for 10:

The scientific names *petroselinum crispum* and *salvia officinalis* give the first two words of the title of a 1966 album by which American folk-rock duo?

Three bonus questions on the American songwriter Oscar Hammerstein:
In each case, identify the musical in which the following song titles appear:
(a) 'A Real Nice Clam-Bake', 'You're A Queer One, Julie Jordan' and 'You'll Never Walk Alone'.
(b) 'People Will Say We're In Love', 'I Cain't [sic] Say No' and 'Oh, What A Beautiful Mornin'.
(c) 'Cockeyed Optimist', 'Honeybun' and 'I'm Gonna Wash That Man Right Outa My Hair'.

28. **Your starter for 10:**
Which gum or resin exuded from the bark of the tree *pistacia lentiscus*, used chiefly in the making of varnishes and, formerly, in medicine, shares its name with a more general term for any of various waterproof, putty-like substances used in the building trade as fillers, coatings, and sealants?

Three bonus questions on historic administrative sub-divisions:
(a) Surviving officially in the names of some counties until 1974, which term comes from an Old Norse word meaning 'a third part' and not, despite beliefs to the contrary, from a distance that could be covered on horseback?
(b) Before the Norman Conquest, although some counties were split into 'Wapentakes' or 'Wards', most such sub-divisions were given what name, familiar today in a parliamentary context?
(c) What archaic term for an administrative division survives in the full names of Jersey and Guernsey?

29. **Your starter for 10:**
What two verbs follow 'Reduce' in the environmentalist slogan sometimes called the 'Three Rs'?

Three bonus questions on paintings about painting:
(a) Generally believed to be a self-portrait, *The Artist in his Studio* or *The Art of Painting*, showing a rear view of an artist painting Clio the Muse of History, is by which seventeenth-century Dutch master?
(b) *L'Atelier du Peintre*, the large canvas painted by Gustave Courbet in 1855, in which a nude model, a little boy and a crowd of onlookers watch the artist at work on a landscape, is in which Paris museum?
(c) Depicting the artist at work alongside the Infanta Margarita of Spain, her maids-of-honour, two dwarfs and a dog, *Las Meninas* is a group portrait of 1656 by which painter?

30. **Your starter for 10:**
From the Sanskrit for 'loom', which tradition in both Hinduism and Buddhism is said to lead the practitioner to spiritual liberation and supernatural powers through mantras, meditation and rituals, and in Hinduism may involve indulgence in normally forbidden taboos?

Three bonus questions on Africa:
(a) Casamance, scene of a low-level civil war for more than a decade, is a region to the south of Gambia in which West African country?
(b) East and West Kasai are, along with Katanga, provinces of which Central African country?
(c) Casablanca is a major city in which African country?

'There's no reason to look dejected — it's a pretty good performance, and when it gets to this stage it's a lot hotter.'

Match Four

1. **Your starter for 10:**
The Bank of England was established to support the public debt in the wars of which monarch?

Three bonus questions on bastards:
(a) Which king of England was the illegitimate son of Robert I of Normandy and his concubine Arlette?
(b) Which French theologian had a celebrated love affair with Héloïse, by whom he had a son named Astralabe?
(c) Julius Caesar was the alleged father of Ptolemy, also known as Caesarion; who was Ptolemy's mother?

2. **Your starter for 10:**
According to the essayist Francis Bacon, what, quote, 'serve for delight, for ornament and for ability'?

Three bonus questions on Shakespearean monarchs:
(a) In Shakespeare's play, which monarch's last words are 'A horse! A horse! My kingdom for a horse!'?
(b) Which Shakespearean king tells the elements, 'I never gave you kingdom, called you children'?
(c) In which play by Shakespeare does the chorus ask for, 'A kingdom for a stage, princes to act, / And monarchs to behold the swelling scene'?

3. **Your starter for 10:**
What is the modern name of the computer peripheral

called by its inventor Douglas Engelbart in his 1967 patent application 'an x-y position indicator for a display system'?

Three bonus questions on volcanoes:

(a) Which peak in central Ecuador is the world's highest continuously active volcano, and is noted for its almost perfectly symmetrical cone?

(b) On which Japanese island is Mount Aso, a volcano with five peaks and a crater that is one of the largest in the world, with a diameter of around 25 kilometres at its widest?

(c) In March 2009, a powerful underwater volcanic eruption in the South Pacific created a new island about 63 kilometres northwest of Nuku'alofa, the capital of which island state?

4.   Your starter for 10:

The word sesquicentenary refers to an anniversary of how many years?

Three bonus questions on constitutional history:

(a) What attempted action by Charles I prompted the then speaker of the House of Commons to say: 'I have, sir, neither eyes to see, nor tongue to speak in this place, but as the house is pleased to direct me, whose servant I am'?

(b) The five members had been accused by the King of treason. For five points, name two of them.

(c) The confrontation between Charles and Parliament had been precipitated by a Commons vote in November 1641 on a list of grievances against the King, known by what two-word name?

5.   Your starter for 10:

According to Ludwig Wittgenstein, what academic

discipline 'is a battle against the bewitchment of our intelligence by means of language'?

Three bonus questions about artistic relatives:

(a) What was the family relationship of Franz Liszt to Richard Wagner?

(b) Known for his use of forced perspective and dramatic foreshortening, which artist born near Vicenza in about 1431 was the brother-in-law of the Venetian painters Giovanni and Gentile Bellini?

(c) The author of the Sherlock Holmes stories, Sir Arthur Conan Doyle, was the brother-in-law of E.W. Hornung, the creator of which 'gentleman' hero on the other side of the law?

6. Your starter for 10:
Referring to King George V, of what is Robert Lacey, in his book *Royal*, writing when he says, 'It ruined his Christmas Day, the King complained. But it made everyone else's'?

Three bonus questions on a Greek city:

(a) Situated on the Gulf of Thermai at the neck of the Halkidiki Peninsula, which seaport is Greece's second-largest city?

(b) Two brothers, born in Thessaloniki in the 820s, are called the 'Apostles of the Slavs'. The younger was appointed Archbishop of Sirmium by Pope Adrian II, and the older gave his name to the alphabet used to write Russian and Bulgarian. Name either.

(c) Born in Thessaloniki in 1881, which First World War military commander founded the Turkish Republic in 1923?

7. Your starter for 10:
Said to have been a favourite of several US presidents,

the title of which 1952 film reflects the time at which
Will Kane has to face his old enemy in the town of
Hadleyville?

Three bonus questions on bells:
(a) Which American-born poet's only novel was *The Bell
    Jar*, published in 1963, the year of her death?
(b) Which novelist is the author of *The Bell*, published in
    1958 and set in a lay community in a country house?
(c) The 1954 film comedy *The Belles of St Trinian's* is
    based on the creations of which British illustrator?

8. Your starter for 10:
The kaka and kakapo are New Zealand species of which
bird?

Three bonus questions on a Caribbean island:
(a) Situated between Martinique and St Vincent, which
    island state shares its name with a fourth-century
    Christian martyr who was blinded and killed after she
    refused to marry a pagan?
(b) The epic poem *Omeros* is a major work of which
    Nobel laureate, born in St Lucia in 1930?
(c) Sir Arthur Lewis, born in St Lucia in 1915, shared
    which Nobel Prize with the American Theodore Schultz
    in 1979?

9. Your starter for 10:
What is the standard dictionary spelling of the third-
person non-personal possessive adjective?

Three bonus questions on a number:
(a) The jointed measuring line traditionally consisting of
    one hundred metal links, used by surveyors and known
    as a 'chain', was how many yards in length?
(b) What is the title of Euclid's classic mathematical work

in which Book Seven begins with twenty-two new definitions such as 'even', 'odd' and 'prime'?

(c) 22 divided by 7 approximates to what mathematical constant?

10. **Your starter for 10:**
Raguly, Barbée, Millvine, Cercelée, Papal and Maltese are all names given to stylised forms of which common symbol?

Three bonus questions on John Ruskin:

(a) Of which English painter did Ruskin write that he was 'the only man who has ever given an entire transcript of the whole system of nature ... the only perfect landscape painter whom the world has ever seen'?

(b) 'Titian colours better, but has not his piety. Leonardo draws better but has not his colour. Angelico is more heavenly, but has not his manliness, far less his powers of art.' This was Ruskin's opinion of which Venetian artist?

(c) In 1845, of which Venetian artist did Ruskin write that he had never been so utterly crushed to the earth before any human intellect as he had been before him?

11. **Your starter for 10:**
Drawing its water from the cave spring near Lynchburg in Tennessee, a distillery registered in 1866 was established by which local teenager who mellowed his product through maple charcoal?

Three bonus questions on a title:

(a) What word denoting a ruler or monarch links the names of a purple butterfly, a scarlet-flowered runner bean, and the largest species of penguin?

(b) Which composer wrote the 'Emperor' String Quartet in C Major, the slow movement of which includes variations on a tune from his 'Emperor's Hymn' of 1797, which was the national hymn of Austria until 1918?

(c) *The Last Emperor*, the Oscar-winning film of 1987 based on the autobiography of Aisin-Gioro Pu Yi, was directed by which Italian film-maker?

12. Your starter for 10:
What word of four letters links a prized white truffle from Italy's Piedmont region, a duchess who was the subject of portraits by Goya in 1795 and 1797, and the Gaelic name for Scotland as a whole?

Three bonus questions on quotations:

(a) 'Wild, melancholy and elevating'; who described a sibling's verse with these words in 1850?

(b) What did the philosopher Francis Bacon describe as, 'a kind of wild justice, which the more man's nature runs to, the more ought law to weed it out'?

(c) Which of her prime ministers did Queen Victoria describe in 1892 as, 'an old, wild and incomprehensible man of eighty-two and a half'?

13. Your starter for 10:
Also known as the 'third eyelid', what term derives from the Latin meaning 'to blink', and denotes the transparent inner eyelid in birds, reptiles and amphibians that closes to protect and moisten the eye?

Three bonus questions on a type of food:

(a) What name is given to the flat, unleavened bread of Mexico, normally made of corn?

(b) Tunstall Tortilla is a name sometimes given to what Staffordshire delicacy?

(c) By what name is the wholewheat, unleavened griddle bread served in Indian restaurants usually known?

14. **Your starter for 10:**

Also known as an Eltonian pyramid, what graphical representation is made of trophic levels and can be indicative of numbers, biomass or energy of a system?

Three bonus questions on Roman numerals which change one word into another:

For example, to get from a male swan to a hairdressing implement, in other words from 'cob' to 'comb', you add the letter 'm', which is 1,000. The answer in each case is the *decimal* equivalent of the Roman numeral:

(a) To get from Stalin's secret police chief to the West African country whose capital is Monrovia, you have to add what number?

(b) From an electrically charged atom to a king of the Lapiths condemned to spend eternity bound to a burning wheel?

(c) From a soft French cheese to an item of horse tack?

15. **Your starter for 10:**

Internal parasites of marine invertebrates, which group of minute worms with no body cavity or organs other than reproductive cells were so named as being supposedly intermediate in structure between protozoans and metazoans?

Three bonus questions on a church:

(a) Begun in 1506 and built on the site of the fourth-century basilica of the Emperor Constantine, which is usually regarded as the largest Christian church?

(b) The original architect of the Basilica, Donato Bramante, died in 1514; which artist, who had recently completed a celebrated cycle of frescoes for the Vatican Papal Apartments, was appointed to succeed him?

(c) The large dome of St Peter's, completed by Giacomo

della Porta and Domenico Fontana, was designed by which artist, who was made the Basilica's chief architect by Pope Paul III in 1546?

16. **Your starter for 10:**
A coin of the Byzantine Empire and the line on a pressure-temperature diagram under which solids are stable, are both named what? It can also mean a forward-slanting line in punctuation.

Three bonus questions on scientists:
(a) The German scientist Rudolf Clausius is regarded as a founder of which branch of physics, having stated the basic ideas behind its second law in 1850?

(b) Clausius's work on thermodynamics built on that of which French scientist who gave his name to a cycle of events that demonstrates the impossibility of total efficiency in heat engines?

(c) Carnot's work was recognised by which British physicist in his 1851 paper 'On the Dynamical Theory of Heat', which sought to reconcile the ideas of Carnot, Joule and Clausius?

17. **Your starter for 10:**
An aspiring academic based in Berlin flies to Stockholm and Warsaw to attend seminars and then continues to Helsinki to take up a new post. When drawn on a map, what capital letter does her route most closely describe?

Three bonus questions on a female name:
(a) With a Hebrew name meaning '(My) Father Rejoices', who in the Bible calls herself King David's handmaid? The name has also come into literary use to mean a lady's maid.

(b) In Christopher Marlowe's drama *The Jew of Malta*,

what method does Barabas use to murder his daughter Abigail?

(c) Abigail is the mischief-making niece of Reverend Parris in which stage work, set in seventeenth-century Salem and first performed in 1953?

18. Your starter for 10:
Who or what, according to Defoe, builds his chapel on a house of prayer; according to Garrick, sends the cooks when heaven sends good meat; according to Shakespeare, understands Welsh; and in a remark attributed to various speakers, has all the best tunes?

Three bonus questions on islands:
(a) Ownership of Tierra del Fuego has been the subject of a dispute between Argentina and which country?
(b) Noted for its monolithic stone statues, which island lies 2,200 miles west of Chile?
(c) The Chilean Juan Fernandez Islands are sometimes known by the name of which fictional character?

19. Your starter for 10:
'The ex-drunk who finds Jesus is a cliché, but the ex-drunk who finds Blair is a perplexing creature.' To which government minister do these words from an opinion column of July 2006 refer?

Three bonus questions on the Indo-European language family:
(a) Spoken in ancient Anatolia in the second millennium BC, which extinct language is the oldest attested member of the Indo-European family?
(b) Often classified as an independent branch within Indo-European, which language with around seven million speakers is the official language of a mountainous, landlocked republic in the Caucasus?

(c) Two languages of the Indo-Iranian branch of Indo-European have more than 200 million speakers. One is Hindi-Urdu, or Hindustani; what is the other?

20. Your starter for 10:
Which chemical element was originally called Cyprian in antiquity?

Three bonus questions on bioluminescence, the emission by living organisms of light without heat:
(a) In bioluminescence, light is emitted when luciferin is oxidised to oxyluciferin. There are several distinct types of luciferin; what enzyme catalyses their oxidation?
(b) What name is given to the specialised, light-emitting glands or organs which are a common feature of bioluminescent deep-water fish and cephalopods?
(c) The rare *Phosphaenus hemipterus* and the common *Lampyris noctiluca* are both native to Britain and, regardless of their common name of glow worms, are not worms but belong to which group of insects?

21. Your starter for 10:
From the Latin for 'little swelling', what name is given to the rounded inflamed swellings typically found on the skin of sufferers of leprosy as a result of infection by *mycobacterium leprae*?

Three bonus questions on a city:
(a) Derbent is the southernmost city of which large country? Its twenty-metre-high walls believed to date to the Sassanid period, it also claims to be that country's oldest city.
(b) Derbent is the second city of which republic of the Russian Federation, whose ethnic groups include the Avars, Kumyk and Lezgin?
(c) Derbent is situated in a historically strategic gap

between the Caspian Sea and which range of mountains?

22. Your starter for 10:
Although he makes no such claim himself, genealogically speaking, Franz, Duke of Bavaria, born in 1933, is the senior heir of which possible alternative British royal house?

Three questions on an English chemist:
(a) Born in 1877, the Nobel laureate Frederick Soddy is noted for the formulation of what concept, defined as 'one of two or more atoms having the same atomic number but differing in atomic weight and mass number'?
(b) Soddy, in conjunction with Sir William Ramsay, found which noble gas to be a product of radium decay?
(c) Which British physicist worked with Soddy at Canada's McGill University in the early 1900s to form the theory of atomic disintegration for which he would receive the 1908 Nobel Prize?

23. Your starter for 10:
Meanings of what term include: in psychology, the physically measured value of stimulation at which an observer's response changes from one category to another; in physics, a limit below which no reaction occurs; and, in taxation, a step usually operative in specific conditions?

Three bonus questions on sinusoidal progressive waves:
(a) What name is given to the distance between successive peaks or troughs of a sinusoidal wave, in other words a wave relating to the sine wave?
(b) What property of the wave is given by its wavelength times its frequency?

(c) By what factor must the frequency of the wave be multiplied to obtain its angular frequency?

24. Your starter for 10:
What is the technical term for the dispersal of spores or seeds by ants?

Three bonus questions on owls:
(a) The owl symbolised which Greek goddess, and also the city under her protection?
(b) Which pioneering woman, who died in 1910 aged 90, frequently carried a small pet owl in her pocket?
(c) Which fictional anti-hero was described by his creator Frank Richards as 'the Fat Owl of the Remove'?

25. Your starter for 10:
In music, what term from the Italian for 'harp' indicates a chord whose pitches are sounded successively, usually from lowest to highest, rather than simultaneously?

Three bonus questions on Ted Hughes's Tales from Ovid:
In each case, give the mythological figure who is the subject of the following lines:
(a) 'So he lived / In the solitary confinement / Of a phobia, / Shunning living women, wifeless / Yet he still dreamed of woman. / He dreamed / Unbrokenly awake as asleep / The perfect body of a perfect woman.'
(b) 'A grace like Minerva's, unearthly / Moved her hands whether she bundled the fleeces / Or teased out the wool, like Cirrus / Or spun the yarn, or finally / Conjured her images into their places. / Surely, only Minerva could have taught her!'
(c) 'Her face hardened / And whitened, as the blood left it. / Her very hair hardened / Like hair carved by a chisel. / Her open eyes became stones. / Her whole body / A stone.'

26. **Your starter for 10:**

What astronomical feature does this describe: sites of concentrated magnetic field, even with central temperatures of about 4,000 Kelvin, they appear dark, because their surroundings are hotter. Their number peaks every eleven years, although, between 1645 and 1715, they were almost completely absent?

Three bonus questions on fathers and sons:

(a) Dionysius the Elder and Dionysius the Younger were successive tyrants of which Mediterranean city state between 405 and 343 BC?

(b) What first name and surname were shared by the German father and son born in 1472 and 1515, both of whom were painters? The Younger's works include a 1550 portrait of the Elder, now in the Uffizi.

(c) What first name and surname were shared by the Austrian composers born in 1804 and 1825? The Elder deliberately sabotaged the early musical career of his son, who is now regarded as having exceeded his father's achievements.

27. **Your starter for 10:**

In economics, what term is sometimes used to refer to the divestment or disposal of subsidiaries and other unwanted activities, but more usually describes the large-scale shedding of employees by major corporations in an effort to reduce costs?

Three bonus questions on manuscripts destroyed by fire:

(a) When his dog Diamond knocked over a candle and set fire to papers representing several years' work, which physicist is said to have cried out 'O, Diamond, Diamond, thou little knowest the mischief done'?

(b) In 1835, John Stuart Mill was sent the first draft of a

history of the French Revolution to read, but his maid, thinking it was waste paper, used it to light a fire, forcing the author to start again from scratch. Who was that author?

(c) The memoirs of which Romantic poet, having been deemed unsuitable for publication by his friends, were burnt in the fireplace of his publisher John Murray in Albemarle Street after his death?

28. **Your starter for 10:**
From the Greek for 'going downhill', what name is given to a wind that blows down a topographic incline such as a hill, mountain, or glacier?

Three bonus questions on engravings:

(a) When colour prints are made with woodcuts or linocuts, there is a different block for each colour, plus one more, usually black, that carries the outline. What name is given to this block?

(b) What was the name of the wood engraver born in Northumberland in 1753 who was known particularly for his wildlife illustrations and was the subject of a biography by Jenny Uglow published in 2006?

(c) What Italian name is given to methods of engraving on metal such as dry-point and mezzotint, in which the ink is in the engraved furrows, rather than on the uncut surface as in wood engraving and woodcuts?

29. **Your starter for 10:**
What do the letters 'T' and 'I' represent in the acronym TIFF, which denotes a graphical file format used to store bit-mapped images?

Three bonus questions on science:

(a) Which group of very hot stars is named after the two French astronomers who identified them in 1867?

(b) The adjective 'Wolffian' refers to which organs in the embryo of vertebrates?

(c) In 1997, Andrew Wiles collected the Wolfskehl Prize, established in 1908, for his solution of what?

30. Your starter for 10:
Derived from the Greek for 'return home' and 'pain', what term was first recorded in a medical dissertation of 1688 for the condition of homesickness and now has the extended meaning of a sentimental longing for the past?

Three bonus questions on characters in opera:

(a) Count Almaviva, a servant called Fiorello, and Rosina, who is Doctor Bartolo's ward, all feature in which opera by Rossini, based on a comedy by Beaumarchais?

(b) Which opera, first performed in Milan in 1926, includes among its characters the Emperor Altoum and a suitor called Calaf?

(c) Beppe, who plays a harlequin in the Commedia dell'arte, and Silvio, who is in love with Nedda, the wife of Canio, are characters in which opera?

> **'Wasn't your greatest hour. But it wasn't an embarrassingly bad performance.'**

HIGHEST WINNING MARGINS
(1994–2010)

1. Open v. Charing Cross Hospital (1997) — 350
2. Corpus Christi, Oxford v. Exeter (2009) — 335
3. Manchester v. Birkbeck, London (1997) — 320
4. Manchester v. Lincoln, Oxford (2009) — 315
5. Open v. Swansea (1997) — 310
6. Nottingham v. New Hall, Cambridge (1998) — 300
7. Magdalen, Oxford v. Cardiff (1998) — 295
8. Lincoln, Oxford v. Queens', Cambridge (2009) — 285
9. Manchester v. St Andrews (2005) — 275
10. Corpus Christi, Oxford Lancaster v. (2005) — 265
11. Imperial, London v. Exeter (1996) — 255
12. Wadham, Oxford v. Robinson, Cambridge (2007) — 255
13. University, Oxford v. Magdalene, Cambridge (2001) — 250
14. Trinity Hall, Cambridge v. Magdalen, Oxford (2006) — 250
15. Christ's, Cambridge v. Keele (2002) — 245
16. Queen's, Belfast v. Bradford (2004) — 245
17. Durham v. King's, London (2000) — 235
18. Corpus Christi, Oxford v. Durham (2009) — 235
19. University, Oxford v. Heriot-Watt (1996) — 230
20. Queen's, Belfast v. St Bartholomew's, London (1998) — 230

Semi-Finals

'Another half-hour of intellectual
Tiddlywinks lies ahead of us, and
whichever team has the most winks
in the pot when the gong sounds
will win themselves a place in the
final.'

THE RULES

We won't waste any time reciting the rules – fingers on the buzzers, here's your first starter for 10.

Match One

1. **Your starter for 10:**
   What name is given to the photosensitive layer of the human eye that consists of rods and cones?

   Three bonus questions on insect secretions:
   (a) What common name is given to the sugar-rich liquid secreted by insects such as greenfly, which is often collected by ants as it is being released?
   (b) The insect whose nymphs protect themselves both from drying out and from predators by secreting the white frothy mass called 'cuckoo spit' has what popular name, derived from its shape and leaping ability?
   (c) What name is given to the resin obtained from a secretion of various insects, including those of the genera *metata chardia* and *tachardia*, which, when melted into thin plates, was formerly used for making gramophone records?

2. **Your starter for 10:**
   Immediately before its independence in 1960, the territory that is now the Somali Republic had been governed in two parts, as a British protectorate, and as a colony of which other European power?

   Three bonus questions on acronyms in electronics:
   (a) In digital broadcasting, scrolling text can be displayed

which gives information about programme content and additional material such as signal strength and traffic reports. The application providing this service is known as DLS; for what do these initials stand?

(b) Mobile cellular telephones contain a smart card with the acronym SIM. For what do the initials S.I.M. stand?

(c) The machine developed in 1957 to produce winning numbers for Premium Bond draws was called 'Ernie', the current version being Ernie mark 4. For what do the initials E.R.N.I.E. stand?

3.   **Your starter for 10:**
What five-letter word follows 'Blue' in the name of a group of avant-garde artists from 1911; 'Pale', in the name of a champion beer from Sheffield; and 'Easy' in the title of a 1969 film starring Peter Fonda and Dennis Hopper?

Three bonus questions on battlefields:
In each case, give the English county that is the location of the following:

(a) The Battle of Bosworth of August 1485, the outcome of which established Henry Tudor on the English throne?

(b) The village of Naseby which, in June 1645, witnessed the last major battle of the main phase of the English Civil War?

(c) The plain of Sedgemoor where the Duke of Monmouth was defeated by James II's troops in July 1685?

4.   **Your starter for 10:**
The original departure point for the Mayflower pilgrims in 1620, for Henry V in 1415, and for RMS *Titanic* in

1912, which port lies between the mouths of the Test and the Itchen rivers?

Three bonus questions linked by a word:

(a) Which two-word term for a cheap café is thought to have originated in the USA during the 1920s?

(b) Who remarked, when he served briefly as Prime Minister in 1868, 'I have climbed to the top of the greasy pole'?

(c) In the *Just So Stories*, which animal's child acquired his distinctive nose when it was pulled by a crocodile in the 'great, grey, green, greasy Limpopo river'?

5. **Your starter for 10:**

Appointed Savilian Professor at Oxford in 1702, which scientist established the law connecting air pressure with height above sea level, persuaded Isaac Newton to publish his *Principia Mathematica* and predicted the return of a comet 76 years after its last sighting?

Three bonus questions on names:

(a) 'Robinson' was a term used during the eighteenth century in both England and France for which device, the name inspired by a portable construction improvised by Defoe's Crusoe in which he stretched animal skins over a frame?

(b) 'Gamp' became a colloquial term for an umbrella in the Victorian era after Mrs Sairey Gamp, the inebriated layer-out of the dead who habitually carries a battered, black example in which novel by Charles Dickens?

(c) *Mrs Jolly's Brolly* is the third in a trilogy of books for children by which prolific British author, who won the *Guardian* Children's Fiction Award in 1984 for *The Sheep-Pig*?

6. Your starter for 10:

Originating in the USA, the Dagwood, the Elvis and the Hoagie are among larger or more extravagant varieties of what prepared food item?

Three bonus questions on geology:

(a) Which rock, formed by the solidification of thin layers of molten lava, comprises much of the surfaces of Mercury, Venus, Mars and the moon?

(b) Basalt is usually composed primarily of crystals of augite or hornblende, olivine and which other mineral that occurs in various forms including labradorite, and makes up more than half the Earth's crust?

(c) Basalt forms the distinctive columnar strata of the Giant's Causeway in Ireland and the similar structures found on which island in the Inner Hebrides, the location of Fingal's Cave?

7. Your starter for 10:

Homeward: Songs by the Way and *The Earth Breath* are among the works of which figure in the Irish literary revival, who used the grapheme 'Æ' as a pen name?

Three bonus questions on debt:

(a) According to *The Oxford English Dictionary*, what familiar two-word term means 'money that a creditor is bound by law to accept if it is [offered] in payment of a debt'?

(b) Only three denominations of money are legal tender for a debt of any amount throughout the United Kingdom. Name two of them.

(c) One penny coins are legal tender throughout the UK only for the payment of sums up to what small amount?

8. Your starter for 10:
In the complex number a + ib, what does the i denote?

Three bonus questions on London:
(a) Which London street takes its name from a grant of land by Edward I to Goldsmiths from an area of what is now northern Italy?
(b) Formerly part of the Great Middlesex Forest, which area of London takes its name from its former ownership by the Knights Hospitallers?
(c) Which London street was renamed after a product made in the vicinity, and has featured in writings by Tarquin Hall, Rachel Lichtenstein and Monica Ali?

9. Your starter for 10:
What subatomic particle was postulated in 1931 to account for the energy that seems to go missing when an atomic nucleus undergoes beta decay, but was not detected for more than 20 years because it interacts only very weakly with matter? Its name means 'little neutral one'.

Three bonus questions on a rodent:
(a) Also known as the quill pig, which new world rodent presents its rear when approached?
(b) Who wrote the provocatively pro-British *Life and Adventures of Peter Porcupine* while living in the USA in 1796?
(c) Nicknamed the Flying Porcupine by Luftwaffe pilots, what sort of aircraft was the Sunderland?

10. Your starter for 10:
The authors of the 1796 gothic novel *The Monk*, the 1914 Vorticist review *Blast*, the 1927 satire *Elmer Gantry* and the 1955 spiritual autobiography *Surprised by Joy* all share what surname?

Three bonus questions on alternative names for chemical elements proposed by the US author Poul Anderson:
The names are coined from Germanic roots instead of Romance or Greek ones. Identify the element in each case:
(a) 'Flintstuff', that is, element number 14.
(b) 'Stonestuff', that is, element number 3.
(c) The inert gas 'sunstuff'.

11. **Your starter for 10:**
'He was wounded for our transgressions, crushed for our iniquities. By his wounds we are healed.' These are the opening words of which controversial film of 2004?

Three bonus questions on US geography:
(a) Which two states have a coastline on Chesapeake Bay?
(b) In addition to Delaware, which US state has a coastline on Delaware Bay?
(c) In which US state is the city of Green Bay, the name also being given to the arm of Lake Michigan on which it is located?

12. **Your starter for 10:**
Which bird is the largest of the ratites?

Three bonus questions on lips in Shakespeare:
(a) 'Alas! Why gnaw you so your nether lip? / Some bloody passion shakes your very frame.' In which of Shakespeare's tragedies do these lines appear?
(b) 'Here hung those lips that I have kissed I know not how oft'. These words, uttered in a graveyard, refer to whom?
(c) 'Life and these lips have long been separated: / Death lies on her like an untimely frost.' To which of Shakespeare's heroines do these words refer?

13. **Your starter for 10:**
Named after the fourth-century Pope said to have baptised Constantine the Great, St Sylvester's night is celebrated, particularly in German-speaking regions, on which day of the year?

Three bonus questions on herbs:
(a) The leaves of which aromatic herb are sometimes known as Chinese parsley or cilantro?
(b) Which herbaceous plant of the ginger family has been used since antiquity as a condiment and as a yellow dye?
(c) Which aromatic herb takes its name from the Latin for 'Greek hay'?

14. **Your starter for 10:**
The Norwegian chemists Christian Birkeland and Samuel Eyde give their names to the commercial process, based on a method devised by Cavendish, that they developed at the start of the twentieth century for the economic production of which acid?

Three bonus questions on pairs of words whose spelling differs by the addition of a 'w' after the first letter, for example 'seep' and 'sweep':
In each case, give both words from the definitions provided:
(a) To separate finer and coarser parts of material, or examine evidence; and a bird of the family *apodidae*, superficially similar to the swallow.
(b) To cultivate soil for crops; and a fabric woven with a network of diagonal parallel ridges.
(c) A seat for a rider; and to wrap an infant in garments or bandages.

15. Your starter for 10:

In which Shakespeare play do the following lines appear: 'There is a tide in the affairs of men, / Which, taken at the flood, leads on to fortune / Omitted, all the voyage of their life / Is bound in shallows and in miseries'?

Three bonus questions on Mexican history:

(a) In 1911, the liberal Francisco Madero ousted which dictator, who had first become President in 1876 and whose rule is known as the *Porfiriato*?

(b) After Madero's death in a counter-revolutionary coup, which commander of the popular army known as the Division of the North fought the military regime and raided the USA in 1916?

(c) Which agrarian reformer joined forces with Villa against the Carranza government? Killed in an ambush in 1919, he gives his name to a guerrilla movement formed in 1994.

16. Your starter for 10:

In stellar evolutionary theory, which physicist born in 1877 gives his name to a term used to describe the mass that a cloud of interstellar gas must have before it can contract under its own weight to form a protostar?

Three bonus questions on legal affairs:

(a) Dalton Trumbo, Ring Lardner Junior and Edward Dymtryk were members of which group of screenwriters who were cited for contempt of Congress and jailed in 1947 for refusing to answer questions about their political beliefs?

(b) The Natwest Three, who were jailed in February 2008 for pocketing $7.3 million of their employer's money, made headlines by their challenge to which 2003 Act of Parliament?

(c) What was the title of the 1993 film directed by Jim Sheridan based on the case of the Guildford Four?

17. Your starter for 10:

What common name is given to a multi-cellular, eukaryotic, photosynthetic organism adapted primarily to life on land?

Three bonus questions on Africa:

In each case, name the African country whose first three letters correspond to the given definition. For example, 'to convert hide into leather' would be 'Tan-zania'.

(a) A machine part that transforms rotary motion into linear motion.

(b) An Old English or Icelandic letter, resembling a barred letter 'd'.

(c) One hundredth of a Japanese yen.

18. Your starter for 10:

Listen carefully to the Latin: 'Numero deus impare gaudet'. In what general class of numbers does the god delight, according to the poet Virgil?

Three bonus questions on World Heritage Sites:

(a) The Minaret and archaeological remains of Jam in the Hari River Valley, and the cultural landscape and remains of the Bamiyan Valley are on the UNESCO list of World Heritage Sites in danger; in which Central Asian republic are they located?

(b) Which sultanate on the southeast coast of the Arabian peninsula lost the World Heritage status of its Arabian Oryx Sanctuary in 2007 after reducing its size by ninety per cent?

(c) Which German city lost its UNESCO World Heritage Site status in June 2009 after the construction of a controversial four-lane bridge over the River Elbe?

19. Your starter for 10:

Over more than ten years, a highbrow quiz programme is broadcast 480 times, each episode being exactly 30 minutes long. In order to boost ratings, a satellite channel broadcasts each and every episode continuously, without breaks. How many days does this 'special season' last?

Three bonus questions on diets:

(a) Which low-carbohydrate, low-calorie diet was published in 1979 by Dr Herman Tarnower, who named it after the area of New York where he practised? The diet soared in popularity when Dr Tarnower was murdered by his lover a year later.

(b) Who popularised the F-Plan diet that advised consumption of high-fibre foods?

(c) The GI diet is based on a ranking system for foods devised in the early 1980s by Dr David Jenkins of the University of Toronto. For what do the letters 'GI' stand?

20. Your starter for 10:

The Beas, Ravi and Sutlej are among the rivers that give which state of north-western India its name, being derived from the Persian for 'five rivers'?

Three bonus questions on a country:

(a) In September 1939, which country was declared by Germany and the Soviet Union to have ceased to exist?

(b) Between the two world wars, which province of Germany was separated from the rest of the Reich by the Polish corridor?

(c) Which enclave was formed from the northern half of East Prussia, ceded to the USSR by the Potsdam Agreement in 1945?

21. **Your starter for 10:**
Which American author and poet wrote these lines? 'A free bird leaps / On the back of the wind / And floats downstream / Till the current ends / And dips his wing / In the orange sun rays / And dares to claim the sky.'

Three bonus questions on forms of rhyme:
(a) A 'vowel rhyme', such as 'feet' and 'sleep', where the vowels but not the consonants are the same, is commonly known by what name, from the Latin verb 'to sound'?
(b) What name is given to rhymes of the 'love-move' / 'come-home' variety, where the ending is spelt the same but pronounced differently?
(c) A feminine or trochaic rhyme has the stress on which syllable of the rhyming words?

22. **Your starter for 10:**
Who once wrote, 'It is worth being shot at, to see how much one is loved,' following a seventh attempt on her life, this time by the well-educated but impoverished Roderick McLean?

Three bonus questions on trees in the Bible:
(a) In Genesis, which tree's nut or drupe is among 'the best products of the land'? Its flowers appear on Aaron's rod in Numbers, and provide the model for a menorah in Exodus.
(b) The father of David, which biblical figure's name is given in the book of Isaiah to the tree stump from which it is said that 'a shoot will come up', the name later being applied to medieval stained-glass depictions of the genealogy of Jesus?
(c) In Genesis chapter three, in which Adam and Eve eat the fruit of the tree of knowledge, which species

of tree native to southwest Asia and the eastern Mediterranean is mentioned by name?

23. Your starter for 10:
Chosen for the badge of the Covenanters of seventeenth-century Scotland and associated in Hinduism with Krishna, which colour was also adopted symbolically by the Whigs and, in the American Civil War, served the Union forces in distinction to the grey of the Confederates?

> **Three bonus questions on twentieth-century philosophy:**
> In each case, name the author of the following works:
> (a) *In Praise of Idleness*, *The Conquest of Happiness* and *Why I Am Not a Christian*.
> (b) *The Logic of Scientific Discovery*, *The Poverty of Historicism* and *Unended Quest*.
> (c) *Tractatus Logico-Philosophicus* and *Philosophical Investigations*.

24. Your starter for 10:
Byssus is a super-fine silk material made from the 'beard' used by which bivalves to attach themselves to rocks?

> **Three bonus questions on a renowned body of water:**
> (a) Running south-west to north-east up the Great Glen, which loch comes next in this sequence: Loch Linnhe, Loch Lochy, Loch Oich?
> (b) Which artist and ornithologist coined the Latin name *Nessiteras rhombopteryx* for the Loch Ness Monster?
> (c) According to legend, which saint used the sign of the Cross to repel a savage monster in the River Ness?

25. Your starter for 10:
27 January 2006 saw a worldwide programme of concerts to mark the 250th anniversary of the birth of which composer?

Three bonus questions on mythology:

(a) In Greek mythology, which of the Titans, the son of Uranus and Gaia, was a benign god who personified the stream of water which was assumed to surround the world?

(b) The Symplegades or 'clashing rocks' through which Jason and the crew of the Argo had to pass were situated at the entrance to which sea, at the far end of which was Colchis, the home of Medea?

(c) Their names varying from source to source, as do their numbers, which creatures were half bird and half woman, and lived according to Homer on an island in the western sea between Aeaea and the rock of Scylla?

26. Your starter for 10:
Which scientist was awarded the 1964 Nobel Prize in Chemistry, principally for her determination of the structure of vitamin B12?

Three bonus questions on US states:

(a) Four US states have borders with only two other states. Washington is one, being bordered by Oregon and Idaho. Name one of the other three.

(b) Which state has short borders with Wisconsin and South Dakota and longer borders with Nebraska, Missouri, Illinois and Minnesota?

(c) Which is the only state to border Maine?

27. Your starter for 10:
What name is given to infections or diseases transferred to humans from non-human vertebrates?

Three bonus questions on a word appropriated by science:

(a) Which two-word term is used in physics for a hypothetical interconnection between widely separated regions of space-time?

(b) Denoting an optical disk used for read-only storage of data, for what, in computing, does the acronym WORM stand?

(c) A worm gear connects non-intersecting shafts at what angle to each other?

28. Your starter for 10:

What is the only chemical element whose English name begins with the letter 'a' but whose symbol does not?

Three bonus questions on the year 1910 in world history:

(a) In August 1910, which country was annexed by Japan and its king, Sunjong, forced to abdicate?

(b) In which country did Francisco Madero proclaim the elections of 1910 void, calling for an armed insurrection against the presidency of Porfirio Díaz?

(c) In October 1910, which European country became a republic after King Manuel II was overthrown?

29. Your starter for 10:

From the Greek for 'race', what name is given, in biological classification, to the taxonomic rank between kingdom and class, and in linguistics, to a group of languages related to each other less closely than those of a family?

Three bonus questions on international organisations based in Geneva:

In each case, name the organisation from its abbreviation:

(a) WIPO, established in 1967.

(b) The ILO, founded in 1919.

(c) Finally: the ICRC, which dates to 1863.

30. Your starter for 10:

What word denotes the exposed area of a stratum or vein of rock on the Earth's surface?

Three bonus questions on names:

(a) In 1996, John Galliano left Givenchy to become head designer at which rival fashion house?

(b) Which cocktail is made with vodka, orange juice and Galliano?

(c) In the 1950 film *Harvey*, which concerned a six-foot invisible rabbit of that name, who played the only person able to see Harvey?

'Well, we're going to have to say goodbye to you, but there is no shame at all in leaving in the semi-final.'

THE RULES

Tedious to recite the rules again at
this stage in the contest – let's just
get on with it.

Match Two

1. **Your starter for 10:**
Scratched into the stone of the Brougham Bridge by William Rowan Hamilton, the fundamental formula of which division algebra states $i^2 = j^2 = k^2 = ijk = -1$?

   Three bonus questions on geology:
   In each case, name the metallic element of which the following are common ores:
   (a) Galena, cerussite and anglesite.
   (b) Rutile and ilmenite.
   (c) Hematite, magnetite and siderite.

2. **Your starter for 10:**
A musical direction meaning 'with passion', what Italian term was given to Beethoven's Piano Sonata No. 23 in F Minor by his publisher?

   Three bonus questions on alliances:
   (a) Partly in reaction to Spain's occupation of Sardinia, which power joined Britain, France and the Dutch Republic in 1718 to form the Quadruple Alliance?
   (b) The War of the Triple Alliance from 1864 to 1870 was fought by Brazil, Argentina and Uruguay against which country, under the dictator Francisco Lopez?
   (c) In 1894, France entered a dual alliance with which other country, in response to the triple alliance of Germany, Austria-Hungary and Italy?

3. Your starter for 10:
Adiposis is the presence of abnormally large accumulations of what substance in the body, an alternative name for the condition being liposis?

Three bonus questions on a year:

(a) The breaking of the Watergate scandal, the Munich Olympics, the release of the first *Godfather* film, and the World Championship Chess match between Spassky and Fischer in Reykjavik all took place in which leap year?

(b) In the same year, which Japanese prefecture was returned to Japan after twenty-seven years of American military occupation?

(c) Also in this year, the Atari company released one of the first generation of video games with a version of which game, roughly simulating table tennis?

4. Your starter for 10:
As an aid to teaching geography, map-maker John Spilsbury is credited with the creation of what device, now most often seen as a pastime that tests ingenuity?

Three bonus questions on an English town:

(a) Which West Country market town on the River Frome was the centre of the organisation of Puritan emigration to America in the seventeenth century, and the site of the trial of the Tolpuddle Martyrs in 1834?

(b) The trial held in the Oak Room of the Antelope Hotel in Dorchester in September 1685 in the aftermath of the Monmouth Rebellion was one of a series known by what name?

(c) What name does Thomas Hardy give to Dorchester in his Wessex novels?

5.   Your starter for 10:
What is the common name for the medical condition *genu valgum*, where the angle between the femur and the tibia is so altered that the leg deviates laterally from the midline?

Three bonus questions on rhyming names:
(a) Which two rhyming names follow 'Ralph' to give the eponymous braggart who aims to woo and win Dame Custance in a mid-sixteenth-century play by Nicholas Udall, often regarded as the first comedy in the English language?
(b) Following a *Blue Peter* competition, the accident-prone schoolboy Wayne, known as 'Wayne's in Pain', first appeared in print in 2007 in the company of his notorious cohorts, known by what collective name?
(c) Cobbler Jack Black dreams of 'chasing naughty couples down the grassgreen gooseberried double bed of the wood' in which work, first broadcast in 1954?

6.   Your starter for 10:
Which building has, on its second floor, rooms called the Queen's Bedroom, the Cosmotology Room, the Lincoln Bedroom and the Truman Balcony? Its grounds include the Rose Garden and the Jacqueline Kennedy Garden.

Three bonus questions on Ancient European languages:
(a) Oscan and Umbrian are among extinct languages formerly spoken in which present-day European country?
(b) The longest single text in which ancient Italian language is housed in the National Museum at Zagreb and was written on a linen book, parts of which were subsequently used as a wrapping for an Egyptian mummy?

(c) What name is given to the main literary dialect of classical Greek, so called because it was written and spoken in and around the city of Athens?

7. **Your starter for 10:**
What surname is shared by a comic novelist called Nigel, a critic called Raymond, a poet called Hugo, an actor-comedian called Robin, a classical guitarist called John, a singer called Robbie and a playwright called Tennessee?

Three bonus questions on lines in Shakespeare:
In each case, name the eponymous tragic hero whose first words in the play are these:
(a) 'So foul and fair a day I have not seen.'
(b) 'Thanks. What's the matter, you dissentious rogues / That, rubbing the poor itch of your opinion, / Make yourselves scabs?'
(c) 'A little more than kin, and less than kind.'

8. **Your starter for 10:**
What is the smallest palindromic prime consisting of three digits?

Three bonus questions on mythological monsters:
(a) In Greek mythology, the monster Typhon was half man, half serpent, and was the youngest son of which primordial goddess, the personification of the Earth?
(b) Typhon's child was which creature, part lion, part snake and part goat? It was killed by Bellerophon with the help of Pegasus.
(c) Which serpent-like water beast with many heads was also the child of Typhon, and was killed by Heracles in the second of his Labours?

9. **Your starter for 10:**
'Hold Your Hand Out, You Naughty Boy', 'I'll Make A Man Of You', 'They Were Only Playing Leapfrog' and 'Hush, Here Comes A Whizzbang' are among the songs in which highly influential stage work, devised by Joan Littlewood's theatre workshop in 1963?

> **Three bonus questions on a shared name:**
> (a) Which of Henry VIII's wives, accused of intent to commit treason, was beheaded in February 1542, two months after the executions of her lovers Francis Dereham and Thomas Culpeper?
> (b) Howard is the family name of which dukes, whose seat is at Arundel Castle?
> (c) Lord Howard of Effingham was Commander-in-Chief of the English forces in 1588 when they faced which fleet under the Duke of Medina Sidonia?

10. **Your starter for 10:**
Its reverse bearing the words 'Saxon' and 'Plural of penny', a fifty-pence piece commemorating the 250th anniversary of the publication of which reference work was issued by the Royal Mint in 2005?

> **Three bonus questions on a country and its states:**
> (a) Durango, Hidalgo and Sonora are three of the thirty-one federal states that comprise which country?
> (b) Which Mexican state shares its name with, and forms the northern end of, the peninsula in south-eastern Mexico that separates the Caribbean Sea from the Gulf of Mexico?
> (c) Which state borders the USA and is the largest by area in Mexico?

11. **Your starter for 10:**
Responding to recent political events, to which city

was Wordsworth referring in a poem of 1802 with the words: 'No guile seduced, no force could violate; / And, when she took unto herself a mate, / She must espouse the everlasting sea'?

Three bonus questions on a shape:

(a) In mathematics, which rule is an approximate method for finding the value of an integral, by regarding the integral as the area of a region between a curve and the x-axis?

(b) In which specific part of the human skeleton is the trapezium bone?

(c) The Trapezium is a cluster of stars lying within the nebula M42 and forming part of the so-called 'Sword' of which major constellation?

12. Your starter for 10:

Which novel by Robert Graves, serialised on television in 1976, is subtitled 'From the Autobiography of Tiberius Claudius, Emperor of the Romans, Born 10 BC, Murdered and Deified AD 54?

Three bonus questions on biological pigments:

(a) What name is given to the group of yellow, orange, red and brown pigments, chemically related to terpenes, with the general formula $C_{40}H_x$, which are responsible for the characteristic colour of many plants products and are accessory pigments in photosynthesis?

(b) Derived from the breakdown of haemoglobin, which pigment is stored in the gall bladder and is responsible for the yellow colouration of the eyes and skin in jaundice?

(c) Which pigments are derived from the amino acid tyrosine, cause the pigmentation of eyes, skin and hair in vertebrates, and help protect against the effects of ultraviolet radiation?

13. Your starter for 10:
Into which rank in most taxonomic hierarchies are families grouped?

Three bonus questions on Italian prime ministers:

(a) Awarded the Jury Prize at Cannes in 2008, *Il Divo*, directed by Paolo Sorrentino, tells the story of which prime minister, of whom Margaret Thatcher said he had 'a positive aversion to principle'?

(b) Which former prime minister was kidnapped and murdered by the Red Brigades in 1978?

(c) Which future prime minister established himself as a residential housing developer around his native Milan with his construction company Edilnord?

14. Your starter for 10:
Which historical figure links an educational web resource developed by John Simkin, a revolutionary movement led by Rosa Luxembourg and Karl Liebknecht and a 1960 film by Stanley Kubrick, starring Kirk Douglas in the title role?

Three bonus questions on American writers and New Journalism:

(a) Co-editor of the 1973 anthology *The New Journalism*, who wrote the non-fiction books *The Electric Kool-Aid Acid Test* and *The Right Stuff*?

(b) Author of the essay collection *Slouching towards Bethlehem*, which writer adapted her memoir *The Year of Magical Thinking* for the stage in 2007?

(c) Regarded as a seminal piece of New Journalism, Gay Talese's 1966 article for *Esquire* magazine profiled which entertainer who, because he had a cold, was described by Talese as 'Picasso without paint, Ferrari without fuel – only worse'.

15. Your starter for 10:
From the clusters in which it grows, what is the common name of *citrus paradisi*, thought to have developed as a hybrid of the pomelo?

Three bonus questions on Arabic titles:
(a) What title for the head of a Bedouin family or tribe is ultimately derived from the Arabic word for 'old man'?
(b) What name for a descendant of the Prophet Muhammad through his daughter Fatima comes from the Arabic for 'noble'?
(c) Meaning 'guardian', what term is used by Muslims for those who know the Koran by heart?

16. Your starter for 10:
Occurring along a diagonal line on the periodic table from boron to polonium, what name is given to elements such as germanium, antimony, silicon and arsenic?

Three bonus questions on diplomatic crises of the late nineteenth and early twentieth centuries:
(a) The Fashoda incident of 1898 brought which two countries to the brink of war over territorial ambitions in Africa?
(b) In the Dogger Bank incident of 1904, ships of which navy fired on hull trawlers, believing them to be Japanese torpedo boats?
(c) A response to the arrival of French troops in Morocco, which country's despatch of a gunboat to the port of Agadir provoked a crisis of July 1911?

17. Your starter for 10:

The pluviometric coefficient refers to the ratio of the mean monthly and the mean annual measurement of what?

Three bonus questions on a war:

(a) The first phase of which war began when King Archidamus of Sparta led an invasion of Attica in 431 BC?

(b) Which Spartan general commanded the fleet that defeated the Athenians at Aegos-Potami in 405 BC, thus effectively bringing the war to its conclusion?

(c) Having fought on the Athenian side during the conflict, which historian is remembered for his *History of the Peloponnesian War*?

18. Your starter for 10:

How many carbon atoms are there in a molecule of methyl benzoic acid?

Three questions about dates in the Christian calendar:

(a) Being the name of a quarter day in Scotland, what term is applied to 2 February, a Christian festival that commemorates the purification of the Virgin Mary and the presentation of Christ in the Temple?

(b) What name is given to the fifth Sunday in Lent that follows Mothering Sunday?

(c) What is the name of the season when Christians traditionally meditate on the Four 'Last Things': Death, Judgement, Heaven and Hell?

19. Your starter for 10:

At the Stockholm Olympics in 1912, which Grand Duchy fielded its own team despite objections from Russia on the grounds that it belonged to the Russian Empire? The team was made to march directly behind the Russians in the opening ceremony, but won nine gold medals in the events?

Three bonus questions on European capitals:
In each case, give the European capital city in which all of the following are located:
(a) The Fisherman's Bastion, Gellért Hill, the Chain Bridge and the statue of 'Anonymous'?
(b) The Huguenot graveyard, the Grand Canal, the Custom House, St Mary's Pro-Cathedral and Temple Bar?
(c) Christiania, Charlottenborg, the Amalienborg Palace and the Tivoli Gardens?

20. Your starter for 10:
What is the definite integral of x^3 with respect to x between the limits 0 and 1?

Three bonus questions on a London square:
(a) In recent years noted for the presence of the anti-war protester Brian Haw, which open space close to Westminster Bridge and HM Treasury was laid out in 1868?
(b) Statues of four nineteenth-century Tory or Conservative prime ministers stand in Parliament Square. For five points, name any two of them.
(c) Among the five remaining statues in the square are two prominent South Africans. Name either one.

21. Your starter for 10:
In biology or zoology, what adjective, derived from the Greek for 'away from' and 'sign', is used to describe colouration or markings serving to warn away predators?

Three bonus questions on English monarchs:
(a) Which monarch did Pope Pius V excommunicate in

1570 as 'a heretic, and aider and fautor [patron] of heretics'?

(b) Which king was excommunicated by Pope Innocent III in 1209; he later surrendered to Innocent's demands and agreed to become his vassal?

(c) Which king was excommunicated by Pope Clement VII in 1533 and by Paul III in 1538?

22. Your starter for 10:

What is a nursehound, caught for food in Britain?

Three bonus questions on horse racing:

(a) During the wartime years of 1915–1918 and 1940–1945, the Epsom Derby was run over the July course of which English racecourse?

(b) In 1940, Thirsk staged which of the five English classics for the only time, the race being won by the Aga Khan's Turkhan, ridden by Gordon Richards?

(c) The St Leger stakes was run in 2006 at which northern racecourse while the traditional venue at Doncaster was being redeveloped?

23. Your starter for 10:

In a sans-serif typeface, if a lower-case letter 'd' is rotated 180° around all three orthogonal axes, which lower-case letter results?

Three bonus questions on a country:

(a) The ancient kingdom of Sheba, whose queen visited King Solomon, is part of which present-day country?

(b) Which Sheffield-based boxer, whose parents are both from Yemen, calls himself 'Prince'?

(c) Which comedian, born in Yemen, co-wrote the sitcom *Cows*, about a bovine family whose son wants to marry a human?

24. Your starter for 10:

To which class of animals does the tuatara, native to islands off the coast of New Zealand, belong?

Three bonus questions linked by a noun:

(a) In a phrase associated with Harry S Truman, what course of action is advocated to those who 'can't stand the heat'?

(b) Which section of the orchestra is sometimes referred to as the 'kitchen department'?

(c) Michael Kitchen played the King in the television adaptation of *To Play the King*, the second in which author's series of novels about Francis Urquhart?

25. Your starter for 10:

Used as a jet and rocket fuel and as a reducing agent, which fuming corrosive liquid is obtained by the reaction between chloramine and ammonia, or by the oxidation of urea? It has the chemical formula N_2H_4.

Three bonus questions on a shared name:

(a) Which device for measuring natural phenomena was invented in the 1880s by the Liverpool-born professor of geology and mining, John Milne?

(b) On which island is Milne Bay, named in 1873 by Captain John Moresby? It was the scene of Japan's first major setback in the Second World War.

(c) Under what title did A.A. Milne adapt Kenneth Grahame's *Wind in the Willows* for the stage?

26. Your starter for 10:

A literary fantasy whose central character 'was a man till the age of thirty, when he became a woman and has remained so ever since', which Virginia Woolf novel, dedicated to Vita Sackville-West, is subtitled *A Biography*?

Three bonus questions on a word:

(a) Which unit of measurement of font size is approximately equal to 0.3 millimetres?

(b) In the Gilbert and Sullivan operetta *The Yeoman of the Guard*, what is the occupation of Jack Point?

(c) Who wrote the novel *Point Counter Point*, first published in 1928?

27. Your starter for 10:

According to Acts in the New Testament, who was chosen by the casting of lots to replace Judas as the twelfth Apostle after his death?

Three bonus questions on a mythological creature:

(a) Which mythical beast was the emblem of the Chinese Imperial family and until 1911 adorned the Chinese flag?

(b) Which legendary king was the son of Uther Pendragon?

(c) The snapdragon is the popular name for any plant of what genus?

28. Your starter for 10:

In the human body, which physiological system includes the heart and the blood?

Three bonus questions on physics:

(a) Which instrument is used to split a light wave into component waves which eventually recombine as patterns that can be used in the quality control of lenses and prisms, and in the measurement of wavelengths?

(b) An interferometer was used in which experiment of 1887, named after the American scientists who conducted it? It failed to detect the motion of the

Earth through the ether, but became a key piece of evidence for the theory of relativity.

(c) The Michelson-Morley experiment was confirmed with the aid of which device, invented in the early 1950s by the American physicist Charles Townes and involving amplification to produce microwaves of a fixed density?

29. Your starter for 10:

What five-letter word can mean: in computing, a set of one or more characters treated as a whole; in geology, a region characterised by having a particular mineral resource; and, in physics, any region, volume or space in which a physical force is operative and influential?

Three bonus questions on similar-sounding words:

(a) Nisan is the name of the first month of the year in which calendar?

(b) To what did the British mining engineer, Lieutenant-Colonel Peter N. Nissen, give his name?

(c) The term 'nisei' means second-generation children born in the USA or Canada of parents who were immigrants from which country?

30. Your starter for 10:

What term can mean: an architectural figure, often a human bust or an animal set on a pillar, used as a boundary marker in Ancient Rome; a final point in space or time; and a station at the end of a railway route?

Three bonus questions on the films of director Elia Kazan:

In each case, name the film from the description:

(a) Marlon Brando stars in an Oscar-winning film about organised crime and union corruption in the New York docks.

(b) Based on a novel by John Steinbeck, James Dean and Richard Davalos play twin brothers on a California farm around 1917.

(c) In a 1951 adaptation of play by Tennessee Williams, Vivien Leigh plays Blanche Dubois, a neurotic woman who decamps to her pregnant sister's home in New Orleans.

> 'It looks bad – it is bad. Anyway, we've got to say goodbye to you, but thank you very much – you were a nice cheerful team, and we were all hugely relieved when you did get some things right. Or get the chance to buzz in – they were very, very, very fast.'

HIGHEST SCORES
(1994–2010)

1. Open (1997) — 415
2. Open (1997) — 395
3. Trinity College, Cambridge (1995) — 390
4. Magdalen College, Oxford (1998) — 375
5. Manchester (1997) — 360
6. Durham (2000) — 360
7. Durham (1999) — 355
8. Open (1999) — 350
9. Corpus Christi College, Oxford (2009) — 350
10. Corpus Christi College, Oxford (2005) — 345
11. Manchester (2009) — 345
12. St John's, Cambridge (2009) — 345
13. Durham (2000) — 340
14. Trinity College, Cambridge (1995) — 335
15. University College, Oxford (1996) — 335
16. Magdalen College, Oxford (1997) — 335
17. Nottingham (1998) — 335
18. Oriel College, Oxford (1999) — 335
19. University College, Oxford (2001) — 335
20. Lincoln College, Oxford (2009) — 335

The Final

'Welcome to the only place where you're expected to demonstrate a familiarity with Schrodinger's cat, Darwin's finches and the Simpsons' family dog.'

THE RULES

Let's skip the rules, here's your first
starter for 10.

The Final

1. Your starter for 10:
The psychologist Raymond Cattell identified 'fluid' and 'crystallised' as factors of what human capacity, defined by one authority as the extent to which one deals 'flexibly and effectively with practical and theoretical problems'?

> **Three bonus questions on timekeeping:**
> (a) What name denotes the class of devices used in clocks that intervene between the motive power and the regulator, causing an intermittent impulse to be given to the regulator and converting rotational to oscillatory motion?
> (b) What form of escapement, invented in the seventeenth century by Robert Hooke, is named after its resemblance to a piece of nautical equipment?
> (c) What kind of escapement, designed in around 1722 by Robert Harrison, is named after a type of insect? A notable modern example is John Taylor's Corpus Clock in Cambridge.

2. Your starter for 10:
A ninth-century poem in Old English contained in the 'Exeter Book', the posthumously published papers of D.H. Lawrence, a novel for children by E. Nesbit and an allegorical poem by Shakespeare all refer in their titles to what mythological bird?

Three bonus questions on a number:

(a) Which number has been described by mathematicians working in artificial intelligence at MIT as 'the least random number', because it was the most common choice of respondents asked to select a number between one and twenty?

(b) The Boeing B-17 heavy bomber aircraft was known by what two-word epithet during the Second World War, partly in reference to its ability to defend itself?

(c) Which Asian verse-form usually consists of seventeen *onji*, a phonetic unit broadly equivalent to the syllable, in three phrases of five, seven and five?

3. Your starter for 10:

An ancient temple site near Luxor in Egypt, the director of *Lolita* and *Dr Strangelove*, and the electronic music group whose albums include *Autobahn* and *Computer Love* all have names that begin and end with which letter of the alphabet?

Three bonus questions on culture:

(a) Author of *Sisterly Feelings*, who, in 1997, became the first playwright to be knighted since Noel Coward in 1970?

(b) Also in 1997, who became only the second composer to receive a life peerage?

(c) And who, in 1997, became the second pop or rock musician to be knighted?

4. Your starter for 10:

The lion, hens and roosters, wild asses, tortoises and the elephant are, in sequence, the first entities introduced in which orchestral suite of fourteen movements, composed in 1886?

Three bonus questions on physics:
(a) The Navier-Stokes equation governs the behaviour of what form of matter?
(b) The ratio of the shear stress to the strain rate in a fluid is commonly known as what?
(c) What is the SI unit of viscosity?

5.   Your starter for 10:
In 1903, the Serbian mathematician Mileva Maric became the first wife of which physicist, who divorced her in 1919 and married his cousin, Elsa Lowenthal?

Three bonus questions on traditional pigments:
(a) Which semi-precious stone was the source of the blue pigment ultramarine, which was used in the Middle Ages for illuminated manuscripts and panel paintings?
(b) From a Greek term meaning a form of yellow, what word has been applied to traditional pigments usually derived from impure iron ores and ranging from yellow to red, brown and purple?
(c) Chemically, the bright green pigment verdigris is a compound of which metallic element?

6.   Your starter for 10:
Recorded by the photographer Iain Macmillan, what event of significance in popular culture took place at about 11.30 a.m. on 8 August 1969, in a road in St John's Wood in London?

Three bonus questions linked by a word:
(a) In Sydney, Australia, what is the Brickfielder?
(b) What, in the USA, is 'brick', which has an elastic texture, is full of holes, and is sold in blocks ten inches by three inches?
(c) In the film version of which Tennessee Williams play

did Paul Newman play Brick Pollitt, who is unhappily married to Maggie, played by Elizabeth Taylor?

7. **Your starter for 10:**
At one time home to a group of expatriate writers including Paul Bowles, William Burroughs and Tennessee Williams, which North African city lies just to the east of Cap Spartel, the promontory where the Mediterranean meets the Atlantic?

Three bonus questions on an ancient manuscript:
(a) The sixth-century *Codex Argenteus*, or 'Silver Book', contains fragments of the four Gospels translated by Bishop Ulfilas, and is a principal source for which extinct East Germanic language?
(b) Rediscovered in the Rhineland in the sixteenth century, the *Codex* became part of the collection of Emperor Rudolf II at which present-day capital?
(c) Captured as booty by the Swedes in 1648, the *Codex Argenteus* is now in the collection of which university, around 80 kilometres north of Stockholm?

8. **Your starter for 10:**
In geology, a coarse-grained clastic rock, composed of angular broken rock fragments held together by a mineral cement or in a fine-grained matrix, is known by what name, an Italian word meaning 'broken stones' or 'rubble'?

Three bonus questions on applause:
(a) The Austrian-born pianist and composer Artur Schnabel called applause 'a receipt, not a note of demand' in explanation of his refusal to do what?
(b) Chief conductor of the BBC Symphony Orchestra from 2000 to 2004, which American conductor, in an essay of 2006, encouraged audiences to applaud when they

felt like it, regardless of whether the final movement had ended?

(c) Which American writer and satirist defined applause as 'the echo of a platitude' in his *Devil's Dictionary*, published in 1911?

9. Your starter for 10:
Flemington Park, in the Australian state of Victoria, is the venue for which classic horse race, run on the first Tuesday in November?

Three bonus questions on a name:

(a) The ratio of the speed of a fluid to the speed of sound in that fluid is named after which Austrian physicist?

(b) David Mach's sculpture *Train* is situated by the line of the historic railway which linked which two sites?

(c) Austrian Field Marshal Mack surrendered to which French commander at Ulm in 1805?

10. Your starter for 10:
Which band was founded in 1986 by Charles Thompson IV, inspired Kurt Cobain to write 'Smells Like Teen Spirit', and is best known for the single 'Monkey Gone To Heaven'?

Three bonus questions on mythology:

(a) The wife of King Tyndareus of Sparta gave birth to two boys, Castor and Pollux, and two girls, Helen and Clytemnestra, after being seduced by Zeus in what form?

(b) The seduction of Europa by Zeus, after he had assumed the form of a bull and carried her on his back to Crete, resulted in the birth of which king, whose own wife, Pasiphaë, later fell in love with a bull?

(c) Which historical figure claimed he was the son of Zeus because his mother, Olympias, insisted she had been impregnated by the god in the form of a snake?

11.   Your starter for 10:
What is the term for a mass of spermatozoa and other products exuded by male fish during spawning?

Three bonus questions on pairs of people who share a given name and surname:
In each case, give the full name from the descriptions:
(a) The second president of the USA, and the composer of the operas *The Death of Klinghoffer* and *Doctor Atomic*?
(b) A professor of particle physics involved with the Large Hadron Collider, and an actor whose roles include King Lear for the National Theatre and the first cinema portrayal of Hannibal Lector?
(c) A senior English naval officer who commanded HMS *Victory* at the Battle of Trafalgar, and a major novelist born in 1840?

12.   Your starter for 10:
Chief of the Eleatic school of philosophy, what Greek philosopher demonstrated that the senses could not be trusted by constructing four paradoxes, including the Achilles and tortoise problems?

Three bonus questions on capital cities:
(a) Which African capital lies at the confluence of the Blue Nile and White Nile?
(b) Which Asian capital is located at the confluence of the Tonle Sap, Bassac and Mekong rivers?
(c) Which European capital lies at the confluence of the Sava with the Danube?

13.   Your starter for 10:
A familiar example being the chirruping heard between

modems before connection, what is the common name of an exchange of signals between two pieces of communicating equipment that announces that each is ready to talk to the other, and on what terms?

Three bonus questions on Shakespeare's Hamlet:
In each case, identify the speaker of the given line or lines:
(a) 'This above all – to thine own self be true.'
(b) 'Let not the royal bed of Denmark be / A couch for luxury and damned incest.'
(c) 'Good night, sweet prince, / And flights of angels sing thee to thy rest.'

14. Your starter for 10:
Which bird of the family *trochillidae* appears on the Bank of England £10 note first issued in 2000?

Three bonus questions on things past:
(a) The phrase 'remembrance of things past', an English title given to Marcel Proust's novel sequence, is taken from a sonnet by which writer?
(b) 'Time present and time past / Are both perhaps present in time future / And time future contained in time past.' Which poet wrote these lines in a work of 1935?
(c) 'Who controls the past controls the future: who controls the present controls the past.' Words from which 1949 novel?

15. Your starter for 10:
An award now coordinated by the Russian magazine *64*, the 'Fascinated Wanderer' is the name given to the statuette presented, usually annually, to the leading international competitor in which game?

Three bonus questions on a Spanish name:
(a) In Shakespeare's *Othello*, which character is in love

with Othello's wife Desdemona, and is killed by Iago?

(b) The twentieth-century Spanish composer Joaquin Rodrigo wrote his *Concierto de Aranjuez* for orchestra and which solo instrument?

(c) What was the title of the eleventh-century Castilian military leader and Rodrigo Diaz de Vivar?

16. Your starter for 10:

Identify the author of these lines: 'Come live with me, and be my love, / And we will some new pleasures prove / Of golden sands, and crystal brooks, / With silken lines, and silver hooks'?

Three bonus questions on heteronyms, that is, words with the same spelling but different pronunciations:

(a) Which heteronyms are the names of a port in Alabama and a type of kinetic art invented in the 1930s by Alexander Calder?

(b) Which two heteronyms are words used to describe workers who have joined together for self-protection, and a chemical compound that has not dissociated electrically?

(c) Which Indian film director and American photographer and Dadaist had heteronymic surnames?

17. Your starter for 10:

In medicine, the term paronychia denotes an infection of the soft tissue around what part of the body?

Three bonus questions on cricket:

In each case, give the decade during which the following captained the England cricket team:

(a) Freddie Brown, Len Hutton and Peter May.

(b) Tony Lewis, Mike Denness and Tony Greig.

(c) Bob Willis, David Gower and Mike Gatting.

18. Your starter for 10:

A regular dodecahedron has twelve faces, but how many edges has each face?

Three bonus questions on place names:

(a) Founded in 1854, what is the largest city and, until 1997, the capital of the Central Asian Republic of Kazakhstan?

(b) The Battle of the Alma was a Russian defeat by British and French forces during which war?

(c) Alamogordo, the site of the detonation of the first atomic bomb in 1945, is situated in which US state?

19. Your starter for 10:

What type of timber decay is caused by various fungi, especially species of *serpula* and *merulius*, that form a white, then red, threadlike surface, which works its way into the timber, making it flaky and brittle?

Three bonus questions on biographies of physicists:

(a) Graham Farmelo described which Bristol-born quantum theorist as 'almost pathologically reticent' in his 2009 biography entitled *The Strangest Man*?

(b) 'Half genius and half buffoon' is a view of which American founding father of quantum field theory, recorded in James Gleick's 1992 biography, *Genius*?

(c) Abraham Pais's 'Subtle is the lord' takes its title from words attributed to which physicist, awarded the Nobel Prize in 1921 for his discovery of the law of the photo-electric effect?

20. Your starter for 10:

Sometimes called the Lady of the Lake, from the magical setting of her palace, which enchantress of Arthurian legend was the mistress of Merlin?

Three bonus questions on dragons:

(a) Kalessin, who transports Ged and Arren to Roke, is the oldest dragon in works by Ursula Le Guin set in which world?

(b) In Tolkien's *Silmarillion*, which dragon is described as 'the first of the Uruloki, the fire-drakes of the North'?

(c) In *Harry Potter and the Philosopher's Stone*, what is the name of the Norwegian ridgeback dragon that Hagrid illegally breeds?

21. Your starter for 10:

The Austrian mountaineer Heinrich Harrer, who died in January 2006, was the author of which book based on his experiences in the 1940s, when he became a tutor to the Dalai Lama? The book was later made into a film starring Brad Pitt.

Three bonus questions on poets' graves:

(a) 'Here lies one whose name was writ in water' are the words of the self-composed epitaph of which poet, on his tombstone in the Protestant cemetery in Rome?

(b) The title of which poem by T.S. Eliot is the name of the Somerset village in whose church his ashes were interred in 1965?

(c) John Masefield was the last poet to be buried in Poets' Corner in Westminster Abbey. Who was the first, in 1400?

22. Your starter for 10:

Meaning 'messenger', what name is given to the Papal Legate, or ambassador, to a civil government?

Three bonus questions on an African country:

(a) In March 1990, Dr Sam Nujoma was installed as which African country's first president after the implementation of a UN resolution for free elections resulted in SWAPO coming to power?

(b) Which national park in Namibia has a name meaning 'Great White Place' and is dominated by a huge pan of salt and clay which was formerly a lake fed by the Kunene river?

(c) A base for SWAPO forces before independence, which former Portuguese colony borders Namibia to the north?

23. Your starter for 10:

In family relationships, what four-word term is used to describe a child of the child of a first cousin of either of one's parents in relation to oneself?

Three bonus questions on Tennyson's Idylls of the King:

(a) Who is the subject of the opening lines of the first Idyll, 'The Coming of Arthur': 'Leodogran, the King of Cameliard, / Had one fair daughter, and none other child; / And she was the fairest of all flesh on earth'?

(b) In the *Idylls*, which young noblewoman declares her love for Lancelot but is dismissed by him with the words: 'Smile at your own self hereafter, / When you yield your flower of life / To one more fitly yours, not thrice your age'?

(c) Tennyson dedicated the *Idylls* to which recently deceased public figure, describing him as one 'who loved one only, and who clave to her'?

24. Your starter for 10:

ITER, the experimental nuclear fusion reactor being built in Cadarache, France, will be fuelled by which two isotopes of hydrogen?

Three bonus questions on Irish aviation history:

(a) Which pair of aviators landed near Clifden in County

Galway after their historic non-stop transatlantic flight from Newfoundland in June 1919?

(b) The invention of which drink is attributed to Joe Sheridan, the head chef at Foynes seaplane terminal in County Limerick, to warm up passengers who landed there on their way to America; a plaque commemorating this may be seen at Shannon Airport?

(c) Which international airport in the west of Ireland was opened in 1986; it was built largely due to the efforts of the local priest, Monsignor James Horan, to enable pilgrims to reach a holy shrine nearby?

25. Your starter for 10:

What word of four letters denotes: in physics, the rate of change of acceleration; in physiology, an involuntary spasmodic muscular movement; and in colloquial speech, a stupid or contemptible person?

Three bonus questions on world history:

In each case, give the Chinese dynasty whose time span corresponds to the following events in Europe and West Asia:

(a) The rise of Rome as the dominant Mediterranean power, and the first two centuries of the Roman Empire.

(b) The beginnings and spread of Islam, and the reigns of Charlemagne and King Alfred the Great.

(c) The aftermath of the Black Death, the Reformation, and the start of the English Civil War.

26. Your starter for 10:

Operating services to Northern Ireland and the Isle of Man, which ferry port on the coast of Lancashire has been conjoined with the neighbouring town of Morecambe since 1928?

Three bonus questions on a culinary spice:

(a) Which spice is an essential ingredient of classic bouillabaisse, and is used to flavour and colour paella, Milanese risotto, pilau rice and biryani?

(b) Saffron is made primarily from which precise part of the Asian flower *Crocus sativus*?

(c) Which relative of the thistle whose seeds are a source of cooking oil is known as 'bastard saffron' because its yellow flowers are often used as a cheap substitute for the spice?

27. Your starter for 10:

Originating from the Latin for 'out' and 'begin to bloom', which adjective describes a substance that has lost moisture and turned to a fine powder on exposure to air?

Three bonus questions on chemical reactions:

(a) An addition-elimination reaction, in which two or more molecules combine to form a larger one with the loss of a small molecule such as water or alcohol, is usually known by what name?

(b) The type of reaction variously called 'double displacement', 'double decomposition' and 'ionic association' is also known by what one-word term?

(c) Reactions between two substances, in which one loses one or more electrons and the other gains them, are commonly referred to by what portmanteau abbreviation?

28. Your starter for 10:

What term is used for a number that cannot be expressed as a fraction p over q where p and q are integers and q is not 0, for example the square root of 2?

Three bonus questions on a radio programme:

(a) Which cult radio programme of the 1950s was originally entitled *Crazy People*?

(b) The 'gooney' is a member of certain species of which seabird?

(c) 'Goon', meaning 'downland' is common in place names in which county of the UK?

29. Your starter for 10:

The title character of which 1972 David Bowie album was inspired by the British rock 'n' roll singer Vince Taylor?

Three bonus questions on brothers:

(a) The better-known brother of the author of the travel books *Brazilian Adventure* and *News from Tartary* was a writer of popular spy fiction. What surname did they share?

(b) In 1902, which two brothers published *The Varieties of Religious Experience* and *The Wings of the Dove*?

(c) *The Liffey Swim* is a picture painted in 1923 by the brother of which Nobel Prize-winning poet?

30. Your starter for 10:

Which famous nineteenth-century short story begins, 'I was sick – sick unto death with that long agony; and when they at length unbound me and I was permitted to sit, I felt that my senses were leaving me'?

Three bonus questions on European national parks:

(a) Established in 1990, the Harz National Park takes its name from the most northerly range of mountains in which EU member state?

(b) The Plitvice Lakes National Park was granted Unesco World Heritage status in 1979 and is a major tourist attraction in which European country?

(c) Including a valley noted for thousands of Bronze Age rock carvings, the Mercantour National Park is in which country?

'Well, if you're going to go out without winning, go out in the final.'

SERIES CHAMPIONS

1963 Leicester
1965 New College,
Oxford
1966 Oriel College,
Oxford
1967 Sussex
1968 Keele
1969 Sussex
1970 Churchill College,
Cambridge
1971 Sidney Sussex
College, Cambridge
1972 University College,
Oxford
1973 Fitzwilliam College,
Cambridge
1974 Trinity College,
Cambridge
1975 Keble College,
Oxford
1976 University College,
Oxford
1977 Durham
1978 Sidney Sussex
College, Cambridge
1979 Bradford
1980 Merton College,
Oxford
1981 Queen's University,
Belfast
1982 St Andrews
1983 Dundee

1984 Open University
1986 Jesus College,
Oxford
1987 Keble College,
Oxford
1995 Trinity College,
Cambridge
1996 Imperial College,
London
1997 Magdalen College,
Oxford
1998 Magdalen College,
Oxford
1999 Open University
2000 Durham
2001 Imperial College,
London
2002 Somerville College,
Oxford
2003 Birkbeck College,
London
2004 Magdalen College,
Oxford
2005 Corpus Christi
College, Oxford
2006 Manchester
2007 Warwick
2008 Christ Church,
Oxford
2009 Manchester
2010 Emmanuel College,
Cambridge

The Answers

1.   Hannibal
     (a) (William) Blake ('Auguries of Innocence') (b) (Samuel Taylor)
     Coleridge (*The Rime of the Ancient Mariner*) (c) (Percy Bysshe)
     Shelley ('Ozymandias')
2.   Iain Banks
     (a) *Cymbeline* (b) A diamond ring (c) Carbuncle
3.   Thrace
     (a) Robert Louis Stevenson (b) Paris (c) Martin Amis
4.   *Las Meninas / The Maids of Honour*
     (a) Fixation of nitrogen (the biological process by which nitrogen in
     the atmosphere is converted into ammonia) (b) Mycorrhiza
     (c) Inquilinism
5.   (*The*) *Flying Scotsman*
     (a) Georgia (b) Ukraine (c) Kyrgyzstan
6.   Redemption
     (a) Kava (b) Qat / khat (c) Kola (nut)
7.   (Jimmy) Carter (in 1980)
     (a) Secretary of State (b) Cyrus Vance (c) Henry Kissinger
8.   Herodotus (of Halicarnassus) (*Histories*, Vol. 4, Book 8, v. 98)
     (a) Derivative(s) (b) Zero / the zero function (c) Acceleration
9.   Flukes
     (a) MySpace (b) iLike (c) Blog early, blog often
10. Israel
     (a) Charlotte (b) Prince Edward Island (c) (Thomas) Jefferson
11. Queen Katherine and Anne Bullen / Catherine of Aragon and Anne
     Boleyn
     (a) Polymerisation (b) Polyphonic (c) Polyhedron
12. Hans Christian (Oersted and Andersen)
     (a) Politics (b) Computer science / computing (c) Economics
13. I.L.P. (Independent Labour Party; Index Librorum Prohibitorum;
     Individual Learning Plan)
     (a) Trier (French: Trèves) (b) Metz (c) Schengen
14. *Through the Looking-Glass (and What Alice Found There)* (not

Alice's Adventures in Wonderland, published 1865; the White Queen only appears in the sequel.)
(a) Dido and Aeneas (b) Tristan and Isolde (c) *Porgy and Bess*

15. Amagat (Emile Amagat, 1841–1915)
(a) *The Flying Dutchman / Der Fliegende Hollander* (b) Exocet (the fish is *exocoetus volitas*) (c) Buttress

16. 290 yards
(a) Shrine (Latin: *scrinium*) (b) Dead Sea Scrolls (c) Cologne (Cathedral)

17. Grounding line
(a) (Fritz) Haber (b) Ernest Rutherford (c) (Linus) Pauling

18. Amphoteric
(a) 2,305 years (accept 2,205–2,405; 490 BC–1815) (b) With flower petals (dropped in great quantity from above) (c) Wedge (Latin: *cuneus*, 'wedge')

19. Memory
(a) Pain (bread) (b) Child (*Kind*) (c) Once

20. Golem
(a) Pablo Neruda (b) Stephen Spender (c) Virginia Woolf

21. Hunter S(tockton) Thompson
(a) (Simple) machine (b) Mechanical advantage (c) Turbine

22. Career
(a) Icosahedron (accept icosahedral (symmetry)) (b) Capsomere(s) (c) Bacteriophage

23. Sodium (accept salt)
(a) (George Frideric) Handel (b) (Dame) Joan Sutherland (c) *Madam Butterfly*

24. The Gaia Hypothesis
(a) Dada / Dadaism (b) David Hockney (c) The cover of The Beatles' *Sgt Pepper / Sgt Pepper's Lonely Hearts Club Band* album

25. Sulphuric acid
(a) Books (b) Death (c) Spending

26. Lipogram
(a) Egypt (b) Pakistan (c) Iran

27. London / Moscow / Helsinki
(a) Cluny la Sorbonne (b) (Georges) Clemenceau (c) Charles de Gaulle Étoile

28. Smiles
(a) *Northanger Abbey* (b) Thomas Love Peacock (c) Waverley Abbey

29. Parma
   (a) St Margaret (b) George III (c) Panorama
30. Bald
   (a) Fastnet Rock (b) Timberlake Wertenbaker (c) Ford Madox Brown

Round One Match Two

1. pH
   (a) Offshore (b) Seville (c) Orkney
2. Colon
   (a) Mercury (b) Elongation (c) 88 (accept 78 to 98)
3. A firkin
   (a) Seville (b) B(a)etis (c) (Ferdinand) Magellan
4. Voltaire
   (a) Kingsley Amis (b) J.L. Carr (c) Oliver Cromwell
5. Of that ilk
   (a) Panama (b) Kentucky (c) Germany
6. Concorde (attributed to Tony Benn)
   (a) Bildungsroman (b) Festschrift (c) Urtext
7. Ogive
   (a) Claptrap (b) Moonshine (c) Hogwash
8. Utilitarianism
   (a) *The Oxford English Dictionary* / OED (b) (John) Walker (c) Edinburgh
9. Hadlee
   (a) (Sir) Colin Cowdrey (b) Ted Dexter (c) Tony Greig
10. Magnetohydrodynamics (accept hydromagnetics)
    (a) Supermarket (b) Allen Ginsberg (c) Dale Winton
11. Turin
    (a) 'Ebony And Ivory' (b) 'Good Morning' (c) 'Helen Wheels'
12. *The Spectator*
    (a) Monsieur Hulot (b) *Strangers on a Train* (c) *Blow-up*
13. Exosphere
    (a) Venture capital (b) (Rate of) flow of a fluid (c) Jim Carrey
14. Polymorphism
    (a) Albion (b) The White Cliffs of Dover (c) Perfidious
15. Edward I and Edward II (married to Henry III and Edward I respectively)
    (a) Tennessee (b) Colorado (c) Wyoming

16. Vitamin A
    (a) Glasgow (b) Scouse (c) Oxford
17. Fartlek
    (a) (Frederick) Delius (b) Shirley Bassey (c) Slim Whitman
18. Nike (or Blue Ribbon Sports, as it was before it became Nike)
    (a) Burgundy (b) Armagnac (brandy) (c) Champagne
19. Northwest Passage
    (a) Mu (b) (August Ferdinand) Möbius (c) Lepton (not meson)
20. Cher
    (a) (Jorge Luis) Borges (b) Iran (c) (Vladimir Ilyich) Lenin
21. Negative capability
    (a) Louis XIV (b) (b) Henri II (c) Louis XV
22. Neutrinos ('no mass' is not strictly true, they have miniscule but
    non-zero mass. Three forms: electron-neutrinos, muon-neutrinos,
    tau-neutrons – accept any, correcting it to just neutrinos)
    (a) (Dr) Samuel Johnson (b) George Orwell (c) Orange Prize
23. Cartouche
    (a) W.H. Auden (b) E.M. Forster (c) *Death in Venice / Der Tod in
    Venedig*
24. Switzerland
    (a) Photoelectric effect (liberation of electrons from the surface of a
    material when electromagnetic radiation falls on it) (b) Princeton
    (c) Watchmaker
25. Portugal
    (a) The Dambusters raids (b) (Sir Neville) Barnes Wallis (c) 'Après
    moi le deluge' / 'After me the flood'
26. Sharp
    (a) Indo-European (b) Greek (c) (West) Germanic
27. 100 (one hundred) (RAM of Ca = 40, RAM of C = 12, RAM of O =
    16. 40 + 12 + 48 = 100; the actual figure is 100.0872 g/mol)
    (a) Trajan (b) Antoninus (Pius) (c) Marcus Aurelius
28. Kaprekar (number)
    (a) St Margaret (b) Edward II (c) Henry VII
29. Perk
    (a) Cornwall (b) (Curved) sword (with a notched blade)
    (c) Northumberland
30. Marilyn (*The Relative Hills of Britain*, 1992)
    (a) Magna Carta (b) Common ownership / state control of industry
    and services (c) Act of Settlement

1.   (John) Updike
        (a) Leeds (b) Chester (c) Isle of Man
2.   Supernumerary
        (a) (Absolute) refractive index or index of refraction (if first medium is a vacuum, ratio is the absolute refractive index of second) (b) Financial Times Stock Exchange (c) Index Librorum Prohibitorum / Index of Forbidden Books (books regarded as 'dangerous to the faith or morals' of Roman Catholics)
3.   Eleven metres per second squared (force = mass x acceleration. 165 = 15 x 11)
        (a) Loris (b) Lemur (Latin: *lemures*) (c) Aye-aye
4.   Pentatope (accept hypertetrahedron)
        (a) Children's literature (b) Ivor Novello Awards (c) (Igor) Sikorsky
5.   Kiev
        (a) Shorn, sheared (b) Stringed, strung (c) Proved, proven
6.   The thirteenth (three: John, 1199–1216; Henry III, 1216–1272; Edward I, 1272–1307)
        (a) The 3 Rs / (reading, 'riting, 'rithmetic) (b) (F.D. Roosevelt's) New Deal (c) Reformat, Reinstall
7.   Woodrow Wilson
        (a) Purple patch / *pannus purpureus* (accept purple passage / purple prose) (b) Porphyry (c) Divinity (accept theology)
8.   Photochromic
        (a) Intravenous (not 'inoculate') (b) Unimportance
        (c) Unsportsmanlike
9.   Peter Cooke
        (a) Tisane (Greek: *ptisane*) (a) Chamomile (or camomile) tea
        (c) Yerba mate / mate (tea) / yerba (tea) / Paraguay tea
10.   Tropism
        (a) (The) Frankfurt (School) (officially Frankfurt Institute for Social Research) (b) Herbert Marcuse (c) New York
11.   Chiasma
        (a) Paradigm (b) Parataxis (c) Paralanguage
12.   Albumin
        (a) Armenia (b) Korea (c) Thailand / Siam
13.   Dordogne and Garonne (not Gironde)
        (a) 1760s (1763) (b) 1920s (1928) (c) 1850s (1856)
14.   A pint of bitter (not lager; the answer must be more specific than

simply 'beer')

(a) (People's Republic of) China (b) Somalia (c) Singapore

15. Gnosticism

(a) Excess of fat in the blood (b) Statins (c) Triglycerides

16. Pinkie

(a) The Royal Society (b) (William) Henry (Henry's Law) (c) (Alfred Russell) Wallace

17. Richter

(a) Fungus (b) Ergot (c) Lysergic acid

18. 1,000 (or 10^3)

(a) Saturn (b) Monoceros (c) Auroras (both Northern and Southern Lights, i.e. Aurora Borealis, Aurora Australis; specifically to study energy releases from the Earth's magnetosphere called substorms, which intensify auroras)

19. (Convention on International Trade in) Endangered Species (of wild flora and fauna)

(a) Setanta (b) Bluetooth (c) Tiscali

20. Flugelhorn

(a) Out and ought (b) Thou and though (c) Nit and night

21. Poetry

(a) Anne Boleyn (b) Anne of Denmark (c) Queen Anne (reigned 1702–1714)

22. Romanesque / Norman

(a) (William) Wordsworth (b) The novel (c) *The Tempest*

23. John

(a) Othello (b) Agincourt (c) Romeo

24. Hadrian's Wall

(a) Eumenides ('the kindly ones') (b) Matricide (accept parricide) (c) (*The*) *Family Reunion*

25. 'Gather ye rosebuds while ye may'

(a) 273.15K (b) 4°C (c) 180°F

26. Hamas (Harakat Al-Muqawama Al-Islamiyya)

(a) Lupin (b) Delphinium (c) Pansy

27. (Henri) Bergson

(a) Barnsley (b) John Arden (c) Joanne Harris

28. Mercury

(a) Capri (b) Tiberius (c) Gracie Fields

29. Iridescence

(a) Alexander (b) Nova Scotia (c) Tunis

30. Belfast (Another couple, one of them terminally ill, was given special dispensation to marry before that, but that was prior to the law coming into effect.)
(a) Rhode Island (b) Los Angeles (c) Buenos Aires (Santa Maria del Buon Aire)

Round One Match Four

1. Allotropes (accept allotropy)
(a) Bay (b) Grey (c) Roan
2. (E.) Annie Proulx
(a) Sandwich men / sandwich-board men (b) Hawaii (c) Thomas Paine
3. Corpus Christi
(a) Capernaum (b) 'Kubla Khan' (c) The Gorbals
4. Mites
(a) (Pierre and Marie) Curie (they were Frederic and Irene Joliot-Curie) (b) Technetium (c) Neptunium
5. Shingle
(a) (Sir George Gabriel) Stokes (b) The Chiltern Hundreds (c) Buckinghamshire
6. Animals
(a) Hades (accept Pluto / Pluton / Dis) (b) The Furies / Erinyes / Eumenides (c) Don DeLillo
7. Grand Theft Auto
(a) (Viscount) Palmerston (b) (Lord) Liverpool (c) (William Ewart) Gladstone
8. Bow (and arrow)
(a) Pembrokeshire (b) Vale of Glamorgan / Bro Morgannwg (c) Powys
9. Telford (in Shropshire)
(a) Richard Parker (b) Howard Spring (c) Penelope Lively
10. Ethnography
(a) Salerno (Scuola Medica Salernitana) (b) Frederick I / Barbarossa (c) Padua (Padova)
11. Smith
(a) Boris Godunov (1552–1605) (b) Alexander I (c) Ivan the Terrible / Ivan IV
12. Berlin, Madrid, Lisbon, Prague, Athens, Vienna, Warsaw
(a) (Albrecht) Dürer (b) (Giovanni Battista) Piranesi (c) (William) Hogarth

13. Peach (not nectarine or apricot)

(a) Stefan-Boltzmann Law (or just Stefan's Law) (Jožef Stefan, 1835–1893; Ludwig Boltzmann, 1844–1906) (b) 3/2 k t (three halves k t / three over two k t) (c) Entropy

14. Yahoo

(a) Primus (b) Prebendary (from 'prebend') (c) Dean

15. Hand / fingers (a shortening of the fascia in the palm. Guillaume Dupuytren, 1777–1835; also known for treating Napoleon Bonaparte's haemorrhoids, and for creating an artificial anus)

(a) *Under the Greenwood Tree* (b) W.B. Yeats ('Sailing to Byzantium') (c) Frida Kahlo

16. Saint Lucy

(a) Costa Rica (b) Belize (c) Ecuador

17. Nigeria (according to a UNESCO report released in 2009)

(a) Brandenburg (not Berlin) (b) Saxony / Sachsen (c) Bavaria / Bayern

18. John Knox

(a) (Marc) Chagall (b) Surrealist / surrealism (c) *Dead Souls*

19. (Henri) Poincaré

(a) Egypt (b) Ptolemaic dynasty (c) Cleopatra (VII)

20. Vinculum (Latin: *vincire*)

(a) Lace (b) Chantilly lace (c) Hydrangea

21. Spain (the War of the Spanish Succession, 1702–1713)

(a) Dorothy Wordsworth (b) Gwen John (sister of Augustus John) (c) Mendelssohn (later Fanny Hensel)

22. (Percy Bysshe) Shelley

(a) (Isaac) Newton (b) 25 (the only such triple in which the numbers are successive integers is 3, 4, 5) (c) One

23. *Hamlet*

(a) Androecium (b) Pithecanthropus (c) Housemaid

24. Copper

(a) Mesosphere (*meso*: 'middle') (b) The Cretaceous period (c) Mesothelium (not mesoderm)

25. Lake Como

(a) Celluloid (accept Parkesine) (b) Bakelite (c) Nylon

26. Prime

(a) Clark's (b) Barbour (c) (Thomas) Burberry

27. Kidneys

(a) Toluene (b) Southern Cross (*Crux Australis*) (c) Aneurin Bevan

28. ZX80
     (a) 1830s (1835 and 1837) (b) 1890s (1895 and 1897) (c) 1920s
     (1921–1923 and 1926)
29. The game of croquet in *Alice's Adventures in Wonderland*
     (flamingos and hedgehogs respectively)
     (a) (Marc) Chagall (b) (Henri) Matisse (c) (Pierre-Auguste) Renoir
30. Ourselves
     (a) Nagasaki (b) *Pacific Overtures* (c) Mike Leigh

Round One Match Five

1. Reeve
    (a) *Bleak House* (b) Mr Jaggers (c) Uriah Heep
2. Love
    (a) Termagant (the deity Tervagan) (b) Virago (c) Shrew
3. Argon
    (a) Sir Aston Webb (b) The Circus (c) Manchester
4. (Common) colds
    (a) (Sir Francis) Drake (b) Vinson Massif (c) Ross Ice Shelf
5. Cobble
    (a) *Cymbeline* (a) Elizabeth Barrett Browning (c) Shelley
6. Libration
    (a) The Aldwych (b) The Prince of Wales (c) The Old Vic
7. 1870s (1871, 1877 and 1872 respectively)
    (a) 1760s (b) 1810s (a) 1850s
8. (Rodolphe) Kreutzer (*The Kreutzer Sonata*)
    (a) (Mikhail) Gorbachev and (Ronald) Reagan (b) *Rainbow Warrior*
    (c) Philadelphia
9. Kent (Kentish rag)
    (a) Helmut Kohl (b) (Kim) Campbell (c) John Howard
10. (Free- or fast-) flowing water
    (a) *Le Grand Meaulnes* (b) (Jean-Auguste-Dominique) Ingres
    (c) (Georges) Seurat
11. FSB
    (a) Tricki-woo (b) Duke Ellington (c) Richard Nixon
12. (Mycobacterium) tuberculosis
    (a) Caryl Phillips (b) Benjamin Zephaniah (c) Derek Walcott
13. Beijing
    (a) The Witch of Exmoor (b) Saul (c) Gingerbread
14. Catenary

(a) Beryl (b) Fifty-five (c) Bangkok / Krung Thep
15. Hypo (originally used of hyposulphite)
(a) Wedding (b) (Gaius Valerius) Catullus (c) Edmund Spenser
16. Balance
(a) Two (b) Jean Genet (c) 34th Street
17. (Indian grey) mongoose
(a) Hip (b) *Drop the Dead Donkey* (c) Boxing
18. Alternative (Investment Market)
(a) Man Ray (b) *Pather Panchali* (c) *Rebel Without a Cause*
19. Theodora / Dorothy
(a) *The Great Gatsby* (b) (Francis Ford) Coppola (c) Sigourney Weaver
20. Stepfather (not uncle, which is not the case in Dickens)
(a) (John) Keats (b) Oscar Wilde (c) Dogs
21. 9 September 1981 (oh-nine, oh-nine, eighty-one)
(a) Greek fire (also known as sea / Roman / war / liquid fire; conjectured to be composed of naphtha, sulphur, quicklime and nitre) (b) Bats (the so-called 'bat bombs', using the Mexican free-tailed bat, *tadarida brasiliensi*) (c) Molotov cocktail
22. Medea (Hypothesis)
(a) Haworth and (Pueblo) Machu Picchu (b) Timbuktu
(c) Battenberg
23. Notre-Dame (de Paris)
(a) United Nations Conference on Trade And Development
(b) United Nations Environment Programme (c) United Nations Educational, Scientific and Cultural Organization
24. Three (Chamberlain to May 1940, Churchill to July 1945, then Attlee)
(a) Oxus (treasure) (b) Michelangelo (Buonarotti) (c) Rosetta Stone
25. (Robert) Hooke (1635–1703)
(a) Exponential function / exp of x / e to the x (b) Sin / sine / sin-x / sine of x (c) One over one minus x
26. Sand (sandboy, George, sandbag)
(a) Hobart (capital of Tasmania, after Robert Hobart, 4th Earl of Buckinghamshire) (b) Brisbane (capital of Queensland, after Sir Thomas Brisbane) (c) Perth (capital of Western Australia)
27. Plaster of Paris
(a) Philip of Anjou / Philip V (accept Duke of Anjou) (b) Pragmatic Sanction (c) (Great) Northern War

28. Butterfly
(a) Charles I (b) (Thomas Wentworth, 1st Earl of) Strafford
(c) (Lady) Jane Grey
29. (Sir William) Herschel (born Friedrich Wilhelm Herschel)
(a) 1920s (1922 and 1929) (b) 1950s (1952 and 1953) (c) 1970s
(1971, 1977, 1979)
30. Puy
(a) Madeira (b) Marsala (c) Sherry

Round One Match Six
1. Pi over 2
(a) Knot (b) Sandpiper / *scolopacidae* (c) English Civil War
2. Chromium
(a) Art for art's sake (*L'art pour l'art*) (b) (James) Whistler (c) MGM
(Metro-Goldwyn-Mayer)
3. (Sir Walter) Raleigh (1552–1618)
(a) Henry VIII (b) Cnut / Canute (c) Henry II
4. Saga
(a) Pamela (b) Geoffrey of Monmouth (c) Jonathan Swift
5. Marcus Trescothick / Andrew Strauss / Robert Key / Ashley Giles /
Steve Harmison
(a) Allotropy / allotropism (b) Isomerism / isomer(s) (c) Catalysis
(accept catalytic power)
6. Des Moines (Iowa)
(a) 'The Kindly Ones' (otherwise 'Eumenides' or 'the Furies')
(b) 'Dead Souls' (c) *A Month in the Country*
7. Winter of Discontent
(a) Ames (test) (b) Enteric bacteria / entero-bacteriaceae / coliforms
(accept bacteria) (c) Benedict's test / solution / reagent
8. Love Wave
(a) Pyongyang (North Korea) (b) Goodwood House (c) (La) Sagrada
Familia
9. *The Faerie Queene*
(a) Chile (b) Peru (c) May (*Sol de Mayo*)
10. The introduction of the Gregorian calendar (2 September was
followed by 14 September)
(a) Hohenzollern (b) Frederick II / Frederick the Great (c) William II
/ Wilhelm II / 'Kaiser Bill'
11. The Crimean War

(a) X (b) (René) Descartes (c) 10,000

12.	Liechtenstein / Uzbekistan
(a) Savoie / Savoy (b) Slovenia (c) Dolomites

13.	Frascati
(a) (Albrecht) Dürer (b) *Infernal Affairs* (c) The Ark of the Covenant / the Ark of God

14.	Four (to make methane)
(a) Libya (b) Benghazi (c) Chad

15.	Skewness
(a) Christopher Marlowe (b) William Blake (in *The Marriage of Heaven And Hell*) (c) *Hamlet*

16.	Royal Prerogative
(a) (Luigi) Boccherini (b) (Joseph) Haydn (c) Cello

17.	(Oliver) Goldsmith (*The Deserted Village*)
(a) Rupert Brooke ('The Old Vicarage, Grantchester') (b) W.H. Davies ('Leisure') (c) Robert Frost ('The Road Not Taken')

18.	Kensington / Kensington & Chelsea (merged in 1965), but not Chelsea alone
(a) Tuber (b) Sycamores / maples (c) Cadaver (Latin: *cadare*)

19.	Cardamom (or cardamon) / elaichi
(a) (Rudyard) Kipling (b) 'A' and 'e' (c) Icelandic

20.	Falkirk
(a) Orhan Pamuk (b) *Clouds* (c) Somerset Maugham

21.	Nacelle
(a) Q (b) (Sir Arthur) Quiller-Couch (c) Paul Young

22.	Robert Graves
(a) *The Prime of Miss Jean Brodie* (by Muriel Spark) (b) Eva Peron (c) *Field of Dreams*

23.	Tycho Brahe (1546–1601)
(a) Set in lower case (b) Set in bold face type (c) Set in small capitals

24.	(Club de) Cordeliers
(a) Chess (b) Bobby Fischer (c) Nigel Short

25.	(Department of HM) Customs and Excise (now known as HM Revenue and Customs)
(a) Frances Hodgson Burnett (b) Hieronymus Bosch (pseudonym of Jerome van Aeken, aka Jeroen Anthoniszoon) (c) Sir Richard Burton

26.	Differential calculus
(a) Nitrous oxide (accept laughing gas) (b) Cocaine (c) Novocaine / procaine (hydrochloride)

27. Computer-Generated Imagery
(a) Dengue fever (b) Yellow fever (c) Malaria
28. Metro (metromania and metronome)
(a) Mozart (b) *Don Giovanni* (c) The Requiem Mass (in D Minor)
29. Australia
(a) Telephone kiosk (b) (Sir) Giles Gilbert Scott (not George Gilbert Scott Jr or Sr, his father and grandfather respectively) (c) The Silver Jubilee of the Coronation of George V
30. *The Princess Bride*
(a) 1890s (1895), to China (b) 1910s (1914), to the USA (c) 1900s (1905), to the USSR

Round One Match Seven

1. Tintoretto (born Jacopo Comin, also known as Jacopo Robusti)
(a) *The Aspern Papers* (b) 'The Beast in the Jungle' (c) 'The Turn of the Screw'
2. Canada
(a) Royal Company of Archers (b) Praetorian Guard (c) Swiss Guard (the Pontifical Swiss Guard of the Vatican City)
3. Italy (Opera de Vigilanza e Repressione Antifascista)
(a) The liquid drop model (b) The semi-empirical mass formula / S.E.M.F. (c) 75 per cent / three-quarters
4. Psychology (Institut fur Experimentelle Psychologie)
(a) Bone marrow (specifically in the hematopoietic stem cells in the bone marrow) (b) Mast cells / mastocytes (c) Spleen
5. (Paul von) Hindenburg / (Erich von) Ludendorff
(a) *Julius Caesar* (Brutus, in Act IV, Scene ii) (b) Marriage (c) Appear on television
6. Tetris (playing Tetris, a visuo-spatial game, was believed to have reduced the frequency of trauma flashbacks, which are also visuo-spatial, according to Oxford's Department of Psychology)
(a) Ulysses S. Grant (b) Chester A. Arthur (c) Rutherford B. Hayes
7. Tongue
(a) Dresden (capital city of Saxony) (b) Poznan (c) Bonn (West German capital, 1949–1990)
8. Matrix
(a) Plough / the Big Dipper / Charles's Wain (b) Lyra / the Lyre (c) Whale
9. Three (Volume = 4 pi r3/3, and surface area = 4 pi r2, therefore for

r/3=1, r=3.)

(a) Phenyl-alanine (b) Glutamine (c) Serotonin (also known as 5-hydroxytryptamine)

10. Pachyderm (this classification has since been superseded)

(a) Coventry (b) It is also on the Greenwich meridian / 0 degrees longitude (c) Aylesbury

11. Webster

(a) Faust (b) Thomas Mann (*Doctor Faustus*) (c) Twenty-four

12. Gambit

(a) Lobster (b) Brittany / Bretagne (c) July

13. Françoise Sagan

(a) Sapphire (b) Beryllium (not beryl) (c) Quartz

14. Mississippi

(a) Glaucoma (b) Vitreous humour (c) Cataract(s)

15. (Drama) critic

(a) Functionalism (b) (Bronislaw) Malinowski (c) Louis Sullivan

16. A square

(a) East Timor / Timor-Leste (b) Sri Lanka (c) Singapore

17. The (English) Channel (not Strait of Dover)

(a) Western Australia and Queensland (b) South Africa, Botswana, Namibia (c) Brazil

18. Bell

(a) Deprecate and depreciate (b) Appraise and apprise (c) Censor and censure

19. Synchrotron radiation (accept curvature radiation)

(a) Bhutan (b) Bournemouth (c) Benjamin Franklin

20. A-o (aorist, aotearoa, aorta)

(a) Jacqueline du Pré (b) Daniel Barenboim (c) Pablo Casals

21. A (thin) crescent

(a) Tayberry (not loganberry or tummelberry) (b) Boysenberry (after Robert Boysen) (c) Grapefruit

22. Teeth-grinding

(a) *Nosferatu (Eine Symphonie des Grauens)* (b) The Golem (c) *The Cabinet of Doctor Caligari*

23. Brazil, Argentina, Paraguay, Uruguay

(a) Thursday (b) Johann Strauss (the Younger) (c) South Korea / Republic of Korea

24. Feisty

(a) Compact Fluorescent Light (b) High-Intensity Discharge

(c) Light-Emitting Diode
25. 'cabbages and kings'
   (a) Laudanum (b) *The Moonstone* (by Wilkie Collins) (c) 'Kubla Khan' (by S.T. Coleridge)
26. The solar system (accept Earth and moon orbiting the sun, as other planets are sometimes excluded)
   (a) *Keep the Aspidistra Flying* (b) *Ballet Shoes* (c) *Gone with the Wind* (by Margaret Mitchell)
27. P-a-n (pantile)
   (a) Henry VIII (b) Crimean (war) (c) Uranus (1781)
28. Bolivia
   (a) 'Happy Birthday To You' (b) *La Marseillaise* (accept French) (c) 'Twinkle, Twinkle Little Star'
29. Overtones
   (a) Chaos (b) The flapping of a butterfly's wing (c) Robert Browning
30. Spring (tides)
   (a) (Justus Freiherr von) Liebig (b) Capacitor (c) Latent heat

Round One Match Eight

1. Hippocampus (from *hippos* and *kampos*)
   (a) Woodhouse (b) Andrews (c) Shirley
2. IIII
   (a) Nagasaki (b) William Shakespeare (c) *Kes* (first published as *A Kestrel for a Knave*)
3. Abel Prize
   (a) Little Big Horn (b) Kentucky (c) 'Get Back'
4. Spitfire
   (a) Melanie Klein (b) Blue (c) No edges and only one surface
5. United Nations High Commissioner for Refugees
   (a) Perspective (b) (John) Constable (c) (Paul) Cezanne
6. Crohn's disease (after Burrill, b. Crohn)
   (a) Oak (b) Willow (c) Yew
7. Diet
   (a) Sandwich (tern) (b) Dover (c) Warbler / *Sylviidae* (Dartford warbler / *Sylvia undata*)
8. Dominion
   (a) Def Jam (b) Capitol Records (c) Island Records
9. Belle (*belles-lettres*, *belle époque*, 'Belle Dame Sans Merci')
   (a) The Birch-Swinnerton-Dyer (B.S.D.) Conjecture / Hypothesis

(b) P versus NP (accept P = NP or P ≠ NP) (c) Riemann Hypothesis (or Conjecture)

10. Muhammad Ali
(a) Father of the House (the MP with the longest unbroken period of service) (b) Hesiod / Hesiodos (c) Texas (the capital, Austin, is named after him)

11. *The Merry Wives of Windsor*
(a) Myelin sheath (b) Adipose cells or adipocytes (accept adipose tissue) (Latin: *adeps*, *adip*-, 'fat') (c) The brain (specifically in the fifth layer of the grey matter of the primary motor cortex, located in the posterior portion of the frontal lobe)

12. Triton
(a) Cardamom (Cardamom Hills in Kerala and Tamil Nadu) (b) Galangal / galingale (c) Turmeric

13. Ice hockey (Canada's official national winter sport)
(a) Rotterdam (b) (*In / The*) *Praise of Folly* (c) Thomas More

14. Squirrel (Greek: *skiouros*; *skia*, shade; *oura*, tail)
(a) Logarithm (b) Exponential (exponential function) (c) Napierian logarithms (after John Napier)

15. Eutectic (system / composition / alloy) (Greek: *eutecktos*, easily melting)
(a) Calypso (b) Trinidad (c) Saturn

16. 7/40
(a) Magnesium (b) Grignard reagents (c) Dolomite

17. *Semper fidelis*
(a) (The era of) the Five Good Emperors (b) (Marcus Cocceius) Nerva, Marcus Ulpius Nerva Traianus / Trajan, (Titus Aurelius Fulvus Boionius Arrius) Antoninus, Marcus Aurelius (Antoninus Augustus) (c) *Meditations* (*Ta eis heauton*, 'Thoughts / Writings addressed to himself')

18. Acton (villages in Herefordshire, Shropshire, Gloucestershire and Staffordshire)
(a) Amber (b) Pliny the Elder (c) Baltic Sea

19. *La Dolce Vita*
(a) (J. Alfred) Prufrock (T.S. Eliot, 'The Love Song of...') (b) 'Howl' (Allen Ginsberg) (c) William Wordsworth ('Ode: Intimations of Immortality from Recollections of Early Childhood')

20. Heat
(a) The point at which the moon is closest to the Earth (b) 27.3 days

/ the same (c) The Sea of Tranquillity / *Mare Tranquillatis*
21. West Lothian
(a) Banal (b) (Charles Pierre) Baudelaire ('Un Voyage à Cythère' in *Les Fleurs du mal*) (c) (Otto Adolf) Eichmann
22. Yagi aerial
(a) Amiens (b) Reims (c) Chartres
23. Safranin
(a) Diarchy (b) India (c) Andorra
24. New York
(a) Emil (elim, mile, lime) (b) Dire (ride, Reid, drei) (c) Liar (rail, lair, lira)
25. The Byzantine Empire
(a) Richard II (b) Henry IV (Bolingbroke) (c) Portugal
26. Bongo(s)
(a) *The Magician's Nephew* (by C.S. Lewis) (b) *Truckers* (c) *The Worst Witch*
27. Poetry
(a) Geoff Thomas (b) James Blake (c) Judo
28. Fibre (or roughage)
(a) *The Turn of the Screw* (b) *The Bell* (c) *The History Boys*
29. Beetle / coleoptera
(a) Paddington (b) Portcullis (accept Parliamentary gate) (c) St Paul's (Cathedral)
30. Doner kebab (not just 'kebab')
(a) Rhone (b) Danube (c) Rhine

Round One Match Nine
1. Western Isles / Outer Hebrides
(a) Skye / Sgitheanach (b) Cairn gorm / Cairngorms (c) Fort William
2. Holy Innocents' Day / Childermas
(a) Mercurial – Mercury (b) Saturnine – Saturn (c) Jovial – Jupiter
3. Stephen Poliakoff
(a) (William) Shakespeare (Sonnet 145) (b) Coral (c) Love
4. *I Pagliacci*
(a) Brackets (not 'parentheses', which is another name for round brackets) (b) Corbel (c) Figure skating (also in roller skating, but this is not an Olympic sport)
5. Twenty20
(a) Lyceum (b) (London) Coliseum (c) (London) Hippodrome

6.   Electoral Reform Society (accept Electoral Reform Services, a subsidiary of the society)
      (a) Panama Canal (b) Tenerife (c) *Easy Rider*
7.   Caustic
      (a) [Erwin] Schrödinger (b) Rats (in Browning's 'Pied Piper of Hamelin') (c) Bottom
8.   Japan
      (a) Cathode Ray Tube (b) Electrons (c) … gun
9.   Frank Hampson
      (a) 42 (b) John Wilkes (c) Clementine
10.   Kazakhstan
      (a) *The Nutcracker* (b) *La Fille mal gardée* (c) *The Sleeping Beauty*
11.   Fox (George Fox, 1624–1691; foxglove; foxtrot)
      (a) London Symphony Orchestra (b) Future Sound Of London
      (c) Original Dixieland Jazz Band
12.   (Johannes) Kepler (1571–1630)
      (a) Finland (b) Bulgaria (c) Belgium
13.   (Mark) Rothko
      (a) (Johann Wolfgang von) Goethe (b) Thomas Mann (c) (Hermann) Hesse
14.   (Mir-Hossein) Mousavi
      (a) Soft Machine (b) Woody Guthrie (c) Virginia Woolf
15.   E (knee, chimpanzee, degree)
      (a) Jack Straw (b) Michael Collins (c) Francis Bacon
16.   (Louis) Pasteur (1822–1895)
      (a) (Henri) Bergson (b) Heraclitus (c) Buddhism
17.   Oboe
      (a) (Tensile) stress (b) (Tensile) strain (c) (Thomas) Young (Young's Modulus)
18.   Dame Vera Lynn (with the album *We'll Meet Again – The Very Best of Vera*)
      (a) Time (sonnets 55, 15, 5, 19, 19 & 16) (b) Love (c) A star
19.   'The affluent society'
      (a) (David) Hume (from the essay 'The Stoic' in *Essays Moral, Political and Literary*) (b) (Dr Samuel) Johnson (in Boswell's *Life*)
      (c) (Jeremy) Bentham (in *An Introduction to the Principles of Morals and Legislation*)
20.   Ergonomics
      (a) *The Marriage of Figaro* (b) *L'Elisir d'Amore* / *The Elixir of Love*

THE ANSWERS

(c) *Carmen*
21. Onan
(a) (Delta – Echo –) Foxtrot (b) (Juliet –) Kilo (– Lima) (c) Whisk(e)y
(– X-ray – Yankee)
22. August
(a) Firth (b) Pentland Firth (c) Moray Firth
23. Glycaemic Index
(a) Gallipoli (b) Utah (c) Korean War
24. AD (accept Anno Domini or the Year of Our Lord)
(a) Cathay (from *khitay*) (b) Tartary (News *from Tartary*)
(c) Barbary
25. Chinoiserie
(a) Republic of Ireland / Irish Free State (b) Burma / Myanmar
(c) (Republic of) Mozambique
26. *We*
(a) *Tribune* (b) Proconsul (c) Département / department (not
'préfecture')
27. Campari
(a) Steroids (b) Triglycerides / triacylglycerols
(c) Glycerophospholipids / phosphoglycerides / phospho-acyl-glycerols
28. John Lightfoot
(a) Pocahontas (b) Paul Nash (c) ''Tis new to thee.' (Prospero to
Miranda in Act V, Scene i)
29. Subcontinental (not 'subcontinent')
(a) John Dryden (b) 'Who watches the watchmen?' / 'Who will
guard the guards (themselves)?' (c) (Dr Samuel) Johnson
30. £210.00 (winnings plus stake on the first race is £70 plus £10 equals
£80; the second race winnings plus stake makes £130, plus £80)
(a) (Frédéric) Chopin (b) Beethoven (c) Tchaikovsky

Round One Match Ten
1. Intelligent Falling ('Evangelical scientists refute gravity with new
"Intelligent Falling" theory')
(a) Polyhymnia / Polymnia (b) Polyneices / Polynikes (c) Polyphemus
2. Capital
(a) Grilling (b) Spatchcock (c) Braise
3. Buenos Aires
(a) Parterre (b) Baked earth (c) Newfoundland
4. Antartica

(a) (Charles) Simonyi (b) Darwin's Rottweiler (c) *The God Delusion*
5. Shirley
(a) (Admiral Lord Cuthbert) Collingwood (b) (Maarten) Tromp (c) John Paul Jones
6. 1989
(a) Sylvia Plath (b) Dorothy Parker (c) 'The Lady of Shalott' (by Tennyson)
7. The college appointed to elect the Holy Roman Emperors
(a) Chile (b) Ginkgo (biloba) / Maidenhair (c) Sydney
8. Ernest Hemingway
(a) AD 444 (sometimes given as 445) (b) 222 BC (c) 333 BC
9. Reflux
(a) Generation X (b) (Valéry) Giscard d'Estaing (c) Midget submarines
10. Monocoque
(a) (Differential) calculus (b) Its excess temperature over that of its surroundings / the difference in temperature between the body and its surroundings (c) Reflecting telescope
11. Rat (18, 1, 20)
(a) Texas (b) Albany (c) Richmond (Virginia)
12. Singapore
(a) Thumb(s) up (b) Chimpanzees (c) *Great Apes*
13. Chancellor of the Exchequer
(a) Nevada (b) Cordillera (c) Flat topped / table-topped (with steep sides)
14. Kangaroo
(a) Casablanca (b) Belgrade (c) New Zealand
15. Five
(a) Tivoli / Tibur (b) Copenhagen (c) The Strand
16. Church / chapel
(a) Tetrahedron (b) 4 (c) Copper
17. Fringe, binge, whinge
(a) (Hernan) Cortés (1485–1547) (b) Charles V (1500–1558) (c) Edward VI
18. Writers Guild of America
(a) Libya (b) Dodecanese (c) Ethiopia
19. Euclid's *Postulates*
(a) Banqueting House (b) Pye Corner (c) Palace of Westminster / Houses of Parliament

20. Ben Goldacre
    (a) Salman Rushdie (b) (Gabriel García) Márquez (c) Tom Wolfe
21. Danube
    (a) Stockholm (b) Budapest (c) Berlin
22. T.S. Eliot
    (a) Anaphylaxis / anaphylactic (shock) (b) Prontosil
    (c) Electrocardiograph / ECG / EKG
23. Yoga
    (a) *The Story of Tracy Beaker* (by Jacqueline Wilson) (b) *Matilda*
    (by Roald Dahl) (c) *Stig of the Dump* (by Clive King)
24. Ribosome
    (a) Rwanda (b) Mozambique and Cameroon (c) South Africa
25. (Airbus) A380
    (a) *Rubber Soul* (1965) (b) *Revolver* (1966) (c) *Sgt Pepper*('*s Lonely*
    Hearts Club Band)
26. Cranial (nerves)
    (a) Hades (accept the underworld) (b) Alph (c) Lorelei
27. (Differential) calculus
    (a) Hybrid (Latin: *hybrida*) (b) F1 (c) Heterosis
28. Pound (lb)
    (a) (César Auguste Jean Guillaume Hubert) Franck (b) (Maurice)
    Maeterlinck (c) Hansen's disease / leprosy
29. Crossword puzzles
    (a) Linus Pauling (b) Purines and pyrimidines (c) (Erwin)
    Schrödinger
30. A (large) canoe
    (a) Melatonin (b) Melanin (c) Melamine

Round One Match Eleven
1. Oxford (almost exactly; no other city is close)
   (a) Nova Scotia (b) Hudson Bay (c) Manitoba
2. Primates
   (a) The Boys (b) The Elephants (Ivory Coast) (c) Nigeria
3. Papua New Guinea
   (a) Epitaph (b) Epitasis (not epistasis, which is a term in genetics)
   (c) Wedding / marriage
4. Sense ('Common Sense' and *Sense and Sensibility*)
   (a) Beluga / white whale (not 'narwhal') (b) Finback whale / fin
   whale (c) Sperm whale / cachalot / *physeter catodon*

5. (Gerald) Ford (on 4 July 1976)
    (a) Alain de Botton (b) Heathrow Airport (c) *Work*
6. (John Stuart) Mill
    (a) Zachary Taylor (b) (Stephen) Grover Cleveland (c) Calvin
    Coolidge
7. 729
    (a) 37 per cent (accept 32–42 per cent; the world population in
    late 2009 being about 6.79 billion) (b) Indonesia and Brazil (230m
    and 190m) (c) Australia (The G20 are Argentina, Australia, Brazil,
    Canada, China, France, Germany, India, Indonesia, Italy, Japan,
    Mexico, Russia, Saudi Arabia, South Africa, South Korea, Turkey,
    United Kingdom, the USA and the EU)
8. Investiture (Latin: *investive*)
    (a) Joseph Chamberlain (b) Randolph Churchill (c) William Pitt the
    Elder / Earl of Chatham
9. Feather (fe - at - h - er)
    (a) De Stijl ('the Style') (b) Piet Mondrian (c) M(aurits) C(ornelis)
    Escher
10. One-twelfth
    (a) France (b) French Polynesia (c) Caribbean
11. Dihedral
    (a) 'Call me Ishmael.' (*Moby-Dick* by Herman Melville) (b) Kurt
    Vonnegut (c) *Leviathan (or The Whale)*
12. (Harlequin) Mills & Boon
    (a) '… pass the ammunition' (b) 'Kiss Me Goodnight (Sergeant-
    Major)' (c) 'Lili Marlene'
13. *Thunderbirds* (no.1 single for Busted)
    (a) Intense, intensive (b) Gracious, graceful (c) Abstention,
    abstinence (accept abstemiousness)
14. St Edmund (*c.*841–870)
    (a) Auscultation (Latin: *auscultare*) (b) Keyhole surgery / minimal
    invasive surgery (of the abdomen) (c) Electrocardiography /
    electrocardiogram
15. Spontaneous generation
    (a) Pastrami (b) Bresaola (c) Kobe
16. Subscriber Identity Module
    (a) Ctrl+alt+del / CAD (b) Piled Higher (and) Deeper
    (c) Questionable Content
17. The euro (architectural designs on the obverse of the notes)

(a) Ambition (b) Amnesty (c) Anoint

18. Zip
(a) 'Beauty and the Beast' / 'La Belle et la Bête' (b) 'Bluebeard' / 'La Barbe Bleu' (c) 'Hansel and Gretel'

19. Darrow (Clarence, 1857–1938; Charles, 1889–1969; Ann)
(a) Pontiac (b) Bologna (c) Opel

20. Vanadium
(a) Error (Latin: *errare*) (b) Gaffe (c) Blunder (ME: *blundren*)

21. (Bubonic) Plague
(a) Dihedral (b) Circumsphere (c) Two

22. France
(a) George II (b) Charles I (c) George V

23. The Lady of Shalott
(a) Romania (b) Switzerland (c) Belgium

24. The vote to ordain women into the priesthood of the Church of England
(a) Sacrament (b) Baptism and the Eucharist / Holy Communion / Supper of the Lord (c) Seven (Baptism, Confirmation, Eucharist, Penance, Anointing of the Sick, Holy Orders and Matrimony)

25. Two forwards, two backwards
(a) *The Heart of Midlothian* (b) City prison (c) St Giles's (Cathedral) / High Kirk of Scotland

26. Geneva
(a) Bridge (b) Deng Xiaoping (c) Omar Sharif

27. (Arthur) Schopenhauer
(a) (John Maynard) Keynes (b) (Pablo) Picasso (c) Ludovic Kennedy

28. Cosmic microwave background
(a) Mausoleum (b) Split (c) General Franco

29. Julius Caesar
(a) Mandolin (b) Rod Stewart (c) Captain Corelli

30. (Striated or striped) muscle
(a) Blue babies (b) (Republic of) Ireland (c) (Hydrated) copper (II) sulphate (accept cupric sulphate)

Round One Match Twelve
1. Alpine (orogeny)
(a) Minorca (b) Malta (c) Cyprus

2. Wilfred Owen ('Greater Love')
(a) (Harry S) Truman (b) (Franklin D.) Roosevelt (c) (Dwight D.)

Eisenhower

3. Anomie (Greek: *anomos*, 'lawless')
   (a) Intelligence (b) (Alfred) Binet (c) g

4. *Das Wohltemperierte Klavier* / *The Well-Tempered Clavier* (the term pre-dates Bach; twelve notes of standard octave tuned such that one can play most music in most major and minor keys and it not sound out of tune)
   (a) Parapet (b) Paraffin (*parum affinis*, 'little affinity') (c) Paraclete (Greek: *para*, 'alongside'; *kletos*, 'to call')

5. Third world / le tiers monde
   (a) Kim Jong-il (b) (Joseph) Stalin (c) Idi Amin

6. Vehicle Excise Duty
   (a) The integers (accept whole numbers, but not positive integers; 'z' for 'Zahlen', the German for 'numbers') (b) Quaternions ('h' for Sir William Rowan Hamilton, their discoverer) (c) The complex numbers

7. Hot
   (a) Nevada (b) Lake Tahoe (Washoe: *dá'aw*) (c) Reno

8. Astronomer Royal
   (a) Rhodopsin (b) Rheostat (c) Rhesus

9. Violin (Suzuki was himself a violinist, but the method is now used with many instruments)
   (a) Eleanor of Aquitaine (b) Elizabeth of York (c) Queen Victoria

10. Canvass
    (a) Ester (b) Soap (c) Hydrolysis

11. Constant
    (a) Scallop / scallop (b) (Sir Benjamin) Britten (the quote is from *Peter Grimes*) (c) (Santiago de) Compostela

12. Steel
    (a) Honduras and Nicaragua (b) Coromandel Coast (c) The Gold Coast

13. God Calls Me God
    (a) Bacchus (not Dionysos) (b) Pietà (c) Royal Academy

14. Octillion
    (a) Nepal (b) (Republic of) South Africa (c) Libya (solid green)

15. Helen (Adams) Keller
    (a) Laverbread (accept laver) (b) Carrageenans (c) Agar

16. Media Player
    (a) Dylan Thomas (*Under Milk Wood*) (b) Patrick Hamilton

(c) (J.R.R) Tolkien (in *The Fellowship of the Ring*, the first book of *The Lord of the Rings*)

17. Nouvelle cuisine
(a) Mesa (b) Guyana and Brazil (c) Angel Falls

18. The Tower of Hanoi
(a) Ajax (*Ajax / Aias Mastigophoros*) (b) *Medea / Medeia*
(c) Aeschylus

19. British Indian Ocean Territory
(a) Sloth (b) *Artiodactyla* / artiodactyls (c) Jerboa

20. Da capo
(a) Jessica (b) Rodney (c) Chloe (Greek: *kloros*)

21. Double-entry bookkeeping / double-entry system
(a) *Richard II* (b) *King Henry VI Part Two* (c) *Richard III*

22. The ferns (or *pterophyta*)
(a) Uralic (b) Novaya Zemlya (c) Caspian (Sea)

23. Smallpox
(a) William of Malmesbury (b) William of Occam (Occam's Razor: 'entities should not be multiplied beyond necessity') (c) William of Wykeham

24. Gough (Gough Island; Steve; Damon; and Darren)
(a) Fourth wall (b) Commedia dell'arte (c) Woody Allen

25. Dynamo
(a) Naming (b) Longest unbroken service as an MP (c) Death

26. Still
(a) (Maxwell's) Silver Hammer (b) The Pope (c) English (Adrian IV, formerly Nicholas Breakspear)

27. Virgo
(a) South Africa (b) 'The Green Eye of the Yellow God' (c) Cavalier Poets

28. Meiji (accept Mutsuhito, his name when alive)
(a) The contact lens (b) Lorgnette (c) Pince-nez

29. Syrinx
(a) Oak (b) Cork (c) Windsor Great Park

30. 10
(a) Neuron(e) (b) Motor neurones (or motor nerves) (c) (Lou) Gehrig

Round One Match Thirteen

1. 91 (31 + 29 + 31)

(a) Driving on the left (b) Suriname (c) Thailand

2.   Opera singers (categorised by range, colour and character of voice)
     (a) Sauvignon / Sauvignon Blanc (not Cabernet Sauvignon, which
     is a black grape) (b) Merlot (*merle*) (c) Gewürtztraminer (*Gewürtz,
     traminer*)

3.   Leek (Greek, bleak, meek)
     (a) Berlin Philharmonic / B.P.O. (b) Venezuela (c) The Hallé

4.   (Statute of) Westminster
     (a) Energy (b) 50 joules (c) 10 metres per second

5.   Libido
     (a) Art nouveau (b) (George) Meredith (c) (John) Ruskin

6.   (John) Cheever
     (a) Lithuania (b) Seattle (c) Budapest

7.   Clouds (*Hamlet*, Act III, scene iii; 'Both Sides Now')
     (a) (Edward Williams) Morley (b) Maya / Mayan (c) Elizabeth I

8.   2k (k is the unit vector in the z direction)
     (a) Hawaii (the volcano Kilauea) (b) Mariana islands (after Queen
     Mariana of Austria, widow of Philip IV of Spain) (c) Aleutian
     Islands

9.   (Evarist) Galois (1811–1832)
     (a) Pound sign (£) (b) Ampersand (c) Hash

10. Occidentalism
     (a) Network (b) Pension (c) Monsieur

11. China
     (a) *The Merry Wives of Windsor* (Mistress Alice Ford and Mistress
     'Meg' Page) (b) *The Two Gentlemen of Verona* (c) *Troilus and
     Cressida*

12. Lawnmower racing
     (a) Dante (Alighieri) (b) (Christopher) Marlowe (from 'Hero and
     Leander') (c) (Captain John) Yossarian (in *Catch-22* by Joseph
     Heller)

13. (John) Milton ('On His Blindness')
     (a) Steel(s) (b) Zinc (c) Mercury

14. Ketone
     (a) Salvador Dalí (b) *The Sea Inside / Mar Adentro* (c) Pedro
     Almodóvar

15. Pig (hog)
     (a) Pea (b) Jay (c) Tea

16. Christina Rossetti

(a) Reggio (nell')Emilia (not Reggio di Calabria) (b) Parma ham (accept Prosciutto) (c) Parma violets

17. Muesli
    (a) James (Grover) Thurber (b) (William) Heath Robinson (c) 'The man who...'

18. Atlas
    (a) 'Lamia' (b) *The Blind Watchmaker* (c) Douglas Adams

19. Goliath
    (a) Polio (Salk vaccine) (b) Meningitis (c) The cow (Latin: *vacca*)

20. Dome
    (a) (Ludwig van) Beethoven (b) (Haruki) Murakami (c) Violin and cello

21. Georgia
    (a) Angola (b) MPLA (Movimento Popular de Libertação de Angola / Popular Movement for the Liberation of Angola) (c) Namibia / Zambia

22. Tea bag
    (a) *A Shropshire Lad* (by A.E. Housman) (b) Silurian (Pridoli, Ludlow, Wenlock and Llandovery) (c) Robert Clive (of India)

23. Black Panther Party (originally the Black Panther Party for Self-Defense)
    (a) St Anthony (b) Ergot / ergotism (c) (Johannes) Brahms

24. Edward Jenner
    (a) Usk (or Wysg) (b) Caerleon / Caerllion (c) The Black Mountains

25. (Dmitri) Shostakovich
    (a) Carnival (b) Venice (c) Fat Tuesday

26. Light (or any electromagnetic radiation)
    (a) Angel (b) Lincoln (c) Tess Durbeyfield / Tess (of the) d'Urberville(s)

27. (Robert) Catesby (originator of the Gunpowder Plot)
    (a) Around / near (b) 'Meta-' (c) 'Dia-'

28. Phoney war
    (a) Vanessa Redgrave (b) Cybill Shepherd (c) Helena Bonham-Carter

29. The Bay of Bengal
    (a) Col-ombia (b) Chi-le (c) Cos-ta Rica

30. Iphigeneia (*Iphigeneia at Tauris*; *Iphigenia in Tauris*; *Iphigenie en Tauride*)
    (a) Hans Christian Anderson (b) *Chocolat* (c) Alexander McCall Smith (in the *No. 1 Ladies' Detective Agency* series)

Round One Match Fourteen

1. Seventy-five per cent / three-quarters
   (a) (Thomas) Jefferson (b) Stephen Hawking (c) Paris Hilton
2. *Tabula rasa*
   (a) Lactose (b) Prolactin (accept luteotrophin / luteotrophic hormone) (c) Beta-carotene
3. D (deltoid, dryad, drunkard)
   (a) James Stirling (b) Léon Krier (c) Zaha Hadid
4. *The Winter's Tale* (Perdita, daughter of Leontes and Hermione, falls in love with Florizel, son of Polixenes)
   (a) The second law of thermodynamics (b) Carnot heat engine (accept Carnot engine) (c) Kelvin scale (accept ideal gas scale)
5. Nicotine
   (a) The gain (b) (Amplitude) Modulation (not Frequency Modulation) (c) Multivibrator
6. Louisiana
   (a) Plutarch (b) (Julius) Caesar (c) (Marcus Tullius) Cicero
7. (St) Thomas Aquinas
   (a) Hotel (b) Oscar (*Oscar and Lucinda*) (c) (*A Passage to*) *India*
8. Invertibility / inverse property (every element must have an inverse, i.e., basically an element that can 'undo' the effect of combination with another given element)
   (a) Thane / Thegn (of Cawdor) (b) *Coriolanus* (c) Malvolio
9. Face
   (a) Edward IV (b) Richard III (c) Richard II
10. The Brothers (Jacob and Wilhelm) Grimm
    (a) Clergy, nobility, commoners (b) Ireland (a) Austerlitz
11. Scalar quantity
    (a) Brocade (b) Absconder (c) Scoreboard
12. Nave
    (a) Smuts (b) (Powdery) mildews (c) Dutch elm disease
13. Rhyolite
    (a) Drake's Drum (b) Cheshire (c) Ephesus
14. A.S. Byatt / Margaret Drabble
    (a) Leonard Cohen (b) (Kwame) Nkrumah (c) H(erbert) G(eorge) Wells
15. Ash
    (a) (Albert) Camus (*L'Étranger*) (b) (*The*) *Invisible Man* (c) *The Sea, the Sea*

16. Ontario
    (a) Switzerland (b) Bavaria (Bavarian Alps) (c) Dolomites
17. 10
    (a) (West) Germany and Italy (b) Denmark and (Republic of) Ireland
    (c) Romania and Bulgaria
18. (Kenneth) Tynan
    (a) Paul Wolfowitz (b) Bangladesh (c) Société Général
19. 10 April
    (a) Casablanca (b) Tehran (c) Yalta
20. Mary, Queen of Scots / Mary Stuart
    (a) (La) Rioja (b) Tuscany / Toscana (c) Burgundy / Bourgogne
21. The Roman Catholic Church
    (a) Chemistry (b) (François) Rabelais (c) Jarrow
22. (Richard) Dalitz
    (a) The British (b) (State) socialism (c) (Lord) Montgomery
23. Denmark
    (a) Bra (b) Verona (c) *Catch-22* (by Joseph Heller)
24. Olympus Mons
    (a) Java (b) New Guinea (c) Borneo
25. East Germany / GDR (German Democratic Republic)
    (a) Noah (b) Benjamin Britten (c) Wakefield
26. Optical activity
    (a) Lou Reed (b) *Trainspotting* (c) Proverbs (Chapter 4, verse 18)
27. 1510–1520 (1519, *c.*1513–1514, 1516, 1517)
    (a) Chlorophyll (b) Haemoglobin (c) Magnesium
28. Quantitative easing
    (a) Kenneth I / Kenneth mac Alpin / Cináed mac Alpin (b) Anne
    (c) Charles II
29. Thorstein Veblen
    (a) Coconut milk (b) Crop milk (c) Magnesium hydroxide $(Mg(OH)_2)$
30. Peru
    (a) *Let the Right One In* (*Låt den Rätte Komma in*; the American
    edition is called *Let Me In*) (b) Martin Beck (c) (Kurt) Wallander

Round One Match Fifteen
1. (Karl Guthe) Jansky (1905–1950)
    (a) Socrates (Socratic method) (b) (André) Breton (c) '… feet freeze?'
2. *Emil and the Detectives* (by Erich Kastner)
    (a) (Henry Mayo) Bateman (b) Sicily (c) Rudyard Kipling

3. Erg
   (a) (Giacomo) Puccini (b) (Antonio) Vivaldi (c) (Edvard) Grieg
4. 20 (twenty)
   (a) Lanthanides (Greek: *lanthanein*) (b) Promethium (c) Lutetium
   (after Lutetia)
5. 1444 (MCDXLIV)
   (a) Milan (b) *Corriere della Sera* (c) Panettone / pannetone
6. South Africa
   (a) Thirteenth (1776, 476) (b) Sedgemoor (in 1685; Bosworth was
   1485, Brixton 1985) (c) 89 (1689, 1789, 1889, 1989)
7. Pope Urban II
   (a) Hadrian (b) Pope Gregory (I / the Great) (c) (Benvenuto) Cellini
8. (Upper) Silesia
   (a) Beige (a) Khaki (c) Sienna
9. David Brent
   (a) Isle of Skye (b) The Old Man of Hoy (c) Finn MacCool / Fionn
   mac Cumhail
10. Quatrains (four-line stanzas)
    (a) Bildungsroman (b) Glockenspiel (c) Schadenfreude
11. 'One learns by suffering' / 'Sufferings are lessons' (accept similar)
    (a) Burma (b) Mughal (c) Dalai Lama
12. Baltic
    (a) Hyperion (b) Selene (c) Endymion
13. Last quarter
    (a) Elephant grass (*Miscanthus gigantens*) (b) Sorghum (*Red
    Sorghum*) (c) Bluegrass / June grass
14. Telemark (*The Heroes of Telemark*)
    (a) William Boyd (in *Nat Tate: An American Artist*) (b) Virginia
    Woolf (in *To the Lighthouse*) (c) Oscar Wilde (in *The Picture of
    Dorian Gray*)
15. Austria
    (a) (Sydney) Pollack (b) *They Shoot Horses, Don't They?* (c) *Out of
    Africa*
16. The American War of Independence
    (a) Edward I (b) Henry III (c) Henry II
17. (Classical) Pentecostal(ism)
    (a) Silicon (b) South-east (c) Knight
18. Quadrature Amplitude Modulation
    (a) Fasting (b) Long unshorn hair (c) Nirvana

19. Alkanes (not 'alkenes': these have the general formula C_nH_{2n})
    (a) Straits of Dover (not the English Channel, which is known as la Manche) (b) Channel Islands (c) Bay of Biscay
20. Crab
    (a) Sinn Féin (b) Plaid Cymru (c) Cornwall
21. The vertebral column (accept backbone or spine)
    (a) Henry Fielding (b) (William Makepeace) Thackeray (c) H.G. Wells
22. Esquire / Esq.
    (a) 'Bill Bailey, Won't You Please Come Home' (b) 'You're So Vain' (c) Half Man, Half Biscuit
23. *The Marriage of Figaro*
    (a) Bel-gium (b) Fra-nce (c) Lux-embourg
24. Portland Vase (formerly known as the Barberini Vase)
    (a) Ash (b) 'a' and 'e' (æ) (c) T.S. Eliot (from 'Little Gidding', the last of the *Four Quartets*)
25. Comprehensive
    (a) Place de la Concorde (b) Place Blanche (c) Place Charles de Gaulle
26. Roller skates (with metal wheels set in a line along the sole)
    (a) Four Color Theorem / Map Theorem (accept Appel and Haken's Theorem) (b) Poincaré Conjecture / Perelman's Theorem (c) Fermat's Last Theorem / Wiles' Theorem
27. Buddhism
    (a) William Faulkner (b) *Barnaby Rudge* (*A Tale of the Riots of Eighty*) (c) Michael Chabon (*The Amazing Adventures of Kavalier & Clay*)
28. Walker (Henry Raeburn's 1790s painting; Sir James, 1863–1935; Alice, 1944)
    (a) Facetious (b) Precarious (c) Education
29. El Escorial
    (a) Helsinki (Accords / Declarations) (b) Reykjavik (c) Oslo
30. Thirty-two
    (a) Limestone (b) Karst (c) Dolomites / *alpi dolomitiche*

Round One Match Sixteen

1. Duty / obligation / compulsion / requirement
    (a) Parasympathetic (do not accept craniosacral; known as the 'rest and repair' division) (b) Parabasis (Greek: *parabainein*)

(c) Paracetamol

2.   Always where under where (always wear underwear)
       (a) *A Portrait of the Artist as a Young Man* (by James Joyce)
       (b) Edward Bulwer-Lytton (c) 'I'

3.   Michael Heseltine
       (a) Noon (b) (Il) Mezzogiorno (c) Arthur Koestler

4.   Clastic rock
       (a) 'Pictures of the floating world' (b) (Katsushika) Hokusai
       (c) Kazuo Ishiguro

5.   Doctor (medical doctor, physician)
       (a) Preston (b) Dunbar (c) Worcester

6.   Leonardo da Vinci
       (a) John F. Kennedy (b) Richard Nixon (c) George H.W. Bush / Bush
       Senior

7.   Castor
       (a) 'The Whitsun Weddings' (by Philip Larkin) (b) 'Eastertide' (from
       'A Shropshire Lad') (c) T.S. Eliot

8.   Locusts
       (a) (Thomas) Graham (b) Colloids (Greek: *kolla*) (c) Emulsion

9.   Conglomerate
       (a) The Mariana Islands (b) Fram (Basin) (c) Java (accept Sunda, as
       it is also known as the Double Sunda Trench)

10.   Bratislava
       (a) *King Lear* (b) *Romeo and Juliet* (c) *Richard III*

11.   Pi
       (a) Bantry Bay (b) Donegal Bay (c) Galway Bay

12.   Psalm 23
       (a) Macaroon (macaroni) (b) Fop / dandy / coxcomb (c) (Macaroni)
       penguin (*Eudyptes chrysolophus*)

13.   Liminality
       (a) Rosaline (b) Lady (Constance) Chatterley (c) Edmund Bertram

14.   Trill
       (a) Maureen Connolly (b) John Brown (c) A thin man

15.   Inner core (not simply 'core')
       (a) Rhodes (b) Sculpture (c) The Colossus of Rhodes

16.   Chile
       (a) Plagiarism (b) 'Research' (c) Tom Lehrer

17.   Four candles (fork 'andles)
       (a) (Sergei) Eisenstein (b) (Aleksandr) Solzhenitsyn (c) (Mikhail)

Glinka
18. Association of Southeast Asian Nations
(a) The Witch of Endor (b) The Witch of Atlas (c) The Witch of Agnesi
19. Cyprus, Cameroon
(a) Conceptualism (b) Naturalism (c) Realism
20. (Marcel) Proust (1871–1922)
(a) *Notes from a Small Island* (b) Patagonia (*In Patagonia*) (c) Paul Theroux
21. Baldwin (1171–1205; James, 1924–1987; Stanley, 1867–1947)
(a) (Alfred) Sisley (b) Berthe Morisot (c) (Camille) Pissarro
22. Midas
(a) (Point-contact) transistor (b) (Django) Reinhardt (c) (Jean) Anouilh
23. (William Makepeace) Thackeray
(a) Estonian (b) Moldova (NB Moldavia is a different entity)
(c) Lithuanian
24. 17 (seventeen) (modulus is the absolute value, i.e., a real number's numerical value without regard to its sign. [8 squared = 64] + [15 squared = 225] = 289 which is 17 squared)
(a) Rubbing wings or legs together to produce sound (b) Locusts
(c) Crickets (*gryllidae*)
25. Alimentary canal / digestive tract (also accept intestine, oesophagus)
(a) Pinot (b) Shiraz (c) Sangiovese (*Sanguis Jovis*)
26. Horse
(a) Sophistry / sophism (Greek: *sophos*, 'wise') (b) Doctrinaire (not 'doctrine') (c) Tyrant (Greek: *turannos*)
27. (Joan) Miro (1893–1983)
(a) Ross and Shaw (b) Rudolf Hess (c) *A Clockwork Orange* (by Anthony Burgess)
28. Terminator
(a) Afghanistan (*Afghan Star* is the title of both the film and the series) (b) Liverpool (c) *Man on Wire*
29. Let or hindrance
(a) China (b) 1937 (c) Poland
30. Gluten
(a) *Vanity Fair* (by W.M. Thackeray) (b) John Buchan (c) *Lord of the Flies*

Round Two Match One

1. Guise
   (a) Temperature (b) Boiling (point) (c) m
2. Theatre
   (a) Dominicans (b) Weepers / Whiners / Snivellers (*Piagnoni*)
   (c) France (under Charles VIII during the first of the Franco-Italian wars, 1494–1559)
3. Magdalen (from Mary Magdalen)
   (a) Specific heat (capacity) (b) (Latent) heat of fusion, enthalpy of fusion (accept enthalpy change of fusion, specific melting heat)
   (c) (Latent) heat of vaporisation / enthalpy of vaporisation (accept heat of evaporation)
4. Prayer mat / prayer rug
   (a) (Herbert Henry) Asquith (b) Chancellor of the Exchequer
   (c) Parliament Act
5. Pedagogue (Greek: *paid*, 'child'; *ago*, 'to lead')
   (a) Michael Collins (b) (William) Cosgrave (c) (Eamon) de Valera
6. 29 (twenty-nine) (three positive integers such that a squared plus b squared equals c squared. [20 squared = 400] + [21 squared = 441] = 841. 29 squared = 841)
   (a) Nervous system (b) Dendrites (c) Myelin (sheath)
7. iTunes Music Store
   (a) Before the Christian / Current / Common Era (b) One million years (from *mega* + *annus*) (c) Before Present (accept Before Physics)
8. (Alexander) Pope ('An Essay on Man')
   (a) Madder (b) Yellow (c) Saffron Walden (formerly Chipping Walden)
9. (Adrien Marie) Legendre (1752–1833)
   (a) *The Ginger Man* (b) *The Go-Between* (c) *Our Man in Havana*
10. Glasgow Coma Scale
    (a) Pembrokeshire Coast Path / Llwybr Cenedlaethol Arfordir Penfro (b) Fife (Coastal Path) (c) Southwest Coast Path
11. Germany (black, yellow and red respectively)
    (a) Iran (b) Brunei (c) Ceylon (accept Sri Lanka, which it became in 1972)
12. Corsica and Sardinia
    (a) St Anselm (b) (William) Paley (c) (David) Hume ('An Enquiry Concerning Human Understanding')
13. Eighteenth

(a) Baked Alaska (b) Danish pastries (c) Trifle
14. Spat
(a) (Henry) Purcell (b) Aphra Behn (c) *A Midsummer Night's Dream*
15. Hungarian
(a) Puglia / Apulia (b) Brindisi / Brundisium (c) Taranto (tarantula and tarantella)
16. Mary Poppins
(a) Achilles and Agamemnon (b) Menelaus and Paris (c) Hector and Andromache
17. Peso
(a) Silver (b) Japan (c) Galena
18. Sigma
(a) Martin Bell (b) Sir Alec Guinness (c) *Airplane*
19. South African
(a) The Queen of (the) Night (b) Puttanesca (c) Sidney Poitier
20. The Pleiades
(a) Mean Free Path (b) Variance (c) 4
21. Therm
(a) (Ellen) Ripley (in the *Alien* films) (b) (*Ripley's*) *Believe It or Not* (c) *Gone with the Wind*
22. Fruits and seeds
(a) Kohl (b) Leishmaniasis (c) Pewter
23. Moldova (the breakaway state of Transnistria was not historically part of Moldova)
(a) Geek and leek (b) Peer and leer (c) Seep and weep
24. Venus de Milo / Aphrodite of Melos
(a) (Wilhelm) Roentgen (X-rays were originally called Roentgen rays) (b) (Dennis) Gabor (c) (Albert) Einstein
25. Florida, Delaware, Louisiana, Mississippi (105m, 137m, 163m, 246m)
(a) Rembrandt (van Rijn) (b) Duke of Wellington (c) *The Scream* by Edvard Munch
26. *A Brief History of Time* (by Stephen Hawking)
(a) *Much Ado about Nothing* (b) 'Two households...' (c) *Antony and Cleopatra*
27. Heliometer
(a) (Jean) Genet (b) (Samuel) Barber (c) (Akira) Kurosawa
28. Lead
(a) Lima bean (b) (Francisco) Pizarro (Gonzaléz, 1st Marqués de los

Atabillas) (c) Stockholm
29. One (sin30 = 0.5; cos 60 = 0.5)
(a) Edward V (b) Capet (c) Albania
30. Spinach
(a) (Vitamin) B12 (b) Dorothy (Crowfoot) Hodgkin (c) Cobalt

Round Two Match Two

1. *Twelfth Night*
(a) Positron Emission Tomography (b) Superconducting Quantum Interference Devices (c) Near Infra-Red Spectroscopy
2. (Cardinal) Richelieu
(a) Galleon (b) Brigantine (not 'brig', which is square-rigged on both masts) (c) (Tea-) clipper
3. Wigner / the Wigner Effect (Eugene Paul Wigner, Hungarian-American physicist and mathematician, 1902–1995)
(a) Or (b) Nor (c) And
4. The railways (the dated Edmondson passenger ticket)
(a) Vermont (b) South Dakota (c) Kentucky
5. Sibyl (Greek: *sibylla*)
(a) Cram and scram (b) Carp and scarp (c) Leek and sleek
6. Aggregate
(a) Knight Bachelor (b) *Baccalaureus* (c) Sherlock Holmes
7. Sport(s)
(a) Lambda (b) (Time-dependent) wave function (c) Pan (pi, alpha, nu)
8. Kopyright Liberation Front
(a) Six (1 + 2 + 3) (b) (Darius) Milhaud, (Francis) Poulenc, (Arthur) Honegger, (Georges) Auric, (Louis) Durey, (Germaine) Tailleferre (c) Cavan, Donegal, Monaghan
9. Five
(a) Autonomic (nervous system) (accept visceral (nervous system))
(b) Vagus (nerve) (Latin: *vagus*) (c) Synapse (Greek: *sunapsis*)
10. Eternity
(a) Iain M. Banks (b) Botanist / naturalist (c) Pelé
11. John Major
(a) Grenadines (b) Barbuda (c) Nevis
12. Bordeaux
(a) *Wuthering Heights* (Emily Brontë) (b) Flambards (c) Terry Pratchett

13. Rivers

    (a) *Twelfth Night (or, What You Will)* (b) Joseph Grimaldi (c) Pablo Picasso

14. Pasha / pasa / pacha

    (a) Caernarfon (b) Adam Dalgleish (c) James Joyce

15. Dante Gabriel Rossetti

    (a) Zimbabwe (b) Amish (c) Football Association

16. Cardinal

    (a) W.H. Auden (b) 'The Blessed Damozel' (c) Bram Stoker

17. *Lumpenproletariat*

    (a) (William) Fulbright (b) Madeleine Albright (c) Berlin Wall

18. (Ludwig) Boltzmann

    (a) Arthur Rimbaud (b) Paul Verlaine (c) Charles Baudelaire

19. Manganese

    (a) Tailor (b) Farmer (c) Smith

20. Hydra

    (a) Morecambe (b) Southport (c) Blackpool

21. Romania

    (a) *Matzohs* (b) Rice (c) Buckwheat flour

22. Ten thousand (Greek: *murioi*, 10,000)

    (a) Gulf of Bothnia / Bothnian Sea (b) 3.5 per cent (so accept 1.5 to 5.5 per cent) (c) Minus 2°C

23. Tom, Dick and / or Harry (Sawyer, Cheney and Truman, of course)

    (a) The Uffizi (b) Catherine (de' Medici) (c) Galileo (Galilei)

24. Birds / Aves (*The Wind-up Bird Chronicle, I Know Why the Caged Bird Sings, The Birds, To Kill a Mockingbird*)

    (a) Leptons (Greek: *leptos*) (b) Positron (accept anti-electron) (c) Photons (accept gamma rays, electromagnetic radiation)

25. Enron (Corporation)

    (a) Hudson's Bay Company (b) Prince Rupert (of the Rhine) (c) Churchill

26. Red blood cells

    (a) (David) Lloyd George (b) Parliament Act (c) Votes for women

27. Skewe's number

    (a) Mississippi (b) Memphis (c) Mark Twain

28. Robot

    (a) Charles I ('the Man of Blood' reigned between James I and VI, and Charles II) (b) 'Lackland' / 'Sans terre' (accept 'Soft-Sword') (King John, son of Henry II, father of Henry III, grandfather of

Edward I) (c) Niece (Victoria was the niece of George IV)

29. Canterbury
    (a) Don Quixote (b) Macbeth (c) Don Juan / Don Giovanni
30. (The fear of) falling man-made satellites
    (a) La Sapienza (b) Salamanca (c) Portugal

Round Two Match Three

1. One
   (a) Galileo (Galilei) (b) Newmarket (c) Khaled Hosseini
2. Bratislava, Slovakia
   (a) Horace (Quintus Horatius Flaccus) (b) Ovid (Publius Ovidius Naso) (c) Catullus (Gaius Valerius Catullus)
3. Babies / children
   (a) Arsenic (b) Pterodactyl (accept pterosaur) (c) Nickel (the alloy chromel, or nichrome)
4. Lip(s) (ellipsis, ellipse, eclipse)
   (a) Scarlatti (Alessandro, 1659–1725, and Domenico, 1685–1757) (b) (Georg Philipp) Telemann (1681–1767) (c) (Antonio) Vivaldi (1678–1741)
5. (Paul) Dirac
   (a) *Mansfield Park* (b) *Three Men in a Boat* (by Jerome K. Jerome) (c) '… and heaven knows I'm miserable now.'
6. Kolmogorov-Smirnov Test (accept KS Test)
   (a) Trieste (b) Berlin (c) Austria, Slovenia, Italy
7. Myanmar (don't accept Burma)
   (a) Kenneth Clark(e) (b) Robert Schuman(n) (c) Matthew Par(r)is
8. Tunisia (in February 1943)
   (a) Haddock (*Melanogrammus aeglefinus*) (b) Salmon (*Salmo salar*) (c) Herring (*Clupea harengus*)
9. Inert
   (a) Nick (b) Robin (c) Peter
10. London, 1908
    (a) Tokyo (b) Steeplechase (c) Baseball
11. *War and Peace*
    (a) Preston (b) *Hard Times* (c) Rayon
12. (Malarial) mosquito
    (a) Sephardic Jews / Sephardi(m) (as opposed to Ashkenazim) (b) (Baruch / Benedictus de) Spinoza (c) Statue of Liberty
13. Shambles

(a) Netherlands / Holland (b) Le Championnat / Ligue Un
(c) Scudetto

14. Buntings
(a) Aachen / Aix-la-Chapelle (b) Lake Constance / Bodensee (c) West

15. Barista
(a) M and n (b) Antinomy and antimony (c) Dumbarton (in the old Dunbartonshire)

16. Prime Minister (*The Prime Minister* and *Yes, Prime Minister*)
(a) Room 101 (b) Nick Hancock (c) *Four Weddings and a Funeral*

17. Astrobleme
(a) Cathedral (b) Town hall (c) *Campanile*

18. Ecuador
(a) Baked Beans (b) (Scarlet) runner bean (c) Pythagoras

19. Accordion
(a) Thomas Hardy (b) Edna O'Brien (c) The Beautiful South

20. Hungary
(a) Austen Chamberlain (b) Ramsay MacDonald (c) (3rd Marquess of) Salisbury (Robert Arthur Talbot Gascoyne-Cecil)

21. Hilary Mantel
(a) Edmund Spenser (b) Latin Secretary / Secretary of Foreign Tongues (c) Zutphen

22. St Boniface (Bonifacius)
(a) Set (b) (Binary) relation (accept dyadic relation / 2-place relation) (c) Function

23. Coriolis (effect / force)
(a) (John) Berger (b) *From A to X* (c) *G*

24. Ester (Gloucester and Worcester, Chester, Winchester)
(a) *Ex gratia* (b) *Ex cathedra* (not *ex officio*, which means 'out of' / 'from', 'duty' [*officium*]) (c) *Ex libris*

25. (Andrei) Markov (1856–1922)
(a) Massachusetts (b) Georgia (c) Arizona

26. (Staatliches) Bauhaus
(a) Lucian Freud (b) Benefits Supervisor (*Benefits Supervisor Sleeping*) (c) Leigh Bowery

27. Thursday
(a) *Serious Money* (b) *Cloud Nine* (c) *Top Girls*

28. Farsightedness (accept hyperopia / presbyopia)
(a) 18 (b) – 12 (c) 9

29. Anarchy (*The International Anarchy, 1904–1914; Culture and*

Anarchy; 'The Mask of Anarchy'; 'Anarchy In The UK')
(a) Great Bear Lake, Great Slave Lake, Lake Winnipeg
(b) Mackenzie (c) Russia (Russia 17 million km²; Canada 9.9
million km²; China 9.5 million km²; USA 9.2 million km²)

30. Grasping / seizing / holding
(a) Quail (b) Partridge (c) Snipe

Round Two Match Four

1. Charleston
(a) Bruce Robinson (b) *The Killing Fields* (c) Hunter S. Thompson
2. (Joseph) Conrad (1857–1924)
(a) Steak tartare (b) Sashimi (not sushi) (c) Ceviche (also cebiche / seviche)
3. (Sir John) Falstaff (Act II, Scene iv)
(a) Don McCullin (b) Tom Stoddart (c) Bryan Adams
4. Halicarnassus
(a) India (b) Azerbaijan (c) Japan
5. (Pierre-Simon, Marquis de) Laplace (1749–1827)
(a) *The Lost World* (b) Roanoke Island (c) Gertrude Stein
6. (O)porto (Latin: *portus cale*)
(a) Haemoglobin / Hb / Hgb (b) Copper (c) Vitamin B12 (accept Cobalamin)
7. Colour blindness or Daltonism
(a) Istanbul / Constantinople (b) W(illiam) H(enry) Davies (c) *As I Walked out One Midsummer Morning*
8. Lewis Carroll
(a) *Richard II* (b) *Timon of Athens* (c) *As You Like It*
9. Laminar flow
(a) India (b) Pakistan (Islamabad Capital Territory) (c) New South Wales
10. Sea anemone
(a) Tour de France (b) (Alberto) Contador (c) The Prologue
11. Jimmy Wales
(a) Veracruz (b) Tunisia (c) Albania
12. Pressure
(a) (Eric) Hobsbawm (b) 'Short twentieth century' (c) Conservative
13. Nottinghamshire
(a) (Sir Isaac) Newton (b) Robert Burton (c) £2 coin
14. Botulism

(a) Watercolour (b) Norwich (School) (c) (Joseph Mallord William) Turner

15. Strait of Hormuz
(a) Nottingham (b) Priest (c) Paternoster

16. Vanadium
(a) Diminished seventh (b) Little Bighorn (Custer's Last Stand) (c) Iron Maiden

17. Polytechnic
(a) Christopher Logue (b) Carrie Fisher (c) David Evans

18. Lord Lieutenants
(a) Fairies (b) Loch Ness Monster (c) Sasquatch / Bigfoot

19. (John) Cage (1912–1992)
(a) Yellow (b) Green dot / Grüne Punkt (c) White Dot

20. Wrist / carpus
(a) Fandango (b) Scaramouche (c) Bismillah

21. Inklings
(a) Occulting (light) (b) Make contact with a tooth (in the opposing jaw) (c) The Harry Potter oeuvre (particularly in *The Order of the Phoenix*)

22. Big (Big Bang theory, big-end, Big Dipper)
(a) (Nikita) Khrushchev (b) (West) Berlin (c) Suez

23. A (regular) dodecahedron
(a) St David / Dewi Saint (b) Pembrokeshire (c) Glastonbury (Abbey / Monastery)

24. John Keats (1795–1821)
(a) Sugar (accept sucrose) (b) Star anise (c) Buckwheat (*fagopyrum esculentum*)

25. Nine
(a) Hardness (of minerals) / scratch resistance (b) Catalytic activity (of enzymes and other catalysts) (c) 373 (degrees)

26. *Four Quartets* (by T.S. Eliot)
(a) Elizabeth I (b) Victoria (c) Charles I

27. Fog
(a) Ship money (b) William Pitt the Younger (c) 1970s (1973)

28. Ferris wheel
(a) Clare Short (b) *Pride and Perjury* (c) Mo Mowlam

29. Earthworms
(a) Lorraine (b) Nancy (c) Cross of De Gaulle / Gaullist Cross

30. Clement Attlee

(a) Tacitus (b) (A) definition (c) *The Pilgrim's Progress*

Round Two Match Five

1. La Mancha (Arabic: *al-mansha*, 'land dry')
   (a) Gub-Gub (*Gub-Gub's Book: An Encyclopaedia of Food*)
   (b) Berkshire (c) Old Major
2. Charles (Charles III, 879–929; IV, 1294–1328; V, 1338–1380; VI, 1368–1422; VII, 1403–1461)
   (a) Ethology (b) Konrad Lorenz (c) Desmond Morris
3. Shorthand / stenography
   (a) Joe DiMaggio (b) Squeeze play (c) Toronto Blue Jays
4. Pi over three (accept 1/3 pi) (the argument is the angle of the complex number in polar co-ordinates)
   (a) Indian Ocean (b) Iceland (c) Pacific Ocean
5. Albedo
   (a) Preston (b) Bradford (c) Royal Armouries
6. Malibu
   (a) 'Ortho-' (wrong answers: 'meta-' – separated by one carbon atom; 'para-' – separated by two carbon atoms) (b) Grasshoppers and (bush) crickets (c) Children
7. Their letters are in alphabetical order
   (a) Crimean War (b) Robert Capa (c) Magnum (Photos)
8. (Boiled) eggs
   (a) Isogloss (b) Diglossia (c) Glottal stop
9. Constant
   (a) Seven Weeks War (b) Florida (c) Suez Crisis
10. The (central part of the) retina
    (a) Pathogenic (b) Phagocytes (accept reticuloendothelial system, but not stem cells) (c) MRSA / Methicillin Resistant Staphylococcus Aureus
11. George C. Scott (1927–1999)
    (a) Élan (b) Étude (c) Émigré
12. The Garden of Eden (Genesis 2:8–14)
    (a) (*The Magic*) *Faraway Tree* (b) Czechoslovakia (c) Soap opera
13. Pakistan
    (a) George III (1760–1820) (b) Edward III (1327–1377) (c) Henry III (1216–1272)
14. Black hole
    (a) (Evariste) Galois (b) (George) Canning (c) *War and Peace* (by

Leo Tolstoy)
15. Mao Zedong
    (a) Edmund Crispin (b) Agincourt (c) The United Nations
16. Red Brigade(s) / Brigate Rosse
    (a) 200 metres (b) Ergot (c) Martin Clunes
17. Copenhagen (interpretation)
    (a) Swaziland (b) Sierra Leone (c) Tunisia
18. Aristotle
    (a) *Jumpers* (b) *Rock 'n' Roll* (c) *Arcadia*
19. Harold Laski
    (a) Antimony (b) (Friedrich) Heusler (c) Zinc
20. Thomas Tallis (1505–1585)
    (a) (Chemical) element (oxygen and hydrogen; *sauerstoff* and
    wasserstoff in German) (b) Atomic theory (Greek: *atomos*,
    'indivisible'; *theoreo*, 'look at') (c) Uranium (in Germanic myth,
    ymir corresponds to the god Uranus)
21. Cycloid
    (a) Bobby Fischer (b) (Benjamin) Britten (c) Hydrocarbons
22. Noodle
    (a) Cambrian (Cambria: Wales) (b) Permian (Perm region) (c) Jura
    (Jurassic)
23. Aluminium (accept magnesium)
    (a) Pulmonary artery (b) (Hepatic) portal vein (c) Aorta
24. Jimmy Carter (James Earl Carter)
    (a) Art (*What Is Art?*) (b) '… patience.' (c) 'Newspaper and
    journalistic activity' (accept similar)
25. Hawkeye / hawk-eye
    (a) Dmitri Shostakovitch (b) Dylan Thomas (c) *Gone with the Wind*
    (by Margaret Mitchell)
26. Rotifera (accept rotifers)
    (a) Pedalfer (b) Laterites / latosols / plinthites / oxisol (c) Clay, silt
    and sand
27. Stock car racing (National Association of Stock Car Auto Racing)
    (a) (Gustav) Klimt (b) (Vienna) Secession / Secessionists (c) Art
    Nouveau
28. Submarines
    (a) (Aristocratic / noble) royal houses (b) Edward VII (c) Karl Marx
29. Teeth
    (a) *Friends* (b) Quakers (c) 'I come to bury Caesar, not to praise

him.'
30. Elliptical / lenticular
   (a) Australian Aborigines (b) Brazil (c) Hungary

Round Two Match Six
1. Starch grains
   (a) Richard II (b) Louis XIV (c) Kaiser Wilhelm II
2. Mood
   (a) 'The Selfish Giant' (b) The Big Friendly Giant (c) Raymond Briggs
3. Angst
   (a) *Mona Lisa / La Gioconda* (b) Marcel Duchamp (c) (Erik) Satie
4. (Aleksandr) Pushkin
   (a) William Wykeham (b) Sir Francis Bacon (c) Sir Thomas More
5. Bay of Naples / Gulf of Naples
   (a) (Kurt) Waldheim (b) Peru (c) Ban Ki-moon
6. Saturn
   (a) Mali (b) Senegal (c) Timbuktu
7. E.E. Cummings
   (a) Mantua / Mantova (not Montferrato or Monteferrat)
   (b) (Andrea) Palladio (c) King Ludwig (II of Bavaria) / Mad King Ludwig
8. Commonwealth War Graves Commission
   (a) Gascogne (accept Gascony) (b) Maine (c) Île-de-France
9. Benjamin Franklin
   (a) Polybius (b) (Charles de Secondat, Baron de) Montesquieu
   (c) (Niccolo) Machiavelli
10. Chattanooga
   (a) Frank Zappa (b) 'God Save The Queen' (by the Sex Pistols)
   (c) 'Another Brick In The Wall (Part II)' (from the album *The Wall*)
11. Lift
   (a) Palazzo Vecchio (b) Bargello (c) Palazzo Pitti
12. Aldous Huxley / C.S. Lewis
   (a) Singleton (b) Singularity (c) Zero
13. Queen Alexandra
   (a) Swiss cheese plant / fruit salad plant / monster plant (b) Rubber plant / Asian fig (c) Mother-in-law's tongue (accept snake plant)
14. Devonian
   (a) Mount Athos (b) Aramis (c) Estée Lauder

15. (Claude) Shannon
    (a) Bruce Willis (b) Keanu Reeves (c) Johnny Depp
16. Silk
    (a) The Impaler (b) Bloodaxe (c) Strongbow
17. An appeaser
    (a) Womb (b) Spleen (c) Liver
18. Popcorn
    (a) Lofoten Islands (in Norway) (b) Hawaii / the Hawaiian Islands
    (c) Finland (the islands are divided between Finland proper, and the
    Aland Islands, an autonomous territory within Finland)
19. Newlyn
    (a) Imaginary numbers (not 'complex numbers': imaginary numbers
    are complex numbers which have real part equal to 0) (b) Minus i
    (accept negative i) (c) Samuel Beckett
20. Burning bush
    (a) 1900s (1902) (b) 1930s (1936) (c) 1920s (1921)
21. Lithuania
    (a) Electro-encephalogram / electro-encephalography
    (b) Electroconvulsive therapy (or ECT) (c) Vibrations of the vocal
    cords (information about the way vocal folds come together)
22. Silk
    (a) *A Clergyman's Daughter* (b) *Keep the Aspidistra Flying*
    (c) Ministry of Truth / Mini-True (the Senate House in London
    is also suggested as an inspiration, and actually fits Orwell's
    description of the building slightly better)
23. Quenching temperature
    (a) Charles Rennie Mackintosh (b) George III (c) *The Singing Butler*
24. (Highland biting) midge (*culicoides impunctatus*)
    (a) (William) Harvey (b) (Thomas) Hobbes (c) Francis Bacon
25. Clavicle
    (a) *Mrs Henderson Presents* (b) ('Being for the Benefit of) Mr Kite'
    (c) (Thomas) 'Fats' Waller
26. Materials science / metallurgy (they determine impact toughness)
    (a) Lynx (*Lynx pardinus*) (b) Sun bear (c) Yangtze / Chang Jiang
27. John Lennon
    (a) Carolingian (from Charles Martel, Carolus Martellus)
    (b) Charlemagne / Charles the Great (c) 'The Bald'
28. Sea anemones
    (a) The Suffragettes / Suffragists / Women's Social and Political

Union (b) The Pietà (in St Peter's) (c) Cricket bat

29. H1 (H One)
(a) Paul Dirac (b) Positrons (accept positive electrons)
(c) Electromagnetic energy / electromagnetic radiation (accept
photons or gamma rays)

30. Lead
(a) Heligoland / Helgoland (b) Plymouth (c) Utsire

Round Two Match Seven

1. Tofu / beancurd / doufu (in Chinese)
(a) William Burroughs (b) Blanche Dubois (in *A Streetcar Named Desire*) (c) Dylan Thomas

2. W.B. Yeats ('When You Are Old')
(a) Cucumbers (b) Radish (c) Lettuce

3. Sixty-nine (Reagan was born 6 February 1911)
(a) L-z-r (b) Polyurethane (c) Michael Phelps

4. Charlotte Brontë (in the opening sentence of Chapter 2)
(a) Franklin (b) Parson (c) Knight

5. Link (12, 9, 14, 11)
(a) France and Spain (b) Russia (Kaliningrad enclave, between Poland and Lithuania) (c) Iceland

6. Aldehyde
(a) W(ystan) H(ugh) Auden (b) William Herbert (c) (W.H.) Davies

7. (René) Magritte
(a) (Henryk) Gorecki (b) (John) Tavener (c) (Benjamin) Britten

8. Emerald (not beryl, aquamarine, though emerald is a variety of beryl)
(a) Legal deposit / Copyright deposit / Copyright libraries
(b) Aberystwyth (c) British Library

9. Richard Cromwell
(a) Bluebell Railway (b) Norfolk (c) Severn Valley Railway

10. Probiotic
(a) Ossian (b) Howard Hughes (c) Hugh Trevor-Roper (Baron Dacre of Glanton)

11. Brent (brent goose; Brent; Brent Hoberman; David Brent)
(a) (Kaiser) Wilhelm II (b) Greece (c) (Tsar) Nicholas II

12. Radio Two
(a) Ambridge (home to *The Archers*) (b) *The Portrait of a Lady*
(c) (Michael) Powell

13. Uranus
    (a) Sir Isaac Newton (b) (Gottfried) Leibniz (c) 12
14. European Health Insurance Card
    (a) *Hamlet* (b) T.S. Eliot (in *The Waste Land*) (c) Homer
15. Black Panthers / the Black Panther Party for Self-Defence (Wolfe's article 'These Radical Chic Evenings' in *New York* magazine)
    (a) (George) Canning (1770–1827) (b) Banjul (c) (Arthur Wellesley, first Duke of) Wellington (1760–1842)
16. Jack
    (a) Alsace (not Alsace-Lorraine, see below) (b) Franche-Comté (c) Lorraine
17. African violet
    (a) W.G. Grace (b) (Sir Alec) Douglas-Home (c) Samuel Beckett
18. 1924
    (a) Samuel Taylor Coleridge (b) T.S. Eliot (c) Robert Frost
19. *Finding Nemo*
    (a) Italian (b) Trainer / sneaker (accept plimsoll, etc.) (c) Mobile phone (cell or cellular phone, etc.)
20. Meteorology
    (a) Typhoid (fever) (accept Salmonella (thypi)) (b) Cholera / *Vibrio cholera* (c) (Bubonic) plague / Black Death / *Yersinia pestis* (accept *Pasteurella pestis*)
21. Polaroid
    (a) (Leonard) Bernstein (b) (Henryk) Gorecki (c) (Dmitri) Shostakovich
22. Breastplate (accept armour / cuirass)
    (a) Topaz (b) *I Capture the Castle* (c) William McGonagall
23. Macramé
    (a) (Giles) Lytton Strachey (b) 'Ignorance' (c) 'I believe I should try to come between them' (accept similar sense)
24. Intelligent Design
    (a) Ablative absolute (b) Mutatis mutandis (c) Vice versa
25. (Max) Planck [the Planck Constant and the Planck time]
    (a) Dodo (b) Passenger (pigeon) (c) Tiger
26. Humbolt current / Peru current
    (a) Sedimentary (b) Limestone (c) Oolitic (limestone) / oolite
27. Argentina / South Africa (Brazil and Indonesia straddle the Equator)
    (a) Integrated Service(S) Digital Network (b) Internet Service Provider (c) Uniform Resource Locator / Universal Resource Locator

28. White
(a) Sad (Sagittal Abdominal Diameter; Special Activities Division; Seasonal Affective Disorder) (b) Scotus (Duns Scotus; Supreme Court of the United States) (c) Sic (silicon carbide; Sicily; Sepang International Circuit)

29. Bosworth (Field)
(a) G.E. Moore (as in Moore's paradox / problem) (b) Zeno (of Elea) (as in Zeno's paradoxes) (c) *The Pirates of Penzance*

30. Sporadic (group)
(a) Bangladesh (b) 246 (accept 221–271) (c) Belgium, Netherlands, Malta (341, 396 and 1,310)

Round Two Match Eight

1. Vivienne Westwood
(a) Somerset (b) Buckingham (c) Clarence

2. The Zeeman Effect
(a) Great house (Greek: *pharaoh*, from Egyptian: *pr'o*) (b) Sublime porte (c) Mikado (Emperor of Japan)

3. Mistral (Frederic, 1830–1914; Gabriela, 1889–1957)
(a) River or stream (b) (Pierre Joseph) Proudhon (c) Giles Coren

4. The lanthanides / lanthanum earth metals
(a) Elizabeth David (b) Eliza Acton (c) Toast

5. Ukraine
(a) Aeschylus (b) Thomas the Rhymer (Thomas Learmonth of Erceldoune) (c) Ephesus

6. Asafoetida
(a) (Thomas) Jefferson (b) Arthur Wellesley (later Duke of Wellington) (c) *The Communist Manifesto*

7. (Robert) Hooke (1635–1703)
(a) Seed (not fruit) (b) Fruit (c) Nut

8. Lisbon
(a) Offa's Dyke Path (b) West Highland Way (c) Edale

9. The US Declaration of Independence
(a) Saint-Saëns (b) Johann Sebastian Bach (c) 'Could It Be Magic'

10. Xenon
(a) Kir-ibati (b) Sol-omon Islands (c) Van-uatu

11. Terawatt (it also equals 1,000 million kilowatts)
(a) (Lady) Margaret Beaufort (also married at the age of 7 to John de la Pole although she later refused to recognise the marriage)

(b) Edward IV (c) Great granddaughter

12. Archimedes ('Transire suum pectus mundoque potiri')
    (a) Rhizome (b) Rhyolite (c) Rhinitis

13. Plough
    (a) Hot spot (b) Switch between normal size and full screen
    (c) Henry IV

14. DNA
    (a) *The Faerie Queene* (Edmund Spenser) (b) Honoré de Balzac (*La Comédie humaine*) (c) (*The Mystery of*) *Edwin Drood* (by Charles Dickens)

15. (Oliver) Cromwell and (George) Washington (in *Certain Trumpets: The Call of Leaders*)
    (a) 1750s (1755) (b) 1900s (1901 and 1906) (c) 1920s (1928 and 1922)

16. Childe ('Childe Roland to the Dark Tower Came'; *Childe Harold's Pilgrimage*)
    (a) *Jane Eyre* (b) Mr Lockwood (c) *Villette* (by Charlotte Brontë)

17. Mathias Grünewald
    (a) Maine (b) *The Cider House Rules* (c) Spain

18. Knickerbockers (Diedrich Knickerbocker)
    (a) Caribbean (Sea) (b) Newfoundland (c) Pacific

19. Red
    (a) *The English Patient* (b) Canada (c) Herodotus

20. Divalent
    (a) Humbug (b) Fudge (c) Bullseye

21. Synagogue (Greek: *sun*, 'together'; *agein*, 'bring')
    (a) Grand Unified (Unification) Theory (b) J.B. Priestley (c) *Red Shift*

22. (Thomas) Bewick
    (a) *Macbeth* (he also apparently contributed to *Measure for Measure*, but that is not a tragedy) (b) (John) Fletcher (c) *Henry VIII* (during which a prop cannon misfired)

23. Root two over root three (accept square root of two over square root of three)
    (a) Life (and) liberty (b) John Adams (the second President)
    (c) (John) Locke

24. Groundhog (if he sees his shadow there will be another six weeks of winter; if not, an early spring)
    (a) Limousin (b) Limoges (c) Eleanor of Aquitane

25. Straight Edge and Compass

(a) A.J. (A.J. Cronin, A.J. Ayer) (b) H.E. (H.E. Todd, H.E. Bates)
(c) C.P. (C.P. Cavafy, C.P. Snow)

26. The speed of light
(a) Beaumaris Castle (b) Henry VII / Henry Tudor (c) Caerphilly Castle

27. Hangman / executioner
(a) Phytoestrogens (b) On or near the bottom of water (accept bottom of the sea) (c) Potato

28. Seine (in Paris)
(a) (Anthony Colin Bruce Chapman) Lotus (b) Active Suspension System (c) Chris Boardman

29. Massé
(a) 1937 (b) 1935 (c) 1933

30. (James) Madison
(a) El Greco (Domenikos Thetokopoulos) (b) (Raoul) Dufy
(c) (Stanley) Spencer

Quarter-Finals Match One

1. Tuscany
(a) Floating point notation (b) Balsa (c) Muhammad Ali

2. Double-entry bookkeeping
(a) Seven Years War (b) Thirty Years' War (c) Seven Weeks' War (accept Austro-Prussian War)

3. Jet Propulsion Laboratory
(a) Babies (with) milk ('There is no finer investment for any community than putting milk into babies.') (b) 'Kubla Khan' (Coleridge) (c) Macbeth (Lady Macbeth in I.v: 'Yet do I fear thy nature; / It is too full o' the milk of human kindness')

4. 496
(a) Cecil Rhodes (b) Vietnam (c) Cookery / food

5. Badminton
(a) Lord's (Cricket Ground) (b) Archery (c) Dubai

6. Thanksgiving
(a) The execution of Charles I (b) William Laud (c) Andrew Marvell ('an Horatian Ode upon Cromwell's Return from Ireland')

7. (John) Keats
(a) (Franz) Liszt (b) (Sergei) Rachmaninov (c) (George) Gershwin

8. Membranes
(a) Horace (b) 'The old lie' (c) Craiglockhart (Hydropathic Institute)

9. Billy Budd
(a) John Rebus (b) (Jack) Frost (c) (Andy) Dalziel
10. Wireless Application Protocol
(a) Warden pear (from Warden Abbey) (b) St Jude (c) *The Winter's Tale*
11. Polyp
(a) Alfred Adler (b) Sherlock Holmes (c) Battle of Britain
12. Oklahoma (Choctaw: *okla homma*, 'red people', meaning the native American people as a whole)
(a) Princeton (b) Campus (c) Cornell, Dartmouth, Pennsylvania, Brown
13. Finland (constructed under the orders of Field Marshall Baron Carl Gustav Emil Mannerheim, regent of Finland and its sixth President)
(a) John Donne ('Song') (b) Wormwood ('and the name of the star is called Wormwood', Rev 8:10, 11) (c) *The War of the Worlds*
14. Mercury (Hg, follows Hf [hafnium] and He [helium])
(a) Picardy (b) Limousin (c) Aquitaine
15. Opus Dei
(a) Winston Churchill (1874) (b) Harold Wilson or Edward Heath (1916) (c) Tony Blair
16. Catalogue raisonné
(a) (Socialist Republic of) Romania (b) Boss / (South African) Bureau Of State Security (c) East Germany
17. Doldrum(s)
(a) Iris (b) Norse (Scandinavian / Germanic, etc) (c) Incas
18. Liège
(a) Afghanistan (b) Bookseller (*The Bookseller of Kabul*) (c) *Charlie Wilson's War*
19. She Who Must Be Obeyed
(a) (Friedrich) Nietzsche (b) Morality (c) Woman
20. (William Thomson, 1st Baron) Kelvin
(a) (William) Wordsworth (in 'The Lost Leader') (b) 'Don Juan' (c) (Percy Bysshe) Shelley
21. Tritium
(a) Denzel Washington (b) Michael (c) Barbarella
22. Liberty (formerly the National Council for Civil Liberties)
(a) Kazakhstan (b) Aral Sea (c) Caspian
23. Covenant
(a) Vitruvius (b) (Gian Lorenzo) Bernini (c) Renzo Piano

24. Three-quarters
(a) (Geoffrey) Chaucer (in *Troilus and Criseyde* and *Parlement of Foules*, as well as some of the *Canterbury Tales*) (b) *Ottava rima* (c) *The Arabian Nights / Thousand and One Nights*
25. Catalunya / Catalonia
(a) *Forrest Gump* (b) Billy Wilder (c) The Marx Brothers
26. The moon
(a) Gutenberg (discontinuity) (b) Rainbow (c) –pause (tropopause, etc)
27. Pencil lead
(a) Polychromy (b) Polysemy (c) Polyandry (not 'polygamy' or 'polygyny')
28. Heel bone (the large bone in the tarsus of the foot that forms the projection of the heel behind the foot)
(a) (Vittore) Carpaccio (b) Soffrito / soffritto (c) Crostino
29. Penelope (*The Penelopiad*)
(a) (Sabine) women (b) (Nicolas) Poussin (c) *Seven Brides for Seven Brothers*
30. (Antonio) Vivaldi
(a) Hanover (b) Lower Saxony / Niedersachsen (c) 'Hannover'

Quarter-Finals Match Two
1. (Edward) Elgar (op. 61)
(a) Ethiopia (b) Italy (c) Aida
2. Skull (the spinal cord extension, the *medulla oblongata*, passes through it)
(a) Chile (b) Uruguay (c) Brazil
3. Abundant
(a) (Sacred) lotus (b) Parasol / umbrella (c) Conch shell
4. Sir Ian McKellen
(a) W.B. Yeats (b) (County) Sligo (c) Willow (Irish: *saileach*, 'willow')
5. (Robert) Musil (1880–1942)
(a) Bologna (b) Siena (c) Florence
6. The axon
(a) Fox and lion (b) War(s) (c) Divide and rule / *divide et impera / divide ut regnes*
7. Volley
(a) Seoul (b) Nigeria (c) Malvolio (*Twelfth Night*)

8. 1850s (1856, 1854, 1857–1858)
   (a) Kintyre (b) Knoydart (c) Skye
9. To the sea (downstream)
   (a) The Simpsons (b) Chloroform (accept ether) (c) Orenthal James
10. The Sun
    (a) (Vladimir) Nabokov (b) Thomas Pynchon (c) J.D. Salinger
11. Mathematics
    (a) *Hidalgo* (Miguel Hidalgo, 1753–1811) (b) *Aguascalientes*
    (c) *Veracruz*
12. Ascent and descent (*Ascent of Man* and *Descent of Man*)
    (a) Golden ratio or mean (accept golden or divine proportion /
    section, golden cut or number, mean of Phidias) (b) (Lower-case)
    gamma (c) E / Napier's Constant (the base of the natural logarithm)
13. Basle / Basel
    (a) Oystercatcher (*haematopodidae*) (b) Beluga (*delphinapterus
    leucas*) (c) Manatee (*trichechidae*)
14. France
    (a) D.O.C. and C.O.D. (*Denominazione di Origine Controllata*;
    Cash On Delivery) (b) G.C.B. and B.C.G. (Knight Grand Cross;
    Bacillus Calmette-Guérin) (c) O.M.G. and G.M.O. (Oh My God;
    Genetically Modified Organism)
15. (Used in communications concerned with) intimacy / love (accept
    sex) ('My Anxious Lips Await Your Arrival', 'Eager to Grab Your
    Pretty Toes', 'Hope Our Love Lasts And Never Dies', 'I Trust And
    Love You', 'Be Undressed and Ready My Angel', 'Please Open
    Lovingly And Never Destroy')
    (a) Kandahar (b) Tajikistan (c) Turkey
16. Peach (*prunus persica*; *James and the Giant Peach*; 'Peaches')
    (a) (Giacomo) Puccini (b) Fifth and Sixth (c) (Franz Peter) Schubert
    (not Robert Schumann, who also composed lieder and admired
    Beethoven, but died in 1856)
17. The sinking of the *Titanic*
    (a) Oscar Wilde (b) John Halifax (*John Halifax, Gentleman*)
    (c) Captain (L.E.G.) Oates
18. Baldric
    (a) Unidentified Flying Object (b) Videotape (c) Stripper
19. Miller
    (a) (Pierre) Laplace (b) (Joseph Louis de) Lagrange (c) (Antoine)
    Lavoisier

20. (John) Milton
    (a) Mulled (b) Tobermory (c) Cornwall
21. Cardioid
    (a) Hero and Hera (b) Apis and Acis (c) Eris and Iris
22. Lord Byron ('Letter to Lord Byron')
    (a) *Tristram Shandy / The Life and Opinions of Tristram Shandy, Gentleman* (by Laurence Sterne) (b) *War and Peace* (by Leo Tolstoy) (c) *The Great Gatsby* (by F. Scott Fitzgerald)
23. Blunderbuss
    (a) War of the Austrian Succession (b) Thirty Years' War (c) Hundred Years' War
24. Hermeneutics
    (a) *Memoirs of a Fox-Hunting Man* (b) *The Go-Between* (by L.P. Hartley) (c) The Ashes
25. Molière
    (a) South Africa (.za) (b) Spain (.es) and Sweden (.se) (c) Ukraine (.ua)
26. Gold
    (a) (George Francis) Fitzgerald (b) John F. Kennedy (c) *The Last Tycoon*
27. Apogee
    (a) (Peter) Rachman (b) G.K. Chesterton (c) Mark Knopfler
28. The Pentagon
    (a) *Tallith / tallit / tallis* (b) *Shtetl* (c) Schlock
29. 23 (E = 2.718 and pi = 3.14159, so E to the power of pi = 23.14069 26327)
    (a) Poland (b) Heidelberg (c) Theology / Religious Studies
30. October (thirty-one days and an extra hour due to clocks going back)
    (a) Coinage (not money, banknotes) (b) Phrygia (the Phrygian cap or bonnet) (c) Halicarnassus

Quarter-Finals Match Three
1. Thomas Hardy ('The Darkling Thrush')
    (a) Muse and mews (b) Marquis and marquee (c) Mote and moat
2. Mole
    (a) Io / Europa / Ganymede / Callisto (b) Titan (Saturn's largest moon) (c) Charon
3. Nitrogen

(a) Sedan (b) Napoleon III (c) (Emile) Zola

4. Dada
(a) Edward Morgan (b) Fruit flies (*Drosophila*) (c) Jamaica

5. *Anthony and Cleopatra* (Enobarbus' speech: 'The barge she sat in, like a burnished throne, / Burnt on the water')
(a) Tl (b) Transistor-Transistor Logic (c) Through The Lens

6. Aeron chair
(a) 100 (b) 80 (c) One-fifth / 0.2 (accept 20 per cent)

7. Winston Churchill
(a) Arsenic (b) Ultramarine (c) Verdigris

8. Luxembourg
(a) Syphilis (b) Magic bullet (accept selective toxicity / silver bullet)
(c) *Ghosts*

9. Digamma / double gamma
(a) Ahmet Ertegun (b) Led Zeppelin (c) Billie Holiday

10. Carat
(a) (Harold) Macmillan (b) Privatisation (c) Africa

11. Red herring
(a) Deep Purple (b) For those wounded in the service of their country (also awarded posthumously to those killed) (c) Rhodopsin

12. Eight (i.e. $8^3 = 512 : 5 + 1 + 2 = 8$)
(a) Alma mater (b) Brain (c) (Franz Joseph) Haydn

13. *Antigone*
(a) The Swan (b) A The Stephen Joseph Theatre (c) Donmar Warehouse

14. Sutton Hoo
(a) Georgia (b) Abkhazia (c) Moldova (NB Moldavia is a different entity)

15. Leitmotif
(a) Nephron (b) Glomerulus (c) Loop of Henle / Henle's loop

16. Quadrature
(a) Bridgewater (Canal) (b) Tatton Park (c) *The Adventures of Huckleberry Finn* (by Mark Twain)

17. Georgia
(a) *A Midsummer Night's Dream* (b) *Much Ado about Nothing* (c) *Romeo and Juliet*

18. Without hairs (or other projections)
(a) Riff (b) Morocco (c) Spain

19. Ukraine (the Ukranian term *holodomor* means 'death by starvation';

Jones's reports were published in the *Manchester Guardian* and the *New York Evening Post*)

(a) Miss Bates (b) Janet Leigh (c) *The Darling Buds of May*

20. Nineteenth

(a) Michael (as in San Michele) (b) Sant'Erasmo (from St Erasmus of Formiae / St Elmo's Fire) (c) Glass

21. Bobby Moore

(a) Trappists (b) Port Salut (c) Beer / ale

22. Arabic

(a) (Antonio) Gramsci (b) Praxis (c) Hegemony

23. Inflation

(a) Gran Chaco (b) Colombia (c) Lake Maracaibo

24. Franklin

(a) Newton (not Halley's, which made a reappearance two years later, 1682) (b) Hale-Bopp (after Alan Hale and Thomas Bopp) (c) *War and Peace*

25. (James Robert) Mann

(a) Orion's Belt (b) Denmark (c) Lonsdale Belt

26. Wealth of Nations (Adam Smith)

(a) Ours (b) Nur (c) Onus

27. Simon and Garfunkel (*Parsley, Sage, Rosemary and Thyme*)

(a) *Carousel* (b) *Oklahoma!* (c) *South Pacific*

28. Mastic

(a) Riding (originally 'Thriding') (b) Hundred (c) Bailiwick

29. 'Reuse' and 'Recycle'

(a) (Jan / Johan / Johannes) Vermeer (b) Musée d'Orsay (c) Velasquez

30. Tantra

(a) Senegal (b) Democratic Republic of Congo / Congo Kinshasa (c) Morocco

Quarter-Finals Match Four

1. William III / William of Orange

(a) William I / William the Conqueror (b) (Peter) Abelard (c) Cleopatra

2. Studies (in 'Of Studies', 1625)

(a) Richard III (b) King Lear (c) *Henry V*

3. Mouse

(a) Cotopaxi (b) Kyushu (c) Tonga

4. 150

(a) The attempted arrest of five members of the Long Parliament (the speaker was William Lenthall) (b) John Pym, John Hampden, Arthur Haselrig, Denzil Holles, William Strode (c) (The) Grand Remonstrance

5. Philosophy

(a) Father-in-law (b) Andrea Mantegna (c) (A.J.) Raffles

6. The Christmas Day broadcast

(a) Thessaloniki / Salonika (b) Saints Cyril and Methodius (c) (Mustafa Kemal) Atatürk

7. *High Noon* (a train carrying Frank Miller, recently released from prison, is due to arrive at noon)

(a) Sylvia Plath (b) Iris Murdoch (c) Ronald Searle

8. Parrot

(a) St Lucia (b) (Derek) Walcott (c) Economics

9. I-t-s

(a) Twenty-two (b) *Elements* (c) Pi

10. The cross

(a) (J.M.W.) Turner (b) (Giovanni) Bellini (father of Jacopo and Gentile) (c) Tintoretto / Tintoret (Jacopo Robusti)

11. Jack (Jasper Newton) Daniel

(a) Emperor (b) Joseph Haydn (c) Bernardo Bertolucci

12. Alba

(a) Charlotte Brontë (of Emily) (b) Revenge (c) Gladstone

13. Nictitating membrane (accept nictitans or membrana nictitans) (Latin: *nictare*, to blink)

(a) Tortilla (b) Oatcake (c) Chappati

14. Ecological pyramids

(a) 51 (LI, 'Beria' to 'Liberia') (b) 9 (IX, 'ion' to 'ixion') (c) 550 (DL, 'brie' to 'bridle')

15. Mesozoans

(a) St Peter's (Basilica) in Rome (b) Raphael (Raffaello Sanzio) (c) Michelangelo

16. Solidus

(a) Thermodynamics (b) (Nicolas Léonard Sadi) Carnot (c) (William Thomson) Kelvin / 1st Baron Kelvin

17. N (somewhat italicised)

(a) Abigail (b) He poisons her (c) *The Crucible*

18. The Devil (the last is commonly attributed to Charles Wesley, the

preacher Rowland Hill, William Booth...)
(a) Chile (b) Easter island (accept Rapanui or Isla de Pascua)
(c) Robinson Crusoe

19. Dr John Reid
(a) Hittite (b) Armenian (c) Bengali (accept Bangla)

20. Copper
(a) Luciferase (accept photo-protein) (b) Photophores (c) Beetles / *Coleoptera*

21. Tubercle
(a) Russia (b) Dagestan (c) Caucasus

22. Jacobite / House of Stuart
(a) Isotope(s) (b) Helium (c) (Ernest) Rutherford

23. Threshold
(a) Wavelength (b) (Propagation) speed (c) 2 pi

24. Myrmecochory
(a) Athena (and Athens) (b) Florence Nightingale (c) Billy Bunter

25. Arpeggio
(a) Pygmalion (b) Arachne (c) Niobe

26. Sunspots
(a) Syracuse (Siracusa) (b) Lucas Cranach (the Elder and the Younger) (c) Johann Strauss (the Elder and the Younger)

27. Downsizing / rightsizing
(a) (Sir Isaac) Newton (b) Thomas Carlyle (c) (Lord) Byron

28. Katabatic wind (Greek= *katabatiko*)
(a) Key (block) (b) (Thomas) Bewick (c) Intaglio

29. Tagged Image (File Format)
(a) Wolf-Rayet stars (b) Renal / kidneys (c) Fermat's Last Theorem

30. Nostalgia
(a) *The Barber of Seville* (b) *Turandot* (by Puccini) (c) *Pagliacci* (by Leoncavallo)

Semi-Finals Match One

1. Retina
(a) Honeydew (b) Froghopper (*cercopoidea*; also known as spittlebug but that doesn't answer the question) (c) Shellac / lac

2. Italy
(a) Dynamic Label Segment (b) Subscriber Identity Module (c) Electronic Random Number Indicator Equipment

3. Rider

(a) Leicestershire (b) Northamptonshire (c) Somerset

4. Southampton
   (a) Greasy spoon (b) Benjamin Disraeli (c) The elephant's (child)

5. (Edmond) Halley
   (a) Umbrella (b) *Martin Chuzzlewit* (c) Dick King-Smith (Ronald Gordon King-Smith; the *Jolly Witch* series)

6. Sandwich (after a comic strip character of the 1930s; a peanut butter, banana and bacon filling; and a 'submarine' or 'sub' respectively)
   (a) Basalt (b) Feldspar / feldspar (c) Staffa

7. (George William) Russell (1867–1935)
   (a) Legal tender (b) £5, £2 and £1 coins (c) Twenty pence

8. Square root of −1
   (a) Lombard Street (b) St John's Wood (c) Brick Lane

9. Neutrino
   (a) Porcupine (b) William Cobbett (c) Flying boat

10. Lewis (Matthew, 1775–1818; Sinclair, 1885–1951; Wyndham, 1882–1957; Clive Staples, 1898–1963)
    (a) Silicon (b) Lithium (c) Helium

11. *The Passion of the Christ* (the words come from the book of Isaiah)
    (a) Virginia and Maryland (b) New Jersey (c) Wisconsin

12. Ostrich
    (a) *Othello* (b) Yorick (in *Hamlet*) (c) Juliet (*Romeo and Juliet*)

13. New Year's Eve / 31 December
    (a) Coriander (b) Turmeric (c) Fenugreek (from *faenum graecum*)

14. Nitric (acid) (HNO_3) (the Birkeland-Eyde process. Not nitrous acid, HNO_2)
    (a) Sift and swift (b) Till and twill (c) Saddle and swaddle

15. *Julius Caesar* (Act IV, scene iii)
    (a) Porfirio Díaz (b) (Francisco) 'Pancho' Villa (c) (Emiliano) Zapata

16. (Sir James) Jeans
    (a) Hollywood Ten (b) Extradition Act (c) *In the Name of the Father*

17. Plant
    (a) Cam-eroon (b) Eth-iopia (c) Sen-egal

18. Odd / uneven numbers ('Numero deus impare gaudet', *Eclogues* viii. 75.)
    (a) Afghanistan (b) Oman (c) Dresden

19. Ten
    (a) Scarsdale diet (b) Audrey Eyton (c) Glycaemic Index (diet)

20. Punjab
    (a) Poland (b) East Prussia (c) Kaliningrad (formerly Konigsberg)
21. Maya Angelou ('Caged Bird')
    (a) Assonance (b) Eye-rhyme / sight rhyme (c) Penultimate
22. Queen Victoria
    (a) Almond (*prunus dulcis*; Genesis 43.11, Numbers 17.8, Exodus 25:33–4) (b) Jesse (Isaiah 11:1; Jesse windows) (c) Fig (the leaves of which they use to cover their nakedness)
23. Blue
    (a) (Bertrand) Russell (b) (Karl) Popper (c) (Ludwig) Wittgenstein
24. Mussels
    (a) Loch Ness (b) Sir Peter Scott (c) St Columba
25. (Wolfgang Amadeus) Mozart
    (a) Oceanus (b) Black Sea (the rocks supposedly located on the Bosphorus) (c) The Sirens
26. Dorothy Hodgkin
    (a) Rhode Island (Connecticut and Massachusetts) / South Carolina (North Carolina and Georgia) / Florida (Alabama and Georgia) (b) Iowa (c) New Hampshire
27. Zoonoses
    (a) Worm hole (b) Write Once Read Many (times) (c) Right angle / 90 degrees
28. Antimony (Sb)
    (a) Korea (b) Mexico (c) Portugal
29. Phylum
    (a) World Intellectual Property Organization (b) International Labour Organization (c) International Committee of the Red Cross
30. Outcrop
    (a) Christian Dior (b) Harvey Wallbanger (c) James Stewart

Semi-Finals Match Two
1. Quaternion (multiplication)
   (a) Lead (b) Titanium (c) Iron
2. *Appassionata*
   (a) Holy Roman Empire (accept Austria) (b) Paraguay (c) Russia / Russian Empire
3. Fat
   (a) 1972 (b) Okinawa (c) Pong
4. Jigsaw puzzle

THE ANSWERS

(a) Dorchester (b) Bloody Assizes (c) Casterbridge
5. Knock knee
(a) Roister Doister (b) The Bash Street Kids (c) *Under Milk Wood* (by Dylan Thomas)
6. The White House (specifically the Executive Residence, the central building of the White House complex)
(a) Italy (b) Etruscan (the *Liber Linteus Zagrebiensis* or *Liber Agramensis*) (c) Attic Greek (accept Greater Attic)
7. Williams
(a) Macbeth (to Banquo, Act I, Scene iii) (b) Coriolanus (responding to Menenius Agrippa and berating the mutinous citizens, Act I, Scene ii) (c) Hamlet (in an aside, refuting Claudius's statement of kinship, Act I, Scene ii)
8. 101
(a) Gaia / Ge (b) Chimera (c) Hydra
9. *Oh, What a Lovely War!*
(a) Catherine Howard (b) Dukes of Norfolk (c) Spanish Armada
10. (Doctor Samuel) Johnson's Dictionary
(a) Mexico (United Mexican States) (b) Yucatan (c) Chihuahua
11. Venice ('On the extinction of the Venetian Republic, 1802')
(a) Trapezium rule (the trapezoidal or trapezoid rule in American usage) (b) Wrist (c) Orion
12. *I, Claudius*
(a) Carotenoid(s) (b) Bilirubin (c) Melanin(s)
13. Order
(a) Giulio Andreotti (b) Aldo Moro (c) (Silvio) Berlusconi
14. *Spartacus*
(a) Tom Wolfe (b) Joan Didion (c) Frank Sinatra (the piece was 'Frank Sinatra Has a Cold')
15. Grapefruit
(a) Sheikh (b) Sharif (c) Hafiz
16. Metalloids / semimetals
(a) Britain and France (b) Russia (c) Germany
17. (Daily) rainfall
(a) The Peloponnesian War (b) Lysander (c) Thucydides
18. Eight ($CH_3C_6H_4COOH$ – methyl implies 1, benzoic implies 6, and the acid group has 1)
(a) Candlemas (b) Passion Sunday (c) Advent
19. Finland

(a) Budapest (b) Dublin (c) Copenhagen
20. One-quarter
(a) Parliament Square (b) (George) Canning, (Robert) Peel, (Edward Stanley, Earl of) Derby, (Benjamin) Disraeli (c) (Nelson) Mandela, (Jan Christian) Smuts
21. Aposematic
(a) Elizabeth I (b) King John (c) Henry VIII
22. Fish (large spotted dogfish)
(a) Newmarket (b) St Leger (c) York
23. 'p'
(a) (Republic of) Yemen (b) Naseem Hamed (c) Eddie Izzard
24. Reptilia
(a) 'Get out of the kitchen.' (b) Percussion section (c) Michael Dobbs
25. Hydrazine
(a) Seismograph (for measuring earthquakes) (b) (Papua) New Guinea (c) *Toad of Toad Hall*
26. *Orlando*
(a) Point (b) Jester (c) Aldous Huxley
27. Matthias (Acts 1.15–26)
(a) Dragon (b) King Arthur (c) *Antirrhinum*
28. Cardiovascular or circulatory system
(a) Interferometer (b) The Michelson-Morley experiment (c) MASER (Microwave Amplification by Stimulated Emission of Radiation; not laser, which amplifies visible light rather than microwaves)
29. Field
(a) Jewish (b) Shelter / hut (c) Japan
30. Terminus
(a) *On the Waterfront* (b) *East of Eden* (not *The Grapes of Wrath*, which was a John Ford film) (c) *A Streetcar Named Desire*

The Final
1. Intelligence
(a) Escapements (b) Anchor (escapement) (c) Grasshopper (escapement)
2. Phoenix ('The Phoenix', 'Phoenix', *The Phoenix and the Carpet* and 'The Phoenix and the Turtle')
(a) Seventeen (b) Flying Fortress (c) Haiku
3. K (Karnak, Kubrick and Kraftwerk)
(a) Alan Ayckbourn (b) Andrew Lloyd-Webber (c) Paul McCartney

4. Saint-Saens' *Carnival of the Animals*
   (a) Fluids (not liquids) (b) Viscosity (c) A Pascal second (also accept poise or Newton second per metre squared)
5. (Albert) Einstein
   (a) Lapis lazuli (b) Ochre (Greek: *ōchros*) (c) Copper
6. The cover photograph for The Beatles' *Abbey Road* album was taken (the four of them walking over the zebra crossing)
   (a) A wind (b) Cheese (c) *Cat on a Hot Tin Roof*
7. Tangier
   (a) Gothic (b) Prague (c) Uppsala
8. Breccia
   (a) Give encores (b) Leonard Slatkin (c) Ambrose Bierce
9. Melbourne Cup
   (a) (Ernst) Mach (b) Stockton and Darlington (c) Napoleon (Bonaparte)
10. The Pixies
    (a) Swan (b) Minos (c) Alexander the Great / Alexander III of Macedon
11. Milt
    (a) John Adams (b) Brian Cox (c) Thomas Hardy
12. Zeno (of Elea)
    (a) Khartoum (Sudan) (b) Phnom Penh (Cambodia) (c) Belgrade (Serbia)
13. Handshake
    (a) Polonius (to Laertes, Act I, scene iii) (b) Old Hamlet / the ghost (of Hamlet's father) (to Hamlet, Act I, scene v) (c) Horatio (to Hamlet as he dies, Act V, scene ii)
14. Hummingbird
    (a) Shakespeare (Sonnet 30: 'When to the sessions of sweet silent thought / I summon up remembrance of things past.') (b) T.S. Eliot (in 'Burnt Norton', the first of the *Four Quartets*) (c) *Nineteen Eighty-Four* (by George Orwell)
15. Chess
    (a) Roderigo (b) Guitar (c) El Cid
16. (John) Donne ('The Bait')
    (a) Mobile and mobile (moh-beel, moh-bile) (b) Unionised and un-ionised (c) Satyajit Ray and Man Ray (wry, ray)
17. (Finger or toe) nail
    (a) 1950s (b) 1970s (c) 1980s

18. Five
    (a) Almaty (accept Alma-Ata, its name until 1993) (b) Crimean
    (c) New Mexico
19. Dry rot
    (a) (Paul) Dirac (b) (Richard) Feynman (reporting the view of fellow
    physicist Freeman Dyson) (c) (Albert) Einstein ('The Lord God is
    subtle, but he is not malicious')
20. Vivien (also Nimue / Nimiane)
    (a) Earthsea (b) Glaurung (not Smaug) (c) Norbert
21. *Seven Years in Tibet*
    (a) John Keats (b) East Coker (the title of the second of the *Four
    Quartets*) (c) Geoffrey Chaucer
22. (Apostolic or Papal) Nuncio
    (a) Namibia (b) Etosha (c) Angola
23. Second cousin once removed
    (a) Guinevere (b) Elaine (c) Prince Albert
24. Deuterium and tritium
    (a) (John) Alcock and (Arthur Whitten) Brown (b) Irish / Gaelic
    coffee (c) Knock Airport (also known as Ireland West and Horan
    Airport but is always shown on flight departures as Knock)
25. Jerk
    (a) Han (b) Tang (c) Ming
26. Heysham
    (a) Saffron (b) Stigmata / stigmas (primarily the stigmata, though
    some style is used; not the pollen) (c) Safflower / *Carthamus
    tinctorius*
27. Efflorescent
    (a) Condensation (reaction) (not dehydration reactions, which are a
    subset of elimination reactions) (b) Metathesis (c) Redox (reaction)
    (reduction and oxidation)
28. Irrational number
    (a) *The Goon Show* (b) Albatross (c) Cornwall
29. (*The Rise and Fall of*) *Ziggy Stardust and the Spiders from Mars*
    (a) Fleming (Peter and Ian) (b) William and Henry James (c) W.B.
    Yeats (Jack Butler Yeats, the painter, was his brother)
30. 'The Pit and the Pendulum' (by Edgar Allen Poe)
    (a) Germany (b) Croatia (c) France